Refusing the Limits of Contemporary Childhood

Critical Childhood & Youth Studies: Theoretical Explorations and Practices in Clinical, Educational, Social, and Cultural Settings

Series Editors: Awad Ibrahim, Gabrille Ivinson, Michael O'Loughlin, and Marek Tesar

Mission Statement

Critical Childhood & Youth Studies is a scholarly series that is concerned with understanding the lived experiences of children and youth in economic, social, cultural, political and historical contexts, and addresses complex experiences only knowable through multidisciplinary lenses. The series seeks to address the following core questions: How do notions of childhood & youth differ across time and space? What new theories and methodologies can we employ to enhance our understanding and wellbeing of young people? What position and meaning is attributed to children and childhoods in/across different societies, and what are the public and political discussions concerning children's general position in society? Is agency possible, or must children live in states of exception? What can it mean to theorize the conditions and processes through which children and young people embody a meaningful existence in light of the histories they inherit?

Advisory Board

Jennifer Adair, Sonja Arndt, Marianne (Mimi) Bloch, Gail Boldt, Steven Bruhm, Erica Burman, Hannah Dyer, Giorgia Dona, Lisa Farley, Joanne Faulkner, Peggy Froerer, Lise Paulsen Galal, Madeleine Grumet, Janette Habashi, Lucia Hodgson, Richard Johnson, Julie Kaomea, Helen May, Zsuzsanna Millei, Leigh O'Brien, Carol Owens, Lacey Peters, Valerie Polakow, Elizabeth Quintero, Jenny Ritchie, Richard Ruth, Paula Salvio, Shilpi Sinha, Margaret Somerville, Kathryn Bond Stockton, Joseph Tobin, Mathias Urban, Honey Oberoi Vahali, Joseph Valente, Dan Woodman, and Handel Wright

Books in Series

Refusing the Limits of Contemporary Childhood: Beyond Innocence Edited by Julie C. Garlen & Neil T. Ramjewan

Precarities of 21st Century Childhoods: Critical Explorations of Time(s), Place(s), and Identities Edited by Michael O'Loughlin, Carol Owens, and Louis Rothschild

Critiquing Social and Emotional Learning: Psychodynamic and Cultural Perspectives by Clio Stearns

Refusing the Limits of Contemporary Childhood

Beyond Innocence

Edited by
Julie C. Garlen and Neil T. Ramjewan

Published by Lexington Books
An imprint of The Rowman & Littlefield Publishing Group, Inc.
4501 Forbes Boulevard, Suite 200, Lanham, Maryland 20706
www.rowman.com

86-90 Paul Street, London EC2A 4NE

Copyright © 2024 by The Rowman & Littlefield Publishing Group, Inc.

"From FOR COLORED GIRLS WHO HAVE CONSIDERED SUICIDE / WHEN THE RAINBOW IS ENUF (PLAY) by Ntozake Shange. Copyright © 1975, 1976, 1977, 2010 by Ntozake Shange. Reprinted with the permission of Scribner, a division of Simon & Schuster, Inc. All rights reserved."

"Dark phrases" in FOR COLORED GIRLS WHO HAVE CONSIDERED SUICIDE / WHEN THE RAINBOW IS ENUF (PLAY) by Ntozake Shange. Reproduced with permission of the Licensor through PLSclear.

All rights reserved. No part of this book may be reproduced in any form or by any electronic or mechanical means, including information storage and retrieval systems, without written permission from the publisher, except by a reviewer who may quote passages in a review.

British Library Cataloguing in Publication Information Available

Library of Congress Cataloging-in-Publication Data

Names: Garlen, Julie C., editor. | Ramjewan, Neil T., editor.
Title: Refusing the limits of contemporary childhood : beyond innocence / edited by Julie C. Garlen and Neil T. Ramjewan.
Description: Lanham : Lexington Books, [2024] | Series: Critical childhood & youth studies : theoretical explorations and practices in clinical, educational, social, and cultural settings | Includes bibliographical references and index.
Identifiers: LCCN 2023041931 (print) | LCCN 2023041932 (ebook) | ISBN 9781666911534 (cloth) | ISBN 9781666911541 (ebook)
Subjects: LCSH: Children—Social conditions. | Child development. | Innocence (Psychology)
Classification: LCC HQ767.9 .R448 2024 (print) | LCC HQ767.9 (ebook) | DDC 305.23—dc23/eng/20231019
LC record available at https://lccn.loc.gov/2023041931
LC ebook record available at https://lccn.loc.gov/2023041932

Contents

Introduction: Moving Beyond Childhood Innocence   1
Julie C. Garlen and Neil T. Ramjewan

1. Who Is Entitled to Childhood Innocence: Black Girls and the Struggle against Racial Bias in Canadian Schools   29
   Kisha McPherson and Chanelle Perrier-Telemaque

2. Unpacking the Adultification–Infantilization Paradox   59
   Sebastian Barajas

3. Childhood Innocence, Sanism, and the Image of the Child: Maddening Childhood Innocence Through the "Problem Child"   79
   Adam Davies

4. Zapatista Childhoods: Children's Participation and the Possibilities for Collective Knowledge   103
   Kathia Núñez Patiño

5. Adultism in Uganda's Child Protection Efforts: A Case of Violence against Children   129
   Doris Kakuru

6. Malleability of Innocence: Reimagining Justice in the Indian Juvenile Justice System   155
   Anusha Iyer

7. Narrating Trauma, Subverting Innocence: Challenging Normative Childhood Representations in Bapsi Sidhwa's *Cracking India*   171
   Mayurika Chakravorty

8 The Arrivant Child: Afrofuturity and Contingent Childhood Agencies   189
Neil T. Ramjewan

9 Troubling Innocence: Staging Scenes of Black Youth Pleasures and Possibilities   219
Dominique C. Hill and Durell M. Callier

Index   241

About the Contributors   253

Introduction

Moving Beyond Childhood Innocence

Julie C. Garlen and Neil T. Ramjewan

Since the beginning of the global COVID-19 pandemic in the early months of 2020, children all over the world have been impacted by public health restrictions, including school and business closures that have led to a dramatic increase in multidimensional poverty in low and middle income countries and a mental health epidemic across North America (UNICEF 2020; Leeb et al. 2020; Yousif 2020). Given the challenging circumstances the pandemic has created for so many children, some have characterized it as a loss of innocence (Frampton 2021; McKinney 2020; O'Connell 2020; Wickersham 2020). In one example, a short opinion piece in an Atlantic Canada newspaper publishing company's website saltwire.com titled "Innocence - One Casualty of the Pandemic," managing editor Pam Frampton (2021) considers the intersecting crises of the pandemic and climate change that threaten children's futures. In this emotive piece, Frampton begins from a somber walk on a spring day unexpectedly interrupted by the 'heart-gladdening' sounds of "children's laughter" in the midst of school closures and their intermittent re-openings. The figure of the happy and innocent child provoked by the sounds of children's laughter is quickly perturbed by the "jarring sight" of children "wearing masks" cleaning up litter from the school grounds reminiscent of "Second World War photographs of British children wearing gas masks during the Blitz." Frampton then makes the evocative claim, "Childhood and mortality should never share such close quarters."

Frampton's concern about the confluence of crises that threaten children's wellbeing is well warranted. While the current physical effects of COVID-19 on children is significantly less severe compared to adults, children continue to face the loss of others in their lives, many of whom they depend on. Furthermore, children continue to account for significant percentages of those infected while the physical, social, economic, and political effects remain to be fully determined. Schools are at the nexus of these intersecting domains in children's lives, and their closures are associated with a growing mental health epidemic experienced by children and young people. In March 2021, McMaster Children's hospital reported a threefold increase in suicide attempts by youth over a four month period compared to the previous year, in addition to the increased use of opioids and eating disorders (Brown 2021). Despite Frampton's ethic towards childhood as ideally devoid of pain and suffering, it is precisely the stark reality that childhood and mortality share very close quarters in this pandemic and beyond that prompt her concern.

These stark realities have recently prompted discourses produced by adults that worry about the children in this moment as yet another "lost generation" whose present delimit their futures (Hafstad and Augusti 2021; Schenzle 2021; UNICEF 2020). Like the last "lost generation" to emerge from World War I and the Spanish flu pandemic, what is being mourned in terms of childhood is quite specific. Again, Frampton's reflections are illustrative. After claiming that childhood should be devoid of suffering, she reminisces on an idyllic school ground scene of play from her own 'less-complicated' childhood to pronounce, "Childhood should be full of such simple magic." Frampton concludes with her hopes for a post-pandemic life in which children can be "shrieking with joy....[and] [i]nnocent, again." Through the narration of her past school ground antics what Frampton ultimately mourns is not the decreasing possibilities of children's wellbeing; rather, it is the loss of her own experience of childhood remembered as joyful and innocent, akin to those poor European children who have suffered a similar fate.

In the same month of Frampton's idyllic Atlantic Canadian lamentations, the ongoing effects of Canadian settler colonialism would make headlines across Turtle Island about the hundreds of unmarked graves of Indigenous children, casualties of the residential schooling system that sought to "kill the Indian [child], and save the man" (Pratt 1880). Just before a series of discoveries of mass graves began, 67 Palestinian children were added to the death toll of the of Israeli occupation and settler colonization of Palestine (Tarc 2021). Just a month before in the United States, another settler colony founded on the enslavement of black people, the ongoing terrorization of Black and Brown children and youth by police was marked by the killing of a 13-year-old Latino Adam Toledo (Nickeas, Andone and Tucker 2021). Adding to the dire conditions for children in the U.S. is the legacy of the Trump administration's immigration policies that separated thousands of children from their parents, as well as the recent unprecedented legislative campaigns to curtail the rights of transgender children in numerous states. Meanwhile, in West and Central Africa, UNICEF reported on a "spiraling protection crisis" in the face of 140 students kidnapped from a school in Nigeria (United Nations 2021). While these selected examples arguably justify a need to protect children from such harms, these children represent those whom the experience of innocence is often unavailable. Rather, Black, Brown, and Indigenous children and people have historically been politically excluded through discourses of childhood innocence (Garlen 2019), while at the same time being framed as perpetually childlike (Nandy 1984), even innocent.

These events, particularly in the midst of a global pandemic, bring compelling evidence that childhood is not a universal or equitable experience and offer a stark reminder that the modern Western conception of childhood as a state of innocence — a universal condition of good and happy ignorance and inexperience — is a myth. Rather, all children bear the experiential knowledge of sadness, grief, fear and disappointment, some earlier and in greater measure than others. For many children, such as those who disproportionately experience the traumatizing effects of disease, natural disasters, poverty, homelessness, refugee dispossession and sexual violence, as well as for Black, racialized or Indigenous children who know racism and colonization first-hand, grappling with adversity is not uncommon. This is particularly true for those who face multiple or intersecting vulnerabilities and barriers which have only been exacerbated by COVID-19. Indeed, critical scholars of childhood and education have sought for decades to disrupt and dismantle the persistent logics of innocence (Bernstein 2011; Duschinsky 2013; Farley 2018; Faulkner 2010; Garlen 2019; Meiners 2016; Robinson 2012; Taylor 2010) but given its long history in the Global North, it remains a stubborn site for critique, a problem that precipitates the need for this collection. In order to situate the intervention that these essays offer within the broader discourse on childhood, we will briefly outline below the emergence of innocence as a dominant childhood ideal and describe how it became associated with racist theories of child development. Then, we will describe how childhood studies emerged as a multi- and inter- disciplinary challenge to these hegemonic discourses and examine some of the critical interdisciplinary work that precedes this volume before returning to the resistive projects initiated by the chapters herein.

DEVELOPING INNOCENCE: A BRIEF HISTORY OF THE "MODERN" CHILD

In Western contexts, as illustrated by Frampton's essay, innocence is frequently taken-for-granted as the appropriate condition of childhood. Often depicted as a universal right of early life, innocence emerged as it has continued, as an entitled lack that, by the time it began to be recognized as such, was already under attack. In other words, Western demands to safeguard children's innocence grew out of philosophical and religious debates about what childhood *should* be, rather than an observation of what it really was. As an *ideal* rather than a factual (or achievable) state of existence, a budding concept of childhood innocence emerged from modern European political philosophy, which, with the authority of the monarchy in decline, sought new forms of government and social control and recognized the importance of the early indoctrination of future citizens. Yet it was the utopian discourse of the Romantic era that brought innocence to prominence, most notably the work of Jean Jacques Rousseau, which provided the foundation for the poets, artists, and novelists who would bring the innocent ideal to life in the popular imagination. Rousseau's 1762 treatise *Emile, or On Education*, was both a manifesto on the innate goodness of humanity and nature and a guidebook for how childhood innocence ought to be protected from the corrupting forces of society.

Innocence as a universal feature of childhood was a controversial construct, as it flew in the face of the Christian doctrine of original sin, which justified the harsh treatment of children, who were believed corrupt, depraved, and in need of discipline to secure their salvation. Education, mostly in the form of religious training, had long been viewed as an important tool for redemption. Romanticism, however, bolstered by increasingly secularized governmental and social structures and faced with the uncertainties and anxieties of industrialization, scientific and technological advancement, and abolition, among others, "embraced childhood as an exemplification of an alternative to the sterility of positivism and technology, urging that society affirm and accept childhood with all its potentialities" (Neustadter 2009, 146). As Bernstein (2011) points out, "To be innocent was to be innocent *of* something, to achieve obliviousness" (6). This state of not-knowing was understood as a "holy ignorance," a phrase coined in an 1822 article in *Blackwood's Magazine* (cited in Bernstein 2011). In the 19th century, innocence offered a reprieve from the harsh conditions of urbanization, linking childhood with the simplicity and wisdom of nature and all the virtues found lacking in modern society. This utopian fantasy located the hope for social progress - a universalization of white middle-class morality and dispositions - within childhood. As Bernstein (2011) remarks, "Childhood was then understood not as innocent but as innocence itself" (4).

Largely in response to concerns about urban children's working and living conditions, a host of organizations, political groups, and institutions emerged across Europe and North America to save childhood, and more importantly, Western society from moral decline. Bernstein (2011), in her historical analysis of childhood innocence as a racial project in the United States context, asserts that by the mid-nineteenth century, the "doctrine of original sin" was "replaced by a doctrine of original innocence" (4). This is not exactly true, as the vestiges of original sin still circulated in the social practices that were enacted to "protect" or "reclaim" children's innocence. Although reform efforts were indeed premised on an innocent ideal that sought to establish childhood as a separate and special period of protection from adult concerns, those efforts, in practice, relied on discipline and control rather than protection. Compulsory schooling, in particular, was a key mechanism for *enforcing* innocence. While public schools were intended as tangible containers for the appropriate conditions of childhood, such an intervention was only necessary for those who did not already occupy such a space by virtue of race and social status. In other words, public schools, particularly but not exclusively racially segregatedl and residential schools, "were not designed to bestow that special status on othered members of society, only to assimilate them into disciplined, rational subjects who could aspire to but never achieve such potential" (Garlen 2021, x). Thus, while the rationale for education shifted from original sin to innate innocence, redemption remained its organizing principle.

The innocent ideal not only co-opted the redemptive imperative of traditional religious dogma, it also found new life in modern scientific discourses, thanks in large part to its close association with nature, as the biological essence of humanity began to be explored. The modern move toward compulsory public schooling coincided with the birth of science as a profession and the rise of evolutionary biology, which led to the emergence of "scientific pedagogy." In the final decades of the nineteenth century, American psychologist G. Stanley Hall founded a field of experimental psychology that became known as the Child Study Movement (Brooks-Gunn and Johnson 2006). Child Study was premised on the scientific investigation of children's "nature" (Hall 1883) as the means for determining the appropriate conditions of their care and education. Hall's theories of childhood and approaches to education were heavily influenced by Social Darwinism, which borrowed from Darwin's theory of biological evolution to explain social change, placing human groups along a continuum with "savage" primitive cultures on one end of the evolutionary spectrum and "civilized" modern societies on the other. This logic was applied to an understanding of childhood by way of culture epoch theory, which assumed that children mirrored, or recapitulated, the biological evolution of human beings from simple and savage to complex and civilized. As Baker (1998) notes, "It is through culture epoch theory that discourses of race and of nature met to define the child" (124). This parallel relationship between biological evolution and children's intellectual and moral development was known as the "law of recapitulation," which declared that the developing child "passes through or represents all the stages of life ... "from that of a single -celled animal to that of present adult civilised man" (Partridge 1912, 28).

Culture epoch theory gave scientific weight to the utopian fantasy of ignorant innocence by conflating a modern construct of childhood with so-called savagery. Of course, the association between children and non-white "others" was not unique to the 19th century; theories of the natural laws of the physical and organic universe had long relied on the figure of the child to justify the colonial invasion, dispossession, and enslavement of Black and Indigenous peoples (Pagden 1982; Wynter 1995). Yet, in Western societies increasingly interested in establishing scientific truths to guide social progress and defend white supremacy in the face of increasing urbanization, immigration, and attention to civil rights, recapitulative theories of child development brought a modern empirical legitimacy. As explained by Hall's protege, George Everett Partridge (1912), the similarities between children and primitive peoples were easily observed:

> In regard to fickleness and lack of power of long- sustained effort, optimism, and freedom from care and work, close relation to nature, the tendency to personify natural objects, and to confuse the animate and inanimate, in readiness to imitate, and to act upon suggestion, the child and primitive man are much alike. Both child and savage confuse the real and ideal, the waking life and the dream life (76–77).

This new, scientific association - what Sylvia Wynter (1995) describes as "a system of representations instituting a bioevolutionary notion of order" (39) was mapped onto a theory of natural selection to justify the superiority of whiteness. As Wynter observes, this system of representations established the premise "of a bio-evolutionarily determined difference of genetic value substance between *one* evolutionarily selected *human hereditary variation* and a therefore *eugenic* line of descent" (39). Within this racial schema, eugenically selected whiteness produced its blackened "dysgenic Others" (39) in order to select the fruits of a colonial science manifest in the fantasy of an idealized child.

This premise was at the heart of child study, which quickly grew to prominence alongside the eugenics movement initiated by English social Darwinist Sir Francis Galton, who sought to engineer a better human race through the regulation of marriage and procreation. As Faulkner (2019) explains, "Within this movement, the figure of the child came to be especially meaningful both as an ideal into which the future of the race was invested, and as a sign of race degeneration" (6). Child study offered a systematic way to produce scientific data about children and race, which could be used to establish developmental norms that informed the curricular and pedagogical decisions needed to educate the future subjects of liberal colonial governments. Thus, as Siegel and White (1982) explain, "Child study greatly fostered the growth of the 'typical child' and the 'average child,' mythical creatures of great usefulness in representing the conditions and possibilities of large numbers of children" (234). Ultimately, child study saw the study of human development as necessary for "racial evolution," which mapped onto genetic traits "bourgeois and culture-specific discourses that gave higher value to the evolution of '[w]hiteness' in the human realm" (Baker 1998, 125). Hall's stages of development, from early childhood to adolescence, traced the evolution from simple ignorant savagery to complex, informed civilization. Thus, the representation of childhood in a way that made racial hierarchies appear natural and inevitable was embedded in the foundations of child development, which framed (and continues to inform) the Western educational and social practices that have shaped the experiences of children.

Although culture epoch theory and recapitulation were discredited in the early twentieth century, its logics produced a developmental discourse within which children are constructed as "human becomings" rather than human beings (James and Prout 1997). This designation of the child as less than fully human not only diminished the experiences and knowledges of the young, but also those of non-white adult others who, in Hall's perception, would perpetually remain the children of the human race. Thus, this hegemonic construction childhood only outgrows itself by way of actively and intentionally excluding and erasing the experiences of Black, Brown, and Indigenous children, who are "adultified" and excluded from an assumption of innocence while their parents and ancestors are rendered perpetually childlike. Innocence, therefore, is a rhetorical strategy that enacts its own epistemological violence through the perpetuation of colonial logics and white supremacy. The long-standing sovereignty of developmentalism has helped childhood innocence achieve an "unimpeachable moral status" (Duschinsky 2013, 764), allowing it to operate as a "trump card" (Meiners 2016, 2) that halts interrogation, limits discourse, and produces the erasure of the politics in which it is involved, specifically the implicit racism that underpins the modern ideal of "the child." Although recent years brought more vigorous efforts to "decolonize childhood" as well as research on childhood and children's rights (Liebel 2020), childhood studies has been heavily informed by a Eurocentric worldview that has often failed to grapple fully with whiteness as an organizing principle of Western childhood.

Questioning Innocence: Deconstructing Development

The Child Study Movement set an important precedent for the scientific study of children and laid the foundation for developmental psychology, which informed the training and professional practice of the Anglo-US teachers, social workers, nurses, counselors, and, of course, psychologists, who would educate and care for children in the twentieth century (Burman 1994). In the

1920s, the linear stage model of cognitive development proposed by Swiss psychologist Jean Piaget would make developmental psychology synonymous with the study of childhood, and therefore, a key mechanism by which childhood was imagined and understood. Developmentalism, which legitimized the irrational, unknowing child subject, became a largely unquestioned way of thinking about children. For most of the twentieth century, developmental logics dominated the social sciences, not only psychology but also history, sociology, and educational research. Children were relatively insignificant in terms of historical analysis, and sociology viewed children through the lens of socialization theory, which understood the process by which children develop into functioning members of society as a unidirectional inculcation of social norms (McNamee 2016). Similarly, educational research was largely focused on the identification and measurement of the cognitive and behavioural norms that marked children's progression toward academic and social proficiency. As Walkerdine (1993) observes, "That children were children and develop has appeared so common-sense a notion that the arguments that have raged have been about models of development not about the existence of those objects called 'the child' and 'development'" (451).

Those hegemonic objects remained as unquestioned and taken-for-granted artefacts of childhood until the final decades of the twentieth century, when a paradigm shift in the social sciences brought them under scrutiny. The postmodern perspectives that materialized across multiple disciplines during this time produced a new, critical understanding of childhood as a social construct emerging from specific cultural and historical contexts and with its own claim to present (not just future) personhood and subjectivity. The shift was preceded by a renewed child-rescue movement that emerged after the First World War under the leadership of Eglantyne Jebb, a white British social reformer and founder of the Save the Children non-governmental organization. The movement focused on raising awareness of the plight of children across the world, particularly in the Global South, and decades later was formally recognized by the Declaration of the Rights of the Child, adopted by the United Nations General Assembly in 1959. This was followed by the proclamation of 1979 as the International Year of the Child, which led to the 1989 adoption of the United Nations Convention on the Rights of the Child (UNCRC), an international human rights treaty that was ratified by every nation except for the United States. Although the international children's rights movement was premised on a normative Western view of childhood and motivated by the same redemptive logics that had framed reform efforts in Europe and North America, the public debates set the stage for academic discourse about children's human rights, which generated questions about children's agency, capabilities, and social status.

Equally important in producing the conditions for critique were mid-century civil rights movements across Europe and North America and the increasing influence of postmodernism on the arts and humanities, both of which were calling into question the hegemony of the "grand narrative" of science and scientific racism (Lyotard 1984, 37). It was in the midst of these ideological shifts that French Historian Phillip Ariés (1960) published a landmark text in which he asserted that childhood --understood as a separate time of dependence and freedom from responsibility-- was not, in fact, a natural, universal truth, but a culturally and chronologically specific social construct that changed over time and across different geographic contexts. Ariés' book, *L'enfant et la vie familiale sous l'ancien regime*, which relied heavily on medieval paintings as a primary source, was translated into English as *Centuries of Childhood* in 1962, sparking debate in the humanities about the extent to which childhood did or did not exist in the Middle Ages and beyond.

While Aries' work and the numerous histories of childhood that followed did much to bring attention to the grand narrative of "the child," they did not offer a critique of developmental discourse as a mechanism through which that child was produced. In fact, as Lenzer (2001) points out children had received very little attention at all from academic disciplines, as they were typically relegated to a subcategory within education, sociology of the family, or behavioural psychology. However, in the 1970s as the influence of deconstruction and other critical ideas associated with poststructuralism rose, the field of psychology experienced an acute disciplinary crisis that called into question its methods, philosophical foundations, and contemporary relevance (Faye 2011). Subsequently, one of the first serious critiques of traditional psychology surfaced with *Changing the Subject* (Henriques et. al 1984), an edited collection that challenged the long accepted theories and practices of psychology, particularly the perceived dichotomy between the individual and society. In this volume, British psychologist Valerie Walkerdine (1998), drawing on the work of Michel Foucault (1979), interrogated "the very lynchpin of developmental psychology, the 'developing child,'" identifying it as "an object premised on the location of certain capacities within 'the child' and therefore within the domain of psychology" (148). In the years that followed, the work of Walkerdine (1984, 1987, 1993) as well as fellow British psychologist Erica Burman (1991, 1992, 1993, 1994a, 1994b, 1996) was crucial in bringing attention to the social constructedness of both "the child" and the notion of development. Their work and others' (i.e. Bradley 1994; Morss 1992, 1996; Rose 1985, 1990) helped set the stage for a radical reconsideration of childhood in the social sciences and humanities.

Disrupting Development Across the Disciplines

In the field of sociology, the work of academics in Europe, especially in the United Kingdom and Nordic region (Alanen 1988; Jenks 1982; James and Prout 1997; James, Jenks and Prout 1998; Qvortrup 1994) as well as the United States (Corsaro 1997; Thorne 1994, Zelizer 1985) brought forth the sociology of childhood as a new subfield. Responding to the growing recognition of children's virtual invisibility in society and the academic disciplines, U.S. sociologist Gertrud Lenzer established the Sociology of Children as a new section within the American Sociological Association in 1991, effectively launching the field of children's studies (Lenzer 2001). This new "social study of childhood" rejected the traditional top-down view of socialization and linear model of development, positioning children as active agents of socialization and capable social actors whose experiences and insights were worthy of academic study (McNamee 2016). This agentic perspective challenged the normative view of children as blissfully ignorant and acknowledged the ways that children's capacities and roles had been overlooked in social theory and in society at large. It also held as a central premise that "childhood is always produced as an object in relation to power" (Jenks 2005, 18), acknowledging the influence of developmental discourses that arise from a colonial mindset.

At the same time that childhood was being established as a legitimate area of study within sociology, interest in children was increasing in the humanities. As social theory and cultural studies were applied to literary studies, children's literature began to gain attention as a site for critiquing normative constructions of childhood. Published in 1984, Jacqueline Rose's *The Case of Peter Pan, or the Impossibility of Children's Literature*, emerged as a foundational text for critical studies of children's literature. Rose, a British literary scholar with an interest in psychoanalysis, challenged the traditional assumption that children's literature is written *for* children, asserting that it is actually meant to address the needs and desires of adults, who project their fantasies onto childhood. Rose's work brought attention to the social construction of childhood, and particularly the adult emotional investment in childhood innocence, illustrating how "Children's fiction draws in the child, it secures, places and frames the child" as an "all-too-perfect presence" (Rose 1985, 1–2).

Efforts to debunk the myth of that "all-too-perfect" Western childhood also emerged among a number of British historians (Cunnigham 1991; Davin 1996) who sought to both extend and challenge the work of Ariés by revealing the long-overlooked histories of children who did not fit the innocent ideal, particularly those who grew up in poverty during modern times. Bringing a different but equally critical perspective to the history of childhood,

British historian Carolyn Steedman (1995) published a book entitled *Strange Dislocations: Childhood and the Idea of Human Interiority* in which she asserts that the very notion of Western selfhood that emerged in the nineteenth century - the way industrialized societies understood themselves - was embodied by the idealized figure of the modern child. Drawing on Freudian psychoanalysis, Steedman illustrates how, in the early twentieth century, an individual's psychic identity became associated with their lost childhood. Steedman's analysis provided further evidence of childhood's social constructedness and highlighted its cultural significance.

This universal child figure that was under scrutiny among critical psychologists, sociologists, historians, and literary scholars during the last decades of the 20th century was also being reexamined by education scholars in the United States who sought to disrupt the normalizing developmental discourses that had long permeated curriculum and pedagogy. Specifically, the emerging scholarship sought to challenge the Guidelines for Developmentally Appropriate Practice (DAP) created by the National Association for the Education of Young Children (NAEYC). In 1989, frustrated by the lack of attention to and space for alternative theoretical perspectives on early childhood education and finding resonance with the reconceptualist movement that had challenged mainstream educational research and traditional principles of curriculum development, Shirley Kessler and Beth Blue Swadener organized a conference session on reconceptualizing early childhood education at the Bergamo Curriculum Theory and Classroom Practices conference, which was followed by a symposium on the same topic at the next year's annual meeting of the American Educational Research Association (Swadener and Kessler 1991). Subsequently, the two co-edited a special issue of *Early Education & Development*, founded an international conference on Reconceptualizing in Early Childhood Research, Theory and Practice, and, the following year, published *Reconceptualizing the Early Childhood Curriculum: Beginning the Dialogue* (Kessler and Swadener 1992). These efforts helped highlight the ways that early education was dominated by a Western childhood ideal, leading to an ethnocentric curriculum that ignored cultural diversity and relied on developmental norms that stigmatized difference and disproportionately identified children of colour as being "at risk." The ideological roots of that ethnocentric curriculum were explored in another significant contribution to childhood theory entitled *In Perpetual Motion: Theories of Power, Educational History, and the Child*, in which Bernadette Baker (2001) performs a close analysis of the works of John Locke, Jean-Jacques Rousseau, Johann Herbart, and G. Stanley Hall to illustrate how developmentalism permeated public schooling discourse in the United States.

In response to a growing demand for critical scholarship across traditional disciplines, which was quickly producing disparate new child-focused subspecialties in new fields such as anthropology, political science, and economics, Gertrud Lenzer led the establishment of a new academic program in children's studies, leading to the foundation of a new interdisciplinary field by the same name. Recognizing the fragmentation resulting from the the many disconnected critical projects being initiated within traditional disciplines, Lenzer (2001) sought to develop an interdisciplinary field that would advance a "a holistic understanding of children rather than reducing them to specialized abstract fragments that then in turn are hypostatized as representing *the child, children or childhood*" (183, emphasis in original). In the years that followed, similar programs began appearing at academic institutions across Europe and North America. In 1993, the international journal *Childhood* offered a new medium for the circulation of critical childhood scholarship. As described by founding editor, Norwegian sociologist Ivar Frønes, the journal was premised on the belief that childhood is a "cultural idea," "a cultural and political point of intersection," and "a mirror of what has been, what is, and of visions of what will be" (Frønes 1993, 1–2). In the three decades since, the field, more often referred to as childhood studies, has grown to include many different epistemologies, methodologies, and cultural contexts. However, the unifying premise amongst all of the critical work on childhood is that both the figure of "the child" and the concept of "development" that it has been defined by are socially constructed and culturally, politically, economically, and historically significant.

Contemporary Resistance in Childhood Studies

Although the field of Childhood Studies emerged, much like other multidisciplinary fields like Women's Studies, Black Studies, and Queer Theory, to bring attention to the underrepresentation and oppression of marginalized populations, most of the literature published in English in Europe and North America has been produced by white scholars. Illustrative of the dominance of white Euro-American perspectives, the 2009 *Palgrave Handbook of Childhood Studies*, which editors saw as "a sign that childhood studies have both matured and experienced a remarkable diversification" (Qvortrup et al. 2009, 1), does not feature a single race scholar or include chapters explicitly focused on race or racism in relation to childhood. While some attention is paid to non-Western contexts regarding children's rights and labour, most contributors are working in and from the perspectives of the Global North. Additionally, although the volume includes a few scholars with expertise in geography, media and culture studies, history, law, and education, the predominance of sociology training among the authors also reflects the historical overrepresentation of sociological perspectives among the disciplines contributing to the interdisciplinary field. The volume's makeup reflects the historical tendency of childhood scholars to work from within a traditional discipline, calling into question the extent to which the field achieves interdisciplinarity (Bass 2010).

Over the last decade, numerous childhood scholars have critiqued the field for its "applicability of Minority World conceptualisations and priorities to the Majority World" (Tisdall and Punch 2012, 250; see also Mayall 2012). In particular, contemporary constructions of children's agency and rights have been criticized for their tendency to perpetuate colonialism and disregard the complex social realities of children in diverse cultural and political contexts (Canosa and Graham 2020; de Castro 2020). Among the Majority World insights that demand further consideration, Mayall (2012) includes alternative conceptualizations of family, intergenerational relationships, citizenship, political participation, migration, and schooling. We assert that, in addition to the lack of Majority World perspectives, there exists a dearth of scholarship on the intersections of race and childhood within the Minority world, where, as Dumas and Nelson (2016) observe of Black children's place within educational research, racialized children's perspectives are "the most invisible, the most under-represented and misrepresented" (33). Although recent years have seen growing interest in historical analyses of African American childhoods (King 2022; Webster 2021; White 2021) and the adjacent field of Black Girlhood Studies (Owens, Callier, Robinson and Garner 2017), there are few examples of projects that seek to "operationalise intersectionality and its radical praxis by rethinking childhood in complex and heterogeneous ways" (Konstantoni and Emejulu 2017, 17). This lack of attention to the intersection of identities within childhood has also resulted in the exclusion of disabled children from "new childhood discourses in which children are constructed as active, agential, and entrepreneurial" (Curran and Runswick-Cole 2014, 1627).

Recent contributions, such as the edited collection on new perspectives in childhood studies (Esser et al. 2016), have highlighted the need to bring more diverse perspectives to the field. However, as Canosa and Graham (2020) point out, although the volume seeks to challenge Euro-centric constructions of childhood agency, the contributors are mostly European. Since then, the latest synoptic text in childhood studies, the *SAGE Encyclopedia of Children and Childhood Studies* (Cook 2020) has emerged, with an intention to better reflect the complexities of interdisciplinarity as well as the "complicated and provocative ways" that intersecting identities, including race, geography, and ability, among others, inform the field. Among the 600 entries by contributors from several dozen countries are entries on Global South childhoods, colonialism, race, racial formation, racism, and racial innocence, although notably only one of those entries is written by anti-racist, anti-colonial scholar of colour (Escayg 2020). This fact is reflective of the historical pre-dominance of white Anglo-US scholars (most often women) in the field. Although the field has certainly expanded the limits of thinking about children and childhood, and has seen a number of recent interventions that refuse such invisibility and resist disciplinary boundaries (i.e. Eskayg et al. 2017; Nxumalo 2017; Shaloub-Kervorkian 2019; Twum-Danso Imoh and Ame 2012), there remains a need for spaces that de-centre white, Eurocentric perspectives where emerging scholars from can dismantle, decolonize, Brown, and Indigenize the domain of childhood.

In their recent literature review tracing the key theoretical developments in childhood studies between 2010 and 2018, Canosa and Graham (2020) find that "perhaps the greatest challenge facing the field of childhood studies" moving forward is "overcoming its very epistemic construction shaped and firmly grounded in an Anglophone and Minority World tradition" (41-42). Although, as we have illustrated here, that epistemic legacy has been continually (and importantly) acknowledged by Northern scholars, we agree with Canosa and Graham's assertion that "acknowledging that Majority World perspectives of childhood are still missing is no longer a sufficient response" (42). Additionally, regarding existing Minority World perspectives within childhood studies, we believe that acknowledging the ways that Black, Brown, and Indigenous childhoods are shaped by colonial discourses of development is equally insufficient given the field's long-standing commitment to social justice. Such criticism, while necessary, tends to recenter rather than dismantle racial and cultural hierarchies. The same can be said for critiques of childhood innocence (Bernstein 2011; Farley 2018; Garlen 2019, 2021; Meiners 2016; Taylor 2010) in which white scholars outline the enduring discriminatory effects and political uses of innocence. While such work offers an important entry point for white monority world???scholars to grapple with their own complicity in the productive violence that creates perpetually childlike and adultified others, this recognition alone cannot move beyond the epistemic framework of innocence versus experience to re-imagine Black, Brown, and Indigenous childhoods, borrowing from the wording of Dumas and Nelson (2016), "with all the agency and freedom envisioned in critical notions of childhood and without the anxiety and sense of limitation" placed upon them by childhood and educational research and discourse (38). Toward the end, we offer this collection of essays as an intervention that seeks to address the lack of both Majority world and nonwhite Minority World perspectives on childhood and make space for critical work that attempts to move beyond the limiting discourses of innocence.

REFUSING THE LIMITS OF CONTEMPORARY CHILDHOOD

When putting together the contributors for this collection, we sought out work from both established and emerging scholars who engage with childhood from a wide range of disciplinary perspectives and drawing from different disciplinary and methodological perspectives. Specifically, we looked for projects that offered interesting opportunities for rethinking the politics of nature, culture, bodies, and subjects in and between intersectional, transnational contexts. Each of the essays in this collection considers what lies beyond the limiting discourses of innocence. Instead of focusing on how children "grow up," as has been the focus of developmental science for over a century, we ask what it might mean for discourses of childhood to finally "grow out" of childhood innocence? We believe that such an endeavour requires actively refusing the limits of normative and normalizing conceptions of *the* child by surfacing and centering complex, multiplicitous configurations of childhood that can challenge existing discourses and social practices to reveal how power operates in and through the child and its uses. Doing so often demands a recognition of the inherent traumas of childhood, but this does not mean succumbing to its damaging potentials. Rather, we seek here to unearth the desires that lie just beneath loss and flow from erasure in order to find presence and meaning from the obliviating violence of childhood innocence.

One of the effects of such erasure is the way that innocence is juxtaposed with agency in a problematic either/or dichotomy, as if childhood innocence can simply be reversed through the assignment of agency. This approach fails to "consider the myriad ways in which children are often constrained or express their agency in problematic ways" (Canosa and Graham 2020, 34). In their chapter on how Black girls' agency is shaped by educational experiences, Kisha McPherson and Chanelle Perrier-Telemaque write in response to traditional research on Black girls that focuses on the failure of North American education systems to meet their needs and priorities. Their chapter is premised on the fact that Ontario schools have historically been inequitable in policy and practice to Black students in general and Black girls in particular. As they observe, attempts to address and reform educational policies practices have been slow and inconsistent, leaving Black girls with the responsibility to support their own educational priorities. Drawing on Black feminist epistemologies, they look for insight from their own autobiographies as former Black girls in the Ontario education system as well as from focus group interviews with six Black girls between the ages of 17 to 21 who are current or former Ontario high school students. Using an intersectional approach, McPherson and Perrier-Telemaque consider the multiple dimensions of Black identities that intersect to create specific forms of inequality. As well, drawing on critical pedagogy, they explore how participants resisted and produced knowledge against oppressive forms of schooling, highlighting their perspectives on, and acts of resistance against, the education system and oppressive practices in Ontario schools. Their contribution not only highlights a long history of "miseducation" that has produced discriminatory and specifically, "adultifying," schooling experiences for Black girls in Ontario, but also offers insight into the ways that Black girls are challenging Eurocentric ideologies of childhood and education.

Offering another perspective on such ideologies, Sebastian Barajas explores in the next chapter the paradox between the adultification of Black children and the infantilization of Black adults, which are not contradictory processes but rather, symbiotic processes that reinforce each other. The former is a process that excludes Black children from the category of childhood, which is reserved for white children who are often characterized as innocent, vulnerable, and dependant. The latter process excludes Black adults from the category of adulthood characterized by the capacity to reason, autonomy, and freedom. However, as Barajas explains, childhood and adulthood are not clearly defined binaries, but rather ambivalent, malleable moral constructs that can be weaponized, particularly as they intersect with racial and developmentalist discourses. As Barajas illustrates by tracing the history of racist discourses relating to child welfare, labour, and criminality in the United States, the ambiguity of both constructs allow for Black children to be excluded from the presumed innocence and protectiveness of childhood while simultaneously being recognized as children to the extent that it could be weaponized against them. Ultimately, Barajas calls for childhood studies to move beyond simply critiquing the consequences of racist ideology and instead, critique the adultist ideologies that perpetuate racism.

Contributor Adam Davies draws attention to another important and largely unexplored way that a Western, colonial and developmental construct of childhood intersects with systems of oppression. Specifically, Davies considers the ways that the hegemonic logics of childhood innocence intersect with normative constructs of sanity to pathologize children through sanism, or the systemic denigration and exclusion of those who are perceived to be or who are classified as mad (Perlin 1992; Leblanc and Kinsella 2016). As Davies illustrates, children and youth who are deemed mad or experience psychiatrization are excluded from ideals of childhood innocence by virtue of their categorization as disordered and potentially dangerous – assumptions that are similarly brought to bear upon Blackness. Accordingly, Davies engages with the work of Sylvia Wynter as well as research on the intersection of Blackness and madness, and theories of childhood innocence, to propose a *maddening* (Davies 2022; LeFrançois 2017) of childhood innocence discourses. In their provocative piece, Davies calls for a consideration of how madness and Blackness disrupt developmentalist constructs of childhood that are premised on Enlightenment notions of rationality.

Presenting another compelling counterpoint to normative white, Western perspectives on childhood, Kathia Núñez Patiño tells a story about childhood and cultural practices within Indigenous communities as told through the voices of the children growing up with the legacy of the Zapatista resistance movement in Chiapas, Mexico. The Ch'ol children who are the focus of this chapter were born into the movement and have lived without access to basic rights to education, healthcare, food, and safety, and yet, in their stories, Núñez Patiño finds possibilities for expanding the diversity of childhoods and reimagining children's power to engage in collaborative research processes. Her chapter offers important insights into alternative ways of reflecting on the diversity of contexts in which children participate and reconsider the importance of their presence and participation in public spaces. As an opening toward a decolonial perspective on childhood, she exposes the power structures that exist between the sites that comprised her project - the community, the school, and the academy - and explores the implications for research with and advocacy for marginalized children.

Núñez Patiño's work highlights some of the tensions between children's rights and children's agency, particularly when the practices and values of particular families and communities are at odds with dominant political structures. Historically, the resolution of such conflicts has been shaped by universalist Western ideologies of child protection that offer overly simplistic solutions, as illustrated in Doris Kakaru's chapter. Kakuru examines responses, remedies, and the rights of victims in laws and policies that address an epidemic of violence against children in Uganda. To do this Kakuru conducts a discourse analysis drawing on the notion of childism which serves as an analytic lens to examine adultism, or how adults enact the domination and subordination of children. For example, adultism manifests through colonial developmental discourses which constitute modern childhood as a precursor to adulthood. Within this logic, the status of childhood as an innocent, ignorant, and vulnerable state of "becoming" justify the exclusion and silencing of children's voices and experiences in law and policy-making practices. In turn, Kakaru shows how adult-centric frameworks driven by protectionist impulses collide with human rights frameworks in contradictory ways that endorse the violation of children's bodies and autonomy in order to protect them. Kakaru's analysis rejects the motives and cultural forces that have positioned children as less-than-human, yielding important insight into the ways that contemporary child protection ecosystems, in Uganda and beyond, can benefit from policies informed by children's participation and child-focused evidence in future research, policy, and law.

As illustrated by Kakaru, protective logics are a common way that innocence is invoked to marginalize children and limit their roles as social actors and community members. Furthermore, as Anusha Iyer demonstrates in the next chapter, childhood innocence operates in the service of political aims rooted in colonial histories of subjectification and social ordering. Iyer describes how a malleable construct of innocence has shaped policy and law within the Indian Juvenile Justice system, specifically the *Juvenile Justice Act* that was amended in 2015. Iyer explains how innocence operates as a political tool that perpetuates ignorance in various ways that shift the focus away from the political stakes of children and works to exclude certain bodies from the category of citizen. In exposing the contradictory and yet profoundly impactful ways that childhood innocence operates to inform children's experiences within the Indian Juvenile Justice system, Iyer makes a bold and compelling case for a turn away from the construct of moral innocence as a basis for children's justice.

Moving away from the domain of law and into the realm of literature, Mayurika Chakravorty offers another perspective on the violence of innocence in discourse that occurs through the erasure of childhood experiences in non-Western contexts. Chakravorty attends to these erasures through her analysis of Bapsi Sidhwa's (1947) *Cracking India,* a rare text that foregrounds children's experience of the traumatic ethnic violence and forced migration in the wake of colonial administrative Partition of the Indian subcontinent in 1947. *Cracking India* offers a contrapuntal narrative in the form of the protagonist Lenny, who illustrates a conceptualization of girlhood that is a radical departure from traditional representations governed by gender, caste, and religious norms. Chakravorty interrogates Western assumptions about childhood by tracing how figures of the child subvert innocence through sexuality and violence, two dimensions disavowed through normative discourses. As well, Chakravorty considers how the child's traversing of spaces made for children and spaces children appropriate (or is left unmonitored by adults) challenges notions of innocence. However, in thwarting innocence manifest through space, the girl child becomes more vulnerable to Partition violence and chauvinistic protectionism as she is ushered into maturity. Ultimately, Chakravorty shows how the child's subversion of innocence in *Cracking India* disrupts the moralizing nationalist sentiments entangled with the myth of childhood innocence.

Neil Ramjewan also turns to the literature of resistance that destabilizes and departs from colonial configurations of childhood as innocent, redemptive, and unconditionally agentic in Nalo Hopkinson's (2000) Afrofuturistic science fiction novel, *Midnight Robber*. Starting from a similar premise in discussions on political freedom that turn to the voices of the enslaved, he also turns to the child of the enslaved to theorize childhood agency. To do this, Ramjewan draws on the notion of the "arrivant" which signifies those forced to the "New World" through colonial practices such as slavery and indentured labour. This term unsettles the settler-Indigenous binary in settler colonial discourse, which evades the nuances, contingencies, and complicities that structure the double bind in which arrivants, faced with the impossibility of returning to a lost home, must make home on stolen Indigenous land. Returning to the aesthetics of Caribbean poetic traditions in which arrival is an active event and structure, Ramjewan reads the child's terms of arrival and the relationship with the Indigenous figures of the New World. He argues that Hopkinson draws on the trauma of slavery, and the conditions of repeated and continued arrival, or arrivance, to reimagine agency as multiple and contingent in addition to individualized capacity concepts of agency. Understanding Hopkinson's speculative fiction to be an intervention to the genre of Euro-American science fiction, Ramjewan considers what a turn to the histories of Black, Brown, and Indigenous children might mean for the field of childhood studies for whom theories of agency have limited engagement with histories of colonization and racism.

Exploring possibilities seems like an appropriate place to end the work of this collection, which is why we chose to conclude the volume with Durrell Callier and Dominique Hill's compelling piece on the possibilities and pleasures of Black youth. Drawing on the cases of South Carolina teen Dynasia Clark and the fictional Black youth in Dee Rees cinematic debut Pariah (2011) Callier and Hill stage two scenes that explore the expansive narratives between Black childhood, queerness, and pleasure. Through these scenes, they illustrate how performance can reorient contemporary understandings of childhood beyond innocence by disrupting commonly held believes about how Black youth, specifically Black queer girls, access pleasure, agency, and knowledge. With each case, Callier and Hill present us with opportunities to think about the ways that race, class, gender, and sexuality problematize and oftentimes obliterate historic and contemporary hegemonic understandings of childhood as mapped through discursive logics of innocence and diminutiveness. By centering Black, queer childhood, their work seeks to illuminate multiple potential opportunities for pleasure, while creatively providing redress to the disembodying experiences of discrimination.

MOVING BEYOND INNOCENCE: TOWARD RADICAL REFUSALS

Part of the significance of this collection is a response to the charges of white supremacy we have raised, evidenced by the absence of racialized scholars even as there has been a recent shift towards a greater diversity of discourses and perspectives (Cook 2020). It is our belief that the inclusion of predominantly Black, Brown and Indigenous scholars in this collection, while not immune from internalized forms of prejudice and discrimination, also comes with lived and autobiographical relationships to the discourses we seek to interrogate *and* the ways we seek to so. In particular, the prevailing globally organizing structures of racism and colonization have salience in the work that this collection of authors bring to childhood studies, which continues to have little traction in terms of central concerns for scholars (Canosa and Graham 2020). These discourses shape what is meant by the social construction of childhood, a persistent theme in childhood studies. In fact, the social constructedness of childhood has become a prevailing assumption by scholars in the field which according to Hammersley (2017) rejects the *"internalization* of norms" which developmental psychology offers and is instead deemed to be a form of determinism that is at odds with another preoccupation of the field, children's agency. Hammersley (2017) suggests that a more radical version of social constructionism driven by discursive theoretical and methodological approaches would invite "very different kinds of work from what currently makes up the field" (118). This is precisely what we aim to do in this collection.

What then does moving beyond innocence require? As we have suggested above, instead of focusing on how children "grow up" along a linear path toward a Western ideal of maturity and rationality, as has been the focus of developmental science for over a century, we ask what it might mean for discourses of childhood to finally "grow out" of childhood innocence? In part this means departing from innocence and other normalized presumptions about childhood from the outset as rationales justifying inquiry. We do this by turning to scholars writing from a variety of contexts, both of Majority and Minority world perspectives and the lived experience of children that have been historically marginalized from the field and its preoccupations. Importantly, growing "out" should be considered distinct from growing "away," since we cannot escape the long historical legacy of innocence and its seductive appeal as a balm of insecurities, complicities, and injustices. Rather, growing "out" might be understood, drawing from the metaphor proposed by Deleuze and Guitarri (1980) as a rhizomatic process, a multiplicitous proliferation of complex and contradictory perspectives on childhood unbounded by linear margins and disconnected from any central source. Such an approach refuses the Western narrative of the ignorant, innocent child as the dominant foundation from which understandings of childhood must grow. Toward that end, we hope that each of the essays in this collection will invite readers to consider the diverse and flourishing forms and experiences of childhood that shape the lived experiences of children today and can inform a more complex understanding of what childhood *is*, not what it *should be*. Specifically, we hope this work will bring more attention to some of the counternarratives to the hegemonic stories that continue to be told about childhood and inspire further inquiry into the multitudinous ways of relating to human experiences across the wide and complex spectrum of identities, including culture, language, location, and age.

REFERENCES

Alanen, Leena. 1988. "Rethinking Childhood." *Acta Sociologica* 31 (1): 53–67. https://doi.org/10.1177/000169938803100105.

Ariès, Philippe. 1960. *L'enfant et la vie familiale sous l'Ancien Régime*. Paris: Plon.

Baker, Bernadette M. 1998. "Childhood in the Emergence and Spread of US Public Schools." In *Foucault's Challenge: Discourse, Knowledge, and Power in Education,* edited by Thomas S. Popkewitz and Marie T. Brennan, 117–43. New York: Teacher College Press.

Baker, Bernadette M. 2001. *In Perpetual Motion: Theories of Power, Educational History, and the Child*. New York: P. Lang.

Bass, Loretta E. 2010. "Childhood in Sociology and Society: The US Perspective." *Current Sociology* 58 (2): 335–50. https://doi.org/10.1177/0011392109354248.

Bernstein, Robin. 2011. *Racial Innocence: Performing American Childhood from Slavery to Civil Rights*. New York: New York University Press.

Bradley, Ben S. 1994. "Darwin's Intertextual Baby: Erasmus Darwin as Precursor in Child Psychology." *Human Development* 37 (2): 86–102. https://doi.org/10.1159/000278242.

Brooks-Gunn, Jeanne and Anna Duncan Johnson. 2006. "G. Stanley Hall's Contribution to Science, Practice and Policy: The Child Study, Parent Education, and Child Welfare Movements." *History of Psychology* 9 (3): 247–58. https://doi.org/10.1037/1093-4510.9.3.247.

Brown, Desmond. 2021. "Number of Youth in Hospital After Suicide Attempt Tripled Over 4-Month Period Under COVID-19." Accessed March 18, 2021. https://www.cbc.ca/news/canada/hamilton/pandemic-safety-measures-children-teen-health-impact-1.5953326.

Burman, Erica. 1991. "Power, Gender and Developmental Psychology." *Feminism & Psychology* 1 (1): 141–53. https://doi.org/10.1177/0959353591011018.

Burman, Erica. 1992. "Developmental Psychology and the Postmodern Child." In *Postmodernism and the Social Sciences*, edited by Joe Doherty, Elspeth Graham, and Mo Malek, 95–110. Palgrave MacMillan UK.

Burman, Erica. 1994a. *Deconstructing Developmental Psychology*. London: Routledge.

Burman, Erica. 1994b. "Poor children: Charity Appeals and Ideologies of Childhood." *Changes: An International Journal of Psychology and Psychotherapy* 12 (1): 29–46.

Burman, Erica. 1995. "Constructing and Deconstructing Childhood." In *Psychological Research: Innovative Methods and Strategies*, edited by John Haworth, 70–184. Routledge. https://doi.org/10.4324/9780203138151.

Canosa, Antonia and Anne Graham. 2020. "Tracing the Contribution of Childhood Studies: Maintaining Momentum While Navigating Tensions." *Childhood (Copenhagen, Denmark)* 27 (1): 25–47. https://doi.org/10.1177/0907568219886619.

"Childhood." *Blackwood's Magazine* 12, no. 67 (1822): 139–45, cited in Robin Bernstein, *Racial Innocence: Performing American Childhood from Slavery to Civil Rights* (New York: New York University Press, 2011).

Cook, Daniel Thomas. 2020. *The Sage Encyclopedia of Children and Childhood Studies. 4*. Edited by Daniel Thomas Cook. Los Angeles: Sage Publications, Inc.

Corsaro, William A. 1997. *The Sociology of Childhood*. Thousand Oaks: Pine Forge Press.

Cunningham, Hugh. 1991. *The Children of the Poor: Representations of Childhood Since the Seventeenth Century*. Oxford: Blackwell.

Cunningham, Hugh. 1995. *Children and Childhood in Western Society since 1500*. London: Longman.

Curran, Tillie and Katherine Runswick-Cole. 2014. "Disabled Children's Childhood Studies: A Distinct Approach?" *Disability & Society* 29 (10): 1617–30. https://doi.org/10.1080/09687599.2014.966187.

Davies, Adam W. 2022. "Professional Ruptures in Pre-Service ECEC: Maddening Early Childhood Education and Care." *Curriculum Inquiry* 54 (2). https://doi.org/10.1080/03626784.2022.2149027.

Davin, Anna. 1996. *Growing up Poor: Home, School and Street in London 1870–1914*. London: Rivers Oram Press.

de Castro, Lucia Rabello. 2020. "Why Global? Children and Childhood from a Decolonial Perspective." *Childhood (Copenhagen, Denmark)* 27 (1): 48–62. https://doi.org/10.1177/0907568219885379.

Deleuze, Gilles, Félix Guattari, and Brian Massumi. 2004. *A Thousand Plateaus: Capitalism and Schizophrenia*. London: Continuum.

Duschinsky, Robbie. 2013. "Childhood Innocence: Essence, Education, and Performativity." *Textual Practice* 27 (5): 763–81. https://doi.org/10.1080/0950236X.2012.751441.

Dumas, Michael J. and Joseph Derrick Nelson. 2016. "(Re)Imagining Black Boyhood: Toward a Critical Framework for Educational Research." *Harvard Educational Review* 86 (1): 27–47. https://doi.org/10.17763/0017-8055.86.1.27.

Escayg, Kerry-Ann, ed. 2020. *The SAGE Encyclopedia of Children and Childhood Studies*. 4 vols. Thousand Oaks: SAGE Publications, Inc. https://doi.org/10.4135/9781529714388.

Escayg, Kerry-Ann, Rachel Berman, and Natalie Royer. 2017. "Canadian Children and Race: Toward an Antiracism Analysis." *Canadian Children* 42 (2): 10. https://doi.org/10.18357/jcs.v42i2.17838.

Esser, Florian, Meike S. Baader, Tanja Betz, and Beatrice Hungerland, eds. 2016. *Reconceptualising Agency and Childhood: New Perspectives in Childhood Studies*. New York: Taylor & Francis. https://doi.org/10.4324/9781315722245.

Farley, Lisa Anne. 2018. *Childhood Beyond Pathology: A Psychoanalytic Study of Development and Diagnosis*. Albany: State University of New York Press.

Faulkner, Joanne. 2010. "The Innocence Fetish: The Commodification and Sexualisation of Children in the Media and Popular Culture." *Media International Australia Incorporating Culture & Policy* 135 (135): 106–17. https://doi.org/10.1177/1329878X1013500113.

Faulkner, Joanne. 2019. "Ghosts of Eugenics' Past: 'Childhood' as a Target for Whitening Race in the United States and Canada." *Critical Race and Whiteness Studies*. https://acrawsa.org.au/category/first-glimpse/.

Faye, Cathy. 2012. "American Social Psychology: Examining the Contours of the 1970s Crisis." *Studies in History and Philosophy of Science: Part C, Studies in History and Philosophy of Biological and Biomedical Sciences* 43 (2): 514–21. https://doi.org/10.1016/j.shpsc.2011.11.010.

Foucault, Michel. 1977. *Discipline and Punish: The Birth of the Prison*. 1st American ed. New York: Pantheon Books.

Frampton, Pam. 2021. "Innocence — One Casualty of the Pandemic." Accessed May 7, 2021. https://www.saltwire.com/atlantic-canada/opinion/pam-frampton-innocence-one-casualty-of-the-pandemic-100585405/#.

Frønes, Ivar. 1993. "Changing Childhood." *Childhood* 1 (1): 1–2. https://doi.org/10.1177/090756829300100101.

Garlen, Julie C. 2019. "Interrogating Innocence: 'Childhood' as Exclusionary Social Practice." *Childhood* 26 (1): 54–67. https://doi.org/10.1177/0907568218811484.

Garlen, Julie C. 2021."The End of Innocence: Childhood and Schooling for a Post-Pandemic World." *Journal of Teaching and Learning* 15 (2): 21–39.

Hafstad, Gertrud Sofie and Else-Marie Augusti. 2021. "A Lost Generation? COVID-19 and Adolescent Mental Health." *The Lancet Psychiatry* 8 (8): 640–1.

Hall, Granville Stanley. 1893. *The Contents of Children's Minds on Entering School*. EL Kellogg.

Henriques, Julian. 1998. *Changing the Subject: Psychology, Social Regulation, and Subjectivity*, 2nd edn. London: Routledge. https://doi.org/10.4324/9780203298886.

Holloway, Sarah L. and Gill Valentine. 2000. "Spatiality and the New Social Studies of Childhood." *Sociology (Oxford)* 34 (4): 763–83. https://doi.org/10.1177/S0038038500000468.

Hopkinson, Nalo. 2000. *Midnight Robber*. Grand Central Publishing.

James, Allison, Chris Jenks, and Alan Prout. 1998. *Theorizing Childhood*. Cambridge: Polity Press.

James, Allison and Alan Prout. 1997. *Constructing and Reconstructing Childhood: Contemporary Issues in the Sociological Study of Childhood*, 2nd edn. London: Falmer Press.

Jenks, Chris. 1982. *The Sociology of Childhood*. Batsford: Academic and Educational Ltd.

Jenks, Chris. 2005. *Childhood: Critical Concepts in Sociology*. Routledge.

Kessler, Shirley A. and Beth Blue Swadener. 1992. *Reconceptualizing the Early Childhood Curriculum: Beginning the Dialog*. New York: Teachers College Press.

King, Nicole. 2022. *Black Childhood in Modern African American Fiction*. Edinburgh University Press.

Konstantoni, Kristina and Akwugo Emejulu. 2017. "When Intersectionality Met Childhood Studies: The Dilemmas of a Travelling Concept." *Children's Geographies* 15 (1): 6–22. https://doi.org/10.1080/14733285.2016.1249824.

Leeb, R. T., R. H. Bitsko, L. Radhakrishnan, P. Martinez, R. Njai, and K. M. Holland. 2020. "Mental Health–Related Emergency Department Visits Among Children Aged <18 Years During the COVID-19 Pandemic—United States, January 1–October 17, 2020." *Morbidity and Mortality Weekly Report* 69 (45): 1675–80.

Leblanc, Stephanie and Elizabeth Anne Kinsella. 2016. "Toward Epistemic Justice: A Critically Reflexive Examination of 'Sanism' and Implications for Knowledge Generation." *Studies in Social Justice* 10 (1): 59–78. https://doi.org/10.26522/ssj.v10i1.1324.

LeFrançois, Brenda A. 2017. "Mad Studies: Maddening Social Work," Filmed November 2017 at Connecting for Canada's 150th: Canadian Visionaries of Critical Social Work, Fredericton, NB, YouTube." https://www.youtube.com/watch?v=QYxM_bBk7fs.

Lenzer, Gertrud. 2001. "Children's Studies: Beginnings and Purposes." *The Lion and the Unicorn (Brooklyn)* 25 (2): 181–6. https://doi.org/10.1353/uni.2001.0022.1675.

Liebel, Manfred. 2020. *Decolonizing Childhoods: From Exclusion to Dignity*. Policy Press.

Lyotard, Jean François. 1984. *The Postmodern Condition: A Report on Knowledge*. Manchester: Manchester University Press.

Mayall, Berry. 2012. "An Afterword: Some Reflections on a Seminar Series." *Children's Geographies* 10 (3): 347–55. https://doi.org/10.1080/14733285.2012.693383.

McKinney, Kim. 2020. "The Coronavirus Brings a Loss of Innocence to Healthcare and the Workplace." Accessed April 24, 2023. https://medium.com/illumination-curated/the-coronavirus-brings-a-loss-of-innocence-to-healthcare-and-the-workplace-16a7f9b5b512.

McNamee, Sally. 2019. *The Social Study of Childhood*. Bloomsbury Publishing.

Meiners, Erica R. 2016. *For the Children? Protecting Innocence in a Carceral State*. Minneapolis: University of Minnesota Press.

Morss, John R. 1992. "Making Waves: Deconstruction and Developmental Psychology." *Theory & Psychology* 2 (4): 445–65. https://doi.org/10.1177/0959354392024003.

Morss, John R. 1996. *Growing Critical: Alternatives to Developmental Psychology*. London: Routledge.

Nandy, Ashis. 1984. "Reconstructing Childhood: A Critique of the Ideology of Adulthood." *Alternatives: Global, Local, Political* 10 (3): 359–75. https://doi.org/10.1177/030437548401000303.

Neustadter, Roger M. 2009. *The Obvious Child: Studies in the Significance of Childhood*. Lanham: University Press of America.

Nickeas, Peter, Dakin Andone, and Emma Tucker. 2021. "Chicago Police Say Bodycam Footage Shows Less Than a Second Passes from When 13-Year-Old

Is Seen Holding a Handgun and Is Shot by Officer." Accessed April 16, 2021. https://www.cnn.com/2021/04/15/us/adam-toledo-police-shooting-body-camera/index.html.

Nxumalo, Fikile and Stacia Cedillo. 2017. "Decolonizing Place in Early Childhood Studies: Thinking with Indigenous onto-Epistemologies and Black Feminist Geographies." *Global Studies of Childhood* 7 (2): 99–112. https://doi.org/10.1177/2043610617703831.

O'Connell, Mark. 2020. "Santa Claus Ain't Coming to Town. Is Childhood Innocence Worth Preserving?" Accessed August 27, 2020. https://www.economist.com/1843/2020/08/27/santa-claus-aint-coming-to-town-is-childhood-innocence-worth-preserving.

Pagden, Anthony. 1986. *The Fall of Natural Man: The American Indian and the Origins of Comparative Ethnology*. Cambridge: Cambridge University Press.

Partridge, George Everitt. 1912. *Genetic Philosophy of Education: An Epitome of the Published Educational Writings of President G. Stanley Hall of Clark University*. New York: Sturgis.

Perlin, Michael L. 1992. "On Sanism." *SMU Law Review* 46: 373–407.

Pratt, Richard H. 1892. "The Advantages of Mingling Indians with Whites." In *Americanizing the American Indians: Writings by the "Friends of the Indian" 1880–1900,* edited by Francis Paul Prucha, 260–71. Cambridge: Harvard University Press.

Qvortrup, Jens. 1994. *Childhood Matters: Social Theory, Practice and Politics*. Aldershot: Avebury.

Qvortrup, J., W. Corsaro, and M. Honig. 2009. *The Palgrave Handbook of Childhood Studies*. Edited by J. Qvortrup, W. Corsaro, and M. Honig, 1st edn. London: Palgrave Macmillan UK. https://doi.org/10.1007/978-0-230-27468-6.

Ramjewan, Neil and Julie C. Garlen. 2020. "Growing Out of Childhood Innocence." *Curriculum Inquiry* 50 (4): 281–90. https://doi.org/10.1080/03626784.2020.1851521.

Rees, Dee, director. *Pariah*. Focus Features, 2011.

Robinson, Kerry H. 2012. *Innocence, Knowledge and the Construction of Childhood the Contradictory Nature of Sexuality and Censorship in Children's Contemporary Lives*, 1st edn. Hoboken: Taylor and Francis.

Rose, Jacqueline. 1984. *The Case of Peter Pan, or, The Impossibility of Children's Fiction*. London: Macmillan.

Rose, Nikolas S. 1985. *The Psychological Complex: Psychology, Politics and Society in England, 1869–1939*. London: Routledge & Kegan Paul.

Schenzle, Steffi. 2021. *Have We Lost A Generation of Children During the Corona Pandemic?* Accessed June 21, 2021. https://sciencenorway.no/children-and-adolescents-opinion-psychology/have-we-lost-a-generation-of-children-during-the-corona-pandemic/1876227.

Shalhoub-Kevorkian, Nadera. 2019. *Incarcerated Childhood and the Politics of Unchilding*. Cambridge: Cambridge University Press.

Shaheed, Ahmed. 2021. *Countering Islamophobia/anti-Muslim Hatred to Eliminate Discrimination and Intolerance Based on Religion or Belief*. United Nations

Human Rights Council. https://documents-dds-ny.un.org/doc/UNDOC/GEN/G21/086/49/PDF/G2108649.pdf?OpenElement.

Sidhwa, Bapsi. 1988. *Cracking India*. Milkweed Editions.

Siegel, Alexander W., and Sheldon H. White. 1982. "The Child Study Movement: Early Growth and Development of the Symbolized Child." In *Advances in Child Development and Behavior*, edited by Hayne W. Reese, 233–85. San Diego: Academic Press.

Steedman, Carolyn. 1995. *Strange Dislocations: Childhood and the Idea of Human Interiority, 1780–1930*. Cambridge: Harvard University Press.

Swadener, Beth Blue, and Shirley A. Kessler. 1991. "Reconceptualizing Early Childhood Education: An Introduction." *Early Education and Development* 2 (2): 85–94.

Tarc, Aparna M. 2021. "Tiny Witnesses of War: Palestinian Children's Voices Should Guide a Renewed Commitment to Peace". *The Conversation*. https://theconversation.com/tiny- witnesses-of-war-palestinian-childrens-voices-should-guide-a-renewed-commitment-to-peace-161768.

Taylor, Affrica. 2010. "Troubling Childhood Innocence: Reframing the Debate over the Media Sexualisation of Children." *Australasian Journal of Early Childhood* 35 (1): 48–57. https://doi.org/10.1177/183693911003500108.

Thorne, Barrie. 1994. *Gender Play: Boys and Girls in School*. Rutgers University Press.

Tisdall, E. Kay M. and Samantha Punch. 2012. "Not So 'New'? Looking Critically at Childhood Studies." *Children's Geographies* 10 (3): 249–64.

Twum-Danso Imoh, Afua and Robert Ame. 2012. *Childhoods at the Intersection of the Local and the Global*. Palgrave Macmillan.

UNICEF. 2020. "Averting a Lost COVID Generation: A Six-Point Plan to Respond, Recover and Reimagine a Post-Pandemic World for Every Child." https://www.unicef.org/media/86881/file/Averting-a-lost-covid-generation-world-childrens-day-data-and-advocacy-brief-2020.pdf.

United Nations. 2021. "UNICEF Calls for Action to Reverse 'Spiraling Protection Crisis' for Children in West and Central Africa". United Nations. https://news.un.org/en/story/2021/07/1095402.

Valentine, Kylie. 2011. Accounting for agency. *Children & Society* 25: 347–58.

Walkerdine, Valerie. 1984. "Developmental Psychology and the Child-Centred Pedagogy: The Insertion of Piaget into Early Education." In *Changing the Subject: Psychology, Social Regulation and Subjectivity*, edited by Julian Henriques, Wendy Hollway, Cathy Urwin, Couze Venn, and Valerie Walkerdine, 148–98. New York: Routledge.

Walkerdine, Valerie. 1987. "No Laughing Matter." In *Critical Theories of Psychological Development*, edited by John M. Broughton, Path in Psychology. Boston: Springer. https://doi.org/10.1007/978-1-4757-9886-9_4.

Walkerdine, Valerie. 1993. "Beyond Developmentalism?" *Theory & Psychology* 3 (4): 451–69. https://doi.org/10.1177/0959354393034004.

Walkerdine, Valerie. 2005. "Developmental Psychology and the Study of Childhood." In *Childhood: Critical Concepts in Sociology*, 3rd edn, edited by Chris Jenks, 13–25. New York: Routledge.

Webster, Crystal Lynn. 2021. *Beyond the Boundaries of Childhood: African American Children in the Antebellum North*. Chapel Hill: University of North Carolina Press.

White, Samantha. 2021. "Black Girls Swim: Race, Gender, and Embodied Aquatic Histories." *Girlhood Studies* 14 (2): 63–79. https://doi.org/10.3167/ghs.2021.140206.

Wickersham, Joan. 2020. "Reading the Coronavirus Pandemic as a Loss of Innocence". The Boston Globe. https://www.bostonglobe.com/2020/05/01/opinion/reading-coronavirus-pandemic-loss-innocence.

Wynter, Sylva. 1995. "1492: A New World View." In *Race, Discourse and the Origin of the Americas: A New World View*, edited by Vera Lawrence Hyatt and Rex Nettleford, 5–57. Washington, DC: Smithsonian Institute Press.

Yousif, Nadine. 2021. "Pandemic School Disruptions Wreaking Havoc on Children's Mental Health, Sick Kids Report Says." *The Toronto Star*. https://www.thestar.com/news/gta/2021/01/22/pandemic-school-disruptions-wreaking-havoc-on-childrens-mental-health-sick-kids-report-says.html.

Zelizer, Viviana. 1985. *Pricing the Priceless Child: The Changing Social Value of Children*. New York: HarperCollins.

Chapter 1

Who Is Entitled to Childhood Innocence

Black Girls and the Struggle against Racial Bias in Canadian Schools

Kisha McPherson and Chanelle Perrier-Telemaque

REFLECTIONS

Kisha: Sitting in my grade 11 English Media class, I just turned 16, and I prepare to make a collage focused on media representations to reflect my identity. There are a number of Black students in the class, but I am placed in a group with three white students, and we were provided with a stack of material, placed in the center of our table, to sift through, identify, and cut out images and words that represent our identity. As I go through the images in the stockpile of resources, I am confused, and I feel my frustration increasing as I am struck by the lack of diversity in the media resources that are provided. I am thinking, how am I, a Black girl, with immigrant Caribbean parents, supposed to identify with images in magazines like Marie Claire and Chatelaine? The materials and resources my teacher supplies for students to complete an identity assignment are extremely Eurocentric. There are several piles, piles of magazines, and newspapers, with white faces, white bodies, white skin, white names, white countries, and in clear contrast, very few images that reflect any type of Black identity.

Still, I am expected to complete this assignment. As a Black student, I, along with the other Black students in the class are placed in this difficult position of completing this assignment without resources that adequately or effectively accounts for our experiences, our culture, and our realities. But no one mentions these concerns, we just do our best. One Black girl in the class cuts out fancy letters from a magazine heading to spell out "BLACK", and she uses brown construction paper to cut out what looks like an afro and draws a face underneath it. Most of us try to make do, and get the work done, under any, and all circumstances.

Chanelle: The stage lights come on in the auditorium of the Toronto arts high school I
attended between 2007 and 2011. My teacher, the artistic director, shouts "from the top", and we all reset. I was 15 years old at the time. The band begins to play the prelude to I Know Where I've Been, we're rehearsing for the musical Hairspray. This is the part of the show where the entire Black cast and ensemble is joined by three "woke" white allies, and the show's protagonist, to sing in protest of the local television network's refusal to integrate Black and white dancers.

As the music continues to build, the artistic director and choreographer join us on stage to physically demonstrate how we should remain grounded throughout the number. She stated, "move as if we were walking in place with shackles and chains on our feet." At this point, she is talking to all the Black students performing in the play. We oblige her, our metaphorical shackles keeping us tethered to the stage floor, as if we were in bondage, until the song comes to a somber yet triumphant end. I look around, my peers are visibly upset, some are even in tears. The artistic director shouts "Great! That was really powerful, make sure you do that every time!" The bell rings, it is now time for fourth period. The teacher takes no time to discuss and certainly takes no further opportunity to unpack the violence that had taken place. We were left with our emotions, thoughts, and fears, to just hurry through the rest of our school day.

INTRODUCTION

The stories shared above describe situations that point to some of the inequitable circumstances that we, as Black female children, faced while attending Canadian schools. Following some of the Black feminist traditions (Henry 1995; hooks 1989; McKittrick 2006) that have emphasized the necessity of reclaiming our voices, we use our own experiences to describe how constructions of our own identities conflict with common, normalized virtues of childhood, such as innocence and protection. As Black women who grew up living in Canada, we recount our own circumstances as children to begin to examine how Black girls experience their childhood in context to education.

Our accounts, and those of Black girls today that we feature in this chapter, demonstrate a callous disregard of girls who look like us, and they illustrate how Black girls' status as children is often ignored. Society has normalized treating Black girls like adults, expecting them, even in childhood, to know and do better in their actions. If they don't, they are stereotyped, marginalized, and punished in ways that their white peers are not. It would be difficult to locate any point in history when Black girls were read as "innocent," as childhood innocence is often commonly associated with non-Black children. In Canada, social systems do not offer Black girls the "protection" that continues to be linked with expectations in childhood. Being seen as innocent and being protected due to this innocence is only a fantasy for many Black Canadian girls. Childhood Studies does problematize the universalist, unrealistic, and racist application of concepts such as "innocence" and "protection" of children in childhood (Farley and Garlen 2016; Garlen 2019), but these ideals tend represent childhood for middle-class or wealthy White children. Black girls, however, have never had the "luxury" of such affordances. We say "luxury" not to suggest that children should in fact be seen as innocent. In our opinion, challenging the concept of innocence as a fact of childhood (Garlen 2019; Taylor 2010) is necessary in scholarship. Still, the mere idea of innocence in relation to childhood continues to be so far removed from the experiences of many Black girls that outlining these tensions in Childhood Studies seems almost too obvious for serious debate. However, the fact that Black girls continued to be excluded from this ideal offers a compelling case for dismantling innocence as a conceptual lens for understanding what childhood is or should be.

Here, by examining education practices, policies, and the experience of Black children in Canadian education systems, we call into question these normalized virtues of childhood (James and Prout 1997), children's rights (Covell, Howe, and Blokhuis 2018), and assumptions about how education impacts child development (Darling-Hammond et al. 2020). We agree that notions linked to childhood (i.e., innocence, protection) are not, and have never been, static within a global context. Any reference to the experience of children must be placed in context to the spatial and temporal nature of childhood in specific regions (Punch 2003; Spyrou, Rosen, and Cook 2018). Even writing from the specific context of Canada, we must be careful not to conflate the characteristics of childhood that are often automatically applied to White Canadian children (Hartas 2010; Wells 2017) with the experiences of all children. Commonly accepted characteristics of childhood include the understanding that children, in general, are different from adults, and as result have different social, emotional needs, and expectations during this stage. However, accommodations that might be made for some children throughout childhood have never been equally applied to all children in Canada. As a settler colonial country, Canada has a long legacy of systemic institutional and cultural inequities that continue to adversely and disproportionately impact the lives of racialized Canadian children (Alexander 2016; Maynard 2017).

Some childhood studies and education scholars have referenced education as a central part of child development (Darling-Hammond et al. 2020; Mills and Mills 2000), and in this context, education is described as practices that help to prepare children for the future, as it "connects biological growth with social and educational processes" (Mills and Mills 2000, 20). While linear, future focused interpretations of education and child development have been heavily critiqued for decades by critical psychologists (Burman 1994; Walkerdine 1993), as well as childhood scholars (Woodhead 2009), it should still be noted that experiences of schooling undertaken in childhood remain fundamental to human subjectivity (Biesta 2013; Sonu and Benson 2016). Considering the importance of education as a site of experience throughout childhood, we emphasize here ongoing concerns with how Black children are treated in Canadian school systems. Evidence of the biased treatment of Black children in school also demonstrates how they are excluded from any entitlement to innocence. Here, we expose concerns related to varied manifestations of racial bias in education to illustrate why childhood innocence is an impossibility for Black girls.

This chapter reflects on the authors' personal accounts of our school experiences and analyzes the narratives of six Black girls to outline some of the circumstances that continue to deny Black girls equitable education in Canada. Underpinned by Black feminist epistemologies, our goal is to advance an intersectional analysis of Black girl's experiences in Ontario schools to expose racial bias in education and highlight the concept of "adultificiation bias" (Epstein, Blake, and González 2017) as an inequitable educational practice that impacts Black girls throughout their childhood. The data, collected as part of a small study, summarizes the perspectives of six Black girls on oppressive practices that they witnessed and experienced. In using this approach, we seek to demonstrate the substantial value of centering Black girls' voices in research on Black children in Canada.

BLACK FEMINIST AUTOETHNOGRAPHY AND EDUCATIONAL RESEARCH

As authors of this chapter, we acknowledge and call on our experience attending Ontario high schools as we discuss the experiences of Black girls in Ontario schools over a period of time. Kisha is a Black, feminist, educator, and scholar with over 15 years of experience developing and implementing formal and community-based teaching and learning practices that support Black youth. Chanelle is a Black, feminist, development practitioner and critical disability doctoral student whose research examines the material implications of disability as complexly embodied by second-generation African-Caribbean women in Toronto. Using Black Feminist Autoethnography (BFA) as a method, we reflect on how our own school experiences connect with the experiences of the Black girls who participated in the study. R.A. Griffin outlines the value of BFA as a research approach, particularly for Black women. She suggests that BFA

> "as a methodology [is] positioned to embrace subjectivity, engage critical self-reflexivity, speak rather than being spoken for, interrogate power, and resist

oppression, autoethnography can be productively coupled with Black feminist thought for Black female scholars to 'look in' (at themselves) and out (at the world) connecting the personal to the cultural" (2012, 142–143).

Here, our Black feminist auto-ethnographic approach is underpinned by intersectional analysis to illustrate the long histories of miseducation that have perpetuated racial and adultification biases toward Black girls within educational systems in Canada.

Intersectionality, (Crenshaw 1989) directs attention toward aspects of identity that are considered marginal and at times ignored in broader discourses on the forms of oppression that shape one's experience. Crenshaw's theorization of the impact of compounding identities on the experiences of Black women is particularly useful when examining the lives and experiences of Black girls. As gender and race continue to inform social systems and policies that impact Black girls in Canada, so do other essential aspects of identity such as class, age, and ability (to name only a few). An analysis of age, for example, means considering how the social and cultural factors related to construction of race and Black identities leads to the normalized "adultification" of Black girls in educational spaces. Epstein, Blake, and González define adultification as, "perceptions of Black girls as less innocent and more adult-like than white girls of the same age—as well as its possible causal connection with negative outcomes across a diverse range of public systems, including education" (2017, 1). In school, Black girls regularly face the manifestations of adultification bias at the hands of educators. Given the ways that age and race interact as factors of oppression in Black children's school experiences, intersectionality provides a helpful framework to underscore and elaborate on how marginalization of Black girls can both influence and affect their development as racialized children.

BLACK FEMINIST KNOWLEDGE

Collins's Black Feminist Thought (2000) helps position the social reality of Black girls in the context of race, gender, age, as well as other intersectional factors. Black feminist epistemologies provide access to research tools that are central to any analyses of Black girls, as they yield strategies for deconstructing the manifestations of racial difference in relation to aspects of identities. In this context, Black feminist approaches to research can and should be used to capture, summarize, and analyze data collected from Black girls to effectively account for all factors and complexities of their experience as Black people. Such approaches validate Black girls' knowledge and experience in ways that account for the compounding layers of Black female identities.

From the perspective of a Black feminist epistemology, the Black girls whose experiences are featured here are knowledge producers; their accounts expose the implications of racism, sexism, and other forms of oppression in their lives. It is their knowledge, the knowledge and understanding that only Black girls themselves can advance, that needs to be included and addressed through scholarship, particularly across fields such as childhood, girls, and feminist, studies. As Black Canadian experiences are implicitly linked to factors, such as age, immigration and settlement in the region, diverse histories, social, political, and economic realities of Blackness, it is not surprising that these factors are also implicated in the accounts of Black Canadian girls. According to Norwood, Canadian Black feminism functions "to transform structural inequities and resist multiple oppressions present in Canadian daily life" (2013, 232). We emphasize connections between the structural inequalities that factor and inform the experiences of Black women in Canada and those that continue to shape the lives of Black girls in their childhood.

REVIEW OF EDUCATION AND CHILDHOOD LITERATURE IN CANADA

The following sections provide a review of literature that underpins our position on inequitable treatment of Black girls in Ontario schools. We situate our inquiry as both drawing from and contributing to existing literature on critical approaches to understanding childhood and education, as well as conceptual scholarship on adultification. From its inception as a field in the late twentieth century, childhood studies scholarship has outlined who is considered a child, advanced childhood as a social construct, examined contemporary virtues of childhood (i.e., innocence and purity), and explored the responsibilities that societies have in protecting children (James and Prout 1997; Tisdall and Punch 2012; Woodhead 2006). Connecting childhood studies with discourses in education presents an opportunity to highlight and emphasize how children's identities connect or, in this case, disconnect them from their agency as independent social beings (Tisdall and Punch 2012; Wright 2015). In particular, research that effectively outlines how Black girls negotiate their education as they encounter oppressive barriers in school is significant to educational and childhood research. Existing scholarship on adultification bias provides an important conceptual framework for understanding these oppressive barriers.

Childhood and Innocence

Childhood studies scholarship continues to reconceptualize some of the traditional notions of childhood. As the field continues to expand, exploring children and childhood in context to traditional theoretical underpinnings in childhood studies remains debatable and at times, highly contested (Garlen 2019; Hartas 2010; Singley 2013; Wright 2015). How children and childhood are framed in academic spaces is often based on the fields of study in which the discourses and themes on childhood are positioned. For example, in the field of psychology, childhood is often tethered to concepts related to physical and emotional development and cognition, whereas in sociology and anthropology, the focus on childhood is most often rooted in socialization and culture (Woodhead 2006). Still, there is a considerable number of normalized, universalist notions of childhood, particularly in Western societies, that links biological immaturity and dependance to reference children as innocent and dependent beings, void of agency (Prout and James 1997; Woodhead 2015). Any assumption of children's lack of agency throughout childhood is also indicative of one way that childhood has been theorized in context to adulthood. This is to suggest childhood as period of life has functioned as a subjective descriptor, a way to designate and describe a period in which children simply prepare to become adults (Prout and James 1997).

Throughout the last few decades, theoretical positions such as those described above, have been and continue to be regularly challenged within contemporary childhood studies scholarship (Garlen 2019; Hartas 2010; Taylor 2010; Woodhead 2015). Even with shifts advancing an inclusive, more realistic approach to studying children, the scholarship indicates that theorizes childhood as period of innocence for children, particularly as it relates to sexuality, remain firmly linked to the conceived "purity" and "naivety" of children (Robinson 2012). This common conceptual understanding of childhood as a period of innocence reflects what Jenkins (1998) described decades ago as the "myth" of innocence. However, the idea of innocence and its relevance to childhood seems to be particularly static in discourses surrounding children particularly outside of academic spaces.

Such a universalization of innocence as a generic condition of childhood ignores how cultural, racial, and geo-political factors shape children's unique experiences across different contexts. When speaking to the experiences of children in Canada, for example, any examination that generalizes children within a Western context is likely to ignore the realities of many children in the country. Considering gross national inequities (Covell, Howe, and Blokhuis 2018) that exist across provinces, it is impossible to establish any concrete or general understanding of this period of life based on nationality or region. In Canada, this issue is further compounded by the lack of intersectional analysis on the experiences of children. Due to a insufficient race-based data, there are limited studies that effectively capture and disaggregate factors, such as race, class, and ability within research on Canadian children.

What seems clear is that discussion on virtues and expectations of childhood and children in Canada can only be used to establish a benchmark for the idealized childhood fantasies that are afforded to and defended for White children. Currently, the embodied experiences of children in Canada are demonstrative of marginalized social constructions and lived realities that many other children do not experience. Racialized children, for example, are faced with the burdens of their identities, which often lead to the oppression that is manifested in their daily lives. Perpetual racial bias is one of several factors that shape the experiences of children with social systems, including education.

Childhood and Education

Focusing on the value and purpose of education during childhood allows for an in-depth and practical examination of factors in education that can lead to disruption and oppression in the lives of children (Desai and Goel 2018). On a basic level, children in Canada should expect their formal education to be directed toward developing their "personality, talents, mental and physical abilities to their fullest potential" (Desai and Goel 2018, 72). Canadian education systems are charged with the responsibility of providing quality education to all children. Evidence collected from the accounts of Black girls on their experiences in school continues to point to the bias and discrimination that they face in educative spaces in Canada, treatment that impacts their ability to exercise their full potential academically (George 2020; McPherson 2022).

Many of the issues Black students face in education begin when they first enter the school system during their childhood (Boutte and Bryan 2021). The ongoing concerns surrounding anti-Black racism in education in Canada reveal patterns of inequities that continue to be experienced at various levels of Black children's education (Lopez 2020; McPherson 2020). For decades, educational researchers have called for multicultural, antiracist, equitable education policies in Ontario to protect Black children in education systems (James 1995); however, efforts to address racial bias in education have been consistently sidelined in Canada. According to James (1995, 31), "institutions operate on the premise that the education they provide is free of cultural bias – that there is no one ethnic group culture that is dominant or informs educational practices and content." In the years since James' 1995 study, more data on the experiences of Black children has been collected that document further concerns with normalized discrimination in school settings (Cudjoe 2010; Livingstone and Weinfeld 2017; Lopez 2020). Such studies demonstrate that the education systems in the country are not designed to accommodate the needs and priorities of Black children. Systemic failures, evidenced by toxic classroom environments as well as normalized racism, sexism, classism, and other forms of oppression (Lopez and Jean-Marie 2021; McPherson 2020), continue to impact the development and wellbeing of Black children within Ontario schools, despite government policies implemented to respond to these concerns and ongoing issues (Anti-Black Racism Strategy 2017; Ontario's Education Equity Action Plan 2017).

Such scholarship reveals that normative concepts applied to childhood, such as "protection" and "innocence," reflect Western expectations for the treatment of children (Jenkins 1998; Robinson 2012) that have never been fully realized for all children in Canada within or outside of institutional educational spaces. Black girls, specifically, are continually excluded from childhood and thus denied equitable access to quality education. Even when Black girls live in regions where the cultural context of childhood as this period of protection and innocence has been structurally normalized and legally accepted (Covell, Howe, and Blokhuis 2018), Black girls' experiences continue to demonstrate their universal marginalization within a childhood context, further exemplifying the "myth" of childhood innocence.

Black Girls' Voice in Education

In an article published in 2005, Evans-Winters' highlighted the concerns with clear absence of scholarship that focuses on the lives and experiences Black girls in the United States. Research on Black children and youth tends to place emphasis on Black boys. Evans-Winters (2005, 9–10) notes that "compared to Black males, Black females have fewer behavior problems. African American girls' behavior is least likely to affect others; thus, research and the resulting reform efforts tend to focus on Black males." In Canada, similar assumptions are made (Dei 1993; James 2012), and although the focus on Black boys is necessary and relevant in Canada, the consequence of focusing on Black boys in education is limited research and material that adequately represents the diverse needs and voices of Black girls. As Joseph et al. point out, "Black adolescent girls are an important group that is often overlooked in schools due to colorblind approaches and complexities of multiple intersectional identities based on race and gender" (2016, 5). Black girls experience racism and sexism in school in ways that differ from the experiences of Black boys (McPherson 2020; McPherson 2022) and continuing to advance research that prioritizes disaggregated data collected from Black children has the potential to present more accurate, equitable findings. As Milner (2017, 4) observes, Black girls consistently experience "structural and systemic barriers" that schools lack the ability to address. The lack of an intersectional focus when addressing issues related to Black children leads to missing histories, experiences, and an absence of data that accounts for specific experiences that continue to impact the overall well-being of Black children in Ontario.

Adultification Bias

As children, Black girls are required to navigate biases that continually place them into situations that many other children never face. Based on the literature that highlights some concerns for Black girls in school (George 2020; Linton and McLean 2017; McPherson 2020), there is a salient connection between the experiences outlined in various accounts of Black girls and what is often described as "adultification bias." A study completed by the Georgetown Centre on Poverty and Inequality found that Black girls in the United States are commonly seen as and treated like adults (Epstein, Blake, and González 2017). This form of racial bias and prejudice, in which children are held to expectations normally associated with adults, disproportionately impacts Black girls as they are more likely to receive harsh and punitive responses to their behavior as compared to their White and other non-Black counterparts (Morris 2016a). Although the Georgetown study describes experiences of Black girls living in the United States, adultification bias continues to be a significant concern in the lives of Black girls across Canada, particularly in the context of education (Linton and McLean 2017; McPherson 2020).

The modern idea that children are entitled to special treatment or expectations to accommodate for a perceived lack of experience and knowledge during the developmental period is particularly significant in the context of education (Darling-Hammond et al. 2020). What adultification bias demonstrates is Black girls, in comparison to their White peers, often do not receive any latitude for their errors in judgment that might result in inappropriate behavior at school (Morris 2016b). Adultification bias also factors in circumstances in which Black girls are treated unfairly, even cruelly (McPherson 2020), illustrating what George (2020) effectively refers to as the "mulling" of Black girls—when Black girls are forced to carry the burden and labor for the circumstances of their discrimination.

Similar to the adultification bias findings in the United States, the implicit bias of educators in Canada leads to adultification of Black girls in a few distinct forms. First, there is a general lack of compassion that educators and administrators demonstrate toward Black girls (McPherson 2022). The actions of teachers and administrations in school settings are discriminatory, and Black girls are left to deal with the repercussions (McPherson 2020). They are not provided the same level of support in school afforded to White girls (Darling-Hammond et al. 2020). Second, when Black girls face adultification bias, any error in their judgment is an extreme risk as they are often treated more harshly with no consideration for their status as children when they display unexpected or unwelcomed behavior (George 2020; McPherson 2020). Another common form of adultification is the hyper sexualization of Black girl bodies, which often leads to different dress code expectations for Black girls, particularly in high school, where they are punished for the development of their bodies (Litchmore 2021; Ray 2022).

RESEARCH METHODS

In exploring the accounts of Black girls in Ontario schools, we engaged Black feminist approaches including intersectional analysis (Crenshaw 1989), use of narratives (Nadar 2014), autoethnography (Griffin 2012), and validating voice in pursuit of self-determination (Collins 1986; Henry 1998) to support the summary and analysis of the study data. In using these holistic, qualitative approaches, our goal was to underscore the role the Black girls play in creating knowledge that supports childhood research. Sarojini Nadar (2014) calls attention to what she describes as three critical points on the contribution that Black feminist theorizing makes to research and production of knowledge.

> One is that the process of research is as important as the product of research. Two, that the identity of the researcher is as important as the participants in the research. And three, as Nnaemeka so aptly states, feminism helps us 'To put a human face on what is called a body of knowledge, and in the process unmasks this presumably faceless body.' This is one of the most profound ways of describing the value that feminist discourse has injected into research and knowledge production. (20)

In this quote, Nadar outlines the central argument as to how and why Black feminist approaches are essential in both childhood and education research. We contend that any research on education is incomplete without an intersectional analysis of the experiences and accounts of Black girls and their schooling.

Data Collection and Analysis

To collect and analyze the narratives, we applied qualitative methods to data drawn from focus groups with Black girls living on the GTA and our own autoethnographic accounts, which highlight our past high-school experiences. The focus group data was collected as part of a small qualitative study that focused on the experiences of Black girls and young women in the Greater Toronto Area (GTA). Through working with The Power to Be International (PTBI), a small grassroots charity in GTA, we were connected with potential study participants who had previously volunteered with the organization and consented to be contacted for research purposes. Six Black girls voluntarily agreed to take part in the study. In the focus group, participants were asked to share their thoughts and perspectives on several topics, including education, media, and representation. The two focus groups included six, self-identified Black girls between seventeen and twenty-one years old living in the GTA. Gabby and Marie are Black of Caribbean heritage, and grew up in Toronto. Keke, Zuri, Mia, and Chantel are of Black of African and Caribbean heritage and live in Durham. Although most of the participants were aged out of the K-12 school system at the time of the focus groups, they all reflect on experiences while attending a GTA school as Black children under the age of eighteen.

The focus groups were recorded via Zoom. The discussions in the groups started with a broad question to capture the general concerns of participants in context to media and education. Then, moving on to more specific issues, participants engaged with questions that focused on their experiences as Black girls in Ontario schools. Some of the questions included: What are some of the challenges Black girls face in school? How do school decisions and policies impact Black girls specifically? Participants were also asked to describe their educational environments and to outline specific interactions (positive and/or negative) with teachers and administrators throughout their school experience. The recorded sessions were transcribed, and the narratives and accounts of the participants were then used to examine how gender, race, age, and other sites of oppression impact the childhood of Black girls in Canada.

FINDINGS

The findings from the study data were divided, summarized, and discussed in relation to participants' school experiences across two themes: (1) exclusion and misrepresentation and (2) missed opportunities and miseducation. Using tenets of Black feminist theorizing to interpret the experiences of Black girls in their childhood, we found that the narratives collected from participants emphasized collective experiences, which are shaped by factors of their identities. In the context of schooling and pedagogy, the accounts that reflect the theme of misrepresentation and exclusion illustrate Black girls' internal struggle with feeling marginalized and isolated due to representations of Black women and girls within society. The second theme that emerged as Black girls recounted their school experiences illustrates how teachers missed opportunities to provide support for Black girls, leaving them to struggle for recognition and support and take responsibility for educating themselves and others on important issues. Throughout the narratives, participants revealed numerous examples of teachers and school administrators failing to offer Black girls protection from or support with circumstances that presented significant challenges throughout their childhood. Direct quotes from participants are reflected in italics to emphasize the voices and perspective of Black girls.

Black Girls on Exclusion and Misrepresentation

When participants were asked about the circumstances that have significant impact on Black girls in school, most of them reflected on their feelings of isolation, not fitting in, or belonging in school based on how their race and gender are stereotyped in society. Marie states:

> *Self-love can be difficult I think, because like just growing up in school, especially the darker you are, the less wanted you are, quote unquote, from just anybody. You feel like there are fewer opportunities for you. So, then you start to feel like, am I worth it? Am I worth these opportunities? Am I worth being in this space? So that follows you all the way up until you are older. However, it's so weird because there's this whole thing now like a strong Black woman, but it's like damn, no I'm super insecure right now and I can't even be in this room without shaking. So, I think it's like having that self-hate internalized from everything that's been shown in the media and in the classroom and from your teachers and your peers and then having to grow up and be like, I'm strong all of a sudden that's like, where did it even come from though?*

Marie's reflection reveals the challenge of having to process the expectation of being "strong" when the feelings she experienced childhood were riddled with insecurities. As Marie's reflection illustrates, the general lack of belonging that is often experienced by Black girls in educational spaces can be difficult for them to comprehend and work through, a challenge that makes it a necessity for Black girls to understand the impact of their identities. Marie expresses what she describes as feelings of "self-hate" when having the added burden of having to be a "strong Black woman" in school.

Echoing one of Marie's points on the cultural standards that exclude Black girls, Gabby notes that, *"beauty standards are something that also impact young black girls growing up in Canada, specifically those who go to schools that are predominantly White and lack diversity."* Further describing her experience, Gabby summarizes what she feels when attending predominantly White schools, explaining, *"You feel ostracized and alone even if you do have close friends who would say that you're their best friend, but it's just like, you're not getting that same experience as me. So, regardless of if you feel lonely and just like dang, I have to really go through this on my own or with a few Black students that you have in your school."* When Black girls are forced into white spaces where they feel excluded, such as the school settings described by Marie and Gabby, there is a high likelihood that racism will impact their development, self-concept, esteem, and achievement (McPherson, 2020). Black children spend a considerable amount of time in school, therefore, unsupportive educational environments that lack diversity and/or any consideration for issues Black children must face due to racial and gender bias, become breeding grounds of self-hate for Black children. Keke's reflection reveals the damaging impact that being excluded as a Black girl in school had on her self-image:

In high school, I was around a lot of White people, I was around a lot of Asian people, and all the teachers could do was make me feel like my skin was a problem. Like even when they didn't say it, I knew it was a problem because the way they would treat me the way they would call me out in front of the class, the way they would just address me as a whole. It made me feel like I had to shrink in order to be okay. And if I wasn't shrinking, the only way for me to get the attention that I needed was acting out.

These accounts from Gabby, Marie, and Keke, demonstrate how school environments maintain and even reproduce practices and stereotypes that contribute to the isolation that Black girls experience in educative spaces. Considering dominant norms around beauty standards and school achievement, from which Black girls' experiences are regularly excluded, how are Black girls supposed to develop a confident sense of self when they are pit against expectations of Whiteness? Without support for understanding racism, how are Black girls, and Black children in general, supposed to cope with the discrimination they experience in school? The failure to address these questions in illustrates how Black girls are not afforded an assumption of innocence. As Faulkner (2013, 128) notes, "the belief in the natural innocence of children obscures the fact that some are more exposed than others . . ." In these instances, there are no resources provided to support Black girls as they deal with racial bias.

In addition to the isolation and exclusion that the participants described, they also identified numerous examples of having been misrepresented through the perpetuation of harmful stereotypes. These experiences had a negative impact on their performance in school. In reflecting on her high-school experience, Keke described how microaggressions based on stereotypes of Blackness affected her ability to learn and participate in school:

I had to deal with all the microaggressions. Like when I first moved, when I first went to high school, there was this one principal who like, he literally would pull me out of class and it was always something that had to do with conflict that I was never involved in. But just because it was a group of Black people, he would point out . . . like he would literally call out all of the Black kids assuming that, "Okay, maybe you know something about it." You know, our names were always associated with conflict. And that hindered me from actually learning, because it makes you feel discouraged, like you start to see yourself from the same lens that they see you.

Similarly, Mia expressed how her treatment in schools as a Black girl was directly associated with her ability to achieve: "I've been through school and there hasn't been a single year that I can say I've been able to excel to my full potential because I was dealing with so many other things that had nothing to do with my education. It just had to do with the fact that school was terrible. Like, the environment was terrible. It was hard on my mental health." One factor that makes the school environment "terrible" for Black girls, as described by Mia, is the lack of representation in the classroom and curriculum paired with prevalent misrepresentation in the media. As Zuri explained:

If we're in class, we're not seeing ourselves in history, we're not seeing ourselves in the classrooms. If you go to a predominantly white school or you don't have Black students in your class or Black peers, you're not going to see yourself in your classrooms. So, we literally don't see ourselves and then when we do see ourselves, it's so negative, in the media or even our teachers are like criminalizing us before we do anything good or bad, so it's like where does that leave us?.

As reflected in these narratives, the educational environments in which Black students are placed —the same environments in which they are expected to thrive—are toxic and unsupportive, resulting in Black girls feeling confused, misplaced, and isolated. While dealing with these feelings as children, Black girls are often expected to cope with the circumstances of this miseducation with no support.

As the preceding excerpts illustrate, Black girls feel that they lack support from their teachers and schools. While there have been recent policy-based attempts to address school environments for Black students across GTA school boards (DDSB Compendium of Action for Black Student Success 2018; Supporting Black Student Achievement and Dismantling Anti-Black Racism at the TDSB 2022). However, many of the approaches implemented do not fully address Black children's concerns. In addition, these resolutions are often created without, or with limited, input from Black children themselves, and in turn they further contribute to harmful misrepresentation. Gabby described her experience with such an initiative:

I went to some kind of cultural equity event that was put on by the school board. They were promoting a resource on how to handle Black students, how to talk to

> them, and stuff like that. It's different things like that, that maintain the problem and for me personally, that was super weird, what are we, dogs? Then we are seen as the problem. You have to train me to be in your class and what they think is resourceful and helpful is actually really damaging because you're singling me out when really it's you, it's not me. I'm in your class trying to learn and you're trying to single me out, learn how to talk to me. I'm really just a person behind this Black skin. So it's kind of just like those things that are super disrespectful. That attacks our identity. People think that because of everything going on, it's helpful in it and it's progressive, but it's really disrespectful and confusing for Black students, I think.

Mia expanded on what Gabby considers, "attacks on identity" detailing how Black girls often feel compelled to perform forms of "Whiteness." *"So, I think that [attacks on identity] is something that also impacts young Black girls, especially in school, just trying to not come off as ghetto or ratchet or like less than and even when you do still talk in your white voice, that often doesn't even change anything."* These shared opinions of participants speak to the overwhelming power that these experiences have over Black girls their education and achievement. Black girls must contend with the stigma of the normalized stereotypes that surround Black women, even though they themselves are children. This places additional inequitable limits and expectations on Black girls in school throughout their childhood.

Chanelle's experience in 2010 with her music theater class further illustrates how Black girls are expected to confirm to certain standards of dress and appearance that approximate whiteness.

> *At the beginning of the semester my teacher would always pick a few students to stand up in front of the class as an example of what we all needed to look like on stage. The exemplary students were always white girls with long sleek ponytails, decked out in TNA or Lululemon and UGGS. I knew the clothes were out of the question, but I could come close, so I begged my disapproving mom for a perm and an 18-inch sew-in weave. Not long after, I became one of those exemplary students and it felt good to be front and center and to be praised but the impact on my self-esteem as a Black woman is something I struggle with to this day as a result.*

As both Gabby and Chanelle describe, Black girls are expected to approximate whiteness in order to succeed inside and outside of the classroom. Often an act of self-preservation, especially in predominantly White spaces, performing Whiteness can seem worthwhile, providing momentary gratification and false respite from the violence of white supremacy and its manifestations. Still, the rewards are fleeting and come at great cost, because as reflected in the narratives of participants, isolation, and lack of belonging continue to have a harmful impact on Black girls throughout our lives even when they step outside identities to try and fit in. As illustrated in Kisha's initial reflection on the pedagogical approach used in her Grade 11 English Media, along with the reflections presented here, it is clear that the lack of diversity in educational spaces creates an environment of exclusion and misrepresentation that negatively impacts the self-esteem and academic achievement of Black girls.

The participants' narratives along with our own recollections of schooling reflect Linton and McLean's study on four Black girls attending high school in Toronto. They note, "this misrepresentation and cultural irrelevance may explain why some Black students frequently skip class or acted out in school, yet these students were often branded as troublemakers and delinquents requiring disciplinary action" (Linton and McLean 2017, 78). The circumstances of Black girl's exclusion in school may cause them to react in a manner that results in discipline and excessive punitive responses to their childhood behavior (Morris 2016b). The disproportionately harsh measures often used to punish Black girls in school is one example of the manifestation of adultification bias as it illustrates the ease in which Black girls' status as children is overlooked and ignored in a system that is supposed to be designed to support their education. Across the girls' accounts of their experiences, there were no attempts to support or address their concern. Yet, when issues relating to unwanted behavior arise, Black girls are quickly silenced and punitively punished (George 2020; McPherson 2020).

Black Girls on Missed Opportunities and Miseducation

The second theme involves what we understand as missed opportunities on the part of teachers and schools to act in ways that might meaningfully address the structural inequalities that exclude and misrepresent Black girls in school. Rather than school serving as a source of positive learning, these missed opportunities result in a form of miseducation, in which students are not provided with adequate resources and information in various curricula areas. In these narratives, Marie, Gabby, and Zuri speak on issues that demonstrate their teachers' lack of knowledge and inability to embrace important teachable moments on race, history, and culture in the classroom. All the participants indicated some of skepticism and lack of trust in system and its teachers for these reasons.

One missed opportunity described by participants was the failure on the part of teachers to recognize Black girls' worth and potential. Chantel, for example, articulates the dangers of allowing school systems to determine or even suggest academic and/or extracurricular directions for Black children. She explains:

> *You have to fight for it to actually . . . like, growing up and going into these white schools, they don't want to see you in these positions of power. And to be honest, I cannot remember a time where a teacher actually suggested that,*

> *you know, I should do something in an academic extracurricular. They always wanted to put me in sports; "do track, do basketball. I want to see you on the team." But where are you when you know there's a philosophy club, where are you when there's student council, where are you where there's debates? I'd put myself into that position. It was never afforded to me, and you can't let that discourage you. You can't let that discourage you, you have to know better than what they expect of you. And throughout my education, there always was a sense that teachers did expect less from me and they would say, you know, it's not because you're black, they would say, "Oh, because you know, look at the other black students, look at what they're doing." And it really is debilitating because it conforms you to the stereotype.*

As Chantel's reflection illustrates, Black girls are often relegated to participating in sports or service activities, as schools spend little time and energy cultivating their academic potential. However, as studies on the rise of suspension, expulsion, and incarceration rates of Black girls in the United States indicate, school systems use considerable resources to excessively punish and isolate them (Crenshaw, Ocen, and Nanda et al. 2017; Morris 2016b). Why are their resources directed toward the punishment of Black girls when resources to cultivate their academic potential remain lacking? More research is needed to examine the impact of the putative measures levied on Black girls in school in Canada, however, research out of the Toronto District School Board (TDSB) notes that excessive discipline rates for Black children in school continues to increase (Black Student Achievement in TDSB 2015).

Another missed opportunity exists in the failure of schools to provide culturally relevant material and experiences, which leaves Black children to educate and teach themselves about their own history. This issue persists despite evidence that supportive, personalized educative environment is one of the key factors in student success (Darling-Hammond et al. 2020). Illustrating the frustrations Black girls feel when they are provided such support, Zuri reflects on her experience with one opportunity her school missed to effectively include and support Black students in school:

> *Even at my school, in grade nine, they weren't doing anything for Black history month, so I called out the principal and they ended up doing something going forward, we ended up putting it on, but it was always led by myself or some friends and we were like the go-to people from that moment to lead the Black history month stuff. So why does it have to be by the students, why aren't the teachers starting it?*

Black children, like all children, deserve to be seen in and validated through their curriculum and in teaching practices. In spite of a clear focus on Eurocentric content and approaches that often demean Black identities (James 1995; Mujawamariya, Hujaleh, and Lima-Kerckhoff 2014; Khushal 2022),

Black children are expected to "achieve" and succeed with the existing curriculum. When they do not or simply cannot succeed using Eurocentric standards, somehow, Black children are blamed for not meeting specific educational and social expectations that they should develop in their childhood.

The participants describe how these missed opportunities, whether unintentional or purposeful, transformed their school experience into a miseducation. Gabby states,

> *Teachers do such a great job at upholding white supremacy and patriarchy and just violence against Black students and honestly, I do think it's subconsciously, I don't think that, and maybe consciously at times, but for the most part, I remember on the basketball team, I was, again, one of the only Black students in my school and we went to a school that was predominantly Black to compete in basketball. We were taking public transit and all the teachers were like, oh my gosh, you guys are going there alone, what? Be careful like that school is so dah, dah, dah, dah, and it's just like what? The fact that you're even saying that it's just insane to me.*

In this reflection, Gabby outlines some of the current stereotypes that teachers use to formulate their judgments on Black people. Teachers then project these, often racist opinions, in their interactions with Black children, causing their further isolation. Gabby, through this account, interpreted how easily her teachers linked race and class to cultivate a fear of violence in spaces that are predominantly Black. In these situations, the miseducation results from the way the teacher's prejudices are projected in their practice. When teacher's attitudes reflect dangerous stereotypes and biases, it is not uncommon to see evidence of their prejudice in their teaching. Chanelle's account from 2010 in one such example, which had Black students in her school practically in tears due to the teacher's misuse of Black racial violence in an educational context. In Chanelle's experience, the teacher used the histories of Black bondage and subjugation as means of inspiring theatrical performance and then left no room, no time, or opportunity to address how these histories impact Black children. These examples clearly point to teachers' lack of capacity to effectively educate Black children, or at the very least, the missed educational opportunities to intentionally support them in Ontario schools. There seems to be no compassion for the historical trauma that Black students encounter.

Another form of miseducation occurs when clear opportunities to include the perspectives and experiences of Black students in the curriculum are overlooked. Gabby describes how this contributed to her experience of miseducation, pointing out her teacher's lack of preparation to reflect the experiences of Black people and culture in her language course.

> *I took French in high school and there's a whole continent called Africa. Many African countries are Francophone countries, they speak French. The fact that that was never even like, oh, let's watch an African French movie this time in class or, oh, let's listen to this song by an African artist. That was just never even on the table and then it just makes it harder for Black students to, I think, dismantle the racism and stigmas in their communities in school. I do think that this Canadian school system beats down black and indigenous students to the point where it's like, it's really the school to prison pipeline or just not good.*

Gabby's reflection calls attention to the ways that the curriculum, and the teachers responsible for its delivery, fails to meaningfully include Black perspectives. This is also apparent in Marie's example; in this case, the teacher ignored a student's assertion that they were misrepresenting an important part of Canadian history in their lesson. Expand here to connect these two examples. Marie recalled:

> *I remember at one time I was in class and one of my teachers was talking about Indigenous people and Canadian settlers and one of the kids in the class was like, you mean the mass genocide and the teacher was trying to dismiss that. I'm like how can you sit there in front of a bunch of people and dismiss that? I even think it even goes down to me as a Black person having to take an elective, having to sign up for a class just to learn about my history, or what my people have gone through.*

Concerns with inaccurate accounts of Canadian history were shared by a few participants. These examples highlight the various ways miseducation can result from a teacher's lack or capacity or preparation to educate students on these fundamental topics. Zuri expresses her frustration of the intentional omissions of specific histories:

> *In elementary school we learned every other history, medieval history, European history. We did not touch any contributions by Black or Indigenous people in Canada. So, it's definitely very problematic for all the reasons that I mentioned before and I was even thinking to myself this week, how well does it factor in white African studies, PhD person, she probably knows more about my own cultural history than I do, which is just so ridiculous to me.*

For Black girls, these omissions feel like a deliberate attack on our racial identities. As Kisha recalled in her similar experience, her teacher failed to provide material reflecting the identities of Black children for an assignment that was based on representation. Pedagogical practices such as this contribute easily to the marginalization of Black children and should be considered gross negligent on the teacher's part. How are Black girls expected to feel any sense of belonging in their education when their racial identities, key factors of who they are, are invisible in their education?

The contemporary educational environment in some Ontario schools continues to center Eurocentric material throughout the curriculum, which further maintains the isolation that Black students, like Kisha, experienced decades before. As Gabby confirmed Zuri's critique on the curriculum, she states, *"the content is just straight-up white people, 24/7, they didn't talk about like Viola Desmond, for example, until I was probably in the 10th grade, when that was like, oh, Viola Desmond is going to be on the $10 bill, with no real context."* Gabby's point elucidates the level of desire that these Black girls must learn histories that reflect their identities and experiences. Black girls clearly want to learn; however, they need teachers who accept the responsibility to properly teach and inform Black Canadian children. In turn, this commitment only serves to benefit all children in Ontario.

When discussing the miseducation they experienced as a result of these missed opportunities, the participants discussed compounding factors such as race, class, gender, culture, and history, unpacking their experiences through an intersectional analysis that was far more advanced than we, the authors, were able to access as Black girls going through similar educational experiences decades ago. Gabby, for example, spoke about the importance of reclaiming the histories that have historically been omitted and overlooked:

> *I think that in putting out Canadian history and providing other perspectives on what happened, it's also giving students context on like, okay, Black people and Indigenous people aren't just trying to rewrite history suddenly, what really was taught to us was white supremacist propaganda and that's not the facts that all of what happened. So, I think that there's so much power in that and so much reclaiming of our power as Black and Indigenous students. Just to know our own history and know our narrative, that has been erased for so long and I think that that is just transformational in and of itself.*

As an educator, recognizing students' intersectionality is central to providing and ensuring equitable education for all students. Students must see themselves throughout their education. The only way to address concerns documented through the experiences outlined here is to acknowledge the gaps and long-term impact that exclusion and misrepresentation create for racialized students.

DISCUSSION

The accounts of participants illustrate a longing for curricular and pedagogical approaches that accurately reflect the history and contemporary realities of their worlds. The reflections of these Black girls indicate both a desire and need for culturally relevant teaching and learning methods. Teachers seem unprepared to provide or cultivate the types of spaces that support the learning and development needed for equitable education of children of diverse backgrounds. The resulting miseducation, including inaccurate historical data and failure to instruct on difficult topics, leads to a general distrust of a discriminatory educational system that Black children are somehow never "protected" from. On the contrary, as the participants described, Black girls are left to struggle for representation and acknowledgement of their needs, capacities, and identities. This idea that Black girls have to "fight" to demonstrate their worth and potential is inhumane and not a characteristic of innocence or protection. For Black girls, this experience of having to "fight," lobby, or advocate for themselves and for educational opportunities that should be available to all children demonstrates the impact and burden of adultification bias on Black girls. It is a form of adultification because most non-Black children are not expected to fight or fend for themselves. Adultification bias results in Black girls being read as older than they are, which excludes them from any accommodations of childhood afforded during this fundamental period of life. When Black girls suffer through adulification and other forms of racial bias, they are excluded from any notion of innocence.

In examining these social realities that Black girls regularly face, schools should offer some accommodation for the standards and norms perpetuated in society that are harmful to Black girls in their childhood. What we can see from these accounts is that there is no protection from the circumstances that maintain Black girls' marginalization (often due to racism) as it appears to envelope their experiences within school settings on a regular basis. This is not to suggest that all children should be treated as people who unable to make sound decisions for themselves. Rather, the difference in the unequal expectation of Black girls, described through the concept of adultification bias, emphasizes that even in school environments with other children, Black girls are often placed in predicaments where their status as child is denied.

It is through this lens on education that Black girls build the skills to resist its failures and situate themselves as their own educators. As theories and discussions of childhood point to this period of innocence and naiveté (Robinson 2014), Black girls are taking on much more than they should be. This too is an example of the manifestations of adultification bias as experienced by Black girls in school. These accounts of miseducation suggest that if Black girls, for example, want to learn about or from their histories as Black people, they must find ways to teach themselves, when Eurocentric histories, connecting to identities of many White children, continue to be considered central in the Ontario curriculum (James 1995; Mujawamariya, Hujaleh, and Lima-Kerckhoff 2014; Khushal 2022). Why are Black children left to shoulder the responsibility of educating themselves about their histories when many White children are not?

Within the broader context of Canada's colonial past and present, teachers of Black children have an additional responsibility to support the learning of Black children by accounting for cultural and historical factors that influence their identities and lived experiences. The constructions of race, gender, and beauty—normalized based on the countries colonial, racist, and discriminatory past and present—continue to exclude Black girls as they naturally exist. Through a series of educational and social policies, at ministry (Ontario's Anti-Black Racism Strategy 2017; Ontario's Education Equity Action Plan 2017) and school board levels (DDSB Compendium of Action for Black Student Success 2018; Supporting Black Student Achievement and Dismantling Anti-Black Racism at the TDSB 2022), Ontario schools necessitate prioritizing teaching practices that seek to decolonize traditional Eurocentric standards. It requires intentionally planning activities and assignments that reflect the identities and histories of all the children in the classroom. It is equally important to approach issues and concerns with Black girls with added care and compassion as the trauma from racism, discrimination, and other forms of oppression complicate the lives of Black people in ways that White people do not have to readily contend with. The circumstances connected to intersectionality and burden of multiple forms of oppression starts even before Black children are born when Black parents face the added pressure of racism when engaging with social systems such as health care. As such, these legacies of oppression that Black children are likely to face due to race are not new (Maynard 2017), and therefore teachers must be prepared to acknowledge and address them as a universal pedagogical approach to teaching in any grade and subject area.

ADDRESSING RACIAL BIAS AS EXPERIENCED BY BLACK GIRLS

It is both interesting and highly frustrating to examine any theorizing of historical or contemporary factors that includes notions "innocence" or "protection" as it relates to embodiments of childhood. Using the term "children" to describe people under a specific age, and then attaching any expectations to that experience is a paradox, because all children are not read and treated in the same way. Protective notions that seem readily connected to childhood have never been generally applied to Black girls or Black children in Canada. How can Black girls be considered innocent children, in need of protection, and be so easily and callously adultified in school at the same time? How can innocent children be expected to shoulder the impact of racial bias in what should be an equitable education system? Based on the accounts of past and present educational experiences of Black girls in Ontario, we are not now, nor have ever been, entitled to the ideals of childhood.

The manifestations of the bias accounted for throughout this chapter points to race as the leading factor, and when coupled with other aspects of Black girl's identities (gender, class, ability), the levels of discrimination that Black girls continue to face in school seems impossible to address. To treat Black girls like the children that they are means giving them space to make mistakes that will not result in harsh, inequitable punishment. It means providing Black girls with the added support needed to deal with the discrimination and exclusion they face due to racism, sexism, and other forms of oppression. It means seeing their bodies as bodies of children even when they appear to be more physically developed than non-Black girls. It means providing them with spaces that help to address the isolation and lack of information due to the racism that continues to be a manifestation of Canada's past and present inequalities. In absence of these considerations, the adultificiation bias is an embodied experience that Black Canadian girls continue to experience in education.

The description of the teachers' behavior in these accounts confirms some of the conclusions drawn from our description of our past experiences in Toronto schools. Facing some of the conclusions that we've come to through our analysis of the accounts of Black girls who are currently in, or have recently completed high school in Ontario, we quickly realized the impact of not having language to articulate our schooling experiences. We needed language to describe concepts, such as "intersectionality" and "adultification," to effectively account for the consequences of the harsh expectations placed on Black girls. These terms also help to demonstrate how we, Black girls, are/were unfairly treated as children in context to our schooling. In our time, we were left wondering about the root of the issues that resulted in our distrust of systems that should support the development children (Darling-Hammond et al. 2020). We were left to navigate through and away from racism, sexism, and biases we experienced and witnessed in school. We are even forced to minimize these circumstances and assimilate into whiteness as if our unique Blackness as girls did not or does not matter or exist.

Education must acknowledge the magnitude of the circumstances that trickle down to produce the slow, steady, and consistent doubt in Black girl children. These biases continually influence the things we do, don't do, the things we say, and the things left in the awkward silence after a racial offense occurs. The role of education in the lives of children requires Black girls be adequately educated and prepared. We know that the school systems not only fail Black girls through unintentional exclusion and missed opportunities but also participate in the ongoing discrimination and marginalization of

Black children. Black girls are often busy either figuring out how to engage in unsustainable white assimilation or merely preoccupied with developing strategies to resist their oppression and educate themselves. This is an insurmountable task that continues to be placed at the feet of Black girl children in Ontario.

Unfortunately, it is clear that adultification bias is only one of the harmful, limiting, and inequitable realities that Black girls face in their childhood. The education system has not changed, and its inequitable persistence necessitates Black girls need to change, to morph, and deny central aspects of ourselves for educational attainment and survival. In Henry's 1998 study *Taking Back Control: African Canadian Women Teachers' Lives and Practice*, she asks three questions: "How much agony and torment can a child bear in silence? How does a young Black girl develop a healthy self-identity in such environments? How often does it happen in school that a Black child is reprimanded for her response to what may be a series of racial incidents?" (Henry 1998, 16). These questions remain unanswered and are, therefore, still relevant in the contemporary lives of Black girls attending school in the GTA and across Canada. The way in which educators casually burden Black girls with the labor of having to navigate their own trauma, while expecting them to perform at the same level of their peers, is unconscionable. Black girls are not adults and should not have to navigate and resolve the failures of education on their own. Imagine being a child and not feeling any sense of belonging within a social system so inextricably linked to childhood. This is the reality of Black girls. Are we entitled to childhood?

How can educators address these long-standing issues of miseducation and exclusion that continue to impact Black girls' and their education? It is first important to acknowledge that Black girls hold a unique and important intersectional gaze that is needed to respond to these concerns in Ontario schools. We are in a time when Black girls are encouraged to articulate their needs and priorities in education and other systems that adultification and other forms of racial bias are seen. We must make validate and make use of this knowledge. Their opinions need to be understood and utilized in any effort toward advancing equity in education. As racism, sexism, and bias dominate Black girls' experiences in education, it is incumbent on the system to address these issues using their perspectives on the concerns that shape their lives. Black girls' voices, though historically muted, remain central to any examination of teaching practices as there is no way to address the failures in education without them.

To direct immediate attention toward concerns, outlined in this chapter, it is essential for education systems to expose all forms racial bias as experienced by children through educational policies and practices. The accounts of discrimination faced by Black girls in Ontario schools, which include to isolating and hostile education environments and teacher's lack of capacity and pedagogical biases, continue to mount, adding only to evidence of racial bias in schools and not to the examples of impactful solutions. Effective educational policy to address longstanding concerns with racial bias can only be developed through a thorough examination of the realities and roots of these issues. Ministry-level and board-level attempts appear to be surface level as there are still glaring inconsistencies that impact education of Black girls in GTA schools. Those at the helm of education boards and ministries need to demand that all educators and administrators within the system treat all children equitably, perhaps by using the treatment of middle-class White children as a standard for all Canadian children. For example, when faced with a concern involving a Black girl in school, teachers can ask themselves, how would I treat this child and/or situation if the child were wealthy and White? Although this may sound like a tongue-and-cheek suggestion, Black girls are running out of options for assisting educators with how to effectively do their jobs and engage in equitable practices that benefit all children.

As Black women, once Black girls who attended Toronto schools, we do not have all the answers to resolve the concerns outlined in the chapter such as Black girls exclusion in educative spaces, or the misrepresentation of Black and Indigenous people, and the inadequate teaching practices that omit fundamental positions throughout history outlined in this chapter. What we do know is that Black girls are children who shouldn't have to continue to suffer in silence. And as children who deserve quality education like all children, educational policies must be met with action so that Black girls can start recalling and sharing different types of narratives about school and childhood experiences.

REFERENCES

Biesta, Gert. 2009. "Good Education in An Age of Measurement: On the Need to Reconnect with the Question of Purpose in Education." *Educational Assessment, Evaluation an Accountability (Formerly: Journal of Personnel Evaluation in Education)* 21, no. 1 (February): 33–46.

Boutte, Gloria, and Nathaniel Bryan. 2021. "When Will Black Children Be Well? Interrupting Anti-Black Violence in Early Childhood Classrooms and Schools." *Contemporary Issues in Early Childhood* 22, no. 3 (September): 232–243.

Bristow, Peggy, and Dionne Brand. 1994. *We're Rooted Here and They Can't Pull Us Up: Essays in African Canadian Women's History*. Toronto: University of Toronto Press.

Covell, Katherine, R. Brian Howe, and J. C. Blokhuis. 2018. *The Challenge of Children's Rights for Canada*, 2nd edn. Waterloo: Wilfrid Laurier University Press.

Crenshaw, Kimberle. 1989. "Demarginalizing the Intersection of Race and Sex: A Black Feminist Critique of Antidiscrimination Doctrine, Feminist Theory and Antiracist Politics." *University of Chicago Legal Forum* 1, no. 8: 139–167.

Crenshaw, Kimberle, Priscilla Ocen, and Jyoti Nanda. 2015. *Black Girls Matter: Pushed Out, Overpoliced, and Underprotected*. New York: African American Policy Forum & Center for Intersectionality and Social Policy Studies.

Darling-Hammond, Linda, Lisa Flook, Channa Cook-Harvey, Brigid Barron, and David Osher. 2020. "Implications for Educational Practice of the Science of Learning and Development." *Applied Developmental Science* 24, no. 2: 97–140. https//doi.org/10.1080/10888691.2018.1537791.

Dei, George J. Sefa. "(Re) Conceptualizing" Dropouts" from Narratives of Black High School Students in Ontario." Paper presented at the Annual meeting of the American Educational Research Association, Atlanta, GA, April 1993.

DDSB (Durham District School Board). 2018. "Compendium of Action for Black Students." Accessed February 15, 2023. https://www.ddsb.ca/en/about-ddsb/resources/Documents/Equity/Black-Students-Compendium.pdf.

Epstein, Rebbeca, Jamilia J. Blake, and Thalia González. 2017. *Girlhood Interrupted: The Erasure of Black Girls' Childhood*. Washington, DC: Georgetown Law Centre on Poverty and Inequality. https://dx.doi.org/10.2139/ssrn.3000695.

Evans-Winters, Venus E. 2005. *Teaching Black Girls: Resiliency in Urban Classrooms*, 2nd edn. Peter Lang.

Farley, Lisa, and Julie C. Garlen. 2016. "The Child in Question: Childhood Texts, Cultures, and Curricula." *Curriculum Inquiry* 46, no. 3: 221–229. https://doi.org/10.1080/03626784.2016.1178497.

Garlen, Julie C. 2019. "Interrogating Innocence: 'Childhood' As Exclusionary Social Practice." *Childhood* 26, no. 1 (February): 54–67. https://doi.org/10.1177/0907568218811484.

Griffin, Rachel A. 2012. "I Am an Angry Black Woman: Black Feminist Autoethnography, Voice, and Resistance." *Women's Studies in Communication* 35, no. 2 (November): 138–157.

Hartas, Dimitra. 2010. *The Right to Childhoods: Critical Perspectives on Rights, Difference and Knowledge in a Transient World*. London: A&C Black.

Henry, Annette. 1998. "'Speaking Up' and 'Speaking Out': Examining 'Voice' in a Reading/Writing Program with Adolescent African Caribbean Girls." *Journal of Literacy Research* 30, no. 2 (June): 233–252.

Hill Collins, Patricia. 1986. "Learning from the Outsider Within: The Sociological Significance of Black Feminist Thought." *Social Problems* 33, no. 6 (December): s14–s32.

———. 2000. *Black Feminist Thought: Knowledge, Consciousness, and the Politics of Empowerment*. New York: Routledge.

Hope, Elan C., Alexandra B. Skoog, and Robert J. Jagers. 2015. "'It'll Never Be the White Kids, It'll Always Be Us' Black High School Students' Evolving Critical Analysis of Racial Discrimination and Inequity in Schools." *Journal of Adolescent Research* 30, no. 1 (January): 83–112.

Howe, Samuel Gridley. 1864. *The Refugees from Slavery in Canada West: Report to the Freedmen's Inquiry Commission*. Boston: Wright & Potter.

James, Carl E. 1995. "Multicultural and Anti-Racism Education in Canada." *Race, Gender & Class* 2, no. 3 (Spring): 31–48.

———. 2010. "Multicultural Education in a Color-Blind Society." In *In Intercultural and Multicultural Education*, edited by Carl A. Grant and Agostino Portera, 205–224. New York: Routledge.

James, Carl E., and Tana Turner. 2017. *Towards Race Equity in Education: The Schooling of Black Students in the Greater Toronto Area*. Toronto: York University.

Jenkins, Henry. 1998. "Introduction: Childhood Innocence and Other Modern Myths." In *The Children's Culture Reader*, edited by Henry Jenkins, 1–38. New York: New York University Press.

Joseph, Nicole M., Kara Mitchell Viesca, and Margarita Bianco. 2016. "Black Female Adolescents and Racism in Schools: Experiences in a Colorblind Society." *The High School Journal* 100, no. 1 (Fall): 4–25.

Khushal, Shezadi. 2022. "Dismantling Racism in Schools Through Anti-Oppressive Frameworks: The Pivotal Role of Leadership in Achieving Racial Equity." *YU-WRITE: Journal of Graduate Student Research in Education* 1, no. 1: 1–15. https://doi.org/10.25071/28169344.11

Linton, Rowena, and Lorna McLean. 2017. "I'm Not Loud, I'm Outspoken: Narratives of Four Jamaican Girls' Identity and Academic Success." *Girlhood Studies: An Interdisciplinary Journal* 10, no. 1 (Spring): 71–88.

Litchmore, Rashelle V. 2021. "'She's Very Known in the School': Black Girls, Race, Gender, and Sexual Violence in Ontario Schools." *Qualitative Psychology* 9, no. 3: 232–250. https://doi.org/10.1037/qup0000221.

Livingstone, Anne-Marie, and Morton Weinfeld. 2017. "Black Students and High School Completion in Quebec and Ontario: A Multivariate Analysis." *Canadian Review of Sociology/Revue Canadienne de Sociologie* 54, no. 2 (May): 174–197. https://doi.org/10.1111/cars.12144.

Lopez, Ann E. 2020. "Anti-Black Racism in Education: School Leaders' Journey of Resistance and Hope." In *Handbook on Promoting Social Justice in Education*, edited by Rosemary Papa, 1935–1950. Berlin: Springer.

Lopez, Ann E., and Gaëtane Jean-Marie. 2021. "Challenging Anti-Black Racism in Everyday Teaching, Learning, and Leading: From Theory to Practice." *Journal of School Leadership* 31, no. 1–2 (January–March): 50–65. https://doi.org/10.1177/1052684621993115.

Maynard, Robin. 2017. *Policing Black Lives: State Violence in Canada from Slavery to the Present*. Halifax: Fernwood Publishing.

Mujawamariya, Donatille, Filsan Hujaleh, and Ashley Lima-Kerckhoff. 2014. "A Reexamination of Ontario's Science Curriculum: Toward a More Inclusive Multicultural Science Education?" *Canadian Journal of Science, Mathematics and Technology Education* 14, no. 3 (September): 269–283. https://doi.org/10.1080/14926156.2014.874618.

McPherson, Kisha. 2020. "Black Girls are Not Magic; They are Human: Intersectionality and Inequity in the Greater Toronto Area (GTA) Schools." *Curriculum Inquiry* 50, no. 2: 149–167. https://doi.org/10.1080/03626784.2020.1729660.

———. 2022. "'The Teacher Said Nothing': Black Girls on the Prevalence of Anti-Black Racism in Greater Toronto Area (GTA) Schools." *Journal of the American Association for the Advancement of Curriculum Studies (JAAACS)* 15, no. 1 (Fall). https://doi.org/10.14288/jaaacs.v15i1.194206.

Mills, Jean, and Richard Mills, eds. 2000. *Childhood Studies: A Reader in Perspectives of Childhood.* London: Routledge.

Milner, Richard H. 2017. "Where's the Race in Culturally Relevant Pedagogy?" *Teachers College Record* 119, no. 1 (January): 1–32.

Morris, Monique W. 2016a. "Protecting Black Girls." *Educational Leadership* 74, no. 3 (November): 49–53.

———. 2016b. *Pushout: The Criminalization of Black Girls in Schools.* New York: The New Press.

Nadar, Sarojini. 2014. "'Stories are Data with Soul'–Lessons from Black Feminist Epistemology." *Agenda: Empowering Women for Gender Equity* 28, no. 1: 18–28.

Norwood, Carolette. 2013. "Perspective in Africana Feminism; Exploring Expressions of Black Feminism/Womanism in the African Diaspora." *Sociology Compass* 7, no. 3 (March): 225–236. https://doi.org/10.1111/soc4.12025.

Ontario Ministry of Child and Youth Services. 2017. "Ontario's Anti-Black Racism Strategy." Accessed February 15, 2023. https://files.ontario.ca/ar-2002_anti-black_racism_strategy_en.pdf.

Ontario Ministry of Education. 2017. "Ontario's Education Equity Action Plan." Accessed February 15, 2023. https://files.ontario.ca/edu-1_0/edu-Ontario-Education-Equity-Action-Plan-en-2021-08-04.pdf.

Parents of Black Children. 2022. "Call to Action: Systems Abuse of Black Students Within Ontario Education System." Accessed February 15, 2023. https://parentsofblackchildren.org/wp-content/uploads/2022/03/PoBC-System-Abuse-Report-_Final_Updated.pdf.

Punch, Samantha. 2003. "Childhoods in the Majority World: Miniature Adults or Tribal Children?" *Sociology* 37, no. 2 (May): 277–295.

Ray, Ranita. 2022. "School as a Hostile Institution: How Black and Immigrant Girls of Color Experience the Classroom." *Gender & Society* 36, no. 1 (February): 88–111. https://doi.org/10.1177/08912432211057916.

Robinson, Kerry H. 2008. "In The Name of' 'Childhood Innocence': A Discursive Exploration of the Moral Panic Associated with Childhood and Sexuality." *Cultural Studies Review* 14, no. 2 (January): 113–129.

Spyrou, Spyros, Rachel Rosen, and Daniel Thomas Cook, eds. 2018. *Reimagining Childhood Studies.* New York: Bloomsbury Publishing.

TDSB (Toronto District School Board). 2015. "Black Student Achievement: Fact Sheet." Accessed February 15, 2023. https://onabse.org/YCEC-TDSBFactSheet1.pdf.

———. 2020. Supporting Black Student Achievement and Dismantling Anti-Black Racism at the TDSB. Toronto, Ontario. Accessed February 15, 2023. https://www.tdsb.on.ca/Portals/ward8/docs/Shelley%20Laskin/2020%2007%20Supporting%20Black%20Student%20Achievement%20and%20Dismantling%20Anti-Black%20Racism.pdf.

Woodhead, Martin. 2006. "Changing Perspectives on Early Childhood: Theory, Research and Policy." *International Journal of Equity and Innovation in Early Childhood* 4, no. 2 (January): 1–43.

———. 2015. "Childhood Studies: Past, Present, and Future." In *An Introduction to Childhood Studies*, edited by Mary Jane Kehily, 19–33. Maidenhead: Open University Press.

Wright, Bryan. 2015. "Re-Founding Childhood Education: Passages in Presence." *Forum on Public Policy Online* 2015, no. 1.

Chapter 2

Unpacking the Adultification–Infantilization Paradox

Sebastian Barajas

INTRODUCTION

Childhood has long been a morally charged category. As childhood studies scholars have argued, almost every form of political rhetoric, moral panic, or social engineering invokes childhood in some way (Garlen 2019; Harris 2004; Saguisag 2019). The refrain of "for the children" remains a central logic justifying state violence (Edelman 2004; Meiners 2016). As Cook (2017) puts it, "childhood arises as a moral project for all—regardless the 'side' taken on a debate or issue—for, everyone, it seems, stands on the 'side' of children." (n.p.) Almost no one—whether in left- or right-wing politics—denies the moral salience of childhood. For all political factions, childhood represents the future and creates a sense of urgency to save it (Sheldon 2016)—though from what is a point of frequent disagreement.

This near-universal agreement on the moral salience of childhood puts it in contrast with race, a category whose moral salience is frequently denied or downplayed—usually through post-racial logic or willful ignorance (Applebaum 2010; Tatum 2017). Indeed, childhood studies have been critiqued for being slow to account for the intersections between childhood and racism (Garlen 2019; Konstantoni and Emejulu 2017). These critiques point out that childhood is not universally available to all but is instead selectively awarded and withheld through the practice of adultification (Gilmore and Bettis 2022; Toliver 2018). In the context of anti-Black racism, adultification is understood to exclude Black children from the category of childhood. Racial bias treats Black children as physically stronger, more sexually knowledgeable, less innocent, less sensitive to pain, and more culpable than white children (Baetzel et al. 2019; Tatum 2017). This exclusion shows that entitlement to the ideal of childhood is not a given but is instead a privilege that is largely exclusive to white children (Bernstein 2011; Garlen 2019; Webster 2021).

However, racism has also disrupted normative development through the seemingly opposite practice of infantilization. Black adults have been viewed as more childlike than white adults, and therefore as not true adults (Breslow 2019; Rollo 2018). In this case, childhood is treated—not as a privilege—but as a form of social, political, and economic oppression: white adultness is constructed as superior to Black childishness (Mills and Lefrançois 2018). Likewise, adulthood is treated—not as a burden or a fallen state—but as a state of power and dignity (Field 2014). In other words, through the logic of infantilization, racism manifests as a type of adultism.

Yet, these two manifestations of racism—adultification and infantilization—seem at odds with one another. How can both be at work at once? How can being treated like a child be simultaneously an advantage and a form of oppression? Despite childhood's unique level of moral importance in society, and despite childhood studies' decades-long critical analysis of that importance, the field has yet to offer a widely accepted moral account of childhood. Does "being a child" tend to confer advantages or disadvantages? Even among childhood studies scholars, the question of what exactly childhood confers is treated with ambivalence (Barajas 2022). Sometimes it is taken for granted that childhood is a burden (Biswas 2022; Liebel 2015; Wall 2017), and sometimes it is taken for granted that childhood is a privilege (Cox 2015; Morris 2018; Webster 2021). They are opposites, and yet both seem to be true. This is what I refer to as the adultification–infantilization paradox.

While some scholarship has investigated this paradox (c.f. Rollo 2018; Webster 2021; Breslow 2019), there is still a dearth of work that investigates how it manages to persist despite (or perhaps because of) its own internal contradictions. In fact, not only does this paradox manage to persist—it has proven to be a remarkably effective ideological system for reinforcing both racism and adultism. Disciplinary institutions and discourses can weaponize childhood in both its forms—as a perfect state to be protected in a gilded cage and as an inferior state to be contained and ultimately purged (Breslow 2019). Conversely, adulthood may also be weaponized in both its forms: as a higher state to be aspired to and as a fallen state to be punished and exploited.

In this chapter, I will use a theoretical approach drawing on historical examples of anti-Black racism in the United States to argue that the adultification–infantilization paradox is produced by the intersection of adultism and racism. I approach this topic as a U.S.based white/Latinx childhood studies researcher with a background in youth rights activism. My goal here is twofold: to amplify antiracist scholars' interventions into childhood studies and to draw on those interventions to bring out what I consider to be the most useful aspect of childhood studies: its critique of adultism. In doing so, I hope to help strengthen childhood studies' own intervention into the humanities and the social sciences as a whole.

The first two sections in this chapter argue that childhood and adulthood are each categories with multiple, often contradictory meanings. I argue that racism operates by exploiting these contradictions. In the third section, I explain how the ambiguities inherent in childhood and adulthood also enable racist ideologies to construct convenient adult–child hybrids—among them, criminals and adolescents. These hybrid constructs are similarly mobilized in the service of white dominance. Finally, I conclude by explaining why childhood studies must do more than simply critique the negative effects of racist ideology on children. Rather, childhood studies can make its most fruitful antiracist contributions by critiquing the adultist ideologies that intersect with, and strengthen, racism.

WEAPONIZED CHILDHOOD: LITTLE ANGELS, LITTLE DEVILS, AND BLANK SLATES

Antiracist interventions into childhood studies have argued that childhood is not equally available to all, but rather has been exclusively available to white children (Garlen 2019; Rollo 2018). Black children in particular are less likely to be viewed as children, but instead are adultified, meaning they are viewed as more criminal, sexual, and independent than other children. This type of adultification is reflected in media portrayals of Black children (Bernstein 2011), school suspension statistics (Morris 2015), cognitive biases (Tatum 2017), and many other areas. Meanwhile, childhood innocence, piousness, and sexual purity have historically been reserved for white children.

However, this understanding of adultification hinges on one particular version of childhood: the innocent child or "little angel." To obtain a more complete picture of how adultification reproduces racism, one must consider other influential constructions of childhood: in particular, the "little devil" and the blank slate. In childhood studies, it is now taken for granted that childhood has had many different meanings throughout Western history (Snyott 2006; Wall 2010; Zelizer 1985). The Rousseauian tradition holds that, compared to adults, children are innocent, pure, and faultless and must be protected from the harsh realities of the world. The Catholic/Puritan tradition holds the opposite: children are savage "little devils" who need to be tamed by a firm hand and taught how to think and behave virtuously. The Lockean tradition holds that children are blank slates, neither inherently good nor inherently bad, but in need of instruction and guidance. Children are controllable and (in various ways) exploitable (Nandy 1984). And in all cases, children are profoundly, almost paradigmatically, Other.

A cursory glance at childhood studies scholarship might suggest that the Rousseauian ideal of childhood innocence has largely dominated the Western imagination since the end of the Progressive Era (Ariés 1962; Higonnet 1998; Zelizer 1985). However, a closer examination shows that the field has long recognized that the truth is more complicated and that many different views of childhood have always coexisted. In fact, in many instances, different contradictory understandings of childhood have been used to justify the same policies or social arrangements.

White Children's Ambiguous Experience of Childhood

Even in seemingly textbook historical examples where white children were recognized as innocent and in need of protection, it was not merely this one view of childhood that came into play (i.e., the innocent child), but multiple views. One specific historical example that illustrates this complexity was Charles Loring Brace's orphan trains project. The project was intended to be an improvement on New York City's policy toward street children (arrest and incarceration with adult criminals) by sending them to be adopted by families in the Midwest (Gray and Graham 1995, 11:50). Brace's project was designed to accomplish multiple purposes at once: remove a dangerous element (i.e., little devils) from the city streets and give them character-building work, while also providing vulnerable children (i.e., little angels) with a loving home. To win over support, Brace invoked notions of children's mutability (i.e., blank slates) and the role that adults could play in sculpting their futures. Even in this paradigmatic example of white child-saving, these different understandings of childhood did not counteract one another, but rather formed a symbiotic relationship, all working together to spur the same social intervention.

Just as the ideologies behind these projects were ambiguous, so too were their outcomes. The line between character-building chores and child exploitation was inherently blurry for Brace's orphans. Many midwestern families were attracted to the free labor that the children could provide. One commentator at the time "claimed that 'Men needing labor, their slaves being set free, take these boys and treat them as slaves'" (Gray and Graham 1995, 33:16). For many children, being saved from dangerous idleness meant being sent into equally dangerous labor. This example illustrates the principle that, even for white children who are fully recognized as vulnerable and deserving of protection, that protection readily goes hand-in-hand with harm. White children's status as children rendered them fair game for ensnarement, both by state actors and by nonstate actors like Brace. Their status permitted adults to legally remove them from their communities and send them to live under the authority of strangers hundreds or even thousands of miles away.

Why Racism Has Historically (Selectively) Recognized Black Childhood

If the lines between protection and harm have been blurry for white children, they have been even more so for Black children. As previously noted, adultification has been a way of refusing to recognize Black childhood innocence. This has led to harsher treatment by law enforcement, economic and sexual exploitation, and diminished state support. In this respect, then, racism manifests as exclusion from the privilege of childhood innocence (Bernstein 2011; Garlen, 2019; Webster 2021). Black activists have fought for centuries for Black children to be seen as children. Since the nineteenth century, they have been committed to "representing Black children as respectable, pious, innocent, and appropriate future citizens" (Webster 2021, 36). In other words, they have been committed to securing Black people's claims to the privilege of being seen as children.

However, racism has not only operated by excluding Black children from childhood but also by selectively recognizing them as children when it served the purposes of racial oppression. From the nineteenth century onward, as openly racist institutions have been gradually replaced by covertly racist ones, the strategic value of recognizing Black children as children in order to ensnare and control them became increasingly apparent. Making Black childhood legible to justify white adult intervention, but not legible as a rationale for protection and support, ensured that the selective recognition of Black childhood could be made into a weapon of white domination.

Crystal Webster's (2021) analysis of the antebellum North shows how Black children's childhood was weaponized against them through racialized systems of child indenture, adoption, and institutionalization. Indentured servitude had always been an explicitly adultist system. It operated on the fundamental principle that the labor of the young belonged to the old:

> During the colonial era, many children and adults from Europe entered the colonies as indentured servants, a system that functioned in Europe in part as a way to mediate the social problem created by orphaned and poor children . . . The contracts, signed by those who were indentured or, in the case of children, by their guardians, granted the 'master' legal ownership of the indentured servant's labor. (Webster 2021, 139)

According to the dominant political philosophy of the time, such arrangements were justified because children lacked the reason necessary to control any resources, but nevertheless owed labor to the adults they depended on for care and decision-making (Locke 2003).

Indenture was originally a system designed to exploit the labor of young white immigrants. It only began to be repurposed for racist ends in the early nineteenth century as Northern states began to abolish slavery. As the explicitly adultist indenture system became less common for white children, it expanded for Black children in order to allow white Northerners to continue legally exploiting their labor. As Webster puts it, "the North's abolition of slavery resulted in a system of indentured servitude that specifically targeted African American children and youth" (145). And yet despite the palpably racist purposes of these initiatives, they always managed to keep the flavors of all the same child-saving rationales that had served for white children: children must be disciplined, children must be protected, and children must be trained. Fulfilling these traditional adult obligations to Black children in no way jeopardized white control over them—in fact, it was the rationale for that control. Slavery premised on racism managed to gain a second life by disguising itself as child-saving premised on adultism. As Webster (2021) explains, "African American children were no longer enslaved, but they were indentured or apprenticed for an extended period, sometimes to their former enslavers. Their exploitation was linked to their institutionalization in orphanages, schools, and reformatories" (24).

Similar patterns of child re-enslavement emerged during Reconstruction. Even organizations ostensibly set up to help Black families such as the Freedmen's Bureau often ended up binding many Black children back into servitude. Mitchell (2012) writes that, "One of the first tasks facing local Bureau agents after the Confederate surrender was to situate freedchildren who appeared to them to be orphans, or as one agent put it, 'the disposal of children practically orphans'" (164). While the stated intention of the Bureau was to help Black children, its goal of finding placements for these "orphans" was also welcomed by former slaveholders who were eager to replace the unpaid laborers they had lost. One common tactic was to declare Black freedchildren to be orphans (whether or not this was actually the case) and then to bind them into labor contracts. Black adults who challenged their children's placement with white former slaveholders typically lost their case. In one instance, a Bureau agent sided with a child's former enslaver (now re-enslaver) against his grandmother—not on the grounds that he was not really a child—but on the grounds that "the former slaveholder (was) the parental figure in (the child's) life" (165).

In this example, the Black children who were placed by the Bureau were not being excluded from childhood. Quite the opposite: their legal status as children and as so-called orphans was being weaponized under the guise of benevolence in order to recapture them into servitude. Although slavery was now technically illegal, "Apprenticeship remained a legal avenue of child welfare, so long as it made no distinction between black and white children." (Mitchell 2012, 164). To put this another way, Black children's status as children remained a perfectly valid legal basis for binding them out to unpaid labor, even though their status as *Black* children technically did not.

Why Racism Continues to (Selectively) Recognize Black Childhood

Although much has changed since the nineteenth century, Black children's legibility as children remains a key component in the reproduction of racism. One of the most notorious examples of this is the continued practice of removing Black children from their families. Still invoking universalist child-saving language and logic (e.g., "best interest"), child protective services remain infamous for disproportionately removing Black children, often placing them with white families. Today, Black children in the United States are two to three times as likely as white children to be in foster care (Kokaliari et al. 2019). Such entanglements with child protective services would not be possible if Black children were not recognized as children. It is through the many-headed logic of child-saving that Black families are systematically targeted and disrupted, often creating generational cycles of state intervention.

Yet another example where Black children's status as children is essential to their oppression is in the case of school discipline. Many antiracist scholars have criticized specific measures, such as Zero Tolerance policies for their role in the school-to-prison pipeline, which contributes to the criminalization of Black youth. The prevailing suggestion is that Zero Tolerance policies do not treat Black children as children (Datari et al. 2020; Ferguson 2001; Morris 2015). However, while it is certainly true that these policies contribute to the criminalization of Black children more often than white children, it is also true that these policies are legally permissible, not despite the fact that they target children, but because of it.

Zero Tolerance policies are explicitly intended to enable the punishment, penalizing, and sometimes arrest of children without the legal checks and balances that are (at least in theory) available to adults. Such exceptions to constitutional rules are permissible because they are not applied to adults, but to schoolchildren. In landmark cases such as *Ingraham v. Wright* and *New Jersey v. T.L.O.*, the Supreme Court has previously ruled that otherwise unconstitutional uses of state power (physical punishment, searches and seizures without probable cause) are permissible in schools because these institutions have a special interest in maintaining control over their students. If Black children were not considered children, they could not (at least in principle) be legally targeted and punished under policies that are unconstitutional for adults. In this respect, being recognized as children renders Black children more easily punishable under the law, rather than less so.

These examples have illustrated a central paradox in Black childhood. On the one hand, Black children are excluded from the presumed innocence and protectedness of childhood. On the other hand, Black children are especially targeted by the institutions designed for the governing and disciplining of childhood. The effect of these opposing patterns is to exclude Black children from innocence, while at the same time capitalizing on their status as children to justify inflicting special forms of state intervention and violence on them. As Webster describes this phenomenon in the nineteenth century, "Reformers excluded Black children from—and sometimes confined them within—physical sites of childhood including schools, orphanages, and reformatories" (22). This phenomenon of exclusion from *and* confinement within childhood is an important aspect of the adultification–infantilization paradox. In short, by investing in child-saving initiatives and openly adultist systems of institutionalization as its new weapons of choice, white supremacy has resolved to exclude Black children from whatever advantages childhood might confer, but not its burdens.

WEAPONIZED ADULTHOOD: REASON AND CRIMINAL RESPONSIBILITY

As with childhood, antiracist scholarship has revealed that adulthood is not equally available to all. As with childhood, attaining adulthood has been a central struggle for historically oppressed groups, including Black Americans (Field 2014). This struggle is based on the assumption that adulthood is the pinnacle of human development and the full fruition of power. To become an adult is to become the "fully productive, fully performing, human being who owns the modern world" (Nandy 1984, 363). Nonwhite people all over the world have historically been excluded from that privilege, and instead have been infantilized: treated as less reasonable, less civilized, and less autonomous than other adults. In other words, infantilization subjects nonwhite people to adultist oppression.

The Privileges of Adulthood

One important privilege of adulthood has been property ownership: a status from which Black Americans have traditionally been excluded. Historically, such property has included people (slaves, children, domestics, wives, etc.). For this reason alone, true adulthood has historically been out of reach for many people. For example, one major historic struggle for Black parents has been to control the labor of their children. Black Americans did not have access to true adulthood in part because they were viewed as less entitled than white people to possess children—even those who were biologically related to them—or to appropriate those children's labor (Webster 2021). Adult personhood, under this kind of patriarchal logic, is attained through the "annexation" (Perry 2018) of others.

In addition to property ownership, Western political philosophy has long held that what distinguishes humans as a species is their ability to reason. Reaching adulthood, the supposed pinnacle of humanness, means reaching the pinnacle of reason (Locke 2003). Criteria for full citizenship too have increasingly gravitated toward reasonableness and away from other factors, such as heredity, property ownership, and labor (Wall 2022).

The Burdens of Adulthood

However, as with childhood, adulthood has multiple, conflicting meanings. In addition to representing the fully powerful and reasonable human, that very power and reason also taints the one who bears it. This is the opposite of childhood innocence: whereas children may at times be viewed as unknowing and therefore faultless and pure, adults may at times be perceived as knowing, and therefore as impure (Higonnet 1998). Thus, adulthood can burden people with increased culpability, making them less likely to be viewed as deserving of support, guidance, sympathy, or protection than children (Meiners 2016).

Consequently, one major avenue through which racism has manifested itself has been the practice of trying children as adults (Feiler and Sheley 1999). The adultism at work when trying children as adults is pernicious, because it creates a version of adulthood that is devoid of adult privileges. While children may be tried as adults in ways that increase their punishability, they may not be tried as adults in ways that would *decrease* their punishability, such as in cases of underage drinking, truancy, running away, or breaking youth curfew. Adult-like qualities are only recognized in children if they justify harsher treatment, not if there is some possible benefit in it for the child. This double standard is especially severe for Black defendants, who are repeatedly viewed as adults (i.e., as moral agents) for the purposes of establishing guilt and sentencing (Burton 2019), but not for any other purposes. Despite the fact that "consenting adults" are assumed to have a nearly unquestioned right to exercise their autonomy, for children who are adultified (or even for Black adults), no exercise of autonomy goes unquestioned. Every expression of Black autonomy from voting to using public sidewalks has been systematically challenged by racist norms and institutions.

Adulthood as an Ambiguous Category

There is an inherent contradiction in the prevailing Western understandings of the independent, reasonable agent. In general, reasonableness has been defined as the ability to follow a general law or formula for making decisions that are in one's own and others' interest. Such a law may be formally agreed upon or it may be what Locke calls the "law of nature" (Locke 2003). By this definition of reason, breaking the law is inherently unreasonable. And yet, paradoxically, holding people criminally responsible for breaking the law requires that they possess adult reason. By this definition of reason, being "tried as an adult"—that is, as a reasonable person—is a contradiction in terms. Reasonable adults cannot be criminalized, because reasonable adults by definition do not commit crimes. Criminals are thus treated like adults only in the sense that they, unlike children, are treated as moral agents. But they are not treated like adults, in the sense that they are not treated as reasonable, and therefore as deserving of deference and noninterference.

The ambiguity between responsible adults, on the one hand, and *criminally* responsible adults, on the other, raises difficult questions about the very concept of responsibility. How can one be held responsible for doing something irresponsible? How exactly can a reasonable person do something unreasonable? While such questions are deeply relevant to unpacking the paradox of adultification, they are also beyond the scope of this chapter. For my present purposes, it is enough to note that this ambiguity between adulthood as an empowering age of reason and adulthood as a disempowering state of criminal responsibility has been a useful weapon for white supremacy.

WEAPONIZED ADULT–CHILD HYBRIDS

I have demonstrated that "childhood" and "adulthood" carry inherent ambiguities that have been weaponized in order to reproduce racist ideologies and practices. Another consequence of this ambiguity is that, by their very nature, adultification and infantilization are always partial, selective processes. Black children who are adultified are treated only according to one definition of adulthood (tainted and agentic), but not others (empowered and respectable). Likewise, Black adults who are infantilized are treated according to one definition of childhood (savage but potentially civilizable), but not others (innocent and in need of protection). The question then becomes, if the social practices of adultification and infantilization do not produce identities that are either fully children or fully adults, what kinds of identities do they produce? What might we call these constructs that are "beyond the boundaries of" (Webster 2021) both childhood and adulthood? I argue that the incoherent natures of adulthood and childhood give rise to the phenomenon of adult–child hybrids, examples of which include criminals, adolescents, white saviors, and "old boys," as well as many others. Hybridity is the inevitable result of attempting to simultaneously deploy contradictory constructs of childhood and adulthood. Given its inevitability, the power to create and enforce hybridity is just as important to maintaining white dominance as the ability to create and enforce purity.

Hybrids for Annexing Childhood Innocence

Each type of hybrid has its own complex function in the racist social order. For example, Bernstein (2011) suggests that white adults are always eager to annex childhood innocence onto themselves in order to mask and absolve racial violence. The white savior is one such hybrid, allowing white supremacy to combine adult reason with childlike compassion and innocence, to create "concentrated repositories of an 1800s Protestant ethic" dedicated to resolving "nonwhite pathologies and problems in need of white control" (Hughey 2014, 9).

Closely related to the white savior is the "old boy": a white man who is simultaneously able to enjoy the power and influence of adulthood while also being able to get away with the "boys will be boys" defense in court (Walsh 2010). The past decade has seen various high-profile cases of white men who have successfully gotten their transgressions at least partially excused or minimized as merely "locker room talk" (Rhodes et al. 2020) or "just a good kid having some fun" (Stenberg 2018). Annexing childhood innocence onto adult power in this way is a crucial element of white supremacy and merits further investigation than is possible here.

Hybrids for Containing Monstrosity

Perhaps the most visibly destructive examples of hybridity in the racist social order are those whose main use is to contain monstrosity—including mixed-race individuals, criminals, and adolescents. Western rationalists have long been terrified by the notion of a creature who is childish, wild, and hostile—but also one that can reason well enough to pose a threat to the social order (Rollo 2018). And yet, white supremacy has even learned to turn this very terror to its advantage. One of the greatest fear tactics used by the racist establishment in the United States has been to raise alarm about the dangers of "miscegenation"—the conception of mixed-race children. This alarm translated into violence against Black men to protect white women. This despite the fact that, as Frederick Douglass (1960) pointed out, by far the most common source of mixed-race children was the assault of Black women by white slaveowners.

However, mixed-race children were not the only hybrid that concerned white supremacy. This became clear in the late nineteenth century as racial and class divisions began to seem destabilized with the legal emancipation of Black Americans and the effects of immigration and urbanization (Rury 2015; Synott 2006). To the racist establishment, it seemed that the social order itself had become monstrous: newly freed Black children were seen attending school, whereas white children were seen working in factories, begging in the streets, or making a living by thieving or sex work (Saguisag 2019; Wells 2018). The racist establishment realized it needed new ways of confronting dangerous hybrids besides simple prohibitions against miscegenation.

Alongside eugenics and social Darwinism, criminology rose to prominence as a way of scientifically re-enshrining the supremacy of wealthy neurotypical white adult males, while also classifying and pathologizing the rising throng of monstrous forms of hybridity that might conceivably threaten it. Perhaps the most notorious and enduring theory to emerge from this vast criminological project was G. Stanley Hall's theory of adolescence. Hall was a criminologist concerned with delineating true adult reason from the "childish" reason of the savage. He believed that criminals

> are almost always unusually sly and cunning, childish, and even animal. Parasites on society like those on animal bodies need a peculiar kind of adaptation, and we may perhaps say that their intelligence is on a low plane, but is extremely well developed... It is the insight of the street boy highly developed, and those accomplished in crime often have a well-developed philosophy of life, strange and bizarre to normal minds, but... remarkably adapted to survival...
> (Hall 1904, 339–344)

Hall's challenge was to make sense of the rise in criminality of white urban youth in a way that remained consistent with white supremacy. His elegant solution to this problem was to propose the transitory period of adolescence. Adolescence was to be a period of criminality that, for white youth, was both normative and temporary. In other words, Hall argued that white youth may be expected to temporarily be what criminals are for life: monstrous beings with the physical strength, appetites, and cleverness of adults, but with the untamed and lawless nature of children. Hall's solution siloed off the criminality (and therefore hybridity) of white youth, first by normalizing it, and second by temporalizing it. This solution to the problem of white monstrosity proved wildly successful. To this day, developmental psychologists continue to informally refer to adolescent neural physiology as a "paradox," because of the combination of childlike and adult-like qualities that contribute to its criminality (Jensen and Nutt 2015). Hall's solution even helped to spur reformers to set up a separate system for "juvenile" offenders: errant white youth who were only going through a transitory monstrosity and were expected to one day transition into more respectable forms of hybridity (white saviors, "old boys," etc.).

Nevertheless, Hall's theory could not eliminate white society's anxieties about its own decline (Jenks 2005; Postman 1982). Even the evolution of child figures in white literature during the twentieth century is a study in white anxiety. Peter Pan, Anne of Green Gables, and the children in *The Secret Garden* were succeeded by the monstrous figures of Lolita, Holden Caulfield, and the children in *Lord of the Flies*. Fears over the fate of white childhood have not diminished, but, if anything, have only grown stronger (Durham 2008; Higonnet 1998). More recent perceived threats to childhood are also products of white culture: explicit media, youth consumer culture, and unregulated digital spaces. New anxieties have even emerged around the sanctity of white adulthood as well, which has been compromised by jobless, unmarried, infantile adults (Cairns 2017; Epstein 2010). In short, when it comes to preserving the sanctity of childhood that is integral to white supremacy, white society has always been its own worst enemy.

Black Exclusion from White Adolescent Temporality

Black people were not included in Hall's temporality model of adolescence. Instead, they were relegated to monstrosity, as they had always been. In her analysis of 19th-century scientific racism, Castañeda (2001) shows how developmental theories excluded Black inferiority from the temporality that marked white youthful inferiority. According to these pseudoscientific theories, Black and white children were on par in terms of intelligence, with Black children often being more precocious. However, after reaching puberty, Black children's intelligence would stop developing and they would remain permanently childish, albeit with the physical strength and sexual appetites of adults. White children alone could continue growing and reach full adulthood. For white youth, monstrosity was temporary, whereas for Black youth, monstrosity was their destiny. One event that helped to popularize this perspective was the infamous 1990s panic over "superpredators" (Males 1996)—precocious but lawless Black adolescents who supposedly had no hope of attaining white maturity. As such, Black Americans have remained trapped in what Breslow (2019) calls an "adolescent citizenship."

Through developmental logic, white supremacy was able to maintain its claim both to the privileges of (reasonable, powerful) adulthood and to the advantages of (innocent, faultless) childhood. It accomplished this in part by containing its own monstrosity within the temporal field of adolescence, where it would be forever passing away ("just a phase"). Constructing white monstrosity as temporal and therefore as excusable was an important step in sanctifying white exceptionalism.

CONCLUSION: GOALS FOR AN ANTIRACIST CHILDHOOD STUDIES

So far, I have argued that the terms "adult" and "child" are each complex and inconsistent. Consequently, the processes of adultification and infantilization can never be complete, coherent processes, but can only ever be incomplete and selective. White children have faced ambivalent treatment as little angels, little devils, and blank slates. Black children have experienced this ambivalence even more dramatically, having been viewed as adult-like moral agents for the purposes of criminalization and sentencing, but also as children for the purposes of justifying state intervention and for undermining their access to legal protections. Likewise, Black adults have been viewed as moral agents, but not as reasonable or entitled to personal autonomy and property (including their own children). Because of their inherent ambiguity, adultification and infantilization logically require the creation of adult–child hybrids, which have also been manipulated to serve the interests of white supremacy. White adults are often able to use hybridity to access both the advantages of childhood and the privileges of adulthood. Meanwhile, white supremacy has successfully scapegoated the monstrous hybrids in which adult power and agency supposedly meet childlike lawlessness. Mixed-race children, criminals, and adolescents have all filled this role. White adolescence in particular has proven useful as a temporal containment chamber for potentially dangerous forms of white hybridity.

Given the complex role of the adultification–infantilization paradox in the reproduction of racism, the question then becomes: What is the task of an antiracist childhood studies? It cannot be merely to advocate for "age appropriate" treatment for all children (i.e., arguing against adultification). For one thing, "age-appropriateness" is in most cases simply a sanitized name for adultism. For another, as discussed above, it is precisely through logics of "age appropriateness" that racism frequently operates (e.g., child protective services). Neither can the task of an antiracist childhood studies be to advocate for a protected, innocent childhood for all, as childhood innocence was among the very first myths the field set out to critique.

Perhaps the most promising path is to continue investigating the intersections of racism and adultism. Indeed, in the literature that theorizes the experiences of Black and Brown children, the historical manifestations of these two ideologies are often difficult to extricate from one another. The childish savage and the savage child have always co-constructed one another (Nandy 1984; Rollo 2018). The marker of inferiority for both is their childishness. Without this anti-child logic to draw upon, racism would be hard pressed to have a logic of its own. How can supposed white superiority be described, if not in terms of the natural right of adult-like power and rationality to protect childlike innocence from adolescent criminality? And how can the project of adultism be described, if not in terms of creating a hierarchy between the animalistic primitive (i.e., children), and the fully human citizen (i.e., adults)? Given the inextricability of these two logics, it is unclear how, or even whether, the basic disciplinary apparatus of childhood—including schools, courts, detention facilities, families, and so on—can be abstracted from racist ideology.

Of course, some have argued that such an abstraction is possible: that the disciplinary apparatus children and "childlike" adults are subjected to is fundamentally sound and requires only antiracist interventions, among others, to become optimized (Purdy 1992). Such a position, however, depends on having a rather superficial critique of racism. In other words, it requires believing that it is morally appropriate in principle for more evolved humans to benevolently dominate less evolved ones. It requires believing that racism errs only in thinking that nonwhite people are, in fact, less evolved. According to this superficial critique, the reason it is not justified for white people to benevolently dominate nonwhite people is because both have been demonstrated to be equally, biologically evolved. Children, by contrast, are rightly dominated because they are verifiably less evolved than adults. However, this superficial critique of racism is insufficient. For one thing, it makes the (il)legitimacy of racism contingent on some set of empirically falsifiable facts. In other words, if racist ideology is only illegitimate because it has failed to turn up certain kinds of (genetic, neurological, etc.) evidence to support it, then in theory, further empirical investigation could turn up new evidence that might strengthen the case for racist ideology.

The interdisciplinary field of childhood studies has the opportunity to promote a much more substantial critique of racism that takes into account its underlying element of adultism. The adultification–infantilization paradox reveals that the categories "child" and "adult" are treacherous terms upon which to base antiracist efforts. As Rollo (2018) puts it,

> Although there may be short-term strategic utility in framing this issue in terms of Black youth being excluded from some idealized vision of protected childhood, the difficulty for modern emancipatory struggles will be finding a way to abjure the misopedic [adultist] grammar of race and colonialism altogether. (324)

As such, simply trying to confine ascriptions of childishness to actual children and ascriptions of adultness to actual adults (however "actual" is defined) cannot render these terms inert, because of the violence such categories inevitably justify. And even if some good could be achieved by drawing a hard line between childish children and adult-like adults, it would not be feasible. Childishness cannot be confined to children, nor adultness to adults, any more than femininity can be confined to women, "madness" to psychiatric patients, or criminality to those who have actually broken a law. They can never be entirely contained and can appear anywhere at any moment, at once contaminated and contaminating. This is what makes childishness and adultness such powerful qualities to invoke in justifying surveillance, policing, and carcerality.

The challenge for an antiracist childhood studies is to remain alert to the ways that the adultification–infantilization paradox might obfuscate as much as it reveals about racism and how it shapes the category of childhood. As Crenshaw (1991) reminds us, racism thrives off its ability to simultaneously obscure, and be obscured by, its interlocking forms of oppression. To truly unpack the relationship between childhood and racism therefore requires going beyond one-dimensional critiques of adultification and infantilization and considering the ways racism and adultism work together to legitimize violence against Black children (as well as Black adults). Accounting for the complexities of this intersection creates additional challenges for childhood studies, as well as for antiracist work in general. However, it also creates additional possibilities for coalition and for the emergence of rich new forms of scholarship and activism.

REFERENCES

Antiblackness and the Adultification of Black Children in a U.S. Prison Nation. 2022. 1st ed. Oxford University Press.
Applebaum, Barbara. 2010. *Being White, Being Good.* Lanham: Lexington Books.
Baetzel, Anne, et al. 2019. Adultification of Black Children in Pediatric Anesthesia. *Anesthesia and Analgesia* 129, no. 4: 1118–1123.
Barajas, Sebastian. 2022. Unearned Advantages? Redefining Privilege In Light of Childhood. *Children's Geographies* 20, no. 1: 24–36.
Bernstein, Robin. 2011. *Racial Innocence.* NYU Press.
Breslow, Jacob. 2019. Adolescent Citizenship, or Temporality and the Negation of Black Childhood in Two Eras. *American Quarterly* 71, no. 2: 473–494.
Burton, Chase S. 2019. Child Savers and Unchildlike Youth: Class, Race, and Juvenile Justice in the Early Twentieth Century. *Law & Social Inquiry* 44, no. 4: 1251–1269.
Cairns, James I. 2017. *The Myth of the Age of Entitlement.* North York: University of Toronto Press.
Castañeda, Claudia. 2001. Developmentalism and the Child in Nineteenth-Century Science. *Science as Culture* 10, no. 3: 375–409.
Cook, Daniel T. 2017. Childhood as a Moral Project. *Childhood (Copenhagen, Denmark)* 24, no. 1: 3–6.
Crenshaw, Kimberle. 1991. Demarginalizing the Intersection of Race and Sex: A Black Feminist Critique of Antidiscrimination Doctrine, Feminist Theory, and Antiracist Politics [1989]. In *Feminist Legal Theory* (1st Ed.), 57–80. Routledge.

Douglass, Frederick, and Benjamin Quarles. 1960. *Narrative of the Life of Frederick Douglass, an American Slave.* Cambridge: Belknap.

Durham, Meenakshi G. 2008. *The Lolita Effect.* 1. publ. ed. Woodstock: Overlook Press.

Edelman, Lee. 2004. *No Future.* Duke University Press.

Epstein, Robert. 2010. *Teen 2.0.* Fresno: Linden Publishing.

Feiler, Stephen M., and Joseph F. Sheley. 1999. Legal and Racial Elements of Public Willingness to Transfer Juvenile Offenders to Adult Court. *Journal of Criminal Justice* 27, no. 1: 55–64.

Ferguson, Ann A. 2001. *Bad Boys.* 1. paperback ed. Ann Arbor: University of Michigan Press.

Field, Corinne T. 2014. *The Struggle for Equal Adulthood.* Chapel Hill: The University of North Carolina Press.

Firestone, Shulamith. 2015. *The Dialectic of Sex.* London: Verso.

Franklin, Bob. 1986. *The Rights of Children.* Oxford: Basil Blackwell Ltd.

Freire, Paulo, et al. 2018. *Pedagogy of the Oppressed.* 50th anniversary ed. New York; London; Oxford; New Delhi; Sydney: Bloomsbury Academic.

Garlen, Julie C. 2019. Interrogating Innocence: "Childhood" as Exclusionary Social Practice. *Childhood (Copenhagen, Denmark)* 26, no. 1: 54–67.

Gilmore, Amir, and Pamela J. Bettis. 2022. Antiblackness and the Adultification of Black Children in a U.S. Prison Nation. In *The Oxford Encyclopedia of Gender and Sexuality in Education,* edited by Chris Mayo, 1–32. Oxford University Press.

Gray, Edward, and Janet Graham. 1995. *The Orphan Trains.* Edited by Susan Mottau, Margaret Drain and Judy Crichton. Documentary film. PBS.

Harris, Anita. 2004. *Future Girl.* New York: Routledge.

Higonnet, Anne. 1998. *Pictures of Innocence: The History and Crisis of Ideal Childhood* Thames & Hudson.

Hines-Datiri, Dorothy, and Dorinda J. Carter Andrews. 2020. The Effects of Zero Tolerance Policies on Black Girls: Using Critical Race Feminism and Figured Worlds to Examine School Discipline. *Urban Education (Beverly Hills, Calif.)* 55, no. 10: 1419–1440.

Hughey, Matthew W. 2014. *The Savior Trope and the Modern Meanings of Whiteness.* Temple University Press.

Jenks, Chris. 2005. *Childhood.* Routledge.

Jensen, Frances E., and Amy E. Nutt. 2015. *The Teenage Brain.* London: Harper Thorsons.

Kokaliari, Effrosyni D., Ann W. Roy, and Joyce Taylor. 2019. African American Perspectives on Racial Disparities in Child Removals. *Child Abuse & Neglect* 90: 139–148.

Konstantoni, Kristina, and Akwugo Emejulu. 2017. When Intersectionality Met Childhood Studies: The Dilemmas of a Travelling Concept. *Children's Geographies* 15, no. 1: 6–22.

Lensmire, Timothy J., et al. 2013. McIntosh as Synecdoche: How Teacher Education's Focus on White Privilege Undermines Antiracism. *Harvard Educational Review* 83, no. 3: 410–431.

Males, Mike A. 1996. *The Scapegoat Generation: America's War on Adolescents.* Common Courage Press.

McIntosh, Peggy. 1988. White Privilege and Male Privilege: A Personal Account of Coming to See Correspondences Through Work in Women's Studies, 83–93 Wellesley: Center for Research on Women.

Meiners, Erica R. 2016. *For the Children?* Minneapolis: University of Minnesota Press.

Mills, China, and Brenda A. Lefrançois. 2018. Child as Metaphor: Colonialism, Psy-Governance, and Epistemicide. *World Futures* 74, no. 7–8: 503–524.

Mitchell, Mary Niall. 2012. "Free Ourselves, but Deprived of Our Children." In *Children and Youth During the Civil War Era,* edited by James Marten, 160–172. NYU Press.

Monahan, Michael J. 2014. The Concept of Privilege: A Critical Appraisal. *South African Journal of Philosophy* 33, no. 1: 73–83.

Nandy, Ashis. 1984. Reconstructing Childhood: A Critique of the Ideology of Adulthood. *Alternatives: Global, Local, Political* 10, no. 3: 359–375.

Perry, Imani. 2018. *Vexy Thing.* Durham: Duke University Press.

Philippe Ariès, and translated from the French by Robert Baldick. 1962. *Centuries of Childhood: A Social History of Family Life.* New York: Vintage Books.

Postman, Neil. 1982. *The Disappearance of Childhood.* 1. print. ed. New York: Delacorte Pr.

Punch, Samantha. 2020. Why Have Generational Orderings been Marginalised in the Social Sciences Including Childhood Studies? *Children's geographies* 18, no. 2: 128–140.

Purdy, Laura M. 1992. *In Their Best Interest?* 1. publ. ed. Ithaca: Cornell University Press.

Rhodes, Jesse H., Elizabeth A. Sharrow, Jill S. Greenlee, and Tatishe M. Nteta. 2020. Just Locker Room Talk? Explicit Sexism and the Impact of the Access Hollywood Tape on Electoral Support for Donald Trump in 2016. *Political Communication* 37, no. 6: 741–767.

Rousseau, Jean-Jacques. 2015. *Emile.* Jefferson publ.

Rury, John L. 2015. *Education and Social Change.* 6th ed. London: Routledge.

Saguisag, Lara. 2019a. *Incorrigibles and Innocents.* New Brunswick: Rutgers University Press.

Sheldon, Rebekah. 2016. *The Child to Come.* Minneapolis; London: University of Minnesota Press.

Stenberg, Shari J. 2018. 'Tweet Me Your First Assaults': Writing Shame and the Rhetorical Work of #NotOkay. *Rhetoric Society quarterly* 48, no. 2: 119–138.

Synnott, Anthony. 2006. Little Angels, Little Devils: A Sociology of Children. In *Childhood Socialization,* edited by Gerald Handel, 25-42. Routledge.

Tatum, Beverly D. 2017. *Why Are All the Black Kids Sitting Together in the Cafeteria?* Third trade paperback edition. Twentieth anniversary ed. New York: Basic Books.

Toliver, S. R. 2018. Alterity and Innocence: The Hunger Games, Rue, and Black Girl Adultification. *Journal of Children's Literature* 44, no. 2: 4–15.

Wall, John. 2010. *Ethics in Light of Childhood*. Washington, DC: Georgetown University Press.
Wall, John. 2017. *Children's Rights*. Lanham; Boulder; New York; London: Rowman & Littlefield.
Wall, John. 2022. *Give Children the Vote*. First published ed. London; New York; Oxford; New Delhi; Sydney: Bloomsbury Academic.
Walsh, Fintan. 2018. *Male Trouble*. London: Palgrave Macmillan UK.
Wells, Karen C. 2018. *Childhood Studies*. Cambridge: Polity.
Zelizer, Viviana A. 1985a. *Pricing the Priceless Child*. New York: Basic Books.

Chapter 3

Childhood Innocence, Sanism, and the Image of the Child

Maddening Childhood Innocence Through the "Problem Child"

Adam Davies

INTRODUCTION

In November 2021, police were called to a school in the Waterloo Catholic District School Board in Kitchener–Waterloo, Ontario, Canada, regarding a four-year-old Black boy's behavior (Duhatschek 2022). Waterloo Regional Police Services arrived at the child's school and "de-escalated" his behavior, called his family, and drove him home (Duhatschek 2022). The four-year-old boy was reported by adults at the school to have been acting "violently" toward himself and others, which mandated calling police services per the school board's agreed-upon protocol for contacting the police in the event of an incident (Duhatschek 2022). What is notable—and especially violent—in this encounter is the adultification of the four-year-old child, in that he was driven home after being approached by police officers (Parents of Black Children 2022). Moreover, the fear of the young child from adult educators resulted in a police officer being called, indicating how Black children are not considered to conform to ideas of "childhood innocence" and are constructed as adult criminals on the basis of anti-Black ideas of lawlessness (Rollo 2018). That is, instead of being protected, Black children, especially Black boys, are deemed a threat to others, even if they are four years old (Bryan 2017; Shalaby 2017).

Grace, the four-year-old child's mother, sued the Waterloo Catholic District School Board, articulating how the school board failed to care appropriately for her child, criminalized him based on race, and created conditions that did not meet his needs, such as not allowing him to go to the washroom until he wet himself and creating a safety plan without his or the family's consent (Ghonaim 2022). Grace communicated her despair over the school board's treatment of her son to media, specifically stating how his teachers "never allowed my child to be a child. They discriminated against him because of his race and his colour. Hopefully they didn't take the child out of him completely" (Ghonaim 2022). Children who are deemed "behavioral problems" or "problem children" (Knight 2019a) do not fit into the universalized category of childhood; they are criminalized and medicalized, reinforcing punitive approaches and the use of pharmaceuticals on young children as a form of social control and normalization (LeFrançois 2020; Ramey 2018).

How might the "unruliness" of madness disrupt normative depictions of children entrenched in ableist, sanist, cis-heteronormative, and white colonial ideologies? Modernist constructions of childhood involve social practices that constitute identities through action; that is, childhood is a *doing* and not just a being (Garlen 2019). Childhood innocence is conceptualized as a temporal, affective period when children, unaware of the challenges and struggles in society, enjoy life with ease and pleasure, and must therefore be protected through parental, societal, and governmental interventions to ensure their purity and safety (Garlen et al. 2021). Such ideas of childhood innocence intersect with developmentalist and Enlightenment ideals that are promoted in developmental psychology and the "ages and stages" conceptualization of children, which consider children unknowing, immature, and developmentally incomplete (Robinson 2008). Yet many children, such as the recent example in Kitchener–Waterloo illustrates, are not allowed a childhood where they are considered free and innocent. These children are classified as "problem children" (Knight 2019a) and are commonly deemed "irrational" through psychological and medical apparatuses, and therefore violence against them is considered justifiable.

In this chapter, I begin the work of linking theories of childhood innocence, madness, and Blackness to illustrate the importance of Mad and decolonial disruptions of Enlightenment ideas of rationality and how such ideas infiltrate constructions of childhood. My political goal in this chapter is to use rationality as an anchor to explicate how Mad childhoods, Black childhoods, and Mad Black childhoods are excluded from the ideal of childhood innocence and considered disruptive to the image of the innocent white child. Moreover, I argue that constructions of childhood innocence are connected to structures of sanism (Perlin 1992; Poole et al. 2012), which are highly racialized in how they are propagated through Enlightenment ideals of reason (Bruce 2017, 2021; Meerai et al. 2016). It is crucial for scholars in childhood studies to continue to dismantle the grip childhood innocence has on the modern imagining of childhood (Garlen 2019, 2021) to consider how its exclusionary effects have material repercussions on children whose childhoods are imagined as unimaginable and impossible (Knight 2019b; Varga 2018). I argue that Mad Studies is an important framework for childhood studies scholars as they work to disrupt the legacies of modern rationality and its racializing logics. I conclude by exploring the beginnings of *maddening* childhood innocence through a Mad Studies and decolonial lens. To begin, I describe childhood innocence and its critiques in and outside the field of childhood studies.

CHILDHOOD INNOCENCE

Childhood innocence is a regulatory mechanism and construct that originated in Victorian notions of children as untouched, pure, close to nature, and in need of protection, thereby reinforcing the adult–child binary (Farley 2020; Garlen 2019; Rollo 2018). Childhood innocence was and *is* a representation of white supremacist and classist values that reinforce the idea that only white upper middle-class children are vulnerable or even considered children to begin with (Farley 2019; Garlen 2021; Jarkovská and Lamb 2019). As noted by Ramjewan and Garlen (2020), "innocence is not a natural state of being that is accessible to all children, but a socially constructed category shaped by differentials of power that enables adults, namely those who are White and colonial, to produce themselves as dominant" (283). Garlen (2019), drawing on the work of Butler (1988) and McMillan (2017), theorizes childhood as discursively produced through *acts* and *social practices* that construct the child as *at risk* and in peril, thereby potentially having the innocence of childhood disrupted. We must consider how childhood innocence is applied unequally; the Victorian construction of childhood innocence did not include Black, Indigenous, racialized, disabled, or poor children as part of its normative model of childhood (Garlen 2019; Varga 2018).

Childhood studies scholars interrogate the construction of children as inherently innocent and vulnerable and ask critical questions about state and paternalistic control of children, including when actions are taken and legal protection extended in "the best interests of children" (Tesar 2016). Scholars such as Mills (2002) have turned to critical questions regarding the nature of childhood innocence to deconstruct the binary that children are either devilish by nature and need to be tamed into "rational," "civilized" adults or born innocent and pure in nature, therefore society is what taints their innocence. Mills delineates how these constructions of children's "nature" and orientations toward innocence impact parenting styles and socio-political goals and initiatives, with innocence having theological, social, moral, and political implications.

Critical childhood studies draws links between ideas of childhood innocence and ongoing structures of white-cis-heteropatriarchy and settler colonialism, particularly in Early Childhood Education and Care (ECEC), where nature-based play and learning beckons images of the romanticized white child "innocently" playing in nature (Nxumalo 2016). Walton (2021) brings queer of color theories together with women of color feminism to critique the whiteness of both childhood innocence and queer theoretical critiques of childhood innocence's cis-heteronormativity. Walton (2021) specifically asks, "why do we demand the queer child must be seen?" (336). Entering into debates in childhood studies about children "being" or "becoming" (Knight 2019a), Walton provokes questions about the place of the Black queer child, asking, "if the queer child is always becoming, and the Black child is always a being, what do we make of the queer Black child who further complicates the bounds of being and becoming, in that they embody at once both and neither?" (338). Noting Black childhood as a "queer temporality," Walton's work asks critical questions about children who are not imagined as part of modernist constructions of children and childhood, such as queer Black children, and the politics of expanding and/or dismantling normative images of childhood innocence that are historically, socio-politically, and onto-epistemologically exclusionary.

Importantly, the Enlightenment, or the Age of Reason, in the seventeenth to eighteenth centuries significantly impacted constructions of children, childhood, and childhood innocence. Childhood became a device employed to mark racialized populations as savage, irrational, and outside the bounds of liberal reason (Rollo 2018; Varga 2018, 2020). As such, the *capacity for consent* became a mechanism to articulate children's "irrational nature" and their inability to embrace liberal humanist notions of reason (Rollo 2018). This line of thinking is still used to deny mad and disabled people autonomy and personhood, illustrating the link between constructions of children and mad people (Kinsella and LeBlanc 2016). As well, white children were considered in need of adult protection to ensure their development into modern, rational beings, which included gender normativity, class privilege, and the ability to make an economic contribution (Varga 2020).

Here, I take Enlightenment and liberal modern constructions of children and rationality, informed by thinkers such as Locke (1692/1998), as influential in modern notions of childhood innocence (see also Davies and Kenneally 2020; Epp and Brennan 2018; Rollo 2018). Locke saw young children as a blank slate that must be guided into "virtuous habits" at an early age to progress toward reason and rationality. The responsibility was on parents to ensure young children received moral training so that they could resist desires and impulses (Epp and Brennan 2018). For Rousseau (1762/1921), the romantic image of the child prevailed: "happy ignorance" was equated with innocence, and children were kept unaware of their sexual desires until adulthood when they took up gender roles that encouraged men to pursue women as wives and women to remain modest (Epp and Brennan 2018). Thus, remaining carefree and ignorant of social struggle became another modern feature of childhood innocence. Philosophers, such as Rousseau (1972/1921), have highly influenced idea about and images of children and childhood in modern early years education (Bertrand 2021), which promote white innocence and developmental stages as the taken-for-granted norm (Davies 2022a; Davies, Watson, et al. 2022; Varga 2018).

Such ideas of white innocence and rationality were promoted through the emergence of child studies and developmental psychology as disciplines, which drew on eugenics recapitulationist thinking; white children's individual development was expected to model the reproduction of the white race.[1] Varga (2018) describes this in her analysis of the twentieth-century children's texts and psychology textbooks: "contentions of recapitulation theory in child development study, as materialized in images and texts from children's books, contributed to the ideological hegemony of possible and impossible childhoods, with white innocence and Black savagery as counterpoints" (187). Before the late nineteenth century, children were medically considered incapable of being "insane" because their development toward reason and rationality was still "in progress" (Richardson 1989). It was with the establishment of child studies, child psychiatry, and developmental psychology as disciplines separate from philosophy in the late nineteenth century and the promotion of treatment centers and psychiatric hospitals for children in the twentieth century that children's "insanity" became a phenomenon to be investigated (Davies, Watson, et al., in press). Such investigations emerged at the same time as the "ages and stages" theories of Arnold Gesell and eventually Jean Piaget, in which children's cognitive capacities are limited until their full development into adulthood (Richardson 1989).

Problem Children: Those Who Are Not Considered Innocent

In understanding the entanglement of the psy-disciplines, white supremacy, ableism and sanism, and ideas of rationality in modern constructions of childhood innocence, I turn to Knight's (2019a) analysis of the "problem child." Knight analyzes Carla Shalaby's (2017) *Troublemakers* to explore how the children described in Shalaby's text evoke crucial questions regarding how notions of being a "problem child" relate to "the temporal borders structuring childhood" (Knight 2019a, 73). Knight investigates the portraits of four children who are "problem children" in Shalaby's text and therefore in need of behavioral, psychological, and pharmaceutical interventions. Knight argues that Shalaby's text brings about questions regarding "what the process of shaping a narrative of some people as being out-of-sync with childhood says about childhood itself" (74). Such questions consider how "children are narrated into troublesome-ness" (76) and the modern colonial ableist and white supremacist boundaries of normative childhoods.

Developmentalist constructions posit a linear progress narrative that moves a child toward typical adulthood and reason, positioning "the rational space of White, Western masculinity" as ideal (Knight 2019a, 79). Childhood innocence has thereby been reformulated from the liberal tabula rasa, or blank slate, to a scientized and biological construction, in which children are incomplete, cognitively underdeveloped, and incapable of understanding the world around them (Knight 2019a). Moreover, Locke's theories of childhood and citizenship were deployed to justify conquering and then infantilizing racialized and Indigenous populations (Lowe 2015, as cited and discussed in Knight 2019a). By the late nineteenth to early twentieth century, the newer scientized construction of childhood innocence prevalent in developmental psychology and child studies had become racialized, meaning that white children were considered more worthy of being researched scientifically and that when racialized and disabled children were researched, it was their deficits that were of interest (Varga 2018, 2020). In other words, madness, racialization, and childhood innocence were interconnected.

CHILDHOOD INNOCENCE AND MAD STUDIES: AN IMPORTANT INTERVENTION

In this chapter, I describe the knowledges and histories growing out of the Enlightenment, arguing that the field of Mad Studies has much to offer by way of critiquing constructions of childhood innocence and modern rationality. Mad Studies, reportedly first coined by Mad Studies scholar and activist, Richard Ingram, in 2008 (Gorman and LeFrançois 2017), is the combination of inquiry, thought, activism, and scholarship that centralizes ideas of madness, mad subjectivities, and activism to disrupt the predominance of psy-disciplines and create new relationships with and imaginations of madness (see also Beresford and Russo 2021). Importantly, activists and scholars in critical psychiatry, Mad Studies, and anti-psychiatry, interconnected but distinct areas of scholarship and research, hold differing opinions on the place of medical intervention and the angles employed to critique psychiatry's dominance over Mad subjectivities (Chapman 2022; Spandler and Poursanidou 2019); however, all have the aim of critique of the psy-disciplines and pathologizing and normalizing logics. Mad Studies scholars critique and deconstruct taken-for-granted genetic and biomedical explanations of mental "illness" and draw attention to how such explanations perpetuate colonial and biologically essentialist ideas of race that have ramifications for racialized communities, such as stereotypical constructions of Black men as violent, dangerous, or Mad (LeFrançois 2020).

Developmental perspectives of childhood position children as distinct beings from adults, meaning that they are incomplete and in progress, ever changing but still not adult in nature (Duncum 2002). As psychiatrists and psychologists became more intent on the study of young children's development, moral concerns and matters pertaining to the personalities and habits of young children were of great interest to developmental psychologists (Richardson 1989), informed by "the parental concept of the normal, asexual infant and child, and the self-controlled, sublimating, continent, and submissive adolescent" (Neuman 1975, 8). Neuman's analysis of the psychiatric medicalization of young boys' masturbation in the nineteenth century illustrates how masturbation became a clinical concern because of parental fears that their child's sexual innocence was being disrupted and also the recognition that their own childhood might not have embodied the innocent, asexual ideal and norms societally espoused. Thus, the everyday childhood habit of masturbation became a clinical, medical, and psychiatric panic and was constructed as a sign of madness and irrationality (Neuman 1975).

Mad Studies challenges the medicalization, pharmaceuticalization, and pathologization of childhood through psychiatric diagnoses, pharmaceuticals, and psychiatric and clinical psychological treatments, which can discredit and gaslight Mad children's experiences and interpretations of mental distress and madness (LeFrançois 2020). Children experience psychiatrization in different ways, meaning that how children who are psychiatrized or who experience mental distress or "illnesses" identify with psychiatric and biomedical classification and navigate these systems is always individual and differential (Beeker et al. 2020). Still, Mad Studies literature explicitly draws connections between psychiatry and scientific racism, illustrating how Enlightenment and modern legacies of rationality and normative personhood have subjugated and pathologized individuals through hierarchies based on white, middle-class rationality (Gorman and LeFrançois 2017).

For example, Ocen (2015) in her study on the intersection of anti-trafficking laws and the policing and prosecution of young Black girls highlights how modern constructions of childhood innocence inherently exclude Black girls from notions of purity and innocence, thereby positioning Black girls "at the margins of childhood" (1594). Thus, Ocen notes how Black girls are in a liminal position in not being considered "legal adults," yet still being criminalized for their sexuality. Ocen's analysis points to how systemic constructions of Black women's sexualities as unruly, deviant, and needing intervention and control are connected to white supremacist and sexist notions of childhood innocence and normative childhood.

Connections between criminality, deviance, and madness in children can be traced to the nineteenth-century criminologist Cesare Lombroso's (Lombroso 2006; Lombroso and Ferrero 2004) connections between "moral insanity" and crime in young children (Varga 2020). He drew on recapitulationist eugenics that reinforced racialized hierarchies based on "naturalized" criminality (Varga 2020). Lombroso associated specific conduct, such as left-handedness, with "pre-civilized" groups of people, children, and "lunatics" and "the insane," thereby connecting racial hierarchy, infantilization, and insanity through deviance (Kushner 2013). In this sense, white children were to be directed away from markers of deviance, such as left-handedness, in order to preserve the image of the white child at the center of childhood innocence.

It is important for childhood studies scholars to engage with diverse theoretical frameworks and approaches to "help de-reify 'the child' and avoid the traps of closure" (Spyrou 2018, 420). Liegghio (2016) traces the interconnections between ideas of childhood innocence, sanism, adultism, and the discreditation of children and young people who are classified as "mentally ill," behaviorally "challenged," or potentially "criminal" in nature. Liegghio notes how childhood innocence presents the ideal of a happy childhood without internal issues, such as depression, and external issues, such as behavioral or attentional "disorders," thereby positioning the "mentally ill" child as needing intervention to ensure their childhood returns to happiness and innocence. Presumptions of what is in the "best interests" of Mad children and the application of adult values and perspectives to children and youth reinforce adultism (LeFrançois 2008), which Liegghio (2016) connects to sanism, childhood innocence, and systemic discrimination against children and youth who are pushed through psychiatric systems. It is important for childhood studies scholars to bring Mad Studies into conversation with de-colonial frameworks to conceptualize how modern notions of rationality and normalcy are employed to criminalize, medicalize, and incarcerate Black emotion, affect, and resistance to white supremacist systems, which inherently associate Blackness with deviancy and violence (Meerai et al. 2016; Wynter 2003).

SANISM AND MAD CHILDHOODS

Sanism, or the systemic pathologization, discreditation, marginalization, and erasure of individuals who are deemed "mentally ill," or Mad, or identify as such (Perlin 1993; Poole et al. 2012; Leblanc and Kinsella 2016) is connected to normative images of children and childhood that draw from ideas of liberal rationality and psychological development (Davies et al. 2022; Davies and Kenneally 2020). Children who are considered unaligned with normative developmentalist trajectories or whose behaviors are deemed abnormal or pathologized are commonly provided medical and pharmaceutical intervention (i.e., Edmunds and Edmunds 2018; Hutchinson and Specht 2020). Knight (2019a), while not naming sanism explicitly, states how

> medication, a regulator that affects people's moods and behaviors around the clock, is an indication that although the label of "troublemaker" originated at school, these children are considered irregular at a bodily level. It is not just their behavior, but an essential part of who they are, that is too out of-sync: it needs to be changed and modified to make them into acceptable children (77).

Sanism operates through pathologizing the feelings, thoughts, and behaviors of children who are deemed irrational and by placing psychiatric and medicalized labels on children instead of listening to their experiences (LeFrançois 2020). Because of "epistemic injustice" (Fricker 2007) or the act of discrediting Mad children's experiences, voices, and interpretations and not providing resources for children to understand and interpret their experiences with madness (Fricker 2007; LeBlanc and Kinsella 2016), children who are deemed mad, mentally unwell, "ill," or "unstable," are seen as *always* needing medication and behavioral interventions.

As Meerai, Abdillahi, and Poole (2016) theorize in their work on anti-Black sanism, the intersection of sanism and anti-Black racism can be traced back to Enlightenment philosophy of rationality that has historically pathologized Blackness and Black subjectivities and organized systems of slavery and psychiatry that regulated Black subjectivities. The child study movement in the late nineteenth and early twentieth centuries (e.g., Hall 1904) and developmental psychology, which continued its legacy, positioned children of color as naturally, intellectually inferior and even feeble-minded with its racialized explanations for children's behavior and reliance on biologically essentialist ideas of race (Kelly et al. 2021; Varga 2018, 2020). Children have been compared with the "insane" throughout developmental psychology, which sought to establish racialized populations as infantilized, irrational, and in need of state intervention, while positioning children diagnosed with mental "illness" and racialized communities (as well as those of lower socioeconomic status) as primitive (Mills and LeFrançois 2018). For example, James Sully, a prominent English psychologist and developmental researcher, wrote in his text *Studies of Childhood* (1896/2020) how

> children's fears have some resemblance to certain abnormal mental conditions. Idiots, who are so near normal childhood in their degree of intelligence, show a marked fear of strangers. More interesting, however, in the present connection is the exaggeration of the childish fear of new objects which shows itself in certain

mental aberrations. There is a characteristic dread of newness, "neophobia," just as there is a dread of water (103–4).

Varga's (2018, 2020) work investigates the racist, transphobic, homophobic, sexist, and ableist histories of the original theorizing of the child study movement, including Sully.

I bring together these varied analyses to suggest that Mad childhoods, or childhoods of children who are deemed Mad or otherwise "mentally ill," are also constructed as "impossible childhoods," following Varga's (2018) work on the racialization of impossible/possible childhoods. Mad childhoods evoke a disruption to modern notions of childhood that are regulated by ideas of innocence and incompletion. Mad children and childhoods defy the sanctity of childhood innocence due to the incommensurability between the happiness and joy of "innocent" childhoods and the woes and negativity of madness and Mad childhoods (Liegghio 2016), particularly in the case of Black, Indigenous, and other racialized children. In the context of disabled childhoods, Curran and Runswick-Cole (2014) describe how "child development creates a set of norms that creates the 'problem' of the disabled child" (1619), indicating the hegemonic power of developmentalism to construct normal and abnormal childhoods (Burman 2016).

Mad childhoods involve cultivating space to honor what Bernard (2018) terms "the inner-compass of the child unable to speak" (2). Mad childhoods refuse societal constraints, despite countless attempts through medical-psychological-pharmaceutical apparatuses to classify and pathologize children's challenges of societal scripts (Maier 2020). Children have been described through developmental research as unrestrained, in need of behavioral intervention and modification, having developmental deficits, and even animalistic traits that are often associated with madness and cognitive "impairment" (Jackson 1997). Yet, despite white children being constructed as innocent and in need of protection throughout the early child studies movement, Black children were depicted in everyday materials, such as articles and children's books, as animalistic, permanently developmentally "delayed," incomplete, and irrational in their living with animals in "pre-modern" settings (Varga 2018). These depictions continued legacies that associated white children with goodness and Black children with permanent irrationality (Varga 2018, 2020).

MADNESS, CHILDHOOD INNOCENCE, AND MODERN RATIONALITY

At this point, I turn to decolonial scholar Sylvia Wynter (1984, 1987, 1994, 2003, 2006) and Black Mad Studies scholar La Marr Jurelle Bruce (2017,

2021) to conceptualize how Enlightenment liberal humanist hierarchies that privilege universalized notions of rationality and "the human" hold sanist and anti-Black logics that mark Mad and racialized Others. As such, the "problem child" (Knight 2019a) is constructed as a problem due to onto-epistemological racialized legacies that continue to hold sway in the present. Anti-Black racism and sanism continue to medicalize, pathologize, and even murder Black children and youth, who are not considered a part of constructs of childhood innocence.

What can critiques of modern rationality contribute to conversations of childhood and in particular, childhood innocence? What do considerations of modern epistemes offer discussions of discursive, rhetorical, and material violence against children who are denied entry into the universal constructions of childhood and innocence? Here, I turn to Bruce's (2017) work on modern reason and the logics of sanism and anti-Black racism that propagate modernist exclusionary epistemes. Bruce (2017) describes "Reason" as a form of modernist Enlightenment logic that propagates anti-Black ideologies:

> I distinguish "reason" from "Reason." Whereas the former describes the generic process of cogitation within a given system of logic, Reason signifies a hegemonic, Eurocentric, Enlightenment-rooted episteme of transcendental objectivism that is too-often entangled—from those very roots—with antiblack, misogynist, colonialist, and other pernicious ideologies. As such, Reason is often pretext for the systematic subjugation of persons deemed unreasonable or mad. (304)

Madness can be thought of as a barrier; that is, if children are imagined in the Enlightenment project as being on a trajectory toward full reason and adulthood, then madness signifies something gone wrong, immaturity, and unreason. As Ramjewan and Garlen (2020) state, such notions originate from the "organizing structures of the Enlightenment from within which modern childhood emerges as a naturalized life stage the individual progresses out of and into being a fully rational and civilized subject" (282). However, Mad childhoods, Black childhoods, and Mad Black childhoods are onto-epistemologically considered irrational through the racialized marking of children's bodies and their denial into the realm of reason and consciousness (Mohanram 1999). When childhood innocence has historically been applied to Indigenous and Black children, it has been through the logics of assimilation into White settler society and presumptions of racial immorality (Garlen 2019).

Mohanram (1999) investigates how Enlightenment notions of identity are underpinned epistemologically by developmentalism and the theories of John Locke and other Enlightenment philosophers. Such theories propagate notions of "marked" and "unmarked" bodies that "become visible or invisible only through the vectors of power and economics and the meaning imputed to these within cultural knowledge systems" (38). Mohanram furthers the point that "unmarked" bodies—ones that hold a white, male, rationalist, heterosexual subjectivity, similar to Locke—are only associated with consciousness and reason because of their relationship with otherness. As such, "these othered bodies are precluded from participating in the rational discourse of the human and of consciousness in Locke, which attempts to expel any traces of the somatic from its midst" (Mohanram 1999, 39). If participation in the "rational discourse of the human," as Mohanram eloquently illustrates, is dependent on an unmarked subjectivity that reinscribes developmental and Enlightenment notions of liberal rationality, it would follow that those who are cast outside of modern ideas of reason are certainly racially marked (Bruce 2017; Mohanram 1999; Wynter 2003).

Sylvia Wynter's (1984, 1987, 1994, 2003, 2006) work on modern epistemes illustrates how modern ideas of irrationality are based on binary logics that hold racializing implications, in that the Enlightenment taken-for-granted "descriptive statement" of the human (i.e., Man) has become "overrepresented" in a falsely universal manner. Wynter (2003) describes how specific "genres of being human" are valorized through the "biocentric nature of the sociogenic code of our present genre of being human, which imperatively calls for the devalorization of the characteristic of blackness as well as of the Bantu-type physiognomy" (115). Such a form of humanness that is encoded in maleness, heterosexuality, able-bodiedness, and modern rationality is reinscribed through biocentric and purely biological constructions of humanness that were propagated through the evolution of science and reason during the Enlightenment. Wynter specifically notes how modernity's invention of the

> "'Rational Self' is in contrast to the peoples of the militarily expropriated New World territories (i.e., Indians), as well as the enslaved peoples of Black Africa (i.e., Negroes), that were made to reoccupy the matrix slot of Otherness—to be made into the physical referent of the idea of the irrational/subrational Human Other" (Wynter 2003, 266).

Such boundaries of rationality and irrationality were codified through the institutionalization of slavery that drew connections between race and madness (Gillman 1985).

It is such ideas of irrationality that deny Black boys from being considered fully human to begin with. Wynter (1994) asks how Black men have come to be "perceived, and therefore behaved towards, only as the Lack of the human, the Conceptual Other to being North American?" (2). It is these logics that are connected with Enlightenment legacies based in Roussean ideas of childhood innocence and developmental psychological theories that presented white children's development as a progression toward white, cisgender, heterosexual rationality and racialized, specifically Black and Indigenous childhoods as always the irrational Other. Pickens (2019) describes this by articulating how "madness becomes the place to engage because racism adheres to a peculiar kind of rationality, predicated on the long history of the Enlightenment and its material effects" (14). The interconnections between madness; the psychiatrization and regulation of children's behaviors, emotions, and psyches; and racialized hierarchies is important to note. I aim to make clear in this chapter the links between modern Enlightenment constructions of childhood and innocence, ideas of rationality that are propagated through developmental psychology theories of the nineteenth and twentieth centuries and systems of sanism that mark Mad racialized childhoods an impossibility.

Such connections pathologized Black people's attempts to resist slavery and located white fears and anxieties within Black bodies (Gilman 1985). Such fears have repercussions in modern times in how ideas of childhood innocence reproduce whiteness and project white anxieties and fears onto Black children, as in the case of the four-year-old Black boy in Kitchener–Waterloo who was constituted as a "problem child" through anti-Black and sanist logics. It is necessary to also note that when Black, Indigenous, and racialized children experience structural violence, developmentalist logics of childhood innocence deem racialized children incompetent to comprehend their very dehumanization (Greensmith and Sheppard 2018). Despite the lack of training in pre-service education programs on epistemology, ontology, and the histories of developmental psychology, these knowledges still inform present-day, normative ideas of rationality (Davies, Watson, et al. 2022; Varga 2020). I now move to exploring what I term a *maddening* of childhood innocence, specifically drawing from Farley's (2018) description of the murder of 15-year-old Leticia King in 2008.

MADDENING CHILDHOOD INNOCENCE: THE DE-ONTOLOGIZATION OF THE PROBLEM CHILD

Considering the hold the ideal of childhood innocence has on modern imaginings of childhood (Epp and Brennan 2018; Garlen 2019), it is necessary to dismantle exclusionary white supremacist, cis-heteropatriarchal, sanist logics that do not reflect the lived realities of children, silence their voices, elide their experiences (Raby and Raddon 2015), and propagate the "seemingly unimpeachable ideal of innocence, which softens the blow of the racist, classist, colonialist logics that drove the demand to school the masses" (Garlen 2021, 26). Such ideals are *maddening* and require *maddening* in terms of a Mad Studies critique (Davies 2022a). The affect produced through madness is interconnected with Mad Studies' challenge of modern notions of rationality and reason (Davies 2022a see also Bruce 2017; LeFrançois and Voronka

2022). The idea of childhood innocence has been critiqued by scholars within and outside of childhood studies for its exclusionary logics, yet there remains a silence on how sanism and racialization intersect with socio-cultural constructs of childhood innocence.

I move to Farley's (2018) analysis of the 2008 shooting of 15-year-old Black transgender student Leticia King during an early morning computer lab, by her 14-year-old white classmate, Brandon McInerney. Farley (2018) references Bruhm's (2012) work on the "counterfeit child" to explore how such a figure, in this case Leticia, is simultaneously an adult disguised as a child while still being clearly recognized as an adult. The counterfeit "is the uncanny personified, where the familiar image of childhood innocence crosses into its opposite" (Farley 2018, 66). Importantly, Leticia's transness and Blackness produced her as counterfeit and then marked her as dangerous in her school and therefore as not under the aegis of childhood innocence (Farley 2018).

Leticia was constructed as a "problem" in her school, E.O. Green Junior High School in Oxnard, California, in particular through her gender expression, sexuality, and Blackness, which were commonly connected with "breaking rules" and refusing to abide by codes of conduct at school (Corbett 2015, 167, cited and described in Farley 2018). Drawing on Corbett (2015), Farley articulates how Leticia's Black femininity marked her as a problem while her killer, Brandon McInerney's white masculinity was unmarked and normalized, and protected him by associating his actions with self-defense. As Farley (2018) notes, "a counterfeit figure, Leticia was constructed as the unhuman maker of her own murder" (76). Farley describes how leading up to her murder, Leticia flirted with Brandon in the hallway, therefore, in Brandon's narrative, placing his masculinity at risk and feminizing him. As such, Leticia's murder was justified through logics of white heteromasculinity, which associates whiteness, normative masculinity, and heterosexuality with innocence, labelling Brandon's act as self-defense and Leticia as "justifiably" murdered (Farley 2018). Such ideologies have connotations for the intersections of childhood innocence, child–adult binaries, racial hierarchies, and exclusionary legacies of Enlightenment liberal humanism.[2]

Farley (2018) references Leticia's "collected diagnoses" (Corbett 2015, 32) as she describes for the reader how Leticia had been diagnosed with pervasive developmental delay, bipolar disorder, depression, obsessive compulsive disorder, attention deficit disorder, gender identity disorder, and attachment disorder. Leticia was prescribed pharmaceuticals, including stimulants, tranquilizers, mood stabilizers, antipsychotics, antidepressants, and neuroleptics (Corbett 2015, 32, cited in Farley 2018), thereby "treating Leticia as the individual problem" (Farley 2018, 72). The individualization and medicalization of Leticia's distress exemplifies the sanist logics that depend on treating Leticia as a problem child, or perhaps one whose development is simultaneously delayed but also early. Knight's (2019a) explanation of temporality and the problem child is useful here for understanding how children who are deemed problematic are always "out-of-sync" with normative developmental trajectories; they are adultified in a way that denies them their childhood while also diagnosed as delayed or with a disorder that interferes with their normative development (Knight 2019a).

Considering Leticia through this analytic provides a way to consider how her Black sexuality, including her transgender identity, her feminine apparel, and flirtatious interactions with boys, became a means to exclude her from childhood innocence (Farley 2018). Still, her medicalization and diagnoses indicate a level of presumption of delay, in that she was considered abnormal vis-à-vis the normative developmental presumptions of childhood and youth (Farley 2018). Leticia's existence threatened the hierarchies entrenched in modern schooling that reinforce docility in and order among students and begs the question if the justification provided to Brandon McInerney would have been acceptable if Leticia was white (Farley 2018; Meerai et al. 2016).

A maddening approach to this situation asks where and how madness presented itself in the murder of Leticia King and in what ways her subjectivity was considered in opposition to "white rationality," which constructs racialized, Indigenous, and Black populations as inherently "irrational, untrustworthy, and odd" (Meerai et al. 2016, 24). In her resistance to being controlled, tamed, denied her gendered subjectivity, and medicalized, Leticia King was de-ontologized, denied her humanness, and deemed not in need of protection, or even, as Farley (2018) notes, a threat to the normative white masculinity of Brandon McInerney. However, Leticia can also be read as exerting her agency and resisting de-ontologization against the white cisgendered sanism that sought to constitute her otherness. Wynter (1984, 2003) describes how the current genre of human—Man—can be overturned through an autopoetic humanity outside of the current form of privileged humanness, thus in relation to "structural oppositional codes" that come to define humanity through hierarchies of behaviors and beings:

> "By marking the mode of Desire—the desire of Life and of Aversion to Death—these structural oppositional codes function to orient the parameters of motivations/behaviors of the order. They are thus the very condition of the collective behaviors through which each human system realizes itself as such a system" (Wynter 1984, 27).

This process of dismantling current conceptions of the human calls for new humanisms or a new articulation of the human that is honored in its own right outside of the "descriptive statements" of Man (Wynter 2003). Reading Leticia King's resistance to the normative demands of white, cisgender sanism, and heteromasculinity entrenched in normative humanism, Leticia was advocating for a form of humanism and humanity that considers the Black queer trans Mad child as always *already* human.

Wynter (2003) notes how "with this process taking place hitherto outside our conscious awareness, and thereby leading us to be governed by the 'imagined ends' or postulates of being, truth, freedom that we lawlikely put and keep in place, without realizing that it is we ourselves, and not extrahuman entities, who prescribe them" (329). In this sense, there is the potential for a new form of Black queer trans Mad humanity that reimagines the human. As Pickens (2019) states, "Blackness and madness exceed and shift the boundaries and definitions of human, specifically how the subject positions of unknowable excess (that is, Black madness and mad Blackness) jeopardize the neatness with which we draw the line between self and other" (16). The logics that normalize the murder of Leticia King draw from violent sanist and anti-Black racist logics that constitute Leticia as a failure. However, maddening such logics emphasizes Leticia's resistance toward new forms of humanness. As LeFrançois and Voronka (2022) note, maddening entails explicit critiques to the logics of positivism and modern rationalism that discredit and deny the knowledges and lived experiences of those who have been medicalized or psychiatrized. This includes an explicitly anti-racist stance that critiques how white rationality (Meerai et al. 2016) results in the death, medicalization, and incarceration of racialized populations (Gorman and LeFrançois 2017).

My argument here is in conversation with critical childhood studies scholars who critique the dominance of Western imaginaries of childhood innocence (Garlen 2019, 2021; Knight 2019a, 2019b; Ramjewan and Garlen 2020). However, I believe that a specific critique of the *rationalities* behind childhood innocence and modern constructions of childhood is necessary to consider those who are never imagined as children to begin with and their biomedicalization. Taking seriously Knight's (2019a) argument about temporality, this chapter argues that a Mad Studies, or maddening, interruption, and dismantling of childhood innocence is crucial to address sanism in relationship with other systems of inequities embedded in notions of childhood innocence. Considering the continual psychiatrization, medicalization, and criminalization of young children, in particular young children of color (see Ramey 2018), Mad Studies offers an incisive critique of the psy-disciplines and their reign over modern imaginings of normalcy and children (LeFrançois 2020).

Opening up spaces for theorizing children and childhood differently loosens the hold that developmental psychology in pre-service spaces, such as teacher education, has over constructions of children in education (Davies, Watson, et al. 2022), thereby also allowing for critiques of the essentialized racial hierarchies that have been instilled in psychology as a profession and disciplinary field (Kromidas 2019). Maddening childhood innocence—disrupting and dismantling Enlightenment and colonial rationalities that are embedded in childhood innocence—is also about reimagining new futurities apart from modern reason (Bruce 2017). Following Bruce (2017), this does not mean an uncritical glorification of madness or the refusal to acknowledge the real pain that psycho-social distress can cause. However, it is important to simultaneously acknowledge how modern forms of rationality propagate logics that have a real material impact on childhoods and children, especially those who are not considered children to begin with, such as the four-year-old boy who was escorted out of his school by the police and a young Black trans girl who was violently shot in her morning class. It is time to madden (Davies 2022a, 2022b; Davies et al. 2022; LeFrançois 2017; LeFrançois and Voronka 2022) the "myth of innocence" (Garlen 2021) and centralize children who do not fit neatly within this ableist, sanist, white, cis-heteropatriarchal construct, in our research, theorizing, and writing.

NOTES

1. The history of the child study movement and its connections to modern Western ideas of rationality are discussed in Varga (2018, 2020). This is discussed in-depth and connected to the necessity of Mad Studies interventions in early childhood education and care in Davies, Watson, et al. (2022).
2. Davies and Kenneally (2020) discuss in the context of Ontario debates regarding sexuality education how liberal humanist political imaginings of children propagate ableist and exclusionary images of children that do not consider disabled children as fully children or within the realm of childhood or childhood innocence.

REFERENCES

Beeker, Timo, Anna Witeska-Młynarczyk, Sanna te Meerman, and China Mills. 2020. "Psychiatrization of, with and by Children: Drawing a Complex Picture." *Global Studies of Childhood* 10(1): 12–25. https://doi.org/10.1177/2043610619890074.
Beresford, Peter, and Jasna Russo, eds. 2021. *The Routledge International Handbook of Mad Studies*. Routledge.
Bernard, Adrian. 2018. "Understanding the Possible: Creative, Approach Madness." *Journal of Humanistic Psychology*. https://doi.org/10.1177/00221678187622203.
Bertrand, Jane. 2021. *Becoming and Being an Early Childhood Professional*. Boston, MA: Cengage.
Bruce, La Mare J. 2017. "Mad Is a Place: Or, the Slave Ship Tows the Ship of Fools." *American Quarterly* 69(2): 303–8. https://doi.org/10.1353/aq.2017.0024.

Bruce, La Mare J. 2021. *How to Go Mad Without Losing Your Mind: Madness and Black Radical Creativity*. Durham, NC: Duke University Press.

Bruhm, Steven. 2012. "The Counterfeit Child." *English Studies in Canada* 38(3): 25–44.

Bryan, Nathaniel. 2021. *Toward a BlackBoyCrit Pedagogy: Black Boys, Male Teachers, and Early Childhood Classroom Practices*. London: Routledge.

Burman, Erica. 2016. *Deconstructing Developmental Psychology*. London: Routledge.

Butler, Judith. 1988. "Performative Acts and Gender Constitution: An Essay in Phenomenology and Feminist Theory." *Theatre Journal* 40(4): 519–31. https://doi.org/10.2307/3207893.

Chapman, Robert. 2022. "A Critique of Critical Psychiatry." *Philosophy, Psychiatry, and Psychology*. https://www.researchgate.net/publication/362430760_A_Critique_of_Critical_Psychiatry.

Corbett, Ken. 2015. *A Murder Over a Girl: Justice, Gender, Junior High*. Henry Holt.

Curran, Tillie, and Katherine Runswick-Cole. 2014. "Disabled Children's Childhood Studies: A Distinct Approach?" *Disability and Society* 29(10): 1617–30. https://doi.org/10.1080/09687599.2014.966187.

Davies, Adam W. 2022a. "Professional Ruptures in Pre-Service ECEC: Maddening Early Childhood Education and Care." *Curriculum Inquiry* 54(2). https://doi.org/10.1080/03626784.2022.2149027.

Davies, Adam W. 2022b. "Teaching with Madness in Pre-Service Early Childhood Education and Care (ECEC): Bringing Autobiographical Mad Subjectivities and Promoting Curiosity." In *International Handbook of Curriculum Theory, Research, and Practice*, edited by P. Trifonas and S. Jagger, 20-38. Cham: Springer.

Davies, A.W. and Noah Kenneally. 2020. "Cripping the Controversies: Ontario Rights-Based Debates in Sexuality Education." *Sex Education* 20(4): 366–82. https://doi.org/10.1080/14681811.2020.1712549.

Davies, Adam W., Kailyn C. Brewer, and Bronte Shay. 2022. "Sanism in Early Childhood Education and Care: Cultivating Space for Madness and Mad Educators." *eceLINK* 6(1): 18–30. https://www.researchgate.net/profile/Adam-Davies-19/publication/361338042_Sanism_in_Early_Childhood_Education_and_Care_Cultivating_Space_for_Madness_and_Mad_Educators_in_ECEC/links/62bb90435e258e67e10de3bb/Sanism-in-Early-Childhood-Education-and-Care-Cultivating-Space-for-Madness-and-Mad-Educators-in-ECEC.pdf.

Davies, Adam W., Drew Watson, Ben Armstrong, Lauren Spring, Kailyn C. Brewer, Bronte Shay, Alexander Purnell, and Simon Adam. 2022. "Exploring Histories of ECEC to Evoke Questions Through Mad Studies: A Critical Proposition for Pre-Service ECEC." EceLINK 6(2): 20–38. https://assets.nationbuilder.com/aeceo/pages/2733/attachments/original/1671133962/eceLINK_Fall-Winter_2022_Exploring_Histories_of_ECEC.pdf?1671133962.

Duhatschek, Paula. 2022, Feb. 23. "Waterloo Catholic School Board Called Police on 4-Year-Old Child, Advocates Say." *CBC News*. https://www.cbc.ca/news/canada/kitchener-waterloo/waterloo-catholic-board-called-police-child-1.6362341.

Duncum, Paul. 2002. "Children Never Were What They Were: Perspectives on Childhood." In *Contemporary Issues in Art Education*, edited by Yvonne Gaudeluis and Peg Speirs, 97–107. Toronto, ON: Pearson.

Edmunds, Alan, and Gail Edmunds. 2018. *Special Education in Canada*. Ottawa, ON: Ottawa University Press.

Epp, Jennifer, and Samantha Brennan. 2018. "Childhood and Sexuality." In *The Routledge Handbook of the Philosophy of Childhood and Children*, edited by Anca Gheaus, Gideon Caldor, and Jurgen De Wispelaere, 271–81. London: Routledge.

Farley, Lisa. 2018. *Childhood Beyond Pathology: A Psychoanalytic Study of Development and Diagnosis*. Albany, NY: SUNY Press.

Farley, Lisa. 2020. "Innocence." In *Trickbox of Memory: Essays on Power and Disorderly Pasts*, edited by Felicitas Macgilchrist and Rosalie Metro, 65–85. Goleta, CA: Punctum Books.

Fricker, Miranda. 2007. *Epistemic Injustice: Power and the Ethics of Knowing*. Oxford University Press.

Garlen, Julie C. 2019. "Interrogating Innocence: 'Childhood' as Exclusionary Social Practice." *Childhood* 26(1): 54–67. https://doi.org/10.1177/0907568218811484.

Garlen, Julie C. 2021. "The End of Innocence: Childhood and Schooling for a Post-Pandemic World." *Journal of Teaching and Learning* 15(2): 21–39. https://doi.org/10.22329/jtl.v15i2.6724.

Garlen, Julie C., Sandra Chang-Kredl, Lisa Farley, and Debbie Sonu. 2021. "Childhood Innocence and Experience: Memory, Discourse and Practice." *Children and Society* 35(5): 648–62. https://doi.org/10.1111/chso.12428.

Ghonaim, Hala. 2022, June 28. "Kitchener, Ont. Family Sues Catholic School Board Alleging Discrimination against 4-Year-Old Boy." *CBC News*. https://www.cbc.ca/news/canada/kitchener-waterloo/waterloo-catholic-district-school-board-civil-suit-discrimination-1.6497704?cmp=rss.

Gilman, Sander L. 1985. *Difference and Pathology: Stereotypes of Sexuality, Race, and Madness*. Ithaca, NY: Cornell University Press.

Gorman, Rachel, and Brenda A. LeFrançois. 2017. "Mad Studies." In *Routledge International Handbook of Critical Mental Health*, edited by Bruce M. Z. Cohen, 107–14. Routledge.

Greensmith, Cameron, and Lindsay Sheppard. 2018. "At the Age of Twelve: Migrant Children and the Disruption of Multicultural Belonging." *Children and Society* 32(4): 255–65. https://doi.org/10.1111/chso.12251.

Hall, G. S. 1904. *Adolescence: Its Psychology and Its Relations to Physiology, Anthropology, Sociology, Sex, Crime, Religion, and Education* (Vols. I & II). New York, NY: D. Appleton & Co.

Hutchinson, Nancy Lynn, and Jacqueline Specht. 2020. *Inclusion of Learners with Exceptionalities in Canadian Schools: A Practical Handbook for Teachers*. Pearson.

Jackson, Ian. 1997. "Paradigmatic Madness in the Public Representation of Childhood." *Australian Journal of Social Issues* 32(3): 257–72. https://doi.org/10.1002/j.1839-4655.1997.tb01296.x.

Jarkovská, Lucie, and Sharon Lamb. 2019. "Not Innocent, but Vulnerable: An Approach to Childhood Innocence." In *The Cambridge Handbook of Sexual Development: Childhood and Adolescence*, edited by Sharon Lamb and Jen Gilbert, 76–93. Cambridge: Cambridge University Press. https://doi. org/10.1017/9781108116121.

Kelly, Evadne, Dolleen T. Manning, Seika Boye, Carla Rice, Dawn Owen, Sky Stonefish, and Mona Stonefish. 2021. "Elements of a Counter-Exhibition: Excavating and Countering a Canadian History and Legacy of Eugenics." *Journal of the History of the Behavioral Sciences* 57(1): 12–33. https://doi.org/10.1002/jhbs.22081.

Leblanc, Stephanie, and Elizabeth Anne Kinsella. 2016. "Toward Epistemic Justice: A Critically Reflexive Examination of 'Sanism' and Implications for Knowledge Generation." *Studies in Social Justice* 10(1): 59–78. https://doi.org/10.26522/ssj.v10i1.1324.

Knight, Hunter. 2019a. "Centering the Problem Child: Temporality, Colonialism, and Theories of the Child." *Global Studies of Childhood* 9(1): 72–83. https://doi.org/10.1177/2043610618825005.

Knight, Hunter. 2019b. "Imagining Institutions of Man: Constructions of the Human in the Foundations of Ontario Public Schooling Curriculum." *Curriculum Inquiry* 49(1): 90–109. https://doi.org/10.1080/03626784.2018.1552071.

Kromidas, Maria. 2019. "Towards the Human, after the Child of Man: Seeing the Child Differently in Teacher Education." *Curriculum Inquiry* 49(1): 65–89. https://doi.org/10.1080/03626784.2018.1549924.

Kushner, Howard I. 2013. "Deficit or Creativity: Cesare Lombroso, Robert Hertz, and the Meanings of Left-Handedness." *Laterality: Asymmetries of Body, Brain and Cognition* 18(4): 416–36. https://doi.org/10.1080/1357650X.2012.697171.

LeFrançois, Brenda A. 2008. "'It's like Mental Torture': Participation and Mental Health Services." *International Journal of Children's Rights* 16: 211–27. https://doi.org/10.1163/157181808X301809.

LeFrançois, Brenda A. 2017. "Mad Studies: Maddening Social Work." Filmed November 2017 at Connecting for Canada's 150th: Canadian Visionaries of Critical Social Work, Fredericton, NB, YouTube. https://www.youtube.com/watch?v=QYxM_bBk7fs.

LeFrançois, Brenda A. 2020. "Psychiatrising Children." In *Exploring Childhood and Youth*, edited by Victoria Cooper and Naomi Holford, 177–90. London: Routledge.

LeFrançois, Brenda A., and Jijian Voronka. 2022. "Mad Epistemologies and Maddening the Ethics of Knowledge Production." In *Unravelling Research: The Ethics and Politics of Research in the Social Sciences*, edited by Teresa Macias, 105–30. Halifax, NS: Fernwood Publishing.

LeFrançois, Brenda A., Robert Menzies, and Geoffrey Reaume, eds. 2013. *Mad Matters: A Critical Reader in Canadian Mad Studies*. Toronto, ON: Canadian Scholars Press.

Liegghio, Maria. 2016. "Too Young to Be Mad: Disabling Encounters with 'Normal' from the Perspectives of Psychiatrized Youth." *Intersectionalities: A Global Journal of Social Work Analysis, Research, Polity, and Practice* 5(3): 110–29. https://journals.library.mun.ca/ojs/index.php/IJ/article/view/1610.

Locke, John. (1692) 1998. "Some Thoughts Concerning Education." In *Internet Modern History Sourcebook*, edited by P. Hassal. New York, NY: Fordham University. http://sourcebooks.fordham.edu/mod/1692locke-education.asp.

Lombroso, Cesare. (1886) 2006. *Criminal Man*. Durham, NC: Duke University Press.

Lombroso, Cesare and Guglielmo Ferrero. (1893) 2004. *Criminal Woman, the Prostitute, and the Normal Woman*. Durham, NC: Duke University Press.

Lowe, Lisa. 2015. *The Intimacies of Four Continents*. Durham, NC: Duke University Press.

Maier, S. E. 2020. "Gendered (De)Illusions: Imaginative Madness in Neo-Victorian Childhood Trauma Narratives." In *Neo-Victorian Madness*, edited by Sarah E. Maier and Brenda Ayres, 281–302. Cham: Palgrave Macmillan.

McMillan, Kevin. 2017. *The Constitution of Social Practices*. Milton: Taylor and Francis.

Meerai, Sonia, Idil Abdillahi, and Jennifer M. Poole. 2016. "An Introduction to Anti-Black Sanism." *Intersectionalities: A Global Journal of Social Work Analysis, Research, Polity, and Practice* 5(3): 18–35. https://journals.library.mun.ca/ojs/index.php/IJ/article/view/1682.

Mills, China, and Brenda A. LeFrançois. 2018. "Child as Metaphor: Colonialism, Psy-Governance, and Epistemicide." *World Futures* 74(7–8): 503–24. https://doi.org/10.1080/02604027.2018.1485438.

Mills, Richard. 2002. "Perspectives of Childhood." In *Childhood Studies*, edited by Richard Mills and Jean Mills, 21–52. London: Routledge.

Mohanram, Radhika. 1999. *Black Body: Women, Colonialism, and Space*. Minneapolis, MN: University of Minnesota Press.

Neuman, R. P. 1975. "Masturbation, Madness, and the Modern Concepts of Childhood and Adolescence." *Journal of Social History* 8(3): 1–27. https://www.jstor.org/stable/3786713.

Nxumalo, Fikile. 2016. "Towards 'Refiguring Presences' as an Anti-Colonial Orientation to Research in Early Childhood Studies." *International Journal of Qualitative Studies in Education* 29(5): 640–54. https://doi.org/10.1080/09518398.2016.1139212.

Ocen, Priscilla A. 2015. "(E)racing Childhood: Examining the Racialized Construction of Childhood and Innocence in the Treatment of Sexually Exploited Minors." *UCLA Law Review* 62: 1586–1640. https://papers.ssrn.com/sol3/papers.cfm?abstract_id=2692829.

Parents of Black Children. 2022. "Statement in Response to the Third-Party Investigation into the Waterloo Catholic District School Board." *Parents of Black Children*. https://parentsofblackchildren.org/statement-in-response-to-the-third-party-investigation-into-the-waterloo-catholic-district-school-board/.

Perlin, Michael L. 1992. "On Sanism." *SMU Law Review* 46: 373–407.

Pickens, Therí A. 2019. *Black Madness: Mad Blackness*. Durham, NC: Duke University Press.

Poole, Jennifer M., Tania Jivraj, Araxi Arslanian, Kristen Bellows, Sheila Chiasson, Husnia Hakimy, Jessica Rasini, and Jenna Reid. 2012. "Sanism, 'Mental Health,' and Social Work/Education: A Review and Call to Action." *Intersectionalities: A*

Global Journal of Social Work Analysis, Research, Polity, and Practice 1: 20–36. https://journals.library.mun.ca/ojs/index.php/IJ/article/view/348.

Raby, Rebecca, and Mary Beth Raddon. 2015. "Is She a Pawn, Prodigy or Person with a Message? Public Responses to a Child's Political Speech." *Canadian Journal of Sociology/Cahiers canadiens de sociologie* 40(2): 163–88. https://doi.org/10.2307/canajsocicahican.40.2.163.

Ramey, David M. 2018. "The Social Construction of Child Social Control via Criminalization and Medicalization: Why Race Matters." *Sociological Forum* 33(1): 139–64. https://doi.org/10.1111/socf.12403.

Ramjewan, Neil, and Julie C. Garlen. 2020. "Growing Out of Childhood Innocence." *Curriculum Inquiry* 50(4): 281–90. https://doi.org/10.1080/03626784.2020.1851521.

Richardson, Teresa R. 1989. *The Century of the Child: The Mental Hygiene Movement and Social Policy in the United States and Canada.* Albany, NY: Suny Press.

Robinson, Kerry H. 2008. "In the Name of 'Childhood Innocence': A Discursive Exploration of the Moral Panic Associated with Childhood and Sexuality." *Cultural Studies Review* 14(2): 113–29. ISSN:1446-8123.

Rollo, Toby. 2018. "The Color of Childhood: The Role of the Child/Human Binary in the Production of Anti-Black Racism." *Journal of Black Studies* 49(4): 307–29. https://doi.org/10.1177/0021934718760769.

Rousseau, Jean-Jacques. (1762) 1921. *Emile, or Education*, translated by B. Foxley. London: Dent. http://oll.libertyfund.org/titles/rousseau-emile-or-education.

Shalaby, Carla. 2017. *Troublemakers: Lessons in Freedom from Young Children at School.* New York, NY: The New Press.

Spandler, Helen, and Dina Poursanidou. 2019. "Who Is Included in the Mad Studies Project?" *Journal of Ethics in Mental Health* 10. ISSN 1916-2405.

Spyrou, Spyros. 2018. "What Next for Childhood Studies?" *Childhood* 25(4): 419–21. https://doi.org/10.1177/0907568218788212.

Sully, James. (1896) 2020. *Studies of Childhood.* Local Vandals Publishing.

Tesar, M. 2016. "Childhood Studies: An Overview of." In *Encyclopedia of Educational Philosophy and Theory*, Michael Peters, 978–81. Singapore: Springer Nature.

Varga, Donna. 2018. "Innocence Versus Savagery in the Recapitulation Theory of Child Study: Depictions in Picturebooks and Other Cultural Materials." *International Research in Children's Literature* 11(2): 186–202. https://doi.org/10.3366/ircl.2018.0274.

Varga, Donna. 2020. "The Legacy of Recapitulation Theory in the History of Developmental Psychology." In *Oxford Research Encyclopedia of Psychology.* https://oxfordre.com/psychology/view/10.1093/acrefore/9780190236557.001.0001/acrefore-9780190236557-e-519.

Walton, Ellie. 2021. "The Queer Child Cracks: Queer Feminist Encounters with Materiality and Innocence in Childhood Studies." *Childhood* 28(3): 333–45. https://doi.org/10.1177/09075682211026948.

Wynter, Sylvia. 1984. "The Ceremony Must Be Found: After Humanism. *Boundary 2*: 19–70. https://doi.org/10.2307/302808.

Wynter, Sylvia. 1987. "On Disenchanting Discourse: 'Minority' Literary Criticism and Beyond." *Cultural Critique* 7: 207–44. https://doi.org/10.2307/1354156.

Wynter, Sylvia. 1994. "'No Humans Involved': An Open Letter to my Colleagues." In *Forum N. H. I Knowledge for the 21st Century/Knowledge on Trial* 1(1): 42–73.

Wynter, Sylvia. 2003. "Unsettling the Coloniality of Being/Power/Truth/Freedom: Towards the Human, after Man, its Overrepresentation—An Argument." *CR: The New Centennial Review* 3(3): 257–37. https://doi.org/10.1353/ncr.2004.0015.

Wynter, Sylvia. 2006. "On How We Mistook the Map for the Territory, and Reimprisoned Ourselves in Our Unbearable Wrongness of Being, of Desêtre: Black Studies Toward the Human Project." In *A Companion to African-American Studies*, edited by Lewis R. Gordon and Jane Anna Gordon, 107–18. London: Blackwell Publishing.

Chapter 4

Zapatista Childhoods

Children's Participation and the Possibilities for Collective Knowledge

Kathia Núñez Patiño

INTRODUCTION

On January 1, 1994, the same day that the North American Free Trade Agreement (NAFTA) came into effect, the Zapatista Army of National Liberation, or Ejército Zapatista de Liberación Nacional (EZLN), declared war on the Mexican government.[1] Led by the Indigenous people of Chiapas, Mexico, the movement sought "work, land, housing, food, health, education, independence, liberty, democracy, justice, and peace" (International Service for Peace 2002, n.p.) in response to centuries of colonial oppression. According to the most recent census information from the Mexican Institute of Statistics and Geographical Information (INEGI) (2020), the Indigenous population in Chiapas represents 36.15 percent of the state's total population. Although Chiapas is one of the wealthiest states in terms of natural resources, it is one of the most marginalized states, and its Indigenous people experience widespread malnutrition, poverty, and lack of access to education and health care. NAFTA, which sought to eliminate trade barriers between the United States, Canada, and Mexico was seen as "a dangerous new stage of global capitalism" (Klein 2019, n.p) that posed a profound threat to Indigenous interests. Although the armed conflict was short-lived, Zapatista resistance has continued as an important social movement and has "not only provoked a domestic awareness of indigenous rights, recognition and self-determination, but also an international awakening on these issues" (Godelmann 2014, n.p.).

As Klein (2019) observes, "The Zapatista uprising stood against the backdrop of colonialism and its legacy—centuries of poverty and inequality, racism, and exploitation" (n.p.). Throughout history, the State's formal recognition of Indigenous cultural practices has served as a device (Agamben 2011) that has given continuity to the structure of colonial power (Quijano 2000). This structure of coloniality addresses the political alternatives offered by the State, which are implemented in a homogenizing way. The Zapatista autonomy movement in Chiapas and the uprising of the Indigenous community for security, justice, and reconstitution of the territory of Cherán K'eri in Michoacán emerged as a challenge to this structure (Autoría Collective 2017). While Zapatista autonomy is built on a daily basis from within its Indigenous communities and practices, the uprising community in Cherán K'eri has upheld the custom of living together and revived a living memory that emerged from the bonfires of the neighborhoods, which were established from the beginning of their movement with the purpose of monitoring and caring for that area (Sixth Commission 2015, 2016). According to Alvarado (2018), the neighborhood bonfires were created as practices of surveillance and points of care in more than sixty locations.

The creation of the bonfires caused the materialization of a new form of social space and sociality, what the Purépecha Indigenous people recognized as "parhanga" (139–140). The idea of the neighborhood bonfires is very similar to the constitutive pillars that the theorists of communality in Oaxaca highlight in the territory, such as the space as a place that is inhabited, the collective work as a daily activity, the party as enjoyment of the fruit of work, and the assembly as the highest authority and decision-maker since these pillars must be understood from the notions of the communal, the collective, the complementarity, and the integrality (Diaz 2004; Martínez-Luna 2015; Maldonado 2015). Beyond the academic analysis, the centrality of these social congregations lies in their contribution to action in processes like organization and political action; processes that come from popular collective changes and actions that can be promoted from the academy for the reconstruction of "the common" (*lo común*) as an alternative to the privatization and individualism that is characteristic of global capitalism.

Drawing on such cultural traditions, this chapters looks to the Indigenous community practices and political thought within the Zapatista autonomy movement to think about the diverse contexts in which children grow up. The Zapatista movement highlights the diversity of contexts in which childhood occurs and leads us question the singular and presumed universal term "childhood." Pluralizing this term to instead consider "childhoods" in all their diversity offers a challenge to the hegemonic term imposed by the urban-bourgeois society. Exploring such diverse contexts allows us to consider the spatial limitations imposed on children, such as the private space of the family held for their "protection" and the space of the school designed for their "socialization." Childhood, the hegemonic term of the urban-bourgeois society that has been imposed at the national level and established as "normal" operates without a clear understanding of the cultural contexts in which children actually grow up. Moreover, such a hegemonic term has served as an instrument to monitor and penalize childhood, particularly the childhood of specific groups of peoples such as the Zapatistas, where the absence of urban-bourgeois family and educational structures place children at risk of falling under the tutelage of the State.

From this framework of thought and knowledge gained from my own work with the Ch'ol community of El Bascán, in Chiapas, Mexico, I discuss horizontal, collaborative, and activist methodologies that serve to decolonize the academy. First, I describe the historical processes of colonization and Western ideas about culture that marginalized Indigenous peoples. Then, I describe how Indigenous community practices can support decolonization and child protagonism or conditions in which children take a primary role in their own development and that of their communities. I suggest a collaborative research approach based on the practices of Zapatista Indigenous communities and the reflective processes related to education and childhood that emerge from Zapatismo, the perspective, and praxis of the Zapatista movement. In the study described here, the main methodological tool is the collective creation of a community library. It is within this space of the library where I address the conditions, challenges, and possibilities of collaborative research, since such a site offers the opportunity to observe the Zapatista's childhood practices at a horizontal level and, with it, build collective knowledge of decolonization through children's participation. To conclude, I present the impact that the participation of children has on the community social life of the library and discuss its possibilities and contributions at the political level.

COLONIZATION, CULTURE, AND COMMUNITY IN MEXICO

The contemporary definition of community is addressed in critical anthropology as a practice rooted in the colonial era. Under this approach, communities were perceived as fixed and static entities as they were analyzed from the perspective of internal coherence. These ideas allowed for the word community to become synonymous with homogeneity and uniformity, contributing, in turn, to the creation of ideological narratives that were transmitted to the scientific field and served to legitimize practices founded on the colonial system. Such traditional perceptions emerged at the historical moment where the production of knowledge served to legitimize once again the global power structure, which not only dispossessed specific populations from their territories but also classified them under discriminatory categories with the purpose of eradicating their knowledges and practices.

The first evolutionary theorists were interested in explaining the cultural changes through a dual and comparative method that assumed the past of cultures based on the current ones and in turn looked to contemporary cultures to explain aspects such as survivals of the past. The scientific realm developed guidelines for the elaboration and classification of ideas by establishing the difference between existing cultures, such as Indigenous groups perceived as "primitive" and modern cultures, or White European groups (Kahn 1975). It was under this classification that it became the duty of what were deemed modern or "civilized" cultures to bring development and progress to those perceived as less developed. As Echeverría (2010) affirms, modernity emerged as an instrument of rescue or salvation and brought with it the enduring commitment that the "new" humanity has with what was perceived as the "archaic" humanity (239). This work of disciplinary systematization had its beginnings in the ideas generated in other areas of knowledge such the evolutionary theory of Charles Darwin (1859). Once published in the nineteenth century, Darwin's evolutionary ideas, along with advances in medical science and statistics, legalized human differences based on a racial hierarchy in which Western Europeans were shown to occupy the top level (Lamus 2012, 71). Echeverría (2010) points out the way in which English ethnological research carried out its first systematization, for example, in the work of Edward Tylor's (1871) *Primitive Culture*. In this work, Tylor, based on his travel experiences in Mexico, drew on evolutionary theory to discuss the relationship between "primitive" societies and "civilized" societies.

Such beliefs about the primacy of Western culture justified colonial domination in what is now called Mexico. During colonial times, two complementary forms of domination were established. The first was characterized by Spanish military power along with the imposition of a hegemonic political order articulated according to the economy of colonial exploitation. The second corresponded to the religious indoctrination and acculturation of the Indigenous peoples under the canons of Western thought (López-Austin 1999). Then, through such venues, coloniality became established, as well as the motivation to develop a capitalist system based on forms of cruelty like exploitation and domination. Indeed, it was in this exploitation and domination where the experiences, histories, resources, and cultural products were articulated in a single order, in this case, around the European hegemony. The way of seeing the social environment based on European hegemony gave way to the creation of a constant adoption of Western forms of knowledge production while the knowledge of colonized peoples was, at all costs, to be eradicated. Thus, there were those forms of Western knowledge which allowed the appropriation and dissemination of specific mechanisms suitable for the development of capitalism (Quijano 2000).

The arrival of the nineteenth century also brought with it the processes of the construction of national states followed by a diaspora of anthropologists in search for traces of "primitive cultures" since it was thought that these would soon be absorbed by the unstoppable force of modernity. In line with the production of knowledge and hegemonic political organization, prejudicial ideas and discriminatory practices were also emerging in Mexico. These discriminatory practices arose in the context of a racist ideology that not only perceived individual personality traits as inferior but also norms, values, or social and cultural ideologies of Indigenous groups that mainly functioned in opposition to the Western dominant group. Thus, under such racist ideologies, Indigenous groups in Mexico came to occupy the lowest place in the Mexican racial hierarchy (van Dijk 2003, 44).

During this historical process, the idea was widely established that ethnic groups, also considered original peoples in constant opposition to Western groups, were the only possessors of culture. Specifically, in Mexico, the category of culture was used to replace the classification of race without even taking into consideration the physical differences among the various groups of Indigenous peoples and/or problematizing their ethnic dimensions. Such a perspective has been recognized as part of the structural racism that has characterized Mexican society, especially discrimination against the different groups of native peoples (Echeverría 2010). In recent years, however, academic scholarship has been engaging in critical reflection on the ethics of research on, and relationships to, Indigenous knowledge and the rights of Indigenous communities.

INDIGENOUS COMMUNITY PRACTICES AS METHODS FOR DECOLONIZATION AND CHILD PROTAGONISM

It is within the space of current studies on Indigenous communities that debates based on Indigenous topics, like the ways in which these studies should be approached, have been opened. For example, among the elements to consider are: the analysis based on how the structure of Indigenous peoples is articulated in relation to the broader society; the process of memory recovery of various Indigenous peoples; the structures of organization that allow them continuity as peoples; the transformations in today's world in the processes of globalization; and, most importantly, the variety of their community contexts (Lisbona 2009). Drawing on these perspectives, I question the way in which different processes of socialization could be experienced, guided, and articulated by children in their specific community contexts. This questioning is carried out to explore how the participation of children is structured in their culture, and thereby, analyze mechanisms of reproduction, appropriation, and transformation. Above all, my inquiry seeks to observe the relationship taking place between child socialization in Indigenous communities and political participation in public spaces.

These relationships and the spaces in which they emerge vary widely within the contexts of *pueblos originarios*, a term used to the Indigenous communities of America, specifically descendants of pre-Columbian cultures. For example, Paradise (2011) states that in

> the educational practices of different indigenous groups in America, it is evident that non-school education, or those based on observation and participation in daily activities, does not constitute a simple spontaneous phenomenon, but rather systematic educational practices, tested over time, that have evolved and are highly effective.

(42) Describing the participation of young Yucatecan Mayan children in their world, Gaskins (2010) warns that "the act of simply describing the children's activity without taking into account the cultural principles of participation that define the context could lead us to serious misunderstandings in the interpretation of the meanings of the activity" (40). Similarly, Medina (2007) points out that specific identity practices arise as a product of the collective historicity of contexts. Based on this, it is crucial to recognize the different childhoods expressed in specific cultural contexts.

From these context-oriented perspectives, children are perceived as active subjects in the process of cultural learning. At the same time, such perspectives reject the premise that culture is an internalized concept of which children are passive recipients. The recognition of contexts takes into consideration the forms and conditions in which the participation of children occur by addressing the various learning methods within their cultural settings, which in the Indigenous community contexts occur in all spaces of community life. In relation to this topic, Corona and Pérez (2007) note:

> The cultural logic of indigenous peoples is based on the notion of belonging to the community that implies a more extended and open inclusion of children in political, social, or ceremonial activities. The notion of participation itself implies that the subject feels part of something larger; among indigenous peoples, it is allowed and even expected for new generations to cooperate, coordinate, and integrate in collective activities that have to do with the "common good", even if, for outsiders, these activities do not take place in environments considered "safe" for children. (12)

Studies that address childhood along with its forms of participation among communities and *pueblos originarios* have led to the creation of a notion of Indigenous childhood, not with the aim of homogenizing the enormous diversity of contexts in which Indigenous children live but with the purpose of questioning the hegemonic definition of identity (Szulc 2015b). In his study of *Mapuche* childhood in Argentina, Szulc (2015b) indicates that in these settings:

> children are assigned tasks and responsibilities and usually tend to move with a considerable margin of autonomy on a daily basis, without a rigid separation between the spheres of action of children and adults. This concept of childhood then contrasts with the hegemonic definition that considers children as separated from the "adult world" [. . .] and as an object in constant supervision, nonproductive, and not fully capable of understanding their actions. (242)

In this manner, the concept of childhood focuses on how to define, name, educate, or citizenize children. As Szulc (2015) points out, in this case, the school emerges as "a stage for interethnic relations, where it tends to trigger the conflict that historically characterizes the presence of the state in these contexts, and where the Mapuche population has historically 'failed'" (238). This challenge is revealed as one of the central problems between culture and power, mostly because when power is emphasized, culture usually becomes undermined. Such a challenge thus leads to an inequality of social and cultural diversity that is expressed, in turn, through a significant structural difference between "intercultural and intracultural" spheres (Dietz 2012, 102).

This scenario also takes place within the *pueblos originarios* of Mexico, as it has been reported in many studies based on the ideological process of *mestizaje* (a Latin American term for interracial and/or intercultural mixing) (Núñez 2005; Gómez-Lara 2011; Gutiérrez 2011; Mora 2011). Research has shown that schools in the country have played a crucial role as useful mechanisms to eliminate ethnic identity in the communities of *pueblos originarios*. Schools serve as spaces to spread and normalize discourses, since from an early age children are colonized through "subtle messages that speak about them" (Viruru and Cannela 2005, 242). Such messages based on discrimination against Indigeneity, culture, language, and rationality were constructed in colonial times, deepening further under the so-called *Sistema de Fincas*— or Farm System, in which transnational corporations began dominating the agricultural section in the twentieth century. These narratives are perpetuated today as part of the colonial legacy that seeks to keep Indigenous populations in extreme conditions of poverty and marginalization (Rico-Montoya 2018). Rico-Montoya (2018) states that it is precisely these subtle messages, or forms of thought, that have acted as mechanisms of colonization and have marked the subjectivity of grandparents, and in turn, their children, and grandchildren, perpetuating "forms of colonization in which 'Indigeneity' as well as culture, language, and rationality have been displaced, racialized, and dehumanized" (63). These subtle messages are also reflected in the daily relationships between teachers and students, thus establishing a relationship between what is taught and what is learned. Velasco and Baronnet (2016) suggest that it is particularly within the space of the school where education becomes promoted in all the spaces and moments in which it takes effect. In this way, the school represents the place where racist ideas can be taught and learned at the same time and where the ideas circulate in different areas of the school such as classrooms, places for breaks, as well as through teaching materials, blackboards, and electronic screens (4).

The panorama of *pueblos originarios* serves as a way to reflect on the participation of children in the public space, not with the intention of falling into homogenizing essentialisms of "Indigeneity" but with the objective of contributing to the analysis of children's diversity and their experiences and to show the plurality that exists within peoples participating in social movements and struggles. The process of political organization and struggle for dignity, unlike other Indigenous contexts linked more to the system of institutional parties, produces a *"muy otro"* [very other] (Guillén Vicente 2003) kind of context of subjectivity in Indigenous Zapatista childhood. This subjectivity arises through a social process of transformation where thousands of Indigenous communities, without even speaking the same language or having the same culture, come together in the political project of Zapatista autonomy (Rico-Montoya 2011, 318). Importantly, the Zapatista movement brings together communities from the different regions of Chiapas where many different languages are spoken. Although the Indigenous cultural contexts are diverse, it can be said that they often share a cultural matrix that allows them to construct from this diversity a project based on Zapatista autonomy. This project is not limited to a context of colonial domination, but the Zapatista struggle to dignify Indigenous identity (Núñez 2018).

The socialization among Indigenous communities offers a means of analysis of the political participation of children in public spaces. Among the public spaces of Indigenous community practices are ritual festivals, community assemblies, the resolution of intercommunity issues or struggles, as well as those that take place around work on the land (such as the cultivation of milpa, vegetables, and the harvesting of fruits, vegetables, and herbs), and at home (gardens and animal husbandry) (Martínez 2021; Corona-Caraveo and Pérez 2018; Rich 2018; Fernandez 2014; Nunez 2018). These contexts of community socialization also serve as places of educational practices; places where *pueblos originarios* have been able to reproduce their culture, what Gómez-Lara (2011) recognizes as Indigenous education. By strengthening the relationships of collaboration, reciprocity, and solidarity, the practices, although never free of conflict, have the benefit of being able to be carried out not only between close and distant families at the local level but also between families and communities at the regional and national level. This unity of practices, where the presence of children takes place at all levels of community life, works in contrast to urban spaces, particularly those of the school and the home in which normalized childhood is designated 'to be protected' almost exclusively.

The practices of socialization of Indigenous communities, although in constant movement, serve as forms of distribution for shared resources, and it is within this space *where pueblos originarios* find the opportunity to resist the structural violence that they have been facing through time. The structural violence implemented during the conquest against Indigenous peoples continue to be present in contemporary times, as violence continues to be enacted through land dispossessions, sacred space vandalization, and forced displacement, as well as the possibility of children's kidnappings. Referring to the effect that organized crime, specifically the narcotics cartels, has had on Indigenous communities, Hernández Castillo (2022) explains that "Now the 'enemy' is inside their houses, speaks their own language and have the knowledge to dismantle the structures of community power, making it ever more difficult to resist" (para. 5). To contest the violence against Indigenous peoples, the public practices among them represent the possibilities for the reconstruction of the social fabric, its reflection, and recreation, as well as their forms of recovery of *lo común*. As defined by Hardt and Negri (2009), "the common represents a radical alternative . . . to the forms of property and the corresponding models of political organisation and sovereignty that have shaped what we have come to know as modernity" (Frassinell 2011, 121–122). As forms of resistance, these community practices offer a space for a horizontal collaboration that can function as a valuable research tool in the interest of decolonization.

THE REFLECTIVE PROCESSES OF THE ZAPATISTA MOVEMENT

Zapatista's communities, which are governed by a diversity of languages and practices, are built under the political project of Indigenous autonomies. The political organization around autonomies offer a mirror to promote reflective methods that show the structure of power relations in indigenous contexts; contexts in which community practices still exist despite the intensity of the colonial legacies of power that continue to prevail. Paradise (2011) notes that the learning process of cultural practices, through daily activities, offers a solid base of daily resistance. These daily activities not only represent the ways in which Indigenous peoples' practices are reproduced but also the historical base that sustains their own cultural reproduction. As illustrated in figure 4.1, it is in these spaces of daily activity practices and learning processes that a reflective environment for the Zapatista social movement is produced (Dietz 2012).

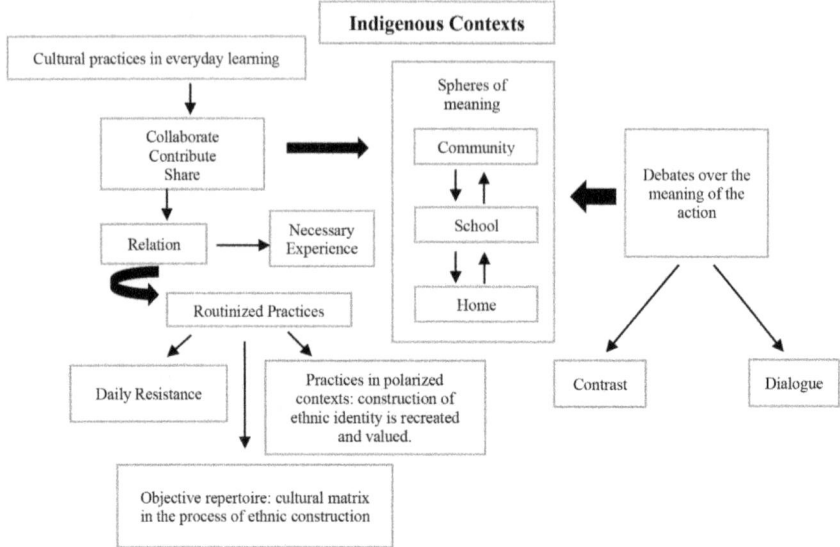

Figure 4.1 Indigenous childhood learning in everyday practices. Author's original figure based on Zemelman (1997) and Dietz (2012)

Figure 4.1 reflects the collective nature of the spaces in which children's learning occurs in Indigenous contexts, a condition that is not encouraged by the neoliberal paradigm that prompted the armed uprising in response to NAFTA. As Stahler-Sholk (2007) explains, "The neoliberal project implies atomization and loss of control to global market forces, posing dilemmas for movements seeking to reassert community identity and grassroots empowerment" (50). According to Hugo Zemelman (1997), the policies based on the value of the individual and private life serve as means to devalue collective projects in which quality of life is linked to the public aspect. In the case of *pueblos originarios*, these policies of individual value are promoted above all in schools, welfare programs, and other projects imposed or promoted by different sectors such as the government, civil institutions, and national or international organizations. These sectors, which are part of the national systematic structure, have been capable of imposing or promoting individualization projects due to the long Eurocentric tradition that still persists in the country; thus, it is this Eurocentric tradition which exalts the value of the human being in its individual aspect and minimizes its value in the collective sphere (Todorov 2008, 72). This type of relationship is established in the community organization as the foundation for Indigenous social movements, such as the Zapatista movement.

In fact, the Zapatista movement is based on Indigenous community practices that emphasize *lo autóctono* (the native) within a country marked by its colonial legacy and thereby promote identities that reveal a multicultural reality. The Zapatista movement demands critical thinking based on the permanent articulation of theory and praxis as expressed in its methodology *el caminar preguntando* (roughly translated as to walk questioning). Under this methodology, the movement generates processes of organization and self-reflection since they are based on the experience and behavior of actors or participants, and it is from here that the actors are able to recover the wisdom and power of the group. Saldoval (2016) mentions that *El caminar preguntando* is important because: "It has provided a critical form of thought built under the path of respect towards a historical-political horizon and under which autonomy has become the project. This requires us to problematize the relationship between reality, subject, and knowledge with the purpose of demonstrating that it is in the deployment of the subject's doing that produces reality and knowledge" (16). This methodological proposal is crucial because it reveals the relationship with the collective. Likewise, it expresses *el mandar obedeciendo* (ruling by obeying) a demand for popular sovereignty that, in addition to implying reflective collective activity, also offers a space for dialogue and agreement for the resolution of community issues. These practices, in turn, refer to the general method also known by Zapatistas as *el periscopio invertido* (the inverted periscope), which alludes to the understanding and transformation of power that requires one to "Let go of the position of 'observers' that insists on your own neutrality and distance" (Kilombo Intergalactico 2010, 9). While "this position can be adequate for the use of the academic microscope," the perspective of the inverted periscope turns our attention inward, allowing us to "break the mirror of power, in order to show that power does not belong to those who rule" (ibid, 10).

In this way, reflection and encounter imply thinking about and observing relationships in everyday life with one another to recognize what the 'norm' is. The ability to reflect allows people to think about oppression and with it, build alternatives to the imposition of "power" implanted from above. It also opens space for the exercise of politics, as this is one of the fundamental qualities of humanity, although humanity has been stripped from it (Arendt, 2008). In this sense, the proposal is based on the centrality of the cultural practices of Indigenous communities as resistance in order to create an organization based on work, face-to-face relationships, assembly, reciprocity, and solidarity in the construction of micropolitics, since one of the best characteristics of politics consists of making the conscious decision to transform with others the lived experiences of misery and violence. In this context, then it is not a question of a new rationality, but rather of a constructive ethical-political approach of concrete alternatives such as those expressed by Hardt and Antonio (2000) who refer to subjective forces as those that act in the historical context; a new scenario in which the different rational acts—a horizon of activities, resistance, wills, and desires—resist the hegemonic order while opening various lines of flight and alternative itineraries (43-44).

ZAPATISTA COMMUNITY PRACTICES AS CONTEXTS FOR CHILDHOOD

The Zapatista approach to organized resistance to state power enabled the creation of free forums as one of the central dimensions in the construction of autonomy and supported the development of new Indigenous subjectivities. These subjectivities have flourished as a result of Zapatismo since such a movement provides the space for the recreation of social relationships, as well as personal alternatives for collective change. In this creation of alternatives that emerge from the Zapatismo organization of rebellion, the "Escuelita (Little School) Zapatista" re-emerged with the purpose of reaching families that represent the base of Zapatista support among them. They sought mostly young people accompanied by family members who also shared the Zapatista way of resistance in their daily lives. It was through these organizations that an arts festival, CompArt por la Humanidad, was convened in 2016 as a space to share creative initiatives for social transformation. The events of the festival were significant because they were accessible to people from the local communities and because they conveyed the idea of art and science as essential tools for critical analysis and therefore of great benefit to humanity.

In this way, the Zapatista movement allows the opportunity for children to build an identity from childhood not as an individual strategic used to obtain support from the State but as a strategy where the Indigenous young person is capable of growing in spaces of freedom in which the logic of neoliberal politics with capitalist consumption models has no place. In an EZLN communiqué recorded on the organizational website Enlace Zapatista (2015), young Zapatista supporter Lizbeth, describes her experience of growing up in the context of such a space of freedom:

> We as Zapatista youth today, we are no longer familiar with the overseer, with the landowner, with the hacienda boss, much less with El Amate [a prison in Chiapas]; we do not know what it is to go to the official municipal presidents so that they can resolve our problems. Thanks to the EZLN organization, we now have our own authorities in each community, we have our municipal authorities, and our Juntas de Buen Gobierno [Good Government Councils], and they resolve whatever type of problem that might arise for a compañera [female comrade] or compañero [male comrade], for both Zapatistas and non-Zapatistas. We now have freedom and rights as women, to have opinions, discuss, and analyze, which is not how it was before.

El Amate, which Lizbeth refers to, is the largest prison in Chiapas, which is formally called the State Center for Social Rehabilitation (CERESO). Located in the municipality of Cintalapa, it is recognized for the large number of Indigenous prisoners unjustly detained there simply for being Indigenous and/or for belonging to the Zapatista movement.

In addition to revealing ideas about power structure, Zapatista women also express their own genealogy of struggle in which, more than before, they demonstrate their political thought based on Zapatismo. It is precisely in this political thought that the emphasis is placed on the creation of alternatives for children with the purpose of promoting an Indigenous community context in which they socialize, think, and behave autonomously. This is also expressed by Selena (Enlace Zapatista 2015) another Zapatista youth supporter, who explains the ways in which the Zapatista youth is capable of resisting low-intensity warfare in which the government and capitalism incite young Indigenous people to leave their villages in order to pursue the illusory model of those perceived as affluent people:

> We Zapatistas are poor, but rich in thinking. Why? Because even though we have shoes and clothes and cellphones, we don't change our thinking or our way of life, because to us as Zapatista youth it doesn't matter to us how we are dressed, or what kinds of things we have. What's important to us is that the work we do is for the good of the community. That is what we Zapatistas want, and it's what we want for the whole world: that there not be rulers, that there not be exploiters, that we as Indigenous people are not exploited.

As Selena suggests, in a program designed collectively, decisions are shared so that everyone benefits. This plan also works in contrast to the one offered by neoliberal capitalism, which promotes limiting individual opportunities for people in a highly unequal context. Hence, the collective project represents the option for multiple alternatives in political decision-making in order to produce subjectivities for resistance and, with it, contest violent forms of capitalism. Among the forms of capitalism in Mexico, there are particularly those that incite poor communities and neighborhoods to participate in activities such as forced migration, extreme exploitation in all its forms, and/or integration into drug trafficking.

The Indigenous community practices that the Zapatista have adopted have made this group distinguished or *"muy otro"* and have become a mirror example of organization for other movements. Thus, their strategies have served to open new venues, among them those focused on decolonizing the academy with the purpose of building "another academy" since the priorities for the Zapatista movement includes breaking traditional forms of politics, opening spaces to establish creative distances between them and the State, maintaining a constant position of innovative ideas directly related to the territory, and establishing processes of political organization (Zagato and Arcos 2017, 77).

Mora (2018) suggests that in the politics of Zapatista autonomy, the everyday acts of *hablar caminando* [walking the talk or following through on spoken commitments] reflect the rejection of the state and the implementation of a multidimensional strategy based on a commitment within the autonomous project of insurrection. These everyday politics reveal other community practices, such as *la asamblea*, the assembly, or the autonomous government in which the construction of the political project is recreated and reinvented. In most of the Indigenous communities of Chiapas, *la asamblea* represents a place where people's practices and relationships are measured in relation to aspects of strengths, forms, and participation. It is here, in *la asamblea*, where people address issues of concern such as granting and taking away communal rights, informing the community about programs and public projects, and dealing with issues that affect the community, especially those involving the usufruct (right to use) of common lands; creating organizations among the communities of the region. Additionally, *la asamblea* is focused on opening spaces for conversations based on semi-independent self-management, as well as offering sites with potential for collective action outside governmental institutions. The way in which the assembly is integrated establishes, in itself, a differentiation within the community, since only those with communal rights are able to participate in it. It is important to mention that along with the participation of community members, their relatives may also participate and women can play a very important role. In this way, *la asamblea* represents a space of possibilities for horizontal and democratic relations, although it is also recognized that in this place individual interests may arise above group interests.

Throughout history, *la asamblea* has faced its own cultural and political changes. For example, Diaz (2004) has recorded the changes that have taken place in *la asamblea* general of Oaxaca. According to Diaz, in the past when the families attended *la asamblea*, there was no silence, because at all times people discussed intrafamilial issues. Thus, in this space, while the authorities had the opportunity to express their views, at the same time, the public had the opportunity to express their opinions in order to reach final agreements. Such agreements were then announced by older individuals, particularly by those accredited under privileged social ranks. However, in recent times, *la asamblea* has taken more institutional forms, for example, through acts such as having to raise one's hand to speak, which has caused change among people's interactions.

For the Zapatista movement, *la asamblea* provides the space for intense processes of political formation and organization. According to Rico-Montoya (2018):

> The Zapatista assembly is a political-social space where agreements are made. The Zapatista organization has tried to strengthen the general assembly by including the principle of "ruling by obeying" as an essential aspect for the construction of social, political, and cultural autonomy. Contrary to the sociocultural and organizational practices of the ejidal assembly, in which only the members (mostly men) have a voice and vote [. . .], in the Zapatista assembly adult women and men vote to make decisions; from the age of 12 boys and girls begin to have a voice.

The structure in which the Zapatista movement is organized responds to a diversity of needs, the resolution of problems presented, and the collective work, whether local or regional, and in which all the community members, including children, are involved. These processes are transforming community contexts where ethnic identity is reinvented and separated from the "bad customs" that have been integrated as part of the State, including ideologies like neoliberalism and capitalism (Núñez 2018). Thus, the Zapatistas dignity has emerged from the structure of resistance and the construction of autonomy.

METHODOLOGICAL STRATEGIES FOR COLLABORATION AND THE CONSTRUCTION OF CHILDHOOD

The reflective processes presented here emerge from research conducted under principles of collaboration such as horizontality, reciprocity, the integration of participants' interests, and the cultural practices that promote the creation of relationships and their organization. Horizontality was established as a result of my political participation at different times in the Zapatista movement, as well as a long process of learning Indigenous community practices throughout my academic career (Corona-Berkin 2012; Denzin 2005; Núñez, Ayora, and Torres 2021; Núñez 2005, 2018). Such strategies have permitted the development of critical reflections on the ways that academic knowledge is constructed. These reflections act as a trench from which the learning of political activism is put into play to build "another academy"—one that integrates local knowledge and praxis in the production of collective knowledge (Olivera 2015). The Zapatista way is taken, in this case, as the process of collecting and systematizing information in order to foster analysis based on organizational political actions (Mora 2015) that support decolonization.

As part of my research, the project based on the community library emerged as a result of reciprocal relationships that were consolidated when I was conducting research for my doctoral thesis in the Ch'ol community of El Bascán. The beginning of reciprocity, through the trajectory of almost twenty years, has woven horizontal relationships that do not hide power relations in the production of knowledge but rather make them explicit by informing and rewarding the investigative process, as well as integrating the interests of those of us who participate in the library (Núñez 2018). The community library is inspired and proposed from my own concerns and personal experiences with books and the project of the community library in the Zapatista autonomous schools, within my participation in the Civil Dialogue Committees that made up the Zapatista National Liberation Front in 1998, and which is consolidated with the close relationship with the literacy methodology developed the organization Bunko Papalote, which seeks to promote dialogue and self-reflection with children through engagement with literature (Núñez, Ayora, and Torres 2021). The community library is installed in the home of one of the families, where Maribel, a mother and aunt to the children who participate in the library, along with other adults, organizes activities and makes books available for the community. For the books, I created a system of collecting books from a sense of sharing them, as life experiences, and not from "donating to the poorest what no longer serves you." Likewise, the purchase of materials arose with my own resources and with the purpose of carrying out artistic and recreational expression activities. In this way, the community library has been built with resources from all the participants. In addition to this, the activities have also been carried out with other colleagues; practices from which the creation of books have emerged, among them, the Libro Cartonero (a hand-bound book with a cardboard book), that brought together children's drawings about home, school, community, and nature (Corona, Núñez, and Rico Montoya 2018). Below I present one of the many ethnographic scenarios that emerged during the process of my research.

The Community Library as a Reflective Practice

One day, my fellow researcher who helped the children create the Libro Cartonero attended the library to talk about the book and to share other examples with them. During the presentation, the children became disinterested in the Libro Cartonero and shifted their interest to the new books brought by the researchers, which they immediately picked up to examine. Given the lack

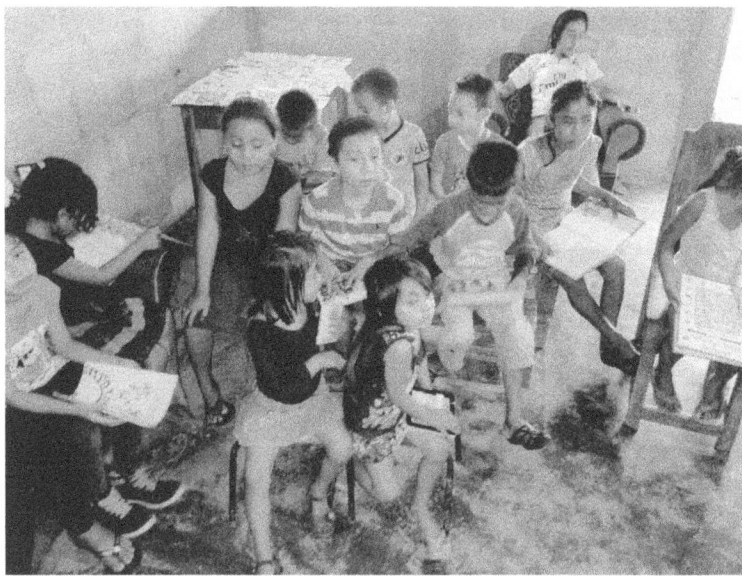

Figure 4.2 Installation of the community library, "El Bascán". Photo taken by Kathia Núñez (author) (El Bascán, September 14, 2015)

of attention of the children toward the presenter, a space for free reading was opened. Maribel, a little embarrassed, asked us if it bothered us that the children did not pay attention to the presenter. We answered that it did not bother us and explained our perspective that when activities are carried out with kids, attention should be paid to their interests in order to redirect activities toward whatever is getting their attention and providing enjoyment. In that moment, we saw an opportunity to reflect on the school and its rigid and static practices, such as punishing and repressing children for not paying attention, which legitimizes the idea of children as passive recipients of adult socialization. In any activity that we carried out, we included a celebration based on sharing, reflecting celebratory practices through which Indigenous communities strengthen their interpersonal relationships in their collective setting. While this context serves to foster horizontal relationships and build trust among the participants, it also offers the opportunity for self-reflection where the inevitable and entrenched power relations can be revealed.

The continuity of the library was supported by resources from a program called Teacher Professional Development (PRODEP 2019–2021), which promotes a framework of critical reflection toward Indigenous community practices and their potential to promote child leadership and collaborative methodologies (Núñez and Plascencia 2020). The program's main objective is to produce a space of horizontal reflection to value, re-signify, and recreate community practices that encourage reflection, such as critical playful reading with children, as well as producing personal materials through drawing and painting (Ayora 2012). At this stage of the project, Maribel and her family, as local collaborators and main managers of the library, achieved their commitment, and the children developed a sense of ownership of the library space as a place that was open to those who needed to use it.

The Workshop Assembly as a Collaborative Methodology

At this stage of the project, the workshop-assembly became established as a central methodology and a living space in which issues related to the library were reported, experiences shared, and decisions made. Initially, it was planned that this workshop-assembly would be held in the community. However, at the most intense stage of fieldwork and given the new conditions

Figure 4.3 Renovation of the community library "El Bascán". Photo taken by Kathia Núñez (author) (El Bascán, July 20, 2020).

that were generated by the COVID-19 pandemic, only parts of the first and the second meetings were held in the community with the participation of the children, the local collaborator, myself, and two university student assistants. The first workshop-assembly was held in two parts. The first part took place at my university, where Mari's experience in the library since its inception was shared and where agreements to continue with the library became ratified. The second part of the meeting took place in the community where the girls, boys, and their families were informed about the continuity of the project. Then we had a *posada* [Christmas party] where piñatas made by the children were broken and sweets, bread, and coffee were shared. The second workshop-assembly followed the same procedure since it was carried out in both the university and the community, but with the difference that in this meeting the objective was based on more explicitly integrating the interests of girls and boys in the space of the library and producing sites for more active participation (Núñez, Ruiz, and Martínez 2020).

Finally, the third workshop was held in the city of San Cristóbal, where Mari, her partner and her daughter, Nish Tye'el, who had become the most responsible participant in the library, were able to participate. There, people shared their experience of the library in the context of the pandemic and discussed strategies for continuing with the project in spite of the pandemic. In this workshop, Mari reflected on the broader meaning of the library and the

Figure 4.4 Second workshop assembly in El Bascán. Photo taken by Kathia Núñez (El Bascán, February 1st, 2020).

Figure 4.5 Second workshop assembly in El Bascán. Photo taken by Kathia Núñez (El Bascán, February 1st, 2020).

relevance of it for the participants. She acknowledged the importance of the children's participation in community affairs, which she had come to realize during her experience with the library. These reflections on the significance of children's participation represent the process that gave meaning and life to the library; a process in which we all learned and shared experiences, talked about our own oppressions and privileges, and explored ways in which changes or transformations could occur. The community library, which we decided to name *Lak ty'añ muk'bä tyi alas* [which means "our word that plays" in the Ch'ol language], is just a seed that has been planted, and we hope it flourishes in the same way in which the Zapatista struggle for human dignity and autonomies has flourished and reclaimed Indigenous community practices.

EXPLORING NEW PATHS TOWARD CHILDREN'S PARTICIPATION

The central methodological axis of the *Lak ty'añ muk'bä tyi alas*, also called the community library of El Báscan, is the fabric of horizontal relationships and collaboration that do not conceal power relations, but instead tries to observe and reflect possibilities for transformation. The collective creation of a community library described here allowed for the observation of relationships and their structures at two levels. First, we can see the liminal space between the community and the school, two spaces where childhood is experienced in the Ch'ol community. Second, we can see the liminal space among children, families, and the library as sites of possibilities for achievements and challenges in the collaboration with, and imagination of, children. Indeed, the library, as a communal site, is perceived as an open space for reflection and political action. However, it should be noted that the strong presence and participation of children in these Indigenous community contexts does not necessarily produce child protagonism. Rather, such a role is already built into the Zapatista struggle by generating a political awareness in childhood and by producing a theoretical basis for autonomous thought and practice.

Here, the story of the community library and the children's participation in its creation offers insight into the power relations within the relationships that have been built between the community and the school and which shape conceptions of what childhood is and should be. In particular, the school is perceived as a space in dispute for the socialization of childhood since it devalues and displaces Indigenous community practices for school practices that limit children's agency and participation. Furthermore, schools reproduce the racist structure in our Mexico and promotes the neocolonial ideology of our times (Núñez, Ayora, and Torres 2021). Likewise, the intention is to observe the relationships that are taking place between those of us who are coming from the academy and engage in these types of projects proposed in conjunction with children and families that participate. These projects have emerged as a result of continuous participation in different moments and spaces of the Zapatista struggle, as well as a desire to redefine what is learned in the academy.

As illustrated in this chapter, the act of reclaiming Indigenous cultural practices such as community assemblies represent an inspiration for reflective methodological practices that create possibilities for transformation as power is produced and reproduced in the creation and recreation of collective knowledge. Although the seed has been sown with *Lak ty'añ muk'bä tyi alas*, there is still a long way to go according to the experiences of liberation that have been highlighted by the Zapatista movement and have served as possibilities for decolonization. The Zapatista movement has not only contributed to methods of organizational knowledge but has also allowed the recovery of the human condition in relation to politics. Above all, while the Zapatista movement has emphasized the creation and recreation of life in the collective, it has de-emphasized capitalism and, with it, the system of representation of the political parties of the country. Therefore, the Zapatista movement and the community practices it has embraced offer a unique site for considering the diversity of contexts in which childhood is experienced and the possibilities for children's participation in community affairs, including political life.

NOTE

1. This chapter was initially translated from Spanish by Veronica Vicencio Diaz, Department of Sociology and Anthropology, Carleton University.

REFERENCES

Agamben, Giorgio. 2011. "¿Qué es un dispositivo?" *Sociológica*, 26(73): 249–264. http://www.sociologicamexico.azc.uam.mx/index.php/Sociologica/article/view/112

Alvarado, Pizana. 2018. "Cherán: la recreación del habitar en común." *Revista Tlamelaua*, 12(45): 131–150. http://www.scielo.org.mx/scielo.php?script=sci_arttext&pid=S1870-69162018000200130

Arendt, Hannah. 2008. *La promesa de la política*. Barcelona: Paidós.

Ayora Vázquez, Gialuanna Enkra. 2012. *Educación intercultural y decolonialidad: de la promoción de la lectura a un enfoque de literacidad para la niñez indígena purhépecha.*). Master's Thesis, University of Veracruz. https://cdigital.uv.mx/handle/123456789/42053?locale-attribute=de

Corona-Berkin, Sarah. 2012. "Notas para construir metodologías horizontales." In Sarah Corona-Berkin and Olaf Kaltmeir (eds.), *Diálogo: Metodologías en Ciencias Sociales y Culturales*, 85–110. Barcelona, Spain: Gedisa.

Corona-Caraveo, Yolanda, Linares Ponton, and Maria Eugenia. 2007. *Participación Infantil y Juvenil en América Latina*. UAM – Childwatch International Research Network: University of Valencia.

Corona-Caraveo, Yolanda, Kathia Núñez Patiño, and Angélica Rico Montoya. 2018. "The right of the Ch´ol children of Chiapas to live in peace in their territories." *Canadian Journal of Children's Rights*, 5(19): 30–55. https://doi.org/10.22215/cjcr.v5i1.1244

Corona-Caraveo, Yolanda and Carlos Pérez. 2018. *La textura infantil de la cultura. La participación de los niños en la vida ceremonial de Tepoztlán*. Mexico: Arkan Ediciones.

Darwin, Charles and Leonard Kebler. 1859. *On the Origin of Species by Means of Natural Selection, or, the Preservation of Favoured Races in the Struggle for Life*. London: J. Murray. https://www.loc.gov/item/06017473/

De León Pasquel, Lourdes. 2010. *Socialización, lenguajes y culturas infantiles: estudios interdisciplinarios*. Mexico City: Centro de Investigaciones y Estudios Superiores en Antropologia Social (CIESAS).

Denzin, N. K. 2005. "Emancipatory discourses and the ethics and politics of interpretation." In Norman K. Denzin and Yvona S. Lincoln (eds.), *The Sage Handbook of Qualitative Research*, 933–958. New York: Sage.

Díaz, Floberto. 2004. "Comunidad y comunalidad." In *Antología sobre culturas populares: lecturas del seminario Diálogos en la Acción*, 365–373. Mexico City: Dirección General de Culturas Populares e Indígenas (DGCPI).
Dietz, Gunther. 2012. *Multiculturalism, Interculturality and Diversity in Education an Anthropological Approach.* New York: Waxmann.
Echeverría, Bolivar. 2010. *Definición de la cultura.* Monterrey: Fondo de Cultura Económica.
Enlace Zapatista. 2015a. "Words of Compañera Lizbeth, Zapatista Base of Support." https://enlacezapatista.ezln.org.mx/2015/05/25/words-of-companera-lizbeth -zapatista-base-of-support/
Enlace Zapatista. 2015b. "Words of Compañera Selena, Listener." https://enlacezapatista.ezln.org.mx/2015/05/25/words-of-companera-selena-listener/
Fernández, Paulina. 2014. *Justicia Autónoma Zapatista. Zona Selva Tzeltal.* Chiapas: Ediciones Autónomas.
Frassinell, Pier Paolo. "Biopolitical Production, the Common, and a Happy Ending: on Michael Hardt and Antonio Negri's *Commonwealth*." *Critical Arts*, 25(2): 119–131. https://doi.org/10.1080/02560046.2011.569056
Gaskins, S. 2010. "La vida cotidiana de los niños en un pueblo maya: un estudio monográfico de los roles y actividades construidos culturalmente." In Lourdes De León Pasquel (ed.), *Socialización, lenguajes y culturas infantiles: estudios interdisciplinarios*, 37–76. Mexico City: Centro de Investigaciones y Estudios Superiores en Antropologia Social (CIESAS).
Gómez Lara, Horacio. 2011. *Indígenas, mexicanos y rebeldes. Procesos educativos y resignificación de identidades en los Altos de Chiapas.* Mexico City: Juan Pablos Editor.
Grimson, A. 2010. "Culture and Identity: Two Different Notions." *Social Identities*, 16(1): 63–79.
Godelmann, Iker. 2014. "The Zapatista Movement: The Fight for Indigenous Rights in Mexico." Australian Institute of International Affairs. https://www.internation alaffairs.org.au/news-item/the-zapatista-movement-the-fight-for-indigenous-rights -in-mexico/
Grosfoguel, R. 2018. "¿Negros marxistas o marxismos negros?: una mirada descolonial." *Tabula Rasa*, 28: 11–22. https://doi.org/10.25058/20112742.n28.1
Gutiérrez Narváez, Raúl. 2011. "Dos proyectos de sociedad en Los Alto de Chiapas. Escuelas secundarias oficial y autónoma entre los tsotsiles de San Andrés." In Mariana Mora Bayo Bruno Baronnet and Richard Stahler–Sholk (eds.), *Luchas "muy otras". Zapatismo y Autonomía en las Comunidades Indígenas de Chiapas*, 237–266. México: Universidad Autónoma Metropolitana, Centro de Investigaciones y Estudios Superiores en Antropología Social, Universidad Autónoma de Chiapa.
Hardt, Michael and Antonio Negri. 2000. *Empire.* Cambridge: Harvard University Press.
Hardt, Michael and Antonio Negri. 2009. *Commonwealth.* Cambridge: Harvard University Press.

Hernández Castillo, R. Aida. 2022. "Narco violencias y juventud indígena." La Jornada. https://www.jornada.com.mx/notas/2022/06/19/politica/narco-violencias-y-juventud-indigena/

Instituto Nacional de Estadística y Geografía. 2020. "Hablantes de lengua indígena." https://en.www.inegi.org.mx/

International Service for Peace (SIPAZ). 2002. "Chiapas Peace Process, War Process." http://www.sipaz.org/en/chiapas/peace-process-war-process/334-1994.html

Kahn, J. 1975. *El concepto de cultura: textos fundamentales.* Barcelona: Anagrama.

Klein, Hilary. 2019. "A Spark of Hope: The Ongoing Lessons of the Zapatista Revolution 25 Years On." The North American Congress on Latin America. https://nacla.org/news/2022/12/21/spark-hope-ongoing-lessons-zapatista-revolution-25-years

Kilombo Intergaláctico. 2010. *Sin referente: una entrevista con Subcomandante Insurgente Marcos.* PaperBoat Press.

Lamus Canavate, Doris. 2012. "Raza, etnia, sexo y género: el significado de la diferencia y el poder." *Reflexión Política*, 14(27): 68–84.

Liebel, Manfred y Iven Saadi. 2012. "La participación infantil ante el desafío de la diversidad cultural." *Desacatos*, 39: 123–140. https://doi.org/10.29340/39.244

Lisbona, Miguel. 2009. *La comunidad a debate. Reflexiones sobre el concepto de comunidad en el México contemporáneo.* Michoacán: El Colegio de Michoacán.

Maldonado Alvarado, Benjamín. 2015. "Perspectivas de la comunalidad en los pueblos indígenas de Oaxaca." *Bajo el Volcán*, 15(23): 151–169. https://www.redalyc.org/pdf/286/28643473009.pdf

Martínez Luna, Jaime. 2015. "Conocimiento y comunalidad." *Bajo el Volcán*, 15(23): 99–112. https://www.redalyc.org/pdf/286/28643473006.pdf

Martínez Ramos, María Fernanda. 2018. "Cherán K'eri. 5 años de autonomía. Por la seguridad, justicia y reconstitución de nuestro territorio." *Ra Ximhai*, 14(2): 233–236. https://www.redalyc.org/journal/461/46158063015/html/

Martínez Ts'ujul, Rocío. 2021. *Fiesta, memoria y autonomía. El K'in Tajimol (Los juegos del sol).* San Cristóbal de Las Casas: El Rebozo Palapa Editorial/Ediciones Bats'il k'op.

Melgarejo, Patricia Medina. 2007. "Configuración de fronteras, interculturalidad y políticas de identidad." *Tramas*, 28: 171–194.

Mora, Mariana. 2018a. *Política kuxlejal: Autonomía indígena, el Estado Racial e investigación descolonizante en comunidades zapatistas.* Mexico City: Centro de Investigaciones y Estudios Superiores en Antropología Social (CIESAS).

Mora, Mariana. 2015. "Reflexiones desde el zapatismo: la producción de conocimientos en una investigación dialógica de compromiso social." In Xochitl Leyva, Jorge Alonso, R. Aída Hernández, Arturo Escobar, Axel Köhler, Aura Cumes, Rafael Sandoval, et al. (eds.), *Prácticas Otras de Conocimiento(s): Entre Crisis, Entre Guerras. Tomo II*, 247–272. Buenos Aires: CLACSO, 2018. https://doi.org/10.2307/j.ctvn96g1f

Mora, Mariana. 2011. "La autonomía indígena y la mujer zapatista frente al legado del mestizaje." In Aparicio Wilhelmi, Marco (ed.), *Contracorrientes. Apuntes Sobre Igualdad, Diferencia y Derechos*, 39–56. Girona: Documenta Universitaria.

Núñez, Kathia. 2018. *Construcción identitaria de niños y niñas en dos comunidades indígenas, desde sus discursos y prácticas de tres ámbitos de sentido: la comunidad, la casa y la escuela.* Doctoral Thesis. Institute of Educational Research, University of Veracruz. http://cdigital.uv.mx/handle/1944/49682.

Núñez, Kathia. 2005. *Socialización infantil en dos comunidades ch'oles. Rupturas y continuidades: escuela oficial y escuela autónoma.* Master's Thesis in Anthropology. Mexico City, Mexico: Centro de Investigaciones y Estudios Superiores en Antropologia Social (CIESAS). http://ciesas.repositorioinstitucional.mx/jspui/handle/1015/789.

Núñez, Kathia, Gialuanna Ayora, and Eliud Torres. 2021. "Bibliotecas comunitarias: dialogismo y colaboración con las niñeces para descolonizarnos." *Linhas Críticas*, 27: 1–19. https://doi.org/10.26512/lc27202135237

Núñez, Kathia, Shally Ruíz, and Ana Cristal Martínez. 2020. "Creando una biblioteca comunitaria con y desde las niñas y niños: Promoviendo el protagonismo infantil. *Sociogénesis.*" *Revista Digital de Divulgación Científica*, 3(3): 26–37. https://www.uv.mx/sociogenesis/divulgacion-conocimiento-sociologico/creando-una-biblioteca-comunitaria-con-y-desde-las-ninas-y-los-ninos/

Núñez, Kathia y M. Plascencia. 2020. "Bibliotecas comunitarias y escolares: diálogos interculturales y protagonismo infantil." In Martín Plascencia González, Maria Lidia Bueno Fernandes, Mathusalam Pantevis Suárez, and Facundo Corvalán (eds.), *Infancias: contextos de acción, interacción y participación*, 167–202. Chiapas: Universidad Autónoma de Chiapas.

Olivera Bustamante, Mercedes. 2015. "Investigar colectivamente para conocer y transformar, en Prácticas otras de conocimiento(s)." *Entre crisis, entre guerras*, Xochitl Leyva Solano et al., Tomo III. Cooperativa Editorial Retos. San Cristóbal Las Casas, Chiapas: 105–124.

Paradise, Ruth. 2011. "¿Cómo educan los indígenas a sus hijos? El cómo y el porqué del aprendizaje en la familia y la comunidad." In Susana Frisancho, María Teresa Moreno, Patricia Ruiz Bravo, and Virginia Zavala (eds.), *Aprendizaje, cultura y desarrollo. Una aproximación interdisciplinaria*, 41–58. Lima: Fondo Editorial Pontificia Universidad Católica del Perú.

Quijano, Anibel. 2000. "Colonialidad del poder, eurocentrismo y América Latina." In Edgardo Lander (ed.), *La colonialidad del saber: eurocentrismo y ciencias sociales. Perspectivas Latinoaméricas*, 201–246. Buenos Aires: CLACSO.

Rico Montoya, Angélica. 2018. "Infancias y maternidades Zapatistas: subjetividades políticas emergentes en las prácticas educativas y de resistencia-rebelde frente a la contrainsurgencia en Chiapas." Doctoral Thesis. Institute of Educational Research, University of Veracruz. https://www.uv.mx/pdie/files/2018/03/Tesis_Norma-Angelica-Rico-Montoya.pdf

Rico Montoya, Angélica. 2018. "De la Colonización al proyecto de emancipación y educación zapatista. Relatos de infancia: Racismo, violencia y memoria colectiva." *Ra Ximhai*, 14(2): 63–84.

Rico Montoya, Angélica. 2011. "Niños y niñas en territorio zapatista. Resistencia, autonomía y guerra de baja intensidad." In Bruno Baronnet, Mariana Mora Bayo, and Richard Stahler–Sholk (eds.), *Luchas "muy otras." Zapatismo y autonomía en las comunidades indígenas de Chiapas*, 267–294. México: Universidad Autónoma Metropolitana, Centro de Investigaciones y Estudios Superiores en Antropología Social, Universidad Autónoma de Chiapa.

Szulc, Andrea. 2015. *La niñez mapuche. Sentidos de pertenencia en tensión*. Buenos Aires: Biblos.

Szulc, Andrea. 2015b. "Concepciones de niñez e identidad en las experiencias escolares de niños mapuche del Neuquén." *Anthropologica*, 33(35): 235–253. http://www.scielo.org.pe/scielo.php?script=sci_arttext&pid=S0254-92122015000200010

Todorov, Tzvetan. 2008. *La vida en común. Ensayo de antropología general*. Madrid: Taurus.

Tylor, Edward B. 1871. *Primitive Culture: Researches into the Development of Mythology, Philosophy, Religion, Art, and Custom*. London: John Murray.

Velasco Cruz, Saúl and Bruno Baronnet. 2016. Racismo y escuela en México: Reconociendo la tragedia para intentar la salida. *En Diálogos sobre educación*, 7(13): 1–17. https://doi.org/10.32870/dse.v0i13.241

Viruru, Radhika and Gaile Cannella. 2005. "La etnografía poscolonial, los niños y la voz." In Susan Grieshhaber y Gaile Cannella (eds.), *Las Identidades en la Educación Temprana. Diversidad y Posibilidades*, 239–259. Monterrey: Fondo de Cultura Económica.

Zagato, Alessandro and Natalia Arcos. 2017. "El Festival 'Comparte por la Humanidad. Estéticas y poíticas de la rebeldía en el movimiento Zapatista." *Revista Digital de la Escuela de Historia*, 9(21): 74–101. https://revistapaginas.unr.edu.ar/index.php/RevPaginas/article/view/273/html

Zemelman Marino, Hugo. 1997. "Sujetos y subjetividad en la construcción metodológica." In Emma León and Hugo Zemelman (eds.), *Subjetividad: umbrales del pensamiento social*, 21–35. Mexico City: Anthropos Editorial.

Chapter 5

Adultism in Uganda's Child Protection Efforts

A Case of Violence against Children

Doris Kakuru

INTRODUCTION

In the 1980s, I attended a boarding school considered among the best girls' high schools in Western Uganda. The school conducted routine pregnancy checks to identify and expel any girl found pregnant, which is still considered inappropriate to date. One Monday morning, we received a memo about how the school management board had decided to conduct a comprehensive medical examination on all learners. The girls who were the first to undergo the examination told everyone what to expect and warned us that refusing was not an option. When a person's turn came, they entered the school nurse's office, where a male physician was waiting. Upon entry, they were to follow specific instructions, which enabled him to perform a medical examination that included inserting his fingers inside them to determine whether they were still virgins. The parents of the girls who were presumed not to be virgins received letters informing them about it. The school setting was so intimidating that none of the 700 girls enrolled had the power to refuse the distressing examination. A few older girls attempted to refuse, but they were threatened with expulsion from one of the best schools in the region.

Such mandatory and involuntary medical examinations can be understood as an extreme and violent form of adolescent "sexual surveillance" (Davies 2014; McClelland & Fine 2013). The need to surveil and manage girls' sexual behavior is perpetuated by adults' construction of children as innocent and immature in child policy-making. While one would expect such a practice to be obsolete, virginity testing is still practiced in Uganda (Leclerc-Madlala 2003), South Africa, Swaziland, and other countries (Leclerc-Madlala 2001;

Olson & García-Moreno 2017). As expressed in the vignette above, virginity testing is not only oppressive for children but also violates their rights, as alluded to by Gibson (2022) and enshrined in various Ugandan laws (Republic of Uganda 1995, 2007). Apart from virginity testing, Uganda's child policy sustains the pervasion of other forms of coerced body intrusion under the guise of "care" and "protection" of young people because they are framed as innocent and vulnerable. For example, the current guidelines for the prevention and management of teenage pregnancy in school settings in Uganda require that "All girls should be examined for pregnancy periodically, at least once termly . . . " (MOES 2020, 18). In addition, pregnant girls are subjected to exclusionary re-entry conditions, which require them to drop out when they are three months pregnant and take a mandatory six-month maternity leave. This context of "decriminalized" violence against children (VAC) due to adult-age power can be understand as an example of "protective practices that seek to preserve the idealized state of innocence" (Garlen 2019, 57) describes as childhood innocence and is the subject of this chapter.

According to the World Health Organization (WHO), violence is "the intentional use of physical force or power, a threat or actual perpetration against oneself, another person, or against a group or community that either results in, or has a high likelihood of resulting in injury, death or psychological harm" (WHO 2014, 3). Every day, millions of children experience violence in the form of physical violence, sexual violence, child labor, child marriage, child trafficking, etc. After decades of dedicated efforts, VAC remains a global phenomenon affecting children in diverse contexts. Over half of the world's children below seventeen years experience violence annually (WHO 2020). According to a recent report by the African Partnership to End Violence against Children (APEVAC) and the African Child Policy Forum, 168 million of the world's children are engaged in child labor (APEVAC & ACPF 2021). The consequences of COVID-19 have disproportionately exacerbated the magnitude of violence in childhood, particularly in the global South where schools were closed for extended periods.

The prevalence of VAC is a particular concern in Africa, which is home to over 20% of the world's children (United Nations, Department of Economic and Social Affairs, Population Division [UNDESA] 2020). It is estimated that 50% of African children have experienced or witnessed some form of physical, sexual, or emotional violence (APEVAC & ACPF 2021). In some African countries, between 22 and 38% of girls below seventeen have experienced child sexual abuse, of which 90% was committed within the family (African Child Policy Forum [ACPF] 2019). In Uganda, it is estimated that 35% of girls aged 18–24 experienced sexual violence before the age of eighteen, and the figure for girls living on the street is 74% (APEVAC & ACPF 2021). Even worse, 67% of female and 65% of male Ugandan children have witnessed violence at home (WHO 2020). Another Ugandan study by Wandera, Clarke, Knight, Allen et al. (2017) found that 29% and 34% of the school children who participated had experienced physical and emotional peer violence, respectively. The perpetrators of violence include family members, community members/neighbors, teachers, school staff, and peers. A study conducted in Uganda by the United Nations Children's Fund (UNICEF) found that 58% of the girls suffer physical violence perpetrated by teachers, and 27% of thirteen to fifteen-year-olds were bullied within thirty days (UNICEF 2014).

Despite the bleak situation, there is evidence of increased global interest in, and commitment to, ending VAC. The United Nations Convention on the Rights of the Child (Article 19) addresses violence against children and the specific protective measures that state parties are required to undertake (United Nations 1989). Both General Comment No. 8 (UN-CRC committee 2007) and General Comment No. 13 (UN-CRC committee 2011) of the UN Committee on the Rights of the Child (UN-CRC Committee) focus on the need for children to enjoy the right to freedom from all forms of violence, including protection from corporal punishment and other cruel or degrading forms of punishment. The United Nations 2030 Agenda for Sustainable Development's target 16.2 focuses on ending abuse, exploitation, trafficking, torture, and all forms of VAC by 2030.

Efforts to end VAC on the African continent have also consistently gained momentum over the past decades. Child protection is reflected in Aspirations 4 and 6 of Agenda 2063: the Africa we want (African Union Commission 2015), as well as in Aspiration 7 of Africa's Agenda for children 2040 (African Committee of Experts on the Rights and Welfare of the Child [ACERWC] 2016). A Pan-African platform—the African Partnership to End Violence Against Children (APEVAC) —was established in 2016 to promote a continent-wide movement to prevent and respond to violence in childhood thereby contributing to global, regional, and national VAC agendas. Unfortunately, COVID-19 disrupted violence prevention and response efforts for at least 121 million children in Eastern and Southern Africa (UNICEF 2020).

Child protection in Uganda occurs within a bedrock of legal and policy frameworks based on international treaties. For example, Uganda ratified the United Nations Convention on the Rights of the Child (United Nations 1989) in 1990. The Ugandan government also ratified the UN committee on the rights of the child (UN-CRC) optional protocol on the sale of children, child prostitution, and child pornography (UN-CRC 2002a), and also the Optional Protocol against the involvement of children in armed conflict (UN-CRC 2002b). Uganda is a party to the 1999 African Charter on the Rights and Welfare of the Child (Organization of African Unity [OAU] 1990) and a path-finding country for the global end violence partnership since 2016. With these national commitments, Uganda is indeed one of the African countries with rich child protection legal and institutional frameworks. There is a host of national laws and policies, some of which are specific to VAC prevention and response. No studies to date have reviewed VAC legislation and policies in Uganda, and this chapter aims to fill this gap.

Toward that end, in the next sections of this chapter, I present a review of previous research on VAC and explain the concepts of childism and adultism, which comprise the theoretical framework for this paper. Next, I provide some context to give insight into Uganda's sociocultural context before explaining the methodology for my discourse analysis of the laws and policies that perpetuate VAC in Uganda. I outline the specific laws and policies addressed in my study and describe the inadequacies, tensions, and silences that emerged from my inquiry. Based on my analysis, I contend that Uganda's VAC prevention and response policies and laws are based on adult-centric, decontextualized Western discourses and ways of knowing developed during colonialism. VAC occurs in a sociopolitical context in which structures of social power and privilege prioritize adult voices while silencing or excluding those of children and young people and recognizing how such inequities inform child-focused policy offers important implications for future reforms.

REVIEW OF PREVIOUS RESEARCH

Previous research on VAC has focused on the situation and magnitude as well as prevention and response strategies. Decades of research on violence in childhood have enhanced understanding of its situation in terms of drivers, experiences, prevalence, and consequences on children and their families. For example, there exists a wealth of evidence on the drivers of VAC to include exposure to intimate partner violence (Kyegombe, Abramsky, Devries, Michau et al. 2015; Wandera, Clarke, Knight, Allen et al. 2017) and lack of adequate parents' and children's understanding of what constitutes abuse (Morris, Kouros, Janecek, Freeman et al. 2016). Other past studies on violence in African childhoods examined its impact. For example, there is a large body of research on sexual violence, which has historically centered on its implications in terms of mental health, physical harm, emotional and physical development, etc. (see Cohen & Nordås 2014; Cohen 2017; Ellsberg, Ovince, Murphy, Blackwell et al. 2020; Eriksson Baaz, Gray, & Stern 2018; Kalisya, Justin, Kimona, Nyavandu et al. 2011; Wells, 2017). Some studies have investigated children's experiences of violence (Nyangoma, Ebila, & Omona 2019; Vohito 2017). Studies that investigated prevalence in Africa and Uganda confirm high levels of violence among children and young people (Collin-Vézina, Daigneault, & Herbert 2013; Khuzwayo Taylor, & Connolly

2016; Devries, Knight, Allen, Parkes et al. 2017). Within this discourse, VAC is analyzed by authors from their adult vantage point or based on research generated with adult-centric methods with adults as experts. There is limited analysis of how age-based inequality in child policy formulation, decision-making, and implementation can deter VAC prevention and response efforts. I expand here upon this existing work by examining how these understandings intersect with adultism to perpetuate VAC.

Another focus of past studies is possible VAC remedies. Notable among the recommendations of scholars is the use of a holistic approach to dismantle unfavorable sociopolitical structures (García-Moreno, Zimmerman, Morris-Gehring, Heise et al. 2014; Michau et al. 2015). According to Temmerman (2014), it is equally important to follow examples of successful community-based approaches, while research by Morris, Kouros, Janecek, Freeman et al. (2016) and Wandera, Clarke, Knight, Allen et al. (2017) recommend the use of school-based violence prevention programs. Kyegombe, Abramsky, Devries, Michau et al. (2015) note that prevention strategies include improving parents' relationships while Jewkes, Flood, and Lang (2014) recommend working with boys and men. The available literature shows that prevention and response mechanisms, albeit important, are based on adult-centric data collected by adults from children and/or their parents. It is well acknowledged that children in the African context are silenced and socialized to respect and obey adults without question (Lake & Jamieson 2016; Wandera, Clarke, Knight, Allen et al. 2017). It is no wonder then that evidence suggests at least 50% of the cases of sexual violence in South Africa are not reported (Mathews, Hendricks, & Naemah 2016).

Another approach to remedying VAC involves examining the rights of victims. For example, Kabaseke and Kitui (2022) analyzed the criminal justice system for female survivors of sexual violence in Uganda. They contend that instead of protecting victims of violence, the law puts emphasis on the rights of suspects and offenders. Citing Hall (2010), they note that "victims in the criminal justice system continue to be passive participants in the courts of law unless they are called upon as witnesses" (62). However, this work was concerned with women and girls in general and not children as a specific category. Therefore, research has not yet adequately examined how the minoritization of children by society and academia extends to policy and practice. This further increases their vulnerability to abuse, exploitation, abandonment.

It is evident that many years of research have produced a wealth of knowledge about the situation of VAC in terms of drivers, experiences, and consequences, as well as prevention and response strategies. However, most published studies have been conducted in the minority world, or the global North, rather than the majority world or the global South, where the majority of the world's children and young people live, and knowledge on what works from the perspective of African children is still limited (Ellsberg, Ellsberg, Arango, Morton, Gennari et al. 2015; Temmerman, 2014). In order to enact meaningful policies that actually function to interrupt VAC, I contend that effective child protection efforts should dismantle the adult privilege and marginalization of children's and young people's voices that characterizes local VAC laws and policies. Childism, as described by Wall (2022), offers a useful lens through which such an interruption can be imagined.

CHILDISM AS A LENS TO DISRUPT ADULTISM IN CHILD POLICY

Childism, first coined by Pierce and Allen (1975) to describe how prejudiced is enacted against children, acts as a lens from which oppressive adultism can be understood. Adultism is the systemic subordination of young people which intersects with other systems of oppression and discrimination such as sexism and racism. It can also be described as ageism against children or the "systemic mistreatment and disrespect of young people" (Bell 1995, 2). It is a form of adult supremacy (DeJong & Love, 2015) manifested in age-based policies that marginalize young people. Betrand, Maneka Deanna Brooks, and Domínguez (2020) equate adultism with abuse, which is internalized differently by adults and young people. Adults tend to draw on developmentalism to justify a belief that they are entitled to act on children without requesting consent because young people are perceived as innocent and vulnerable "becomings." Adultism emerges "out of the cultural, social and political construction of childhood" (Kennedy, 2019, 27). This is where childism becomes relevant as a critical lens for dismantling systemic adultism in society.

Childism is an extension of childhood studies (Qvortrup 1985), a discipline that began as an impetus to challenge the dominant, developmentalist construction of children as "becomings" rather than beings in their own right (Wall 2019). Childism sees child and youth age as a social dimension that has not previously influenced academic research in the same way as have others such as gender, race, class, disability, sexuality. It offers a useful framework to explore children's experiences and voices that are ignored in child-focused research, policy, and practice. According to Wall (2022), it is a lens "for critiquing the deeply engrained adultism that pervades scholarship and societies and reconstructing more age-inclusive research and social imaginations" (258). It "focuses on transforming understandings and practices, not just around children themselves, or even around child-adult inter-generationality, but also around the pervasive normative assumptions that ground scholarship and societies overall" (4). It does so by addressing the entrenched marginalization of children not only in academia but also in society. It is therefore vital for deconstructing, dismantling, and decentering the adult-centric nature of scholarship and social relations and centering children and youth as members of society. In other words, it is an activist movement to correct systemic adultism, prejudice, and discrimination against children and young people. In this chapter, childism acts as a lens to analyze how adult-dominated social and political milieu and the associated child legal policy frameworks marginalize children and youth thereby perpetuating systemic adultism on which violence in childhood thrives. This cycle occurs because violence has many drivers and lack of choices is one of them (Santaella-Tenorio and Tarantola 2021; UNICEF 2014). In what follows, I analyze child policy as providing an avenue through which adultism is shaped and supported. I apply the concepts of adultism and childism to disrupt the adultist aspects of Uganda's child protection policies against the backdrop of decontextualized Western, developmentalist, and normative agenda that marginalizes children in society and academia.

VIOLENCE AGAINST CHILDREN IN PERSPECTIVE

Violence against children in Uganda occurs in a sociocultural context in which certain beliefs and values automatically give adults privilege based on age. Children belong to parents, and they can do with them as they please. In this context, adults are presumed to be competent knowers and doers. They believe they know what is good for children, and they use this purported knowledge to make decisions affecting children's lives. Adults use their privilege when they physically, sexually, and emotionally abuse children. They also use the same privilege to mute children's voices in research, policy, programming, and practice. This being the case, the well-meaning efforts to prevent VAC become fruitless because the perpetrators are also the policymakers. This is particularly crucial because child protection efforts have historically focused more on response rather than prevention.

Moreover, in this context, 54% of the population is under the age of eighteen with children (Uganda Bureau of Statistics [UBOS] 2021). According to a 2017–2018 report by the MGLSD, there were 2,878 reports of VAC were made to the Uganda Child Helpline, also known as Sauti 116, a government toll-free telephone service for reporting, tracking, responding, and referring cases of VAC (MGLSD 2018). These reports included cases of child exploitation, child neglect, child trafficking, emotional abuse, murder, online child sex and violence, physical abuse, and sexual abuse. Child neglect was the most reported form of violence with 1,791 cases followed by sexual violence with 753 cases. Additionally, it is estimated that between 2013 and 2017, more than 414 child marriages occurred in Uganda, of which 96.9% involved girls (MGLSD, 2018). Recent evidence demonstrates the impact of COVID-19 containment measures on escalating VAC (see Bukuluki, Mwenyango, Katongole, Sidhva et al. 2020; Kamusiime et al. 2021; Sserwanja, Kawuki, & Kim 2021; Parkes, Datzberger, Howell, Knight et al. 2020). According to UBOS (2021), 36% of Uganda's children were laborers during the COVID-19 pandemic, up from 21% pre-pandemic. The prevalence of VAC is therefore high despite the strong legal and policy frameworks.

METHODS

This chapter is a review of existing VAC laws and policies in Uganda. The review analyzed the laws and policies from the point of view of childism to identify any inadequacies and silences. I gathered Ugandan laws and policies from the four relevant government ministries—Ministry of Gender, Labor, and Social Development (MGLSD); Ministry of Education; Ministry of Health; and Ministry of Justice and Constitutional Affairs. I drew on extant VAC literature accessed through different search engines (such as Scopus, Google Scholar, and Pubmed). In examining the policies themselves, I applied discourse analysis using the What's the Problem Represented to Be? (WPR) method (Bacci 2012). Discourse analysis helps to establish a deeper understanding of the text. The WPR method is a modified discourse analysis that assumes that reality is constructed based on the discourses within society. The WPR method is an important policy analysis tool that enables the user to interrogate specific policies and documents (Bacchi 2009; Bacchi & Eveline 2010). The WPR approach provides six questions that can guide the policy analysis, and from those six, I applied the following three:

1. What's the problem represented to be?
2. What assumptions underpin this representation?
3. What effects are produced by this representation?

Guided by these questions, I carefully read and critically interrogated each of the policies to identify inherent inadequacies and silences that perpetuate VAC from the point of view of childism and adultism.

NATIONAL VAC LAWS AND POLICIES

Uganda's laws and policies that are specific to VAC include the Constitution (Republic of Uganda 1995), the Gender in Education Sector Policy (Ministry of Education and Sports [MOES] 2016), the National Child Policy (MGLSD 2020, the National Policy on the Elimination of Gender-Based Violence in Uganda (MGLSD 2016a), the National Orphans and other Vulnerable Children Policy (MGLSD 2004a), and the National Child Labor Policy (MGLSD 2006). Acts of Parliament include the 2016 Children (Amendment) Act (Republic of Uganda 2016), Penal Code Act 8 (Amendment) (Republic of Uganda 2007), the Prohibition of Female Genital Mutilation (FGM) Act (Republic of Uganda 2010), the Domestic Violence Act (2010), the Employment Act (2006), the Prevention of Trafficking in Persons Act (2009), the Sexual Offences Bill (2019), among others. Although the number of laws and policies is continuously growing, evidence suggests that the prevalence of VAC in Uganda is still high. The high prevalence of VAC despite the plethora of policies and laws creates a need to interrogate the legal and institutional framework in which VAC prevention and response occur. Table 5.1 summarizes the relevant laws and policies.

Between 2006 and 2008, in addition to the amendment of the Penal Code Act, the Magistrate Court Act, and the Trials and Indictment Act by parliament were amended to improve the management of cases of sexual violence. The said amendments empowered Chief Magistrates Courts to handle nonaggravated defilement cases, compensation for survivors, discretionary hearings, and HIV testing. In addition to the national laws, Uganda also has various policies, development frameworks, action plans, and strategies. For example, in 2012, Uganda established the National Child Protection Working Group under the MGLSD. In 2015, the government implemented the African Union Campaign to End Child Marriage in Africa (African Union 2013), as well as the national strategy to end child marriage and teenage pregnancy (2014/2015–2019/2020). Uganda is also among the countries that have embraced the International Safe to Learn Initiative which aims to end violence in and through schools by providing an environment where children can learn and thrive freely. Safe to Learn has a shared vision of working with governments, civil society organizations, communities, teachers and children to end the violence that undermines education and make sure all children are safe to learn by 2025 (Global Partnership to End Violence Against Children 2020).

Various government strategies remain in place to address VAC. In addition to the Uganda Child Helpline mentioned above, which was launched in 2014, the government established the National Children Authority in 2016 to provide a structure and mechanism for ensuring proper oversight, coordination, monitoring, and evaluation of all child rights policies and programs. Uganda has guidelines for Reporting, Tracking, Referral, and Response (RTRR), a National Strategic Plan on Violence against Children in Schools (MOES 2015), a National Strategy for Girls' Education in Uganda (MOES

Table 5.1 Relevant Laws and Policies

VAC laws and policies	Provisions and mandate	Formulation process
1. The constitution of the Republic of Uganda (1995)	The supreme law protects all citizens including children from any form of torture, cruel, or degrading punishment (the Republic of Uganda, 1995).	The current constitution (amended in 2005 and 2018) is an output of the 1994/95 constituent Assembly which reviewed the previous constitutions
2. The Penal code Act 8 (Amendment) (2007)	Prohibits defilement and corporal punishment	Passed and amended by parliament
3. The National Child Policy (2020)	Coordinates efforts of the different sectors that have a direct and indirect mandate on children and deliver a comprehensive package of services encompassing all the four cardinal rights of the child in a multi-sectoral approach. It is structured around survival, development, participation, & system strengthening	Emerged out of a review of older policies including the National Orphans and Other Vulnerable Children Policy (2004), the National Social Protection Policy (2015), National Youth Policy and Action Plan (2016), the Universal Primary Education (UPE) Policy (1997), National Adolescent Health Policy for Uganda (2004), National Policy on Disability in Uganda (2006), Universal Secondary Education (USE) Policy (2007), the Second National Health Policy (2010), the Special Needs and Inclusive Education Policy (2011), the National Framework for Alternative Care (2012), the East African Community Child Policy.
4. The National Policy on the Elimination of Gender-Based Violence (2016)	The goal of the policy is to eliminate gender-based violence through fostering an environment of zero tolerance, providing a comprehensive response, care, and support services to survivors, and eliminating impunity. Pages 14-16 specifically speaks to the elimination of VAC	Developed as an initiative of the Ministry of Gender Labor and Social Development after conducting wide consultations with stakeholders specified as "line ministries, departments, development partners local governments, civil society, and faith-based organizations" (MGLSD, 2016a: vii)
5. The National Child Labor policy (2006)	Provides an enabling environment for the prevention, protection, and elimination of child labor	The policy is a product of the Ministry of Gender Labor and Social Development

6. The National Orphans and other Vulnerable Children Policy (2004)	Protects orphans and other vulnerable children including those affected by armed conflict, neglected, and abused children, those living on the streets, in conflict with the law, affected by HIV/AIDS, and children living under the worst forms of child labor	The policy is a product of the Ministry of Gender Labor and Social Development in consultation with a cross-section of duty bearers and rights holders
7. The Prohibition of Female Genital mutilation (FGM) Act (2010)	Prohibits female genital mutilation	Act of parliament
8. The children Act (amendment) (2016)	Provides a legal framework for the protection of children's rights, their protection from harmful customary practices and harmful employment. It also prohibits any form of physical punishment and other forms of violence against children	Act of parliament
9. Domestic violence Act (2010)	Provides for the elimination of violence in the context of the family. The policy defines of domestic violence, domestic relationship, and the basis for legal protection of those threatened with domestic violence	Act of parliament
10. The employment Act (2006)	Restricts the employment of children under 14 years	Act of parliament
11. The prevention of trafficking in persons Act (2009)	Prohibits all forms of trafficking and specifies penalties for perpetrators	Act of parliament
12. The sexual offences bill (2019)	Aimed at preventing sexual violence, enhancing punishment against sexual offenders, and providing additional protection to survivors. The bill reiterates a ban on same-sex relations as codified in the Penal Code	Adopted by parliament in 2021 and is yet to be promulgated

2013). Analysis of the available laws and policies shows that violence prevention mechanisms have historically been rooted in the use of punishment and threats. In the following section, I discuss the inadequacies in Uganda's VAC legislation and policies.

INADEQUACIES IN UGANDA'S VAC LAWS AND POLICIES

Analysis of the inadequacies in the key child protection policies and laws through the lens of childism reveals two major concerns. First, there is inadequate child participation in policy development, which breeds tensions and silences about critical VAC issues that are stipulated in pan-African and international laws and treaties. Second, the analysis revealed that a major assumption underlying the laws and policies is that children and young people are innocent and vulnerable beings who require protection through policies and laws created by adults. Consequently, their participation in legislative processes is described in cryptic ways as I elaborate in the next sub-section.

Analysis of the laws and policies shows that while the constitution as the supreme law which requires that "the state shall be based on democratic principles, which empower and encourage active participation of all citizens at all levels in their own governance" (Republic of Uganda 1995, 1), article 59 (1) and (2) only give voting rights to adults: "(1) Every citizen of Uganda of eighteen years of age or above has a right to vote. (2) It is the duty of every citizen of Uganda of eighteen years of age or above to register as a voter for public elections and referenda" (88). Article 80 (1) of the constitution specifies the eligibility criteria for qualifying to be a member of parliament: "(a) is a citizen of Uganda; (b) is a registered voter; and (c) has completed a minimum formal education of Advanced Level standard or its equivalent" (Republic of Uganda: 97). Together, these articles confirm that young people's participation in policy formulation is restricted since only citizens above eighteen years can vote or stand for a political office. This controversy in the supreme law is rooted in childism in the form of developmental psychology, an oppressive adultist discipline modeled on a Western construction of children as immature, irrational, and incompetent. The Constitution of the Republic of Uganda marginalizes and automatically excludes children from all conversations about VAC laws and policies.

Several of the key VAC laws and policies were passed by parliament where children have no opportunity to represent themselves. These include the Prohibition of Female Genital Mutilation (FGM) Act (2010), the Children Act (amendment) (2016), the Domestic Violence Act (2010), the Employment

Act (2006), and the Prevention of Trafficking in Persons Act (2009). Uganda has a National Youth Council, which was also established by an act of parliament (National Youth Council Act Cap 319) in 1993 and amended in 2003 and 2010. The council caters to the interests of youth (defined as people aged 18–30) and has five representatives in parliament, as well as in district and sub-county local government councils. While the National Youth Council provides the youth with opportunities to participate in policy development and reviews, the National Children's Authority, which monitors and evaluates child rights programs and policies, does not provide room for children's engagement or participation. Many key policies in Uganda were developed by government technocrats, including the National Child Policy, the National Policy on the Elimination of Gender-Based Violence, and the National Child Labor Policy, as well as other key documents such as the National strategic plan on violence against children in schools [2015–2020] and the National strategy to end child marriage and teenage pregnancy.

Specifically, The National Child Policy, developed after a review of older child-focused policies, provides a useful example of how adultism shapes policy-making on behalf of children. While the following quote shows that the policy was developed by members of a technical working group that included children, there is no clear information about how children participated, which is important given the adultist culture that characterizes the Ugandan society.

> In 2016, the Ministry of Gender, Labour and Social Development constituted a multi-sectoral Technical Working Group (TWG) to oversee the National Child Policy development process. The TWG steered a participatory process that entailed extensive consultations with a wide range of stakeholders at national, regional, district, and community levels. Stakeholders including technical and political leaders from relevant Government Ministries, Departments and Agencies (MDAs) and LGs, Development partners, Academic and Research Institutions, Civil Society Organizations, cultural and religious leaders, Private Sector and children. (MGLSD 2020, 6)

The excerpt above shows that although children participated, various categories of adults oversaw the process. The National Child Policy acknowledges the limitations to child participation due to deep-seated adultist social and cultural beliefs and attitudes as expressed later in the same policy statement:

> ... in some cultures, it is a deeply rooted belief that children should be silent in the presence of adults, considering that they lack the competence and that such participation encourages bad behaviour. Failure to allow children to participate often has negative consequences. Moreover, there are no actual penalties or forcible measures imposed on the various actors who do not engage children

in meaningful participation pertaining the issues and decisions affecting them. There are also limitations with regard to the capacity of government and civil society officials to facilitate children's participation, which requires capacity and a wide range of skills and experience. The existing participation initiatives have limited coverage as they are typically associated with specific programmes funded and implemented by International and Local NGOs. (MGLSD 2020, 24)

As this example illustrates, although some efforts have been made to achieve child participation, it is not clear whether such efforts reach the most excluded children whose voices are likely ignored in national policies.

A similar example of an attempt to include children in policymaking can be seen in the Orphans and other Vulnerable Children (OVC) policy (MGLSD 2004a), which was developed "through a consultative and participatory process involving a cross-section of duty-bearers and rights holders" (iii). The OVC policy led to the National strategic program plan of interventions (NSPPI) for orphans and other vulnerable children (MGLSD 2004b) and the Quality Standards for the Protection, Care, and Support of Orphans and Other Vulnerable Children in Uganda (MGLSD 2007). While these developments are applaudable particularly for specifying the program-level quality standards and indicators, they remain adultist in nature because of the level of the involvement of young people in their formulation. Furthermore, in cases where national recommendations are revised, such as the guidelines for the prevention and management of pregnancy in school settings, the changes are developed by adults based on other policies that were established through adult-centric processes.

TENSIONS IN UGANDA'S VAC LAWS AND POLICIES

Apart from the inadequacies cited above, some tensions exist within various Ugandan laws and policies, as well as among international treaties. For example, although pregnancy checks are endorsed by Uganda's Ministry of Education and Sports (see MOES 2020) to enhance prevention and management of pregnancy in schools, they can also be perceived as a breach of the guiding principles of the same policy, and also some of the stipulations of the United Nations Convention on the Rights of the Child (UNCRC), as well as the penal code. According to MOES (2020), "do no harm" is one of the guiding principles of the guidelines for the prevention and management of pregnancy in school settings: "Uphold the do no harm principle – all interventions to prevent early pregnancy, discrimination of pregnant girls and adolescent mothers in schools should minimize possible longer term harm, or support the adolescent mothers and their children in ways that facilitate long-term development" (MOES 202, 13). However, some of the practices of conducting pregnancy checks have historically included methods such as touching breasts and other sexual organs that can be interpreted as violation of children's rights to privacy as enshrined in article 16 of the UNCRC (1989). Article 16 states that "No child shall be subjected to arbitrary or unlawful interference with his or her privacy, family, home or correspondence, nor to unlawful attacks on his or her honour and reputation," and furthermore establishes the child's "right to the protection of the law against such interference or attacks" (5). Here, childism in the form of a paternalistic state protectionism that monitors the bodies and sexual autonomy of children, trumps the child's right to privacy and ultimately further inflicts the harm it seeks to reduce.

These rights are also guaranteed by the Penal Code Act, which prohibits indecent assault, defined as "Any intended act that involves unlawful physical contact or force applied to the body of a child and which has the intended effect of reducing the dignity of that child. The assault and circumstances accompanying it, must be capable of being considered by right minded persons as indecent" (MGLSD 2016b, 13). Furthermore, Section 128 (2) states that "It shall be no defence to a charge for an indecent assault on a girl under the age of eighteen years to prove that she consented to the act of indecency" (Republic of Uganda 2007, 33). Furthermore, while the rationale for the MOES guidelines articulates the importance of changing " . . . attitudes toward pregnant girls, their continuation in school, and subsequent re-entry to school," which are "gender-biased, violate the girl child's right to education, and thus require concerted efforts to change" (MOES 2020, 13), the same guidelines require schools to periodically examine girls for pregnancy, which indirectly perpetuates negative attitudes and beliefs about adolescent pregnancy and also violates their rights to privacy and personal freedom. There is therefore an unresolved tension between the protectionist stipulations of the penal code and the MOES guidelines, and also the human rights established by the UNCRC (as well as the MOES). This can be read as a disjuncture between children viewed as human becomings to be protected and full human beings entitled to state rights and their protections. The persistence of sexual surveillance of adolescent girls' bodies through pregnancy checks and virginity testing can be attributed to such tensions which continue to persist due to the inherent adultism of policy development processes.

Therefore, while Uganda ratified the UNCRC and many other international and pan-African instruments, the unresolved tensions discussed here illustrate that its child protection laws remain rooted in adultist, prejudiced, and developmentalist views of children as immature, irrational, and incompetent. The Ugandan VAC laws and policies do not acknowledge children's evolving capacities (United Nations 1989). The notion of evolving capacities recognizes that as children grow, their capacity to take responsibility for decisions affecting their lives increases. As Lansdown (2005) notes, there is a need for urgent action in law, policy, and practice to include the contributions of children, especially if VAC is to be eliminated in a nation whose children constitute a majority of citizens. Moreover, there is adequate evidence to suggest that perpetrators of 25% of the violence suffered by children in school are peers (Wandera, Clarke, Knight, Allen et al. 2017), and therefore it is essential that children themselves be a part of any solution.

SILENCES IN UGANDA'S VAC LAWS AND POLICIES

While it is clear from the preceding analysis that available laws and policies address many strategies for protection, prevention, and access to human rights further scrutiny reveals many silences. In particular, age linked to an assumed sexual innocence operate to sidestep accountability by the state institutions. For example, the 2007 Penal Code Act 8 amendment emphasizes punishment and threats, including the definition of defilement and the penalty/sentence for perpetrators of aggravated defilement. Section 129 of the code states:

> (1) Any person who performs a sexual act with another person who is below the age of eighteen years, commits a felony known as defilement and is on conviction liable to life imprisonment. (2) Any person who attempts to perform a sexual act with another person who is below the age of eighteen years commits an offence and is on conviction, liable to imprisonment not exceeding eighteen years. (3) Any person who performs a sexual act with another person who is below the age of eighteen years in any of the circumstances specified in subsection commits a felony called aggravated defilement and is, on conviction by the High Court, liable to suffer death. (Republic of Uganda 2007, 2)

While steep penalties are set forth for aggravated defilement, there are no clear consequences for perpetrators of corporal punishment for those under the age of eighteen years, in spite of the fact that it was also formally abolished (Republic of Uganda 2007, Act 8:2). In this way, ageist laws that view children as innocent, and therefore innocent of sexual desire, intervenes to punish sexual violations while remaining silent about adult brutalization of children in non-sexual ways.

These silences that maintain adult supremacy also bleed into peer relationships. For example, Article 24 of Uganda's national constitution, which states that "No person shall be subjected to any form of torture, cruel, inhuman, or degrading treatment or punishment" (Republic of Uganda 1995, 73) it does not specify consequences for perpetrating such acts. Article 17 also specifies that citizens are expected "to protect children and vulnerable persons against any form of abuse, harassment or ill treatment" (68). However, it provides no space where any of these concepts are defined or clarified. Of particular importance is the silence on peer perpetrators of violence in spite of the fact that various studies have documented the persistence of justice denial for survivors and victims of repeated peer sexual violence in Uganda (Kawanguchi 2021). The 125 girls abducted by the Lord's Resistance Army abducted from St. Mary's College, Aboke, in Northern Uganda in 1996 did not get reparations due to silences in the existing legislative frameworks (Denov & Drumbl 2020; Ndagire 2022). Such silences can be partly attributed to the low involvement of young stakeholders in policy formulation, an effect of adultist age discrimination that evades attention to lateral forms of violence.

Another significant silence that emerges from the analysis of the existing policies is regarding what happens to a child who has been violated. Some of the laws are strong on stipulating consequences for the offenders but there are hardly any alternative care or options prescribed for children who have been neglected, trafficked, or have suffered corporal punishment. Worse more, children are further silenced in the criminal justice system because their testimonies are received with caution in courts of law. As noted by Kabaseke and Kitui (2022), "During trial there are some procedures that remain challenging to under-age girls who are victims of sexual violence. According to the law, the evidence of a child has to be corroborated after a voire dire—a trial within a trial—has been conducted" (72). The existence of such procedures demonstrates that children are not trusted by adults who are obviously in charge of the justice-seeking procedures. The same adults inflict harm on children, doubt their testimonies, and deny them supports due to adultism against survivors of violence. The silence on supports for children who have experienced violence can be attributed to the adultist nature of the formulation and implementation of child protection policies rooted in beliefs that question children's capacities to reason through speech and testimony. The silences in the existing policies and laws pave the way for VAC to persist despite the rich legal and institutional framework.

DISCUSSION

As demonstrated by the preceding analysis, Uganda has a wide array of laws and policies that are intended to address violence against children, some of which cut across various sectors. According to Michau et al. (2015), a holistic approach in which various sectors work together using diverse strategies to create change within sociopolitical structures and for individuals and communities could eliminate VAC. By taking such a multisectoral approach, the government of Uganda has demonstrated a commitment to a holistic approach to reform sociopolitical structures as alluded to García-Moreno, Zimmerman, Morris-Gehring, Heise et al. (2014). This recommendation is also echoed in the UNCRC, which calls for a holistic, child rights-based approach to child caregiving and protection in recognition of children's agency and evolving capacities (UN Committee 2011). However, given the inadequacies, tensions and silences surfaced by my analysis, it is clear that VAC prevention and response efforts, based on adultism that perpetuates childism through developmentalism and ageism, perpetuates VAC.

The missing piece in Uganda's commitment would be enhancing inclusivity through eliminating barriers to child participation in policy-related conversations. As my analysis illustrates, governmental VAC prevention efforts continue to exclude children not only in policy formulation and decision making but also in VAC research, despite sustained discourse on children's voice in child protection research and practice. This is particularly unfortunate given that 54% of Ugandans are children (UBOS 2021), and previous research found that peer violence contributes to at least one-quarter of the physical violence in schools (Wandera, Clarke, Knight, Allen et al. 2017). Hence, although there is a well-acknowledged view that preventing VAC through research and legal and policy reform is a good approach, evidence has also demonstrated that research, policies, and implementation strategies that exclude children and young people have not yielded much (Oldfield, Tinney, & Dodington 2018). Having a plethora of policies, laws, initiatives, strategies, etc. based on research and discourse in which targeted beneficiaries (children and young people) are absent does not necessarily yield the desired impact. The findings of this study are in agreement with those of Kabaseke and Kitui (2022) who discuss how the rights of perpetrators of violence are protected more than those of survivors, the majority of whom are children and young people.

From the perspective of childism, the inequalities in epistemic power grant different levels of authority and intelligibility to adults and children. Uganda's VAC laws and policies, as well as academic literature are therefore rooted in such epistemic injustice or the kind of unfairness suffered by a person in their capacity as a "knower" (Catala 2015). For child participation in policy formulation and decision making to be effective, it must begin with the recognition that children deserve the same level of epistemic justice (Klyve 2019) as that granted to adults. The political, epistemological, and hegemonic structures inherent in society invisibilize and minoritize the beneficiaries of these processes. Disrupting and decolonizing the methodologies used in stakeholder consultations that precede policy decision-making and formulation as well as the research that informs policy decisions is urgent.

CONCLUSION

While my analysis has focused specifically on policies related to child protection in Uganda, it is important to note that VAC is a global phenomenon driven and exacerbated by contextual factors, and therefore prevention and response measures cannot be standardized. Additionally, VAC has diverse enablers, including a context where some people are not given options because children and young people experience, witness, and in some cases are perpetrators of violence. As this chapter reveals, Uganda's VAC laws and policies assume that punishment and threats are powerful means through which VAC can be eliminated, with a key assumption being that children and young people are not capable of engaging and contributing meaningfully to the creation of laws and policies. The result is that VAC persists because the law creators are also the enforcers.

In order to meaningfully confront and resolve the inadequacies, tensions, and silences discussed in this chapter, it is important to consider children as human beings regardless of age as a dimension of social order and power. Otherwise, the child protection laws and policies continue to be punctuated by age-based inequality or adultism, which has been described as being at the core of child maltreatment (Dziri 2021). From the perspective of childism, child protection should be rooted in age-inclusive and child-focused laws, policies, institutions, frameworks, guidelines, and plans of action. Excluding children's voices from policy conversations on top of being an injustice sends them the message that since they are young and immature, they do not understand that violence is bad, and they may go ahead and commit it. Children and young people should therefore be supported in order to develop an understanding of the root causes of violence and to understand and develop skills to collect, analyze, and disseminate data relevant to their communities. Their lived experiences should be useful in impacting, policy, praxis, and philosophy. This includes involving them in policy development consultations and decision-making. This would lead to the creation of age-inclusive laws, policies, and institutions.

Before inclusive reforms to child-focused policy can be advanced, it is also important to contextualize violence prevention by rethinking the underlying principles, guidelines, and policy-making processes. Most importantly, it is necessary to acknowledge and counteract the nature of adultism inherent in the child protection policy-making processes, principles, values, and interests. Achieving an accelerated reduction in violence against children will also depend on legislative review and policy makers' openness to formulating child-focused evidence-driven violence prevention reforms, policies, and practices. Adultist child policies and laws negatively affect children all over the world, especially since most of them are based in international and regional instruments and treaties. The African Union, for example, provides an excellent platform (ACERWC 2016; African Union Commission 2015; United Nations 1989; UNCRC 2007). Future research should explore children's involvement in child-focused policy reform at global, regional, and national levels.

REFERENCES

African Child Policy Forum. 2019. *Sexual Exploitation of Children in Africa - A Silent Emergency*. Addis Ababa: African Child Policy Forum. Available at: https://violenceagainstchildren.un.org/content/sexual-exploitation-children-africa-silent-emergency-report-african-child-policy-forum.

African Committee of Experts on the Rights and Welfare of the Child (ACERWC), AGENDA 2040. 2016. *Africa's Agenda for Children: Fostering an Africa Fit for Children*. Addis Ababa: African Union.

African Partnership to End Violence against Children (APEVAC) & African Child Policy Forum (ACPF). 2021. *Violence Against Children in Africa: A Report on Progress and Challenges*. Addis Ababa: APEVC & ACPF.

African Union Commission. 2015. *Agenda 2063 report of the commission on the African Union Agenda 2063 The Africa We Want in 2063*. Addis Ababa: African Union.

African Union. 2013. *Campaign to End Child Marriage in Africa: Call to Action*. Addis Ababa: African Union. Available at: https://au.int/sites/default/files/pages/32905-file-campaign_to_end_child_marriage_in_africa_call_for_action-_english.pdf

Bacchi, Carol, and Joan Eveline. 2010. *Mainstreaming Politics: Gendering Practices and Feminist Theory*. University of Adelaide Press.

Bacchi, Carol. 2012. "Introducing the 'What's the Problem Represented to be?' Approach." In *Engaging with Carol Bacchi: Strategic Interventions and Exchanges*, edited by Blestas Angelique, and Chris Beasey, 21–24. Adelaide: University of Adelaide Press,.

Bacchi, Carol. 2009. *Analysing Policy*. Pearson Higher Education AU.

Bell, John. 1995. "Understanding Adultism." *A Major Obstacle to Developing Positive Youth-Adult Relationships*. Somerville, MA: YouthBuild USA.

Bertrand, Melanie, Maneka Deanna Brooks, and Ashley D. Domínguez. 2020. "Challenging adultism: Centering youth as educational decision makers." *Urban Education*. https://doi.org/10.1177/0042085920959135

Bukuluki, Paul, Hadijah Mwenyango, Simon Peter Katongole, Dina Sidhva, and George Palattiyil. 2020. "The Socio-Economic and Psychosocial Impact of Covid-19 Pandemic on Urban Refugees in Uganda." *Social Sciences & Humanities Open* 2(1): 100045.

Catala, Amandine. 2015. "Democracy, Trust, and Epistemic Justice." *The Monist* 98(4): 424–440.

Cohen, Dara Kay, and Ragnhild Nordås. 2014. "Sexual Violence in Armed Conflict: Introducing the SVAC Dataset, 1989–2009." *Journal of Peace Research* 51(3): 418–428.

Cohen, Dara Kay. 2017. "The Ties That Bind: How Armed Groups Use Violence to Socialize Fighters." *Journal of Peace Research* 54(5): 701–714.

Collin-Vézina, Delphine, Isabelle Daigneault, and Martine Hébert. 2013. "Lessons Learned from Child Sexual Abuse Research: Prevalence, Outcomes, and Preventive Strategies." *Child and Adolescent Psychiatry and Mental Health* 7(1): 1–9.

Davies, Sharyn Graham. 2014. "Surveilling Sexuality in Indonesia." In *Sex and Sexualities in Contemporary Indonesia*, edited by Linda Rae Bennet and Sharyn Graham Davies, 47–68. New York: Routledge.

DeJong, Keri, and Barbara J. Love. 2015. "Youth Oppression as a Technology of Colonialism: Conceptual Frameworks and Possibilities for Social Justice Education Praxis." *Equity & Excellence in Education* 48(3): 489–508. https://doi.org/10.1080/10665684.2015.1057086

Denov, Myriam S., and Mark A. Drumbl. 2020. "The Many Harms of Forced Marriage: Insights for Law from Ethnography in Northern Uganda." *Journal of International Criminal Justice* 18(2): 349–372.

Devries, Karen M., Louise Knight, Elizabeth Allen, Jenny Parkes, Nambusi Kyegombe, and Dipak Naker. 2017. "Does the Good Schools Toolkit Reduce Physical, Sexual and Emotional Violence, and Injuries, in Girls and Boys Equally? A Cluster-Randomised Controlled Trial." *Prevention Science* 18: 839–853.

Dziri, Nourhene. 2022. "Adultism at the Root of Youth Maltreatment in AS King's Still Life with Tornado." *Children's Literature in Education* 53(1): 18–32.

Ellsberg, Mary, Diana J. Arango, Matthew Morton, Floriza Gennari, Sveinung Kiplesund, Manuel Contreras, and Charlotte Watts. 2015. "Prevention of Violence Against Women and Girls: What Does the Evidence Say?" *The Lancet* 385(9977): 1555–1566.

Ellsberg, Mary, Junior Ovince, Maureen Murphy, Alexandra Blackwell, Dashakti Reddy, Julianne Stennes, Tim Hess, and Manuel Contreras. 2020. "No Safe Place: Prevalence and Correlates of Violence Against Conflict-Affected Women and Girls in South Sudan." *PLoS one* 15(10): e0237965

Eriksson Baaz, Maria, Harriet Gray, and Maria Stern. 2018. "What Can We/Do We Want to Know? Reflections from Researching SGBV in Military Settings." *Social Politics: International Studies in Gender, State & Society* 25(4): 521–544.

García-Moreno, Claudia, Cathy Zimmerman, Alison Morris-Gehring, Lori Heise, Avni Amin, Naeemah Abrahams, Oswaldo Montoya, Padma Bhate-Deosthali, Nduku Kilonzo, and Charlotte Watts. 2015. "Addressing Violence Against Women: A Call to Action." *The Lancet* 385(9978): 1685–1695.

Garlen, Julie C. 2019. "Interrogating Innocence: "Childhood" as Exclusionary Social Practice." *Childhood* 26(1): 54–67. https://doi.org/10.1177/0907568218811484

Gibson, B. Isaac. 2022. "The Portion of Goods that Falleth to Me: Parental Rights, Children's Rights, and Medical Decisions after COVID-19." *Family Court Review* 60(3): 590–601.

Global Partnership to End Violence Against Children "*Safe to Learn*". 2020. End Violence Against Children: Available at: www.end-violence.org/safe-to-learn.

Hall, Matthew. 2010. "The Relationship Between Victims and Prosecutors: Defending Victims' Rights?" *Criminal Law Review* 1: 31–45.

Jewkes Rachel, Michael Flood, and James Lang. 2015. "From Work with Men and Boys to Changes of Social Norms and Reduction of Inequities in Gender Relations: A Conceptual Shift in Prevention of Violence Against Women and Girls." *The Lancet* 385(9977): 1580–1589.

Kabaseke, Charlotte, and Barbara Kitui. 2022. "Access to Justice for Female Victims of Sexual Violence in Uganda." *Violence Against Women and Criminal Justice in Africa: Volume II: Sexual Violence and Vulnerability*: 53–85.

Kamusiime, Annah, Derrick Ssentumbwe, and Doris Kakuru. 2021. "Child Labour Boom; As Uganda Is Hit with 2 Million, Experts Ask- How Many Children Must Suffer Before We Act." *Red Pepper Daily*. Last modified December 17, 2021. https://www.redpepper.co.ug/2021/12/child-labour-boom-as-uganda-is-hit-with-2-million-experts-askhow-many-children-must-suffer-before-we-act/

Kawaguchi, Chigumi. 2021. "Why GBV Survivors Cannot Seek Help: The Case of South Sudanese Refugees in Uganda." In *Risks, Identity and Conflict*, edited by Ratuva, S., Hassan, H. A., Compel, R. Palgrave Macmillan, Singapore. https://doi.org/10.1007/978-981-16-1486-6_13

Kennedy, Heather. 2019. "Disrupting Adultism: Practices That Enable or Constrain Intergroup Contact Between Youth and Adults." PhD diss., University of Denver.

Khuzwayo, N., M. Taylor, and C. Connolly. 2016. "Prevalence and Correlates of Violence Among South African High School Learners in uMgungundlovu District Municipality, KwaZulu-Natal, South Africa." *South African Medical Journal* 106(12): 1216–1221.

Klyve, Guro Parr. 2019. "Whose Knowledge? Epistemic Injustice and Challenges in Hearing Childrens' Voices." *Voices: A World Forum for Music Therapy* 19(3): 1–10.

Kyegombe, Nambusi, Tanya Abramsky, Karen M. Devries, Lori Michau, Janet Nakuti, Elizabeth Starmann, Tina Musuya, Lori Heise, and Charlotte Watts. 2015. "What Is the Potential for Interventions Designed to Prevent Violence Against Women to Reduce Children's Exposure to Violence? Findings from the SASA! Study, Kampala, Uganda." *Child Abuse & Neglect* 50: 128–140.

Lake, Lori, and Lucy Jamieson. 2016. "Using a Child Rights Approach to Strengthen Prevention of Violence Against Children: CME." *South African Medical Journal* 106(12): 1168–1172.

Lansdown, Gerison. 2005. *The Evolving Capacities of the Child*. Florence: UNICEF Innocenti Insights.

Leclerc-Madlala, Suzanne. 2001. "Virginity Testing: Managing Sexuality in a Maturing HIV/AIDS Epidemic." *Medical Anthropology Quarterly* 15(4): 533–552.

Leclerc-Madlala, Suzanne. 2003. "Protecting Girlhood? Virginity Revivals in the Era of AIDS." *Agenda* 17(56): 16–25. https://doi.org/10.1080/10130950.2003.9676017.

Malemo Kalisya, Luc, Paluku Lussy Justin, Christophe Kimona, Kavira Nyavandu, Kamabu Mukekulu Eugenie, Kasereka Muhindo Lusi Jonathan, Kasereka Masumbuko Claude, and Michael Hawkes. 2011. "Sexual Violence Toward Children and Youth in War-Torn Eastern Democratic Republic of Congo." *PloS One* 6(1): e15911.

Mathews, Shanaaz, Natasha Hendricks, and Naeemah Abrahams. 2016. "A Psychosocial Understanding of Child Sexual Abuse Disclosure Among Female Children in South Africa." *Journal of Child Sexual Abuse* 25(6): 636–654.
McClelland, Sara I., and Michelle Fine. 2013. "Over-Sexed and Under Surveillance: Adolescent Sexualities, Cultural Anxieties, and Thick Desire." In *The Politics of Pleasure in Sexuality Education*, edited by Louisa Allen, Mary Lou Rasmussen, and Kathleen Quinlivan, 12–34. Routledge.
Michau, Lori, Jessica Horn, Amy Bank, Mallika Dutt, and Cathy Zimmerman. 2015. "Prevention of Violence Against Women and Girls: Lessons from Practice." *The Lancet* 385(9978): 1672–1684.
Ministry of Education and Sports. 2014. *Reporting, Tracking, Referral and Response (RTRR) Guidelines*. Kampala: MOES.
Ministry of Education and Sports. 2020. *Revised Guidelines for the Prevention and Management of Teenage Pregnancy in school settings in Uganda*. Kampala: MOES.
Ministry of Education and Sports. 2016. *The Gender in Education Sector Policy*. Kampala: MOES.
Ministry of Education and Sports. 2015. *The National Strategic Plan on Violence Against Children in Schools*. Kampala: MOES.
Ministry of Education and Sports. 2013. *The National Strategy for Girls' Education in Uganda*. Kampala: MOES.
Ministry of Gender, Labour and Social Development. 2018. *Uganda Child Helpline Annual Statistical Report on Cases of Violence Against Children FY2017/18*. Kampala. https://mglsd.go.ug/wp-content/uploads/2020/01/UCHL-ANALYSIS-ANNUAL-REPORT-2017-18.pdf
Ministry of Gender, Labour and Social Development. 2016. *A Handbook for Case Management in Child Protection; A Resource for Multi-Sectoral Case Management*. Kampala. https://www.socialserviceworkforce.org/system/files/resource/files/Handbook%20for%20Case%20Management%20in%20Child%20Protection.pdf
Ministry of Gender, Labour and Social Development. 2007. *Applying National Quality Standards for the Protection, Care and Support of Orphans and Other Vulnerable Children in Uganda*. Kampala: MGLSD.
Ministry of Gender, Labour and Social Development. 2006. *National Child Labour Policy*. Kampala: MGLSD.
Ministry of Gender, Labour and Social Development. 2020. *National Child Policy*. Kampala: MGLSD.
Ministry of Gender, Labour and Social Development. 2004. *National Strategic Programme Plan of Interventions for Orphans and Other Vulnerable Children*, Kampala: MGLSD.
Ministry of Gender, Labour and Social Development. 2004. *The National Orphans and Other Vulnerable Children Policy*. Kampala: MGLSD.
Ministry of Gender, Labour and Social Development. 2016. *The National Policy on the Elimination of Gender-Based Violence in Uganda*. Kampala: MGLSD.
Morris, Matthew C., Chrystyna D. Kouros, Kim Janecek, Rachel Freeman, Alyssa Mielock, and Judy Garber. 2017. "Community-Level Moderators of a School-Based

Childhood Sexual Assault Prevention Program." *Child Abuse & Neglect* 63: 295–306.

Ndagire, Josephine. 2022. "Prospects for Reparations for Victims of Conflict-Related Sexual Violence in Uganda." In *Violence Against Women and Criminal Justice in Africa: Volume II: Sexual Violence and Vulnerability*, edited by Ashwanee Budoo-Scholts and Emma Charlene Lubaale, 201–234. Cham, Switzerland: Palgrave Macmillan.

Nyangoma, Anicent, Florence Ebila, and Julius Omona. 2019. "Child Sexual Abuse and Situational Context: Children's Experiences in Post-Conflict Northern Uganda." *Journal of Child Sexual Abuse* 28(8): 907–926.

Oldfield, Benjamin J., Barbara J. Tinney, and James M. Dodington. 2018. "Partnering with Youth in Community-Based Participatory Research to Address Violence Prevention." *Pediatric Research* 84(2): 155–156.

Olson, Rose McKeon, and Claudia García-Moreno. 2017. "Virginity Testing: A Systematic Review." *Reproductive Health* 14(1): 1–10.

Organization of African Unity (OAU). 1990. *African Charter on the Rights and Welfare of the Child*, CAB/LEG/24.9/49. Last modified June 7, 2002. https://www.refworld.org/docid/3ae6b38c18.html

Parkes, Jenny, Simone Datzberger, Colleen Howell, L. Knight, J. Kasidi, T. Kiwanuka, Rehema Nagawa, Dipak Naker, and Karen Devries. 2020. *Young People, Inequality and Violence During the COVID-19 Lockdown in Uganda*. London. https://discovery.ucl.ac.uk/id/eprint/10111658/1/Young%20People%20COVID%20lockdown%20Uganda.pdf

Qvortrup, Jens. 1985. "Placing Children in the Division of Labour." In *Family and Economy in Modern Society*, Edited by Close, Paul and Collins, Rosemary, 129–145. London: Macmillan.

Republic of Uganda. 2016. *Prohibition of Female Genital Mutilation 2010*. Entebbe: Republic of Uganda.

Republic of Uganda. 2019. *Sexual Offences Bill 2019*. Kampala: Ministry of Justice and Constitutional Affairs.

Republic of Uganda. 2016. *The Children Act (Amendment) 2016*. Kampala: Republic of Uganda.

Republic of Uganda. 1995. *The Constitution of the Republic of Uganda*. Kampala: Republic of Uganda.

Republic of Uganda. 2007. *The Penal Code (Amendment) Act 8 of 2007*. National Legislative Assemblies. Last modified March 19, 2013. https://www.refworld.org/docid/59ca5a694.html

Santaella-Tenorio, Julian, and Daniel Tarantola. 2021. "Youth Violence: Prevention and Control." *American Journal of Public Health* 111(S1): S8–S9.

South Africa. 2005. Children's Act no 38 of 2005. *Government Gazette* (28944).

Sserwanja, Quraish, Joseph Kawuki, and Jean H. Kim. 2021. "Increased Child Abuse in Uganda Amidst COVID-19 Pandemic." *Journal of Paediatrics and Child Health* 57(2): 188–191.

Temmerman, Marleen. 2015. "Research Priorities to Address Violence Against Women and Girls." *The Lancet* 385(9978): e38–e40.

Uganda Bureau of Statistics. 2021. *Uganda National Household Survey, 2019/20*. Kampala: Uganda Bureau of Statistics.

UN Committee on the Rights of the Child (UN-CRC). 2010. *Optional Protocol on the Sale of Children, Child Prostitution and Child Pornography: List of Issues to Be Taken Up in Connection with the Consideration of the Initial Report of Belgium (CRC/C/OPSC/BEL/1)*. Last modified March 7, 2010. https://www.refworld.org/docid/50b3565e2.html

UN Committee on the Rights of the Child (UN-CRC). 2002. *Optional Protocol to the Convention on the Rights of the Child Against the Involvement of Children in Armed Conflict. General Assembly Resolution A/RES/54/263*, 2002b. Last modified Feb 12, 2002. https://childrenandarmedconflict.un.org/tools-for-action/optional-protocol/

UN Committee on the Rights of the Child. *General Comment No. 13 (2011): The Right of the Child to Freedom from All Forms of Violence*, 18 April 2011, CRC/C/GC/13. 2011. Last modified April 19, 2011. https://www.refworld.org/docid/4e6da4922.html

UN Committee on the Rights of the Child. 2006. *General Comment No. 8 (2006): The Right of the Child to Protection from Corporal Punishment and Other Cruel or Degrading Forms of Punishment (Arts. 19; 28, Para. 2; and 37, inter alia)*. Last modified March 6, 2007. Available at: https://www.refworld.org/docid/460bc7772.html.

United Nations Children's Emergency Fund (UNICEF). 2020. *Protecting children from violence in the time of COVID-19: Disruptions in prevention and response services*. Geneva: UNICEF.

United Nations, Department of Economic and Social Affairs, Population Division (UNDESA). 2020. *World population prospects 2019: Highlights* (ST/ESA/SER.A/423). United Nations, Department of Economic and Social Affairs, Population Division.

United Nations. 1989. *Convention on the Rights of the Child. Treaty Series, 1577, 3*.

Vohito, Sonia. 2017. "Violence Against Children in Africa." In *Violence Against Children*, edited by Lenzer, Gertrude, 104–124. New York: Routledge.

Wall, John. 2022. "From Childhood Studies to Childism: Reconstructing the Scholarly and Social Imaginations." *Children's Geographies* 20(3): 257–270.

Wandera, Stephen Ojiambo, Kelly Clarke, Louise Knight, Elizabeth Allen, Eddy Walakira, Sophie Namy, Dipak Naker, and Karen Devries. 2017. "Violence Against Children Perpetrated by Peers: A Cross-Sectional School-Based Survey in Uganda." *Child Abuse & Neglect* 68: 65–73.

Wells, Karen. 2017. "Children's Experiences of Sexual Violence, Psychological Trauma, Death, and Injury in War." *Conflict, Violence and Peace* 11: 19.

World Health Organization. 2014. *Global Status Report on Violence Prevention 2014*. Geneva: WHO.

World Health Organization. 2020. *Global Status Report on Preventing Violence Against Children*. Geneva: WHO.

Chapter 6

Malleability of Innocence

Reimagining Justice in the Indian Juvenile Justice System

Anusha Iyer

INTRODUCTION

Using the amendment in the Juvenile Justice (Care and Protection of Children Act, 2015) (henceforth JJA) as a case example, this chapter demonstrates how innocence as a malleable rhetorical device provides differential treatment to children in conflict with the law (CCL) in the Indian society. This amendment in the legislation came into being after a brutal gangrape of a 23-year-old woman (pseudonym being Nirbhaya) on a late December evening in the capital city of New Delhi in 2012. The accused included five adults and a juvenile who was seventeen years and six months old. Police investigations revealed that the accused juvenile was responsible for leading the goriest acts of violence during the crime. However, because of a mere technicality of not having completed eighteen years of age on the day of commission of the offence, it was decided that the accused youth be tried as a juvenile in the Indian legal system. The aftermath of this incident led to a strong outcry from social activists, feminist groups, politicians, and even the general public, against the trial of the accused as a juvenile and not as an adult. As a quick-fix response to these mass protests and repeated media trials, the amendment in JJA 2015 was introduced allowing for children in the age group of sixteen to eighteen years to be treated as adults (conditionally) in the justice system. This amendment marked a punitive turn for the Indian juvenile justice system as it retreated from the reformative ideology of rehabilitating *all* children and instead, limiting it to specific sections of the child population.

More specifically, I describe how innocence and malleability, as conceptualized in the Juvenile Justice Act, operate in the service of other political aims that are rooted in colonial histories of subjectification and social ordering.

The construction of childhood as innocent-malleable invisibilizes the colonial history of the justice system in India and further aids in reinforcing existing social hierarchies in current times. By bringing forth the erasure of the colonial history of the juvenile reformatory and its implications on the current juvenile justice system in India, I argue for a justice system for juveniles that moves beyond moral conceptions of childhood as innocence and delinked from malleability. By unpacking the various possibilities foreclosed by the political mobilization of innocence, I will argue for a justice system that goes beyond moral liberal ideas of innocence. In addition to pushing the boundaries of the Indian juvenile justice system, such a line of questioning will also help in problematizing the childhood category that is essentially contoured by innocence and plasticity. This chapter is divided into four major sections. The first section provides a general overview of the Juvenile Justice Act, which is the legal instrument authorizing the various tenets of the Indian juvenile justice system. The latter part of this section will briefly shed light on the debates surrounding the amendment of 2015. The second section provides the background literature on the postcolonial framework of "juvenile periphery." The malleability of childhood as presumed by colonizers in the juvenile periphery is a critical framework within which I will situate the amendment of JJA 2016. This section will describe how the malleability of childhood was used for the colonial project of civilizing and modernizing native populations, but also to maintain and reproduce a specific social order along the lines of age, class, and caste. The third section delves into the political mobilization of innocence especially focusing on its use through the category of childhood. By interpreting innocence through an ethico-moral register, this section will show how the presence/absence of innocence equals an ability/inability to be reformed and hence a right to childhood. It discusses the implications of the Juvenile Justice Act, 2015, on real children by introducing the processes of "prolonging" and "suspending" childhoods. The last conclusion section argues for constructing the juvenile justice system in India beyond the purview of innocence.

THE JUVENILE JUSTICE SYSTEM IN INDIA

The JJS in India is currently being governed by the Juvenile Justice (Care and Protection of Children) Act, 2015 (henceforth JJA). Beginning from its first centralized legislation that was passed in 1986, this act has gone through several amendments and revisions at different points in time. Through all its versions, this legal instrument covered two distinct yet interrelated groups of vulnerable children in India: Children in Conflict with Law, or CCL, and Children in Need of Care and Protection, or CNCP. Legally, a CCL is defined as "a child who is alleged or found to have committed an offence and who has not completed eighteen years of age on the date of commission of such offence" (The Gazette of India 2015, 3) Missing children, runaway children, orphans, abandoned children, street children, children forced into begging, and similar groups of vulnerable children are broadly included under the category of CNCP (The Gazette of India 2015, 3).

Here, I focus on Children in Conflict with Law (or CCLs) by first examining the construction of the CCL figure through a postcolonial framework and then its likely impact on the children who are found to be in conflict with the law. The 2015 amendment of JJA focuses on the minimum age of criminal responsibility, or MACR. The minimum age of criminal responsibility (MACR) is the minimum age below which an individual is deemed incapable of committing a criminal offence. The MACR follows from the principle of *doli incapax* (a Latin legal maxim that roughly translates to "incapable of doing harm" thus providing legal immunity to children below different ages in different countries across the world). In the 2015 legislation, the JJA reduced the minimum age of criminal responsibility for children from eighteen years to sixteen years for a specific group of cases legally termed as "heinous offences." According to the Indian Penal Code (Indian Penal Code, or IPC, is the official criminal code of India that covers all substantive aspects of criminal law), "heinous offences" are those offences for which the minimum punishment is imprisonment for seven years or more and broadly includes crimes related to rape, murder, and human trafficking.

This definition means that if a child between the age of sixteen and eighteen years of age commits a "heinous offence," then based on certain conditions, the child can be treated as an adult in the criminal system instead of being sent to the juvenile justice system. These conditions are decided by the Juvenile Justice Board (JJB). This is the point where the essentialized conception of childhood as innocence comes into play. The JJB is a district-level bench of three individuals who possess the judicial and magisterial powers to assess cases and pass orders related to CCLs. In the case of "heinous offences," the JJB conducts a preliminary assessment to assess the child's "mental and physical capacity to commit such (an) offence, ability to understand the consequences of the offence and the circumstances in which (the CCL) allegedly committed the offence" (The Gazette of India 2015, 13). It is important to note here that the assessment is testing and looking for "innocence as ignorance" conception of childhood. Childhood is not merely a distinct period of life marked by age but is also formulated as a social construct that maintains its identity through the performance of innocence (Garlen 2019). In common parlance, the concept of innocence has various connotations of purity, ignorance, freedom from moral wrong, and absence of guilt or sin. Specific to childhoods, innocence implies the absence of all kinds of adult knowledge such as those related to violence, sin, and sexuality (Garlen 2019). In the Indian adult justice system, the term "innocent" means that the offender has been proven to not have committed/not been involved in a criminal act, usually because of a lack of evidence. But in the Indian juvenile justice system, the child is declared as "innocent" not because of "lack of guilt" but as a result of the absence of "adult" knowledge such as the nature and consequences of the crime. Thus, the boundaries of innocence for the CCL are drawn by the lines of obliviousness. It is only the figure of the innocent child that enables "ignorance" of the criminal act's consequences to be used as a means to judge the intentions of the accused.

Depending on the results of this assessment, the CCL is either considered as a "child" and goes through the processes of the juvenile system or is treated as an "adult" in the legal system. In the former case, the CCL could be sent to the Observation Home/Special Home (juvenile institutions in India) or can be released on bail or payment of fine. In the latter scenario, the case is forwarded to the Children's Court where a series of further assessments are undertaken. Children's Court is a special court established for the protection of children under the Commissions for Protection of Child Rights Act, 2005, or a Special Court under the Protection of Children from Sexual Offences Act, 2012. If the child is proven to be innocent there, they are sent back to the juvenile justice system or else the CCL undergoes an adult trial. If the child is still found to be *not innocent* of the "heinous offence," then they are sent to a "place of safety" (instead of a juvenile institution) until they reach twenty-one years of age (The Gazette of India 2015, 15). (Note that I am using the term "not innocent" here instead of guilty because they have different connotations. While "guilty" seems to be based on proof of evidence, the term non-innocent denotes a moral stance wherein the knowledge of the criminal act and the criminal act itself is distanced from each other). After this time, the Children's Court evaluates if the child in the "place of safety" has "undergone reformative changes and if the child can be a contributing member of the society" (The Gazette of India 2015, 15). This evaluation determines if the child is released or transferred to a jail in the adult criminal system. Although, the minimum age of criminal responsibility has been historically debated in the Indian legal context, JJA 2015 is particularly critical as it not only violates international mandates such as the United Nations Convention on the Rights of the Child but also emerges as a band-aid response to mass protests in response to the Nirbhaya case.

While this move appealed to the general public at large, several legal scholars pointed out the ideological discrepancies in this law. Scholars have pointed out how this amendment is a violation of Article 21 of the Indian Constitution that accords "equality before the law" and "life or personal liberty." The reduction in the age of criminal responsibility is also against the United Nations Convention on the Rights of the Child that prescribes child-friendly approaches and emphasizes dealing with cases in the best interests of children. During the legal proceedings of the 2012 rape case, some lawyers argued that it is not fair to reduce the age of criminal responsibility to sixteen years if the same child is legally not allowed to drive, vote, or marry (Kumar 2019, 127). Concerns were also raised with respect to the arbitrariness of the assessment and the level of power vested in the hands of the JJB that decides the future of a child. Although the JJB consults with psychologists during this process, it is not as straightforward to determine the ability of the child to understand the crime and its consequences (Singh 2019, 16).

Building on these legal perspectives making a case against JJA amendment, I would like to draw attention to the logics upon which the JJS, and specifically this act, has been built. The figure of the CCL as imagined by the colonizers was a critical construction within this logic. It was in and through the figure of the CCL that other perverse goals of the colonial civilizing mission were often enacted. Questioning and pushing these foundations will aid in developing a justice system, for CCLs in contemporary times that does not strictly rely on the conception of childhood as innocence.

THE JUVENILE PERIPHERY

In order to unpack the implications of the amendment in current times, it is pertinent to trace the logics of the broader prison system and the juvenile justice system, in particular, using a postcolonial lens. Using the theoretical framework of the "juvenile periphery," this section will review the colonial history of producing the figure of the native Indian child as a site of reform, discipline, and modernity simultaneously. Broadly speaking, the "juvenile periphery" is the set of experimental and institutional spaces that were utilized for producing knowledge regarding natives, race, and civilization (Sen 2004). This abstract zone between the "modern" life of the colonizers and the "native" (read as uncivilized) life of the colonized consisted of practices like flogging of criminals; institutions, such as Borstal schools; and legislations, such as the Reformatory Schools Act (Sen 2005). According to the colonial administrators, the native child figure was simultaneously constructed as both incorrigible and redeemable and the colonizers deployed either of these approaches depending upon different social markers of age, class, caste, and gender.

The physical space as well as the administrative structures of the prison system during the colonial era functioned to constantly regulate the bodies within. For instance, it has been observed that the prison system for adults was used to create a labour pool for the British Raj, conduct experiments for producing knowledge and ultimately advance the civilizing mission (Arnold 1994, 159). Scholars of colonial prisons also state how colonizers concluded that producing virtuous citizens from the criminal classes of the Indian society was almost impossible. Unlike the Benthamian perspective of moral reform for prisoners, the British rulers did not consider the native population to be "citizens capable of moral reform" (Waits 2017, 19). Connected to this notion of the unteachable Indian adult was an idealized notion of childhood that made the colonial civilizing mission not only possible but also expedient. The theoretical framework of the "juvenile periphery" thus provides a lens for examining how the innocent–malleability dyad continues to construct the figure of the child in conflict with law as a discriminatory modernization project.

Childhood was viewed as an unfinished transitional state on the way to adulthood, normality, full socialization, and humanness. Additionally, colonizers viewed the child as an inferior and weak but usable version of the fully productive, fully performing, human being who is capable of owning the modern world. Since the colonial society constructed the evolutionary continuity between premodern and modern societies through the social inculcation of the native child (Nandy 1984, 364), this child figure bore the burden of civilization as it transitions to a fuller adult being. Therefore, the native adult was assumed to be incorrigible while the native child still held the potential of being reformed, and consequently civilized. It is the latter figure that is central to the analysis here as it lies at the core of the juvenile justice system.

This imaginary zone of "juvenile periphery" is characterized by a fundamental difference of 'progress' between the modern colonizer and the native population and was thus instrumental for colonizers to bridge the gap between the metropole and the colony. The real children found at this periphery were in a unique position as they were located at the margin of both the adult and modern world, thus emerging as a perfect site for testing different kinds of social models. Unlike the adult, this child figure was a malleable entity and held the potential of leaving the "native" behind and becoming modern. The colonizers viewed this as an opportunity to recuperate modernity, that is, civilization through the figure of the child (Sen 2005) making it a lucrative site for "experimentation, reform and modernization" (Sen 2004). In the process, a series of experiments on different figures of the child, such as the delinquent child, the deviant child, the educated child, the princely child, was carried out through legislations like the Reformatory Schools Act and institutions like the juvenile reformatories and Borstal schools. Borstal schools were detention centres for youth offenders, especially adolescents, aimed at reforming young delinquents in the colonial era.

In addition to the pre-conceived notions of malleability, the Western notions of innocence associated with childhood also became key to these experiments. The figure of the White child that was constructed as innocent and ignorant served as a benchmark against which actual native children were often compared. Within the colonial civilizing mission, there were opposing views of whether the real native children possessed the innocent nature like the White child of the metropole or could these children be nurtured into a state of innocence from their native precocious state. For instance, the colonizers experimented on separating the delinquent child from the family to assess whether the child was born with criminal attributes as "nature" or can the delinquent child be "nurtured" into a productive member of the society. Such an experiment was used to test if the separation of the child from the family into the reformatory could preserve its innocence or not (Sen 2005, 44). These experiments were conducted to prove that the native child category is capable of reform and hence malleable. More importantly, the project was used to test whether the child is capable of preserving, developing, or subverting the element of innocence. Thus, the accomplishment of the colonial project did not merely rely on the outcome of a modern native adult from the native child. In fact, the experiments carried out from 1850 to 1945 was instrumental in producing knowledge about the ability of native populations to be civilized through the innocence–malleability dyad embodied in the native child.

Social Order of Juvenile Periphery

All the experiments in the periphery resulted in two strands of consequences, both of which were equally worthy for the civilizing mission. In the more "successful" experiments where the native child was modernized, its innocence was established akin to the White child of the metropole. Such experiments supported the notion that White children, and native children were essentially the same – innocent and malleable and thus could be part of the modernization project. On the other hand, the "failure" of the experiments was useful to validate the incorrigible nature of the Indian child, and by extension, the uncivilized attribute of the whole native population (Sen 2005, 160). Although such experiments failed in the actual sense, that is, the native Indian child remained uncivilized, it still implied "success" since it verified that the native population is beyond reform.

The bifurcated set of results as "success" and "failure" was used to assign innocence and malleability differentially to different sections of the child population. The assumption of the child figure as innocent and plastic was instrumentalized by the colonizers toward ensuring a specific social order along the lines of class, caste, and age within Indian society. With respect to other matters such as those pertaining to child labour, it has been noted that the arbitrariness regarding the boundaries of age imposed by the colonial state was founded upon caste and region-specific "cultural logics" to justify various exceptions to the law (Balagopalan 2017, 35). This historical tracing discovered that the so-called universal child category of the metropole was broken down in the colony to accommodate the cultural particularities of native children (Balagopalan 2017, 35). Hence, the colonial project rationalized the need for a biological age and a moral age for different sections of the native child population depending on the issue. In the case of delinquency, it was the use of age as a disciplinary tool in tandem with the pre-conceived notions about certain Indian communities that aided in exacerbating the prevalent social inequalities.

Toward the end of the 1870s, the upper edge of childhood as a distinct life-stage was being highly debated by various inspectors who oversaw the juvenile institutions. The administrative officers appointed in the metropole were debating the rationale for creating separate justice systems for children. It was the Reformatory Schools Act of 1897 that legally stipulated fifteen years as the upper age limit for admission into the juvenile reformatory (The Reformatory Schools Act 1897). This act brought the focus of the delinquency debates to older children or adolescents and not the entire age range of childhood. On the one hand, the Jails Committee of 1922 recommended that criminals between the age of sixteen and twenty-one years should not be sent to adult jails. On the other hand, native experts like SC Contractor, the Chief Inspector of Certified Schools in Madras, believed that adolescents' criminal habits could still be rectified to turn the individual into "a useful and honest citizen" (Sen 2005, 76). At the root of these differing views was the plasticity of the child figure to be geared toward modernization and civilization. The central concern was to determine the age of admission into the reformatory based on the expiration of the plasticity of childhood which is termed as the "ceiling of childhood" (Sen 2005, 75). These debates highlighted "the faint line between adolescence and delinquency in the Indian reformatory" (Sen 2005, 73). Resultantly, the significance of the category of adolescence increased as it could maintain this imprecision between criminality and innocence that could be manipulated and moulded to fit the civilizing mission of the colonizers.

Colonizers distinguished two different kinds of CCL figures: one that is biologically or genetically flawed and hence irreformable and one that is socially flawed and hence reformable (Sen 2005). These two categories were identified as "deviant" and "delinquent," respectively. The former child figure was born "deviant" thus proving its native nature of being precocious. This deviance was not particularly linked to a criminal act but the presumption of native children lacking innocence altogether. As a result, this child did not have the ability to be reformed into a future modern adult. The latter category of delinquent children had an opportunity to have their innocence redeemed within the reformatory. The delinquent children still had the potential to be moulded into modern adults by the influence of the state. Emerging from this distinction was a presumption that some kinds of native children were more "soft" or malleable than others (Sen 2005, 62). Even within the category of adolescence, the innocence–malleability dyad actualized itself along the axes of caste and class.

Criminal Tribes, or CTs, were a group of communities that were assumed to be "born criminals" by their mere association with a specific caste group. Individuals belonging to these groups were known to possess and embody criminality as an attribute, even without committing an offence. Some of these tribes included Sansi, Pakhiwara, Harni, and Bhat. For instance, W.F. Thomas of the Chingleput Reformatory had a circulating register of thieving castes and strongly believed that criminality is biologically transmitted from an adult to the child (Sen 2005, 58). A child that belonged to a CT family was officially excluded from the reformatory because they were assumed to be incorrigible. The urban equivalent of the Criminal Tribe groups was the "habitual offender" as constructed by J.D. Gordon in Mysore. According to him, certain children in the urban areas nurtured criminal habits because of idleness and indifference to the state authorities. As a miniature replica of his parent, the "habitual" child was a small adult without "good conduct and industry" (Sen 2005, 60). These were also left out of the colonial reformatory because they were assumed to be beyond reform.

The other CCL figure emerged from the middle-class population whose innocence was also naturalized and could thus be recuperated toward a modernizing end. For example, the 1894 annual report of the Chingleput Reformatory School describes juveniles in this reformatory as having, "inherited a more or less absolute want of moral sense which was aggravated by poverty, wicked associates and other disadvantages which the lowest classes of people are subject to" (Balagopalan 2017, 30). Stating that some criminals were "different," J. Campbell Forrester of the Tanjore Borstal Association recommended Borstal regimes for the redeemable group of children. The middle-class Indians were using Borstal schools to police the boundaries of class (Sen 2005, 77) by not only sending middle-class children to these Borstal schools but also introducing class-appropriate behaviour supposedly associated with the notion of a normative innocent childhood. Key to such practices was the exposure of the adolescent offender to "industrial training, primary education and games" otherwise absent in other kinds of juvenile reformatories and surely the adult jails (Sen 2005, 33). This presumption of a certain group of adolescents being capable of reform, through access to education and training, led to political and material consequences for the actual children who were found to be violating the law. Hence, the ideas and logics of the colonial reformatory functioned to preserve the innocence of the "non-habitual" and "delinquent" child figure that was mostly an adolescent belonging to the upper class and caste groups. The next section will show, using the social order of the juvenile periphery, how the 2016 amendment politically invokes the innocence–malleability dyad toward creating a divisive society.

THE POLITICAL MOBILIZATION OF INNOCENCE

In this section, I present the moral and ethical dimensions of the liberal concept of "innocence" in order to expose the structural and historical underpinnings that it renders invisible. By interpreting the concept of innocence as implied in the 2016 amendment of the act through an ethico-moral register, this section will demonstrate that the presence/absence of innocence translates directly into an access/exclusion from childhood. Furthermore, it also discusses the implications of the Juvenile Justice Act, 2015, on real children through the processes of "prolonging" and "suspending" childhoods by bringing forth the interlinkages of innocence, reformability, and participation in society (to be detailed later).

In order to understand the political work of innocence, we must begin from a larger body of literature that critiques liberal values and thought itself. For example, Wendy Brown tracks the complexity of "tolerance" closely tied with power structures by examining its "political deployments . . . as historically and culturally specific discourses of power with strong rhetorical functions" (Brown 2009, 9). Similarly, Berlant interrogates the emotional complex of 'compassion' to argue that this moral value serves "as a social and aesthetic technology" (Berlant 2014, 5). Using a similar framework, I will reveal the political workings of the liberal conception of innocence to bring forth the structural and historical inequalities that the 2016 amendment potentially reproduces.

Such an analysis has already been attempted for innocence that calls for opening the "political, moral and affective grammars beyond innocence" (Tiktin 2017, 578). Through the four figures of the child, the refugee, the trafficked victim, and the animal, Tiktin shows how the concept of innocence maps itself on to structures and institutions thus producing certain political possibilities and impossibilities. A new politic gets formed and another gets dismantled by instilling and redrawing the contours of innocence upon existing social, political and economic systems through the logic of expansion (Ticktin 2017, 584). In other words, new figures and new territories of innocence are constantly discovered to shift the focus away from the actual political debates at stake. Conversely, the logic of expansion automatically renders certain spaces and figures to be left out of the discourse of innocence as well. Thus, innocence serves as a socially constructed rhetorical tool that has the potential to create differentials of power. Historically, childhood innocence has served as the perfect alibi to violent acts of erasure by deliberately overlooking its violent actors (Ramjewan and Garlen 2020, 283), wherein it is guised in the language of ignorance, protection, and vulnerability. Under the garb of ignorance of the criminal act committed by the child and the protection of women (refer to Nirbhaya case at the beginning of this chapter), the Indian juvenile justice system is politically marked by innocence. Through the amendment of 2016 that reduced the age of criminal responsibility from eighteen years to sixteen years the figure of the CCL in this age group has been rendered as a liminal zone wherein innocence marginalizes the children from lower castes and classes implicated in the juvenile justice system. As discussed earlier, the treatment of the child in conflict with the law between the age of sixteen and eighteen years is decided by the assessment of the JJB that tests "the capacity of such child to commit and understand the consequences of the alleged offence." In other *heinousness* of the crime and its consequences which is perceived to be adult knowledge. The presence or absence of knowledge of the criminal act determines whether the child be treated as a juvenile or an adult (refer to section on the juvenile justice in India earlier). Classifying certain kind of knowledge as adult is rooted in the construction of childhood as innocence. In common parlance, innocence is defined as a state of "not knowing" or "blamelessness." The etymology of the word innocence as in- + noscere i.e., "not to know," is significant in this context (Ticktin 2017, 578). The boundaries of childhood were marked by specific kinds of knowledge such asthose related to violence, sin, and sexuality (Garlen, 2019). In contradiction to the earlier Calvinist doctrine of infant depravity, Enlightenment philosophers like John Locke and Jean-Jacques Rousseau were formulating childhood as a site of innocence and purity (Bernstein 2011, 4). Over time, the social construct of childhood was naturalized and justified its foundation of innocence as ignorance, characterized by the absence of all kinds of adult knowledge.

With the 2016 amendment, the assessment by the JJB is invoking childhood marked by the "innocence as ignorance" conception. The state of innocence was not merely an absence of knowledge but "an active state of repelling knowledge" (Bernstein 2011, 6). The boundaries of innocence for the CCL are drawn by the absence of adult knowledge—knowledge of the nature and consequences of the crime, but also through the active repulsion of this knowledge, made possible through the psychological assessment introduced in the amendment. In this way, the socially construed meaning of childhood allows the judgement of children in the justice system not on a legal basis proven through evidence but through the ethico-moral concept of innocence as ignorance construction of childhood. The sorting of children into the juvenile and adult justice system is not a liberal humanitarian response to sexual violence against women. Rather, the 2016 amendment is a violent colonial technology that manufactures an imaginary line between corrigible and incorrigible bodies through the political rhetoric of innocence in contemporary times. Following the subjectification of bodies and social ordering of the juvenile periphery of the colony, the 2016 amendment has thus created two distinct experiences for the children in conflict with law.

"PROLONGING" AND "SUSPENDING" CHILDHOODS

Here, I will finally discuss the implications of these CCL figures on the real children who are/ will be in conflict with law in contemporary Indian society. This will be done by superimposing the structures of the "delinquent" and "deviant" child figures from the colonial period on to the actual children accused under the current juvenile justice system and through a moral reading of innocence as implied within the 2016 amendment. The state focuses its efforts on specific groups of children with the goal of reintegrating them into the society. Section 20 (1) of the JJA 2016 states that

> "when the child in conflict with the law attains the age of twenty-one years and is yet to complete the term of stay, the Children´s Court shall provide for a follow up by the probation officer or the District Child Protection Unit or a social worker or by itself, as required, to evaluate if such child has undergone reformative changes and if the child can be a contributing member of the society"

(The Gazette of India 2015, 15). In case the child does not prove to be a contributing member of the society, then "the child shall complete the remainder of his term in a jail" (The Gazette of India 2015, 15). By focusing my attention on the phrase ". . . if the child can be a contributing member of the society," I will interrogate how the innocence–malleability dyad plays out on the CCL. In the process of declaring certain children innocent, the assessment presumes and determines the malleability of childhood. By interpreting innocence as a rhetorical political tool instead of an evidence-based proof, it becomes evident how the state mobilizes childhood innocence (as ignorance) to ultimately determine contributing and productive members of society.

The first category is the child that is found to be "innocent" and is therefore treated as a juvenile in the legal system. Accordingly, the innocent child is sent to an institution within the Indian juvenile justice system such as the Observation Home or the Special Home and has access to rehabilitative services like education, skilling, and therapy/counselling. Concomitant to being declared innocent, the CCL is given a chance to be reformed. Through the 2016 amendment of reducing the criminal age from eighteen years to sixteen years, some children who are in conflict with the law have a right to be part of childhood and hence given an opportunity to be moulded into future productive adult citizens. This category of the innocent CCL experiences a "prolonging" of childhood or a state wherein participation in childhood, as constructed through the lenses of innocence and malleability, can be unhindered and sustained.

On the other hand, a child who is not innocent of knowledge and therefore aware of the crime and its consequences is considered as an "adult" in the legal system. The not-innocent child undergoes "adult" criminal processes like trials at Children's Courts, and if they are found to be guilty, they are sent to a "place of safety" until the age of twenty-one. This "place of safety" is basically an institution which is neither a Special Home of the juvenile justice system nor a prison of the adult justice system wherein their childhood experiences can be "suspended." This means that even in the best case scenarios, such children are reformed in isolation, and in the worst case scenarios, they are sent to an adult jail at the age of twenty-one. Placing these children in a "place of safety" excludes them from the innocence of childhood and the potential productivity of adulthood.

The vaguely set age markers and the arbitrary assessment by the JJB mirror an institutionalization of the differentiated malleability systems of the colonial era. Like the adolescents of the colonial era who were sent to Borstal schools to receive special training, the amendment of the 2016 allows only a specific age group to be able to access the juvenile justice system. Furthermore, by excluding lower caste groups from the Indian colonial reformatory and by including the middle-class Indians, not all children were deemed worthy of the colonial project of modernity (Sen 2005, 76). In the same vein, only some children within this age group can access rehabilitation and deemed fit to be a "productive member of the society." The Indian JJS accordingly creates two levels of hierarchies. First, this amended Act is creating age-based hierarchies as it is applicable only for a specific age group of sixteen to eighteen years old. This amendment is attempting to determine what Sen termed as the "ceiling of childhood" in the colonial era. The site of adolescence that is described as the process from childhood to adulthood (Sen 2005, 7) qualifies this contingency that has been reinforced through this amendment. Moreover, the logic of considering certain bodies more malleable than others indicates a control akin to the creation of colonial caste and class-based subjectivities. Moulding native children, considered as reformable, into modern adults is paralleled within this amendment, goal of which is to construct contributing productive members of society from the CCL. In the colonial era, the bifurcation of children into the juvenile and adult justice system was determined on the basis of phrenological aspects or caste nativity. What would it mean for children to be classified as innocent and "not innocent"; based on the assessment of the JJB? Will these also follow the colonial era patterns of adultifying vulnerable populations like children belonging to lower caste and classes of society, and thus exclude them from contributing to society? Or will it create a different kind of divisive system, say through religion? This grave step holds the dangerous potential to reproduce the class and caste inequalities of Indian society by providing differential access to not just childhood but also membership to society. Irrespective of the social hierarchy it may produce or reproduce, what stays constant is the site of childhood that enables the creation of this divisive society.

CONCLUSION

In this chapter, I have illustrated how the construction of the native Indian child as innocent and malleable in the service of the civilizing project has been instrumentalized as a political tool in the 2016 amendment of the Juvenile Justice Act in India. The consequence of constructing the CCL through the innocent–malleability dyad is two-fold. First, it overlooks the structural and historical inequalities that construct the contemporary figure of the CCL. Such an erasure absolves the violent actors of the colonial era and assumes that the CCL is an ahistorical, naturalized being predisposed to heinous crimes. Second, it has the effect of creating a discriminatory society due to vague determinations of innocence in the act made possible through legal assessments by the JJB. By creating disparate experiences of prolonging and suspending childhoods, the Indian JJS is creating a segregated society that not only decides their inclusion into the category of childhood but also their participation and productivity in society. Through the political working of innocence, the 2016 amendment not only obscures the reproduction of the colonial history of divisiveness but also overlooks the moral-ethical conflation of innocence with evidence-based legal judgments.

Given that such narrow and romanticized conceptions of childhood can lead to marginalization of specific children, I wonder if it is possible to imagine a justice system beyond innocence. Irrespective of evidence or knowledge of the crime or even the nature of the crime, can we conceptualize a justice system that does not merely rely on ethico-moral concepts like innocence? As we witnessed, innocence is fluid and has been used as a political tool toward the erasure of historical and structural inequalities foundational to the Juvenile Justice system. This especially affects children since the category of childhood itself is founded upon the abstract concept of innocence. Perhaps it is time to rethink the ideas of justice beyond binaries of innocence–guilty and reformability–nonmalleability to develop an Indian JJS that takes into account colonial histories and the existing hierarchical social inequalities. Such a justice system would require that we perceive the children beyond this innocence–malleability dyad delinked from their potential usefulness for the future.

REFERENCES

1897. "The Reformatory Schools Act." *Indian Kanoon.* https://indiankanoon.org/doc/1551389/.
Arnold, David. "The colonial prison: Power, knowledge and penology in nineteenth-century India." *Subaltern studies 8* (1994): 148–87.
Balagopalan, Sarada. "Colonial modernity and the 'child figure': Reconfiguring the multiplicity in 'multiple childhoods'." In *Childhoods in India*, edited by T.S. Saraswathi, Shailaja Menon and Ankur Madan, pp. 23–43. Routledge, 2017.
Berlant, Lauren. "Introduction Compassion (and withholding)." In *Compassion*, edited by Lauren Berlant, pp. 1–13. Routledge, 2014.
Bernstein, Robin. "Introduction." In *Racial Innocence*. New York University Press, pp. 1–70. 2011.
Brown, Wendy. "Regulating aversion." In *Regulating Aversion*. Princeton University Press, pp 1-25, 2009.
Garlen, Julie C. "Interrogating innocence: 'Childhood' as exclusionary social practice." *Childhood* 26, no. 1 (2019): 54–67.
Kumar, Shailesh. "Shifting epistemology of juvenile justice in India." *Contexto Internacional* 41 (2019): 113–140.
Nandy, Ashis. "Reconstructing childhood: A critique of the ideology of adulthood." *Alternatives* 10, no. 3 (1984): 359–375.
Ramjewan, Neil, and Julie C. Garlen. "Growing out of childhood innocence." *Curriculum Inquiry* 50, no. 4 (2020): 281–290.
Sen, Satadru. "A juvenile periphery: The geographies of literary childhood in colonial Bengal." *Journal of Colonialism and Colonial History* 5, no. 1 (2004).
Sen, Satadru. *Colonial Childhoods: The Juvenile Periphery of India 1850–1945.* Anthem Press, 2005.
Singh, Deepak. "An analysis of section 15 of the Juvenile Justice Act, 2015." *Christ ULJ* 8 (2019): 1.
The Gazette of India. 2015. "The Juvenile Justice (Care and Protection of Children) Act, 2015." *CARA.* December 31. http://cara.nic.in/PDF/JJ%20act%202015.pdf.
Ticktin, Miriam. "A world without innocence." *American Ethnologist* 44, no. 4 (2017): 577590.
Waits, Mira Rai. "Carceral Capital: The Prison Industrial Complex in Colonial India 1." In *Across Space and Time*, edited by Patrick Haughey, 19–46. Routledge, 2017.

Chapter 7

Narrating Trauma, Subverting Innocence

Challenging Normative Childhood Representations in Bapsi Sidhwa's Cracking India

Mayurika Chakravorty

Bapsi Sidhwa's *Cracking India* (1991), set against the tumultuous history of Partition of the Indian subcontinent in 1947, is distinct within the corpus of Partition literature, as it foregrounds children's experiences as well as the children's perspective in the narration of the traumatic communal violence and forced migration in the wake of Partition. Ascribing rare narratorial agency to a girl child, during a traumatic moment in the personal and national history of the Indian subcontinent, the novel draws into sharp focus the connection between narration, memory, trauma, and innocence, making it an important site of analysis. This chapter will focus on how, in addition to the remarkable centrality of the child's perspective, the text problematizes the conceptualization of a unitary or universal notion of childhood marked by innocence and patronizing protectionism. Focusing on the experience of trauma and its literary representation, it interrogates the assumptions around childhood as a stage of human life that hovers between nostalgia and utopian optimism (Jenks 2005) and one that is often enshrined as a state of incorruptible innocence marked by its separation from the corrupted adult realm. Specifically, it explores how sexual and communal violence leading to individual and national trauma, when filtered through the eyes of children, disrupts and deliberately subverts the tropes of innocence associated with childhood. I argue that the subversion of innocence through the stark representation of violence in the novel provides a contrapuntal approach to the "aestheticizing impulse of the nation-state" (Pandey 2001, 4) that bolsters larger nationalist claims and denials. In addition, owing to the inherently gendered nature of Partition violence, I discuss how the subversion of innocence accentuates the intersection between childhood and gender, as girlhood is subjected to assumptions of maturation and therefore denied the traditionally hallowed cloak of childhood innocence that is more readily bestowed on boyhood. The intersection between childhood and gender is also concurrently mediated by the categories of religion, class, and caste in the novel.

In the following sections, I discuss the critical role of literature in narrating the Partition violence and trauma, situate *Cracking India* within the corpus of Partition literature, and bring into focus the lack of representation of children's experience of violence and trauma of Partition. I also analyze how the narrative subverts the notion of childhood innocence by positing the young protagonist, Lenny, as a "knowing" and "desiring" child who transgresses into domains of knowledge and "places [not] for children" (Rasmussen 2004, 155). Furthermore, I shall explore the nature and effect of the violence and the ensuing trauma on the children during Partition and how it leads to (premature) maturation. Together, these narratives of violence represent a chorus of children's voices hitherto rendered silent in mainstream narratives.

WRITING PARTITION

Cracking India is set against the background of the Partition of the Indian subcontinent, which marked a moment of catastrophic rupture—"a violent, fratricidal sundering of a country" (Menon and Bhasin 1998, 4). In 1947, India gained independence after almost two hundred years of British rule, but the subcontinent was divided along religious lines into two independent nation states—India and Pakistan. Dividing the subcontinent involved the partitioning of the two demographically diverse states or provinces of Punjab in the west and Bengal in the east. Hindus, Muslims, and Sikhs, who had lived side by side for centuries and were ethnically, linguistically, and culturally contiguous and similarly were torn apart because of their religious differences. Most egregiously, the separation was executed in haste and in an arbitrary manner. Lord Mountbatten, the last Viceroy of India, brought in Sir Cyril Radcliffe, a barrister from London who had notoriously never travelled east of Paris, to draw the borders between India and Pakistan. Sir Cyril was put up in a hotel in Lahore with enlarged maps of the border districts. Using an outdated census, he carved out the border without even once visiting the land that he was dividing, literally cracking India. People who had lived in their ancestral land for centuries were displaced overnight and became refugees. About 12 million people crossed the borders and more than 1 million people perished (Butalia 2000, 3). Besides displacement and forced migration, Partition was also marked by unprecedented and horrific communal violence that erupted between the Hindus and Sikhs, on the one side, and the Muslims, on the other.

Commensurate with the tremendous impact of Partition, there is a voluminous body of writing on Partition in the form of newspaper and media reports, official records, agreements, and historical texts, as well as private papers, memoirs, and autobiographies. However, scholars have pointed out that, while there has been an abundance of political histories of Partition, there is a startling paucity of social histories that explore its cultural, social, and psychological ramifications (Menon and Bhasin 1998, 6). Although the more official accounts contain the minutiae of facts and figures, records, and agreements, it is in the unofficial, often oral, family histories and anecdotes that were passed down that one can access more nuanced, de-nationalized narratives of lived experiences, which include both the stories of horror and brutality and that of friendship and sharing, constituting an "underside" of the official history (Butalia 2000, 10). Scholars have, however, pointed out a turn in historical studies to incorporate unofficial anecdotal narratives and literary fiction (Didur 2006; Mushirul Hasan 1993; Gyan Pandey 2001). It is also worth noting that while the official records, reports, and historical accounts were written in English, many of the personal accounts and anecdotes continued to be written in the indigenous languages of the border such as Urdu, Hindi, Punjabi, and Bangla, thereby reaching beyond the urban English-educated readership. Partition literature also played a significant role in filling the gaps and presenting more nuanced and yet visceral narratives of trauma. As Menon and Bhasin (1998) says, "[w]hat seems to have stepped in, at least partly, to record the full horror of Partition, is literature" (6-7). Another critic, Alok Bhalla (1999), points out how Partition literature not only contains contemporary reports of localized and micro-experiences of Partition horror, but according to him, "the best of them . . . do not repeat what the historians already know" (3120). Instead, "they seek to make connections with the social and cultural life of a community in its entirety within a historically specific period" (Bhalla 1999, 3120). Therefore, a novel like *Cracking India* becomes an important site of analysis by giving space and voice to children, whose experiences of trauma are often rendered silent in mainstream narratives.

It is important to note that scholars have explored the significant discursive function of literature, especially literary fiction, in the narration of trauma in other contexts, too. As Granofsky (1995) observes, "the collective disasters of the contemporary world . . . have inspired a variety of novelistic responses" (3). Trauma theorist Cathy Caruth (1996), in *Unclaimed Experiences*, notes that: "If Freud turns to literature to describe traumatic experience, it is because, literature, like psychoanalysis, is interested in the complex relation between knowing and not knowing. And it is, indeed at the specific point at which knowing and not knowing intersect that the language of literature and the psychoanalytic theory of traumatic experience precisely meet" (3). Shoshana Feldman (1992), in *Testimony: Crises of Witnessing in Literature, Psychoanalysis, and History*, argues that ". . . literature and art [can be seen] as a precocious mode of witnessing—of accessing reality—when all other modes of knowledge are precluded" (xx). *Cracking India* bears witness to and proffers a counter-discourse to the dominant narratives on Partition and independence. It does so by subverting the nationalist historiographies and focusing instead on subaltern voices and the everyday life of common, ordinary people from a broad cross-section of society in Lahore. It highlights the realities of servants, laborers, artisans, who are caught up in the uncertainty of events that are not their doing and over which they have no control, while they are the ones who bear the brunt of the trauma. In addition, it also accentuates the "complex relation between knowing and not knowing" (Caruth 1995, ix) through the use of a child-eye perspective in the experience and narration of trauma.

TRAUMA, GENDER, AND CHILDHOOD

While the brunt of Partition violence was felt by everyone along the border, the gendered nature of the violence cannot be overstated, as about 75,000 thousand women were abducted and raped as victims of the "sexual savagery" (Butalia 2000, 3). Thousands more women were "sacrificed" by their own kin to safeguard the honor of their families and communities before they could be "desecrated" by the men of the "other" communities, and they became co-opted into the narrative of martyrdom of Partition. Yet scholars (Butalia 2000; Das 1989; Menon 2004; Menon and Bhasin 1998) have rued the absence of women's voices in Partition history. As Menon and Bhasin (1998) write in *Borders, Boundaries, Women in India's Partition*, "It is not that women are altogether absent from Partition histories or official records; it is just that they figure in the same way as they have always figured in history: as objects of study, rather than subjects. They are present in some reports and policy documents, and no account of Partition violence for instance, is complete without the numbing details of violence against women. Yet they are invisible" (11). Painstakingly and resolutely piecing together oral testimonies and narratives of survivors, feminist scholars like Ritu Menon, Kamala Bhasin, Urvashi Butalia, and Veena Das have written about women into the narrative of Partition through fictional texts that record "women's voices, speaking for themselves" (Menon and Bhasin 1998, 12). Recent scholarly works on gender (Didur 2006; Misri 2014) have remedied this gap even further.

Another persistent gap in Partition narratives has been the invisibility and absence of children's perspectives. In *The Other Side of Silence*, Butalia (2000) includes a few Dalits and children as they were "the smaller, often invisible players" (11). She writes, "No history of Partition that I have seen so far has had anything to say about children.... Where Partition is concerned, this is particularly important. So much of this history is woven around children that their invisibility now, in it, is tragic" (249) In her field notes, she observes, "virtually everyone mentioned hundreds of abandoned, destitute, lost children" (197) and like the women they were also "sacrificed" by their families before they could be brutalized by the rival community. In this context, I argue that much like in the case of gender, this absence and the lack of children's voices may at least be partially remedied by analyzing the literary representations of children's experiences during Partition. A text like *Cracking India* is particularly significant as the narrative not only foregrounds children's experiences of Partition but it also bestows rare narratorial authority to the child protagonist as the events are filtered through a child's eye perspective.

Most of the critical scholarship on *Cracking India* has explored the novel as a postcolonial feminist text that foregrounds the experience of Ayah (whose real name is Shanta), a pivotal character in the novel, who becomes a paradigmatic figure representing the gendered nature of Partition violence as she is abducted, raped, and forced into prostitution by an erstwhile suitor from the rival community (Ahn 2019; Bahri 1999; Daiya 2008; Didur 2006; Hai 2000; Dey 2018). As a postcolonial feminist text, *Cracking India* subverts the grand narrative of nationalist historiographies that valorize (or demonize through "othering") key political figures like Gandhi, Nehru, Jinnah, and others. Uniquely, the story is filtered through the perspective of Lenny, a young eight-year-old disabled Parsee girl, who is nanny Ayah's main charge in the text. There are autobiographical elements in the novel as, like Lenny, the author, Bapsi Sidhwa, was a young Parsee girl during the time of the Partition had contracted polio in childhood. While the development of Lenny's character is influenced by the author's adult consciousness (like any other character in a fictional text), Sidhwa has pointed out that "the central character of the child is not me per se. I had to create some distance between the child Lenny and myself as a child" (Sidhwa and Singh 1998, 19). *Cracking India* is thus not a purely autobiographical text, but a work of fiction where the adult author recreates and revisits her child-self in order to come to terms with the lingering effects of trauma.

As the noted literary critic Gayatri Spivak (1990) has pointed out, "as you proceed along the narrative, the narrative takes on its own impetus as it were, so that one begins to see reality as non-narrated. One begins to say that it's not a narrative, it's the way things are" (19). Deriving from Freud's

(1939) use of the term "latency" in *Moses and Monotheism*, through which he describes trauma as the successive movement of an event from its repression to its return, Cathy Caruth (1996) observes that "trauma is not a simple experience of events but that events, insofar as they are traumatic, assume their force precisely in their temporal delay" (17; 7-9). For example, even when the narrative space is afforded to a young (fictional) Lenny, the adult Lenny interjects throughout the narrative to ask, "How long does Lahore burn? Weeks? Months?" and questions the reliability of her memory saying, "[but] in my memory it is branded over an inordinate length of time: memory demands poetic license" (Sidhwa 1991, 148–149). These instances draw attention to the "complex relation between knowing and not knowing" (Caruth 1996, ix) in the representation of trauma. What is also noteworthy is the child-centricity in the recounting of violent events as they touched the lives of children. Young Lenny, along with other children including Papoo, Ranna, and even the unnamed twelve-year old mother in Dr. Bharucha's office, however marginalized or peripheral, together weave a parallel narrative of loss, violence, and wounding, arguably less dramatic than Ayah's but equally traumatic and rupturous in magnitude and impact. Lenny's centrality and perspective through which Ayah's narrative is presented also discursively frees the girl child from being subsumed into larger "adult" feminist discourses of Partition and allows for an agentic and independent representation that disrupts normative the Western ideal of childhood innocence as a state of ignorance.

SUBVERTING INNOCENCE

In his insightful analysis of childhood innocence, Robbie Duschinsky (2013) points out how "[i]nnocence appears to be the mere expression of a neutral and universal essence attached to childhood" (768) and observes that the "discourses of childhood innocence seem to have an unimpeachable moral status" (764). However, scholars have also argued that contrary to social perceptions that deem innocence in such universal and originary terms, "the connection between childhood and innocence is not essential but is instead historically located" (Bernstein 2011, 4). Although innocence appears to be a "neutral and universal essence" (Duschinsky 2013, 768), it is anything but a universal category. In the Western context, innocence is intrinsically related to the question of race, "raced white" as Bernstein (2011, 4) argues, and it continues to function as an exclusionary category (Duschinsky 2013; Garlen 2019).

In the South Asian context, some scholars have resisted easy correlation between childhood and innocence, owing to the belief in reincarnation and a cyclical conception of life so that the child is not simply born as a tabula rasa but carries within themselves traces of a previous life (Das 1989, 289). Meanwhile, others have pointed out that in more recent times,

> "coexisting with theories that posit that children bring with them memories of a previous life, are modernist discourses that conceive of childhood in terms of a linear progression into sovereign adult/subjecthood. These modernist constructions of childhood reveal a tendency to think of children as 'uncontaminated' by the temporal world in which they live and, therefore, as a space of purity" (Mankekar 1997, 58).

Furthermore, Mankekar points out that in nationalist discourses, "children readily become all that is 'pure' in the nation" due to the tendency of conceiving childhood as untainted and natural (55). What is imperative, however, is to note that these formulations are not uniform and are contingent on the socio-economic location of the child in the Indian context, especially along the lines of class, caste, gender, and religion, besides other local specificities.

In *Cracking India*, innocence, or the lack thereof, is an important recurring theme. By drawing attention to and foregrounding the violence at the birth of the nations, sexuality and sexual awareness in childhood, as well as discursive use of spatiality in demarcating spaces for and not for children, etc., the text challenges a normative juxtaposition of childhood and innocence. In the following sections, I explore some of the relevant instances from the text.

Nation, Violence, and Subversion of Innocence

In *Cracking India*, remarkably, there is no simple assumption of innocence in the depiction of childhood, and the narrative in fact subverts innocence by multiple discursive inversions. In addition, I would suggest that in the context of the nationalist project in South Asia, the *naissance* or the birth of the two nation states—India and Pakistan—was imbricated within a larger project of innocence and, in particular, its connections to childhood. Despite the concurrence of the violence of Partition and the celebration of Independence, there was a nationalist thrust to disentangle the two and imagine the birth of the nation as untainted, pure, and full of hope, thereby inscribing it with a notion of innocence much like it traditionally enshrines the newborn child. As Lenny's great-aunt, the "Slave-sister," says in the novel, "we've all produced a baby . . . we've given birth to a new nation" (Sidhwa 1991, 117). It is also telling that one of the new nation-states was given the name Pakistan, which means land of the pure or the unsullied in Urdu and Persian. Colonialist, nationalist, and even liberal-humanist perspectives agreed that "the grandeur of the drama of Independence, of the formation of two post-colonial nation-states, necessarily overshadowed the regrettable, aberrational, violent sub-plot of Partition" (Kaul 2002, n.p.). Nationalist historians have bristled against scholars who have concentrated on the violence of Partition (Pandey 2001). It has been pointed out that early historians seldom focused on the accounts of survivors not only because "they were committed only to histories of state politics and large-scale transformations but because they, like the survivors themselves, were dedicated to a recovery from the carnage and suffering of 1947–48" (Kaul 2002, n.p.). It was essential that these acts of violence "should be left behind, should be forgotten, so that people may live in peace, socially normal everyday life, politically as well individually" (Pandey 2001, 59). Partition violence, from this perspective, is seen as essentially aberrational, a random act of insanity against the grain of civilizational ethos—a tainting anomaly that came in the way of imagining the nation as pure and innocent at the moment of birth. By bringing into sharp focus the accounts of violence experienced by common people, the novel resists this perspective. It also rejects the idea that Partition violence was just a "regrettable phenomenon that could be wished away" (Kaul 2002, n.p.) and subsumed within the larger narrative of nationalism, thereby challenging any attempt at imagining the nation as unproblematically "innocent" at birth.

Sexuality and Subversion of Innocence

Though cloaked as universal, the concept of childhood innocence is intrinsically linked to the question of normativity. As Duschinsky (2013) writes about "the essential proximity of *normal* children to an ideal of innocence" (764), he draws from Foucault's genealogy in *Abnormal* where he assigns sexuality the primary responsibility for "a fall from an imputed Edenic state" (769). This makes sexuality "an ever-present danger to and within childhood" (770) As Egan and Hawkes (2010) note in their study on the sexual child in modernity, "although the child and sexuality have been fertile sites of research, their intersection has been, for the most part, absent" (5). As a counterpoint to the normalizing desirability of childhood innocence, childhood sexuality was regulated, surveilled, and disciplined by the state through legitimizing discourses of protectionism and social reform (7).

In his insightful work on juvenile delinquency in colonial India between 1850 and 1945, Sen (2005) highlights the distinction made between "genuine children, who were sexually innocent, and what might be described as underage adults or young girls rendered adult by their association with prostitutes" (72). For Sen, the separation of sexual and a/pre-sexual children was of paramount importance in the cause of protectionist reform and preservation of morality. In this context, *Cracking India* subverts the assumptions of innocence through the incursion of sexuality into the realm of childhood, first through Lenny's proximity to Ayah and her sexual encounters with her suitors, and also through the sexual explorations of the children, namely,

Lenny and Cousin. Lenny's sexual awareness is striking in its precocity. Only a few pages into the novel, she describes Ayah's body and the effect it had on passers-by as:

> Ayah is chocolate-brown and short. Everything about her is eighteen years old and round and plump. Even her face. Full-blown cheeks, pouting mouth and smooth forehead curve to form a circle with her head. Her hair is pulled back in a tight knot. And, as if her looks were not stunning enough, she has a rolling bouncy walk that agitates the globules of her buttocks under her cheap colorful saris and the half-spheres beneath her short sari-blouses. The Englishman no doubt had noticed. (Sidhwa 1991, 13)

In addition to these observations, Lenny describes with remarkable candidness the sexual intimacy between Ayah and her suitors, especially the Ice-candy man and the Masseur. As she observes: "They [Masseur's] are knowing fingers, very clever, and sometimes, late in the evening, when he and Ayah and I are alone, they massage Ayah under her sari. Her lids close. She grows still and languid. A pearly wedge gleams between her lips and she moans, a fragile, piteous sound of pleasure. Very carefully, very quietly, I maneuver my eyes and nose" (28). Here, Lenny is not merely a passive observer; she takes advantage of Ayah's admirers— "Massage me! I demand, kicking the handsome masseur" (ibid.) —and also keeps a sharp eye on overzealous suitors, thereby taking an active part in the complex amorous games and rituals that Ayah and her suitors indulge in throughout the first half of the novel:

> [t]hings love to crawl beneath Ayah's sari. Ladybirds, glow-worms, Ice-candy-man's toes. She dusts them off with impartial nonchalance. I keep an eye on Ice-candy-man's toes. Sometimes, in the course of an engrossing story, they travel so cautiously that both Ayah and I are taken unawares. Ice-candy-man is a raconteur. He is also an absorbing gossip. When the story is extra good, and the tentative toes polite, Ayah tolerates them. Sometimes a toe snakes out and zeroes in on its target with such lightning speed that I hear of the attack only from Ayah's startled "Oof." (28-9)

As she experiences these adult sexual games and rituals, she "intuit[s] the meaning and purpose of things. The secret rhythms of creation and mortality. The essence of truth and beauty. I recall the choking hell of milky vapors and discover that heaven has a dark fragrance" (28).

As evidenced by these passages, Lenny is a knowing child, and it is through the ascription of knowledge and astuteness on childhood that the novel counters the myth of innocence that is typically characterized by the lack of, or shielding from, "corrupting" knowledge. She is also a desiring child. Later in the novel, she confesses to Cousin that like her beloved caretaker Ayah, she, too, had found Masseur attractive although he was so much older, and her confession catches both Cousin and herself by surprise: "I surprise myself. Mouthing the words articulates my feelings and reveals myself to me" (230). As she herself grows older and comes to terms with her own sexuality, she finds that "no man is too old to attract me. Or too young" (230). As Duschinsky (2013) observes, "fighting children, working children, or desiring children—or those with sustained experience or agency in contexts 'riven' by conflict, labor, or desire—are less likely to be discursively understood as true innocents" (773). Although Lenny is quite distinct from the Freudian erotic child who is driven by "insatiable libidinal wants" but is still "devoid of reason and rationality" on their way to adult completeness (Egan and Hawkes 2010, 101–102), she is simultaneously desiring, knowing, and agentic, and therefore manages to evade the myth of innocence.

Spatiality and Subversion of Innocence

Another way that the text disrupts normative constructions of childhood innocence is through discursive manipulation of spatiality. Throughout the novel, Lenny constantly disrupts the assumptions and expectations of innocence by literally and figuratively straying into spaces that are not "places for children." Kozlovsky (2013) points out how the discourse of spatiality is informative of asymmetrical power relations, especially as "childhood is the most intensely governed sector of personal existence" (2). Rasmussen (2004) makes a distinction between "places for children" that are created and designated by adults facilitating governance and control and "children's places" which result from the appropriation of the more official "places for children" but also refer "to informal places, often unnoticed by adults." Places for children include the home, the school, and recreational institutions. (155). Afflicted with childhood polio, Lenny is excluded from the school, playground, and other "places for children," but she gets access to places like the park (where Ayah typically meets her suitors), bazaars, and cheap wayside restaurants, unnoticed by her parents or other figures of authority. Even at home, she has privileged access to her parent's bedroom in the night and is privy to their moments of conflict and love alike—"[h]aving polio in infancy is like being born under a lucky star. It has many advantages—it permits me access to my mother's bed in the middle of the night" (Sidhwa 1991, 20). Beyond their immediate sphere in Lahore, Lenny accompanies Imam Din, the cook, to his ill-fated village Pir Pindo, which would witness one of the worst massacres during the lunacy of Partition violence. Each of these spaces becomes an important site of gaining knowledge, experience, and/or relationships for Lenny, and this unique mobility affords her proximity to events before and after Partition, including the unprecedented violence in its wake, from which the adults of her Parsi community are shielded, as the violence primarily targeted Hindus, Muslims, and Sikhs.

In the final and perhaps most transgressive and critical ingress into a place not for children, Lenny visits Ayah in Hira Mandi, the notorious red-light district of Lahore, where the latter had been coerced into prostitution after her abduction, rape, and forced marriage with Ice-Candy Man. In the narrow, sordid lanes of the Hira Mandi (Diamond Market), Lenny observes:

> The bold girls, with short, permed hair, showing traces of stale makeup, stare at us as if we are freaks. They whisper and burst into giggles when we pass and bury their faces in each other's shoulders and necks. Their crumpled kamizes are too short and the pencha-bottoms of their shalwars too wide. Even I can tell they are not well brought up. (271)

Although a model of girlhood that is instinctively othered by Lenny from her vantage of privilege, from which she is considered to be "well brought up," her deep bond with Ayah necessitates her entry into Hira Mandi and thereby connects her to this "place not for children," which becomes a site of experience/knowledge.

Other Subversions of Innocence

In addition to the ways in which innocence is challenged by the recognition of the violent birth of the nation(s), the acknowledgement of sexual awareness, and Lenny's defiance of spatial boundaries, there are several other means through which Lenny subverts the trope of an innocent and benign child. For example, Lenny and other children in the text, including Cousin, are also engaged in acts of jealousy and cruelty in their harassment of Adi, Lenny's brother, by making his lips bleed to check if he is wearing lipstick (34) and hurting him in sleep, foreshadowing larger, more harrowing episodes of cruelty and revenge in the wake of Partition later in the text. It is noteworthy that in the text, while no one calls Lenny innocent, she herself refers to the "exuberant quality" of her mother's "innocence" (50). Later, as she reflects on the photograph of the Parsi wife of Jinnah (the first prime minister of Pakistan), who died of broken heart according to Lenny's mother, she notices her "large eyes, liquid brown . . . declaring innocence" and observes how "only her image in the photograph and her innocence—remain intact" (170). In her own case, it is only subversively that she attributes innocence, as in the false performance of it, to impress her father, at her mother's bidding (88). As she witnesses the confrontation between Godmother and the Ice-candy Man over the latter's treatment of Ayah, Lenny comments on the fragility of innocence, noting that the experience "opened [her] eyes to the wisdom of righteous indignation over compassion, [to] the demands of gratification

– and the unscrupulous nature of desire. To the pitiless face of love" (264). Thus, through portrayal of Lenny as both the knowing and desiring child as she repeatedly transgresses into the spaces, experiences, and realms of knowledge that are not meant for children, the narrative effectively subverts the assumptions and expectations of innocence in the depiction of childhood.

TRAUMA, CHILDHOOD, AND MATURATION

In the following section, I shall further explore the nature and effect of the violence and the ensuing trauma on the children during Partition and how it leads to (premature) maturation and to what effect. While the easy mobility outside the surveilled places for children that Lenny enjoys discursively allows her to thwart the myth of innocence within the narrative, it also makes her acutely vulnerable to the violence and trauma of Partition. Through her experience of the trauma of Partition, along with other children's like Ranna, *Cracking India* brings to light an unrepresented side of Partition violence, that is how it was experienced by the children, some more directly than others. There are three most distinct moments when Lenny directly experiences the horrors of Partition violence in the narrative. During one of their outings to the familiar Queen's Garden, Lenny and Ayah are caught in the melee when Sikh and Muslim mobs attack each other, and the Ice-Candy man hustles them up to his tenements, from where they watch in horror as Shalmi, a neighborhood in Lahore burns in the distance. Lenny also witnesses the bloodbath on the street below and the grisly sight of "a naked child, twitching on a spear struck between her shoulders, waved like a flag" (144). Describing the scene, she explains, "The terror the mob generates is palpable – like an evil, paralyzing spell. The terrible procession, like a sluggish river, flows beneath us. Every short while a group of men, like a whirling eddy, stalls – and like the widening circles of a treacherous eddy dissolving in the mainstream, leaves in its center the pulpy red flotsam of a mangled body" (145).The experience of witnessing such cruelty generates as much fury as fear in Lenny, and later at home, in an act of violent mimicry, Lenny disembowels a doll to find release : "I examine the doll's insides and, holding them in my hands, collapse on the bed sobbing. Adi crouches close to me. I can't bear the disillusioned and contemptuous look in his eyes. 'Why were you so cruel if you couldn't stand it?' He asks at last, infuriated by the pointless brutality" (148). Through Lenny's re-enactment of a violent act while coming to grapple with the experience of violence, the narrative further subverts the trope of childhood innocence.

A more direct experience of brutality and death comes when Lenny and Hari, the cook, discover the mangled body of the Masseur, Ayah's suitor and her true love. In a rare moment of bewilderment and convergence of death and desire, Lenny realizes that the Masseur had been "reduced to a body. A thing. One side of his handsome face already buried in the dusty sidewalk" (186). With the Masseur's death, his earlier promise to Ayah that "no will touch a hair on [her] head" (168) rings hollow, and Ayah is reduced to a "token" (101) of her religious identity and is ruthlessly abducted by a violent mob led by the Ice-Candy Man. With this horrific act of revenge, both personal (due to Ayah's preference of Masseur over Ice-Candy Man) and communal (as it symbolically targets the "other" community), "the signification of Ayah's body subtly shifts from sexually attractive femininity to vulnerable Hindu femininity" (Stokes 2008, 64 as quoted in Dey 2018, 35). As Ayah suffers from "unspeakable" trauma, "that is both psychological and psychosocial" (Bahri 1999, 221), this marks a moment of acute and lingering trauma for Lenny too, first, because of her act of betrayal and guilt—as Ice-Candy man tricked her into revealing Ayah's hiding place—and second, this marks a pivotal moment of rupture, severance, and profound loss. Katharine Capshaw Smith (2005) highlights how "the construction of children's responses to trauma generally adhere to two poles," both connected with the idea/ideal of childhood innocence: "Because children are imagined as innocent, they are figured almost iconographically as the ultimate victims of trauma, those who require above all else adult protection and guidance . . . Alternately, because children are imagined as innocent, they are also figured as the survivors of trauma, those who can offer adult spiritual advice in how to triumph over pain through simple, honest, essential values like love, trust, hope, and perseverance" (116).

However, how is a child, like Lenny in this case, who is not ascribed with innocence within the narrative in the first place, represented as responding to the trauma? Lenny, for example, is neither afforded victim status nor is she bestowed a survivor/savior position. Lenny says of Sharbat Khan, one of Ayah's erstwhile suitors, "[s]ometimes he looks at me as if he is trying to probe my soul and search out the aberrations in my personality that made me betray Ayah. Then he shakes his head and bitterly says: 'Children are the Devil . . . They only know the truth'" (Sidhwa 1991, 204). In Lenny's case, the experience of trauma and the ensuing loss leads to a process of maturation. Referring to American Literature, Eric Tribunella (2010) points out how "irrevocable loss, especially of something dear is experienced as a trauma" and is used "as a way of provoking or ensuring the development of children" (ix). Trauma is seen as a necessary catalyst to hasten the process of growing up—"[it] is as if loss generates the escape velocity of youth. It is the fuel used to achieve the speed necessary for escaping the gravitational force of childhood . . . love and loss work as a catalyst for maturation" (ix) In Ayah's absence, Lenny's vicarious participation in the performance of Ayah's unabashed sexuality is replaced by self-knowledge and awareness of her own body and desires (Sidhwa 1991, 230). The process of maturation for the girl child is inevitably gendered and inflected by the patriarchy that stipulates the normative course to womanhood through marriage and motherhood, a reminder of what Col. Bharucha, Lenny's doctor, had noted earlier in the text: "She'll marry – have children – lead a carefree, happy life. No need to strain her with studies and exams" (25). Lenny, who had feistily resisted sexual advances from Cousin with his "carnal cravings," comes to a compromise with him. Lenny explains, "I will keep an open mind and let bygones be bygones, and Cousin will stop wooing me and wait a couple of years before touching my breasts again. We shall see how I feel about it then" (245).

Lenny also becomes cognizant of the fate of women, including Hamida's and other so-called recovered women who fall outside the socially sanctioned normative spaces for women and become objects of stigma and/or pity, shunned by an apathetic society and the paternalistic state. Another narrative of acquiescence runs through the episode of Papoo's marriage where the young, feisty girl is browbeaten and drugged into marrying a middle-aged dwarf chosen by her own parents (199). Being the daughter of the untouchable sweeper in the Sethi home, she carries the extra burden of caste, in addition to her compromised position of being a girl with no control over her fate and future. It is not a coincidence that within the narrative, this incident directly comes on the heels of Ayah's abduction, both of which Lenny witnesses.

Yet another instance of violence against and as experienced by children during Partition is to be found in "Ranna's story." Although *Cracking India* is filtered through Lenny's perspective, in an unusual narratorial shift, a section entitled "Ranna's Story" is embedded as an eye-witness account of Partition violence, narrated by Ranna, Imam Din's great-grandson, who is Lenny's age and comes from the fated and predominantly Muslim village of Pir Pindo. Through Ranna's narrative, we get a glimpse of the unspeakable horror and violence that befell his village, including the children and youth. Architecturally speaking, within the main narrative, Ranna's narrative presents what may be called an *enfilade of trauma* as we access one story of trauma through another, sequentially, together representing a chorus of collective trauma, which historically had rendered these voices, including that of the children, silent. The narrative bears testament to the fact that although absent from the pages of history, children were not only not spared during the Partition violence but were ruthlessly tortured and butchered for being the progeny of the enemy community, becoming victims of this gory tale of communal nationalism. Through Ranna's eyes, we see young girls brutally raped and killed by grown men and "babies, snatched from their mothers, smashed against walls" (Sidhwa 1991, 219). The ferocity of violence that Ranna, his siblings, and the rest of his family face because of their religion (Islam) and location (rural Punjab) could not be narrated through Lenny's privileged position as an upper-class urban Parsi from Lahore. Yet, when Ranna arrives as the lone survivor, to Lahore, bearing a visible mark of the trauma described as "a grisly scar like a brutally gouged and a prematurely bald spot" (216), there is empathy and bonding with Lenny. A similar bond and solidarity can be seen between Lenny and Papoo, who are also separated by class status, religion, and caste. These instances of juvenile solidarity that transcend religion, class, and caste, especially in dealing with trauma, run contrapuntal to the violence that adults inflict upon each other in the name of religion.

CONCLUSION

Thus, *Cracking India*, in its recounting of the tumultuous and harrowing experiences of Partition violence in the subcontinent, presents us with a remarkable narrative that foregrounds children and their experience of trauma while also dispelling the myth of innocence that shrouds traditional representations of childhood. As Lenny's story makes space for Ranna's and through his leads the readers to countless other stories of brutality and violence committed against children during the Partition, the text discursively fills the gap and the deafening silence in Partition narratives with regard to the children's experiences and remedies their tragic invisibility, as rued by scholars and field workers (Butalia 2000, 249). It counters the triumphalist narratives of nationalism as well as nationalist historiographies that put forth the "proposition about the secondariness of violence, its essential *irrelevance* compared to the tortured search for our moral being" (Pandey 2001, 64), where, in reality, Partition violence constituted nothing short of a war waged especially against the enemy community's women *and* children. (68) [Italics added] In fact, as a narrative that particularly focuses on children's experiences and bestows narratorial authority to children, *Cracking India* acutely problematicizes any quest for moral coherence and the establishment of the new nation as a "natural moral community" (160), as it is left to grapple with the brutalities committed against thousands of defenseless children. The "immoral" acts of violence thus shatter the myth of innocence at the birth of the nation, which is mirrored within the text in the subversion of the tropes of innocence and protectionism that shroud normative representations of childhood. The text underscores how a traditional and normative framework of innocence of childhood does not capture the lived experiences of children touched by rupturous violence and lingering trauma, and also how these lived experiences are distinctly mediated by gender, religion, class, caste, dis/ability, and other categories, thereby thwarting any attempt of a universal construction of childhood innocence. The premature maturation of the girl child, that may be understood as a function of trauma and its lingering legacies, forces a reckoning instead, of the culpability of the adult perpetrators of all involved communities and insists on a more mature, humane, and chastened approach to nationalism and the nation at the moment of its birth.

REFERENCES

Ahn, Hakyoung. 2019. "Queer Eyes and Gendered Violence in Bapsi Sidhwa's *Cracking India*." *Journal of Postcolonial Writing* 55(5): 602–613. https://doi.org/10.1080/17449855.2019.1627570

Bahri, Deepika. 1999. "Telling Tales: Women and the Trauma of Partition in Sidhwa's *Cracking India*." *Interventions: International Journal of Postcolonial Studies* 1(2): 217–234. https://doi.org/10.1080/13698019900510321

Balagopalan, Sarada. 2011. "Introduction: Children's Lives and the Indian Context." *Childhood* 18(3): 291–297. https://doi.org/10.1177/0907568211413369

Bhalla, Alok. 1999. "Memory, History and Fictional Representations of the Partition." *Economic and Political Weekly* 34(44): 3119–3128.

Bernstein, Rachael. 2011. *Racial Innocence: Performing American Childhood from Slavery to Civil Rights*. New York, NY: New York University Press.

Butalia, Urvashi. 2000. *The Other Side of Silence: Voices from the Partition of India*. Durham, NC: Duke University Press.

Caruth, Cathy, ed. 1995. *Trauma: Explorations in Memory*. Baltimore, MD and London: The Johns Hopkins University Press.

Caruth, Cathy. 1996. *Unclaimed Experience: Trauma, Narrative, and History*. Baltimore, MD and London: The Johns Hopkins University Press.

Daiya, Kavita. 2008. *Violent Belongings: Partition, Gender, and National Culture in Postcolonial India*. Philadelphia, PA: Temple University Press.

Das, Veena. 1989. "Voices of Children." *Daedalus* 118(4): 263–294.

Dey, Arunima. 2018. "The Female Body as the Site of Male Violence during the Partition of India in Bapsi Sidhwa's 'Ice-Candy-Man.'" *Complutense Journal of English Studies* 26: 27–45. https://doi.org/10.5209/CJES.54661

Duschinsky, Robbie. 2013. "Childhood Innocence: Essence, Education, and Performativity." *Textual Practice* 27(5): 763–781. https://doi.org/10.1080/0950236X.2012.751441

Didur, Jill. 2006. *Unsettling Partition: Literature, Gender, Memory*. Toronto: University of Toronto Press.

Egan, R. Danielle and Gail Hawkes, eds. 2010. *Theorizing the Sexual Child in Modernity*. New York, NY: Palgrave Macmillan.

Feldman, Shoshana and Dori Laub. 1992. *Testimony: Crises of Witnessing in Literature Psychoanalysis and History*. New York, NY: Routledge.

Garlen, Julie C. 2019. "Interrogating Innocence: 'Childhood' As Exclusionary Social Practice." *Childhood* 26(1): 54–67. https://doi.org/10.1177/0907568218811484

Granofsky, Ronald. 1995. *The Trauma Novel: Contemporary Symbolic Depictions of Collective Disaster*. New York, NY: Peter Lang.

Hai, Ambreen. 2000. "Border Work, Border Trouble: Postcolonial Feminism in Bapsi Sidhwa's 'Cracking India.'" *Modern Fiction Studies* 46(2): 379–426. https://doi.org/10.1353/mfs.2000.0028.

Jenks, Chris. 2005. *Childhood*, 2nd edn. London and New York: Routledge.

Kaul, Suvir. 2002. "Remembering Partition: Violence, Nationalism and History in India" (Review). *Journal of Colonialism & Colonial History* 3(3), n.p. https://doi.org/10.1353/cch.2002.0068

Kozlovsky, Roy. 2013. "Architectures of Childhood." In *The Children's Table: Childhood Studies and the Humanities*, edited by Anna Mae Duane, 124–143. Athens, GA: University of Georgia Press.

Mankekar, Purnima. 1997. "'To Whom Does Ameena Belong?' Towards a Feminist Analysis of Childhood and Nationhood in Contemporary India." *Feminist review* 56(1): 26–60. https://doi.org/10.1057/fr.1997.14

Menon, Ritu and Kamala Bhasin. 1998. *Borders and Boundaries: Women in India's Partition*. New Brunswick, NJ: Rutgers University Press.

Menon, Ritu. 2004. *No Woman's Land: Women from Pakistan, India and Bangladesh Write on the Partition of India*. New Delhi: Women Unlimited.

Misri, Deepti. 2014. *Beyond Partition: Gender, Violence and Representation in Postcolonial India*. Urbana, IL: University of Illinois Press.

Pandey, Gyanendra. 2001. *Remembering Partition: Violence, Nationalism, and History in India*. Cambridge: Cambridge University Press.

Rasmussen. 2004. "Places for Children – Children's Places." *Childhood* 11(2): 155–173. https://doi.org/10.1177/0907568204043053

Sen, Satadru. 2005. *Colonial Childhoods: The Juvenile Periphery of India, 1850–1945*. London: Anthem Press.

Sidhwa, Bapsi. 1991. *Cracking India*. Minneapolis, MN: Milkweed Editions.

Sidhwa, Bapsi and Preeti Singh. 1998. "My Place in the World." *Alif: Journal of Comparative Poetics* 18: 290–298. https://doi.org/10.2307/521890

Smith, Katharine Capshaw. 2005. "Forum: Trauma and Children's Literature." *Children's Literature* 33(1): 115–119. https://doi.org/10.1353/chl.2005.0023

Spivak, Gayatri Chakravorty and Sarah Harasym. 1990. *The Post-Colonial Critic: Interviews, Strategies, Dialogues*. New York, NY: Routledge.

Tribunella, Eric L. 2010. *Melancholia and Maturation: The Use of Trauma in American Children's Literature*. Knoxville, TN: University of Tennessee Press.

Chapter 8

The Arrivant Child

Afrofuturity and Contingent Childhood Agencies

Neil T. Ramjewan

INTRODUCTION

Nalo Hopkinson's (2000) second novel, *Midnight Robber,* can be read as an allegory of colonial trauma in which the discursive figure of the Afrofuturistic child, Tan-Tan, continues to navigate the geographies and politics of settler colonial relations of power in the speculative future. In this coming-of-age story (bildungsroman), Hopkinson explores the agency of what I frame as the arrivant child or the child that is forced to a new interdimensional prison planet in a way that speaks to the dislocations of colonial imperialism. At first, Tan-Tan is but a pawn in between her parents' tumultuous relationship but she is eventually kidnapped by her father, Antonio, who is fleeing to the "New World" to escape state punishment for the unintentional killing of his wife's lover. As the pair arrives, they are immediately greeted by an Indigenous nonhuman figure, Chichibud, who is differentiated by species (the douen) but can speak "anglopatwa" and guide them to a human settlement. Here, Tan-Tan struggles with the traumatic loss of home and eventually the loss of selfhood through sexual violence inflicted by her father, a symbol of paternalistic colonial violence. This violence psychically splits the child giving birth to a critical agent within. The Midnight Robber, traditionally a male carnival figure based on the African griot, is a bombastic storyteller, trickster, and a figure of identification and liberation for Tan-Tan that consolidates in response to ruptural colonial violence. Again, she is dislocated, this time as an act of care by Chichibud, who takes her to his homeland, the existence of which is unbeknownst to settlers. Tan-Tan works through her trauma between this strange place and the familiar human settlements she clandestinely visits as she tries to heal and remake home. Through the historicity of the Midnight Robber as a resistor to colonial order and an agent of justice, she reclaims her voice, integrates her losses, tells her story, and intervenes to disrupt adult settler affairs as the feminized vigilante Tan-Tan Robber Queen. However, this integration of trauma and the emergence of a seemingly individualized agency is contingent on, and not without cost to, the relationship with Indigenous figures that care for and protect the Afrofuturistic child in the wake of the *longue durée* of colonial violence.

Midnight Robber holds relevance for the field of childhood studies, which is also concerned with children's futures and their agencies. Oftentimes, the literary child is an agentic protagonist who redeems imagined futures from the catastrophes of the past and present. While there is an abundance of scholarship that attends to children's agency, they rarely attend to the futures of Black, brown, and Indigenous children. For example, the recent collection of essays by Ingrid Castro, Jessica Clark, and Gary Westfahl (2019), *Child and Youth Agency in Science Fiction: Travel, Technology, Time,* recognizes the child as a colonial figure that often represents dominant social anxieties but makes no sustained analysis that centers either race or colonization to understand childhood or agency. Additionally, in childhood studies' scholarship, the starting point for examining agency often begins from traditional conceptions of agency that is in tension with social structures (i.e., structure-agency debates), which in turn shape the agent's personalized capacities to act and illicit change in the world (Raithelhuber 2016). Despite these omissions and conservations, there is an existing body of work that attends to the persisting legacies of colonial violence, such as postcolonial theorizing of childhood (Balagopalan 2014; Canella and Viruru 2004; Sen 2005) some of which question the meaning of agency altogether. Additionally, there is an emerging body of work that takes into account the existing practices of ongoing settler colonization such as the brutalizing practices of residential schooling in Canada, efforts of reconciliation, and the construction of childhood in the midst of these discourses (Dyer 2017; Land 2023; Nxumalo, Pacini-Ketchabaw, and Rowan 2011; Taylor, Pacini-Ketchabaw, de Finney, and Blaise 2016; Rollo 2016).

While such work brings critical attention to the ways that colonial legacies continue to inform understandings of childhood, one criticism of settler colonial scholarship is that it reifies a binary between settlers and Indigenous people. To rectify this, Chickasaw scholar Jodi Byrd (2011) revisits the social category of arrivants, or those forced into the New World through the practices of imperial colonialism such as transatlantic slavery. These circuits of forced dislocation persist for arrivants such as myself, a descendant of Indian indentured laborers who were brought to the Caribbean plantation to break the post-abolition strikes of formerly enslaved African arrivants. In the wake of plantation colonialism, I was brought to the Canadian settler state as a child of my parents in search of a better life, but at the cost of losing the only life we knew, to again, become implicated in an ongoing project of colonialism. The turn to the category of arrivant risks settler moves to innocence (Mawhinney 1998), which can reproduce settler logics and practices of land dispossession and erasure (Saranillo 2018). However, the social position of the arrivant understood as an ambivalent kind of double bind can add nuance to the relationship, alliances, and complicities between Indigenous peoples, racialized settlers, and white settlers. These themes of psychological, physical, and sexual abuse, settler violence and expansion, and Indigenous–arrivant relations are explored in *Midnight Robber* and invite reflection on what it means to build a shared future through the figure of the child, who often stands in for and saves the future. Just as Hopkinson's body of work has been disruptive to science fiction, I turn to her literary children, specifically the arrivant child, to stage a similar kind of disruption to reconceptualize notions of childhood and its agencies.

In what follows, I begin with a review of the central concerns around agency in the field of childhood studies and present postmodern critiques of an individualized possessive form of agency in favor of multiple, distributed, contingent, and relational forms of agency. Hereafter, I consider the intervention that Afrofuturism offers to Euro-American science fiction paying close attention to its temporal and decolonial possibilities. To define my reading strategy, I then turn to the work of Chickasaw scholar, Jodi Byrd, and their inspiration, Afro-Caribbean poet, Kamau Brathwaite, and his poetics of arrivance. Through the analysis, I attend to the repeated scenes of arrival in the novel to make two arguments. First, I argue that Hopkinson (2000) recuperates the agency of the arrivant child through an Afro-Caribbean imaginary that is attentive to the trauma of slavery. One form of violence that I discuss in detail is the repeated rape of the child by the father which serves as a metaphor for the violence of colonialism and can be triggering for some readers. In doing so, she illustrates how the arrivant child's agencies shift and multiply in response to violence across colonial geographies as a form of resistance and refusal. Next, I argue that the growth and development of the arrivant child's agency as she comes of age is also a form of relational agency contingent on the care and protection of the Indigenous figures. Careful to not romanticize this relationship, Hopkinson (2000) attends to the im/possibilities of making home on usurped Indigenous homeland through the arrivants destabilizing presence. In short, Hopkinson's (2000) child navigates a double bind between protecting the self (healing) and resisting settler injustice, in which it is impossible for the child to not be complicit in their own oppression. In turn, Hopkinson (2000) offers the interstitial space of the maroon as a site of possibility. I conclude with a consideration of the double bind in which the arrivant is located and call for childhood studies scholars to turn to Black, brown, and Indigenous archives to continue to imagine childhood and its agencies otherwise.

BACKGROUND LITERATURE

Nalo Hopkinson is currently a professor of creative writing at the University of California. In 2021, she was the first Black woman, and the second Black recipient after Samuel Delaney, to receive the prestigious Grand Master Award from the Science Fiction and Fantasy Writers of America in its almost fifty-year history. Hopkinson was born in Jamaica in 1960 while it was still a British colony. Her family arrived in Toronto, Canada, in the mid-1970s by way of Guyana, Trinidad, and the United States so her father could receive medical treatment unavailable in the colonies. Hopkinson's (1998, 2000, 2003) work is consistently attentive to such colonial geographies, politics, and the dislocations of its regularly neglected and silenced subjects, such as the Afro-Caribbean girl child. In what follows, I review the literature on childhood studies and the scholarship attending to childhood agency. Next, I consider critiques of the dominant narrative in Euro-American science fiction including its preoccupation with the future which sets a backdrop against which I trace a brief genealogy of Afrofuturism. Finally, I consider the decolonial possibilities of Afrofuturity.

Childhood Studies and Childhood Agency

The central commitments put forth by James, Jenks, and Prout in the 1990s are regularly referred to as the "new paradigm" in childhood studies and include the ideas that children are worthy of study in their own right, childhood is a social construction, and children are to be treated as active agents (Esser, Baader, Betz, and Hungerland 2016). In broad terms, the focus on children's agency is committed to the social emancipation of those who are subject to minoritized and often silenced positions in structures of what Alanen (2009) calls generational power. These efforts are well warranted as a corrective to developmentalist paradigms, in particular the reach of psychology into educational spaces, which objectifies the child and subsumes it into a universal and deterministic model of linear growth (Burman 2017). In the field of childhood studies, the commitment to understanding and supporting children's agency has become a taken-for-granted mantra (Tisdall and Punch 2012), yet research on what agency *is* and its differences between cultures and contexts remains limited.

While childhood studies is an interdisciplinary field, the centrality of children as active agents is a corollary of sociological approaches that remain dominant. The turn to value children, their voices, and participation in social life begins from the premise that they are social actors and in turn possess and utilize personal and individualized forms of agency (Raithelhuber 2016) or what Passoth, Peuker, and Schillmeier (2012) call the "capacity concept of agency" (1). Within this paradigm, the analytic focus continues to be dominated by structure-agency debates (Raithelhuber 2016) or examinations of social reproduction in and through social structures and the reflexivity of subjects to change said structures (Bollig and Kelle 2016). In contrast to these modernist theories of agency, postmodern and poststructuralist influences sought to decenter an already fragmented subject. These theories have helped to understand agency as relational such that "agency is not a human capacity opposed to society [structure] but is socially produced and distributed amongst different human and non-human actors" (Esser 2016, 53). In this way, agency can be thought of as assemblages where "agency is contingent on multiple social and cultural factors" (Garlen, Sonu, Farley, and Chang-Kredl 2022, 2) such that the social relationships at the centers of production "*constitute the very structure and form of agency itself*" (Burkitt 2016, 336). With this focus on *the relationship* between subjects and objects, Burkitt (2016) argues for reconceptualizing actors as "interactants or interdependents and that agency appears only among people in their relational contexts" (332), and to which I add non- and more-than-human beings.

However, the poststructuralist turn in childhood studies has been critiqued as taking agency away from actual children in favor of figurative children (Oswell 2013). In response, Frie (2002) argues that postmodernism's influence on psychoanalysis, another field where voice, experience, and agency matter, has not led to such abandon of the subject in conceptualizations of agency. Frie (2002) reminds that in clinical settings, patients' voice, such as those of children, and the narration of one's life experiences are the lynchpin of the therapeutic process and require a certain sense of personal agency. Therefore, the effects of networks of interactants that consolidate into a sense of personal agency experienced by the individual remain important to projects such as Afrofuturism that aim to recover those voices that have been historically silenced. The tensions of both these forms of agency are evident in *Midnight Robber* and which I highlight to examine how childhood agency is contingent on relationships with others and land.

One important silence in the field of childhood studies that invites reflection is that of the voices of enslaved children or arrivants and their descendants. Only in recent years has there been any attention by historians to the children of slavery, such as the work of Robin Bernstein (2011), Wilma King (2011), and Crystal Lynn Webster (2021). Political theorist, Neil Roberts (2015), in *Freedom as Marronage*, makes the argument that any notion of freedom is inseparable from modern slavery. For Roberts (2015), drawing on

Toni Morrison, the dawn of modernity is marked by chattel slavery in which race is the foremost structure of social difference. Roberts (2015) critiques modern-era political philosophers arguing that their theories of freedom draw on ancient notions of slavery and freedom and omit the category of race. He challenges this omission by turning to the agency of the enslaved and practices of marronage or rebellious acts of taking flight from enslavement. I take a similar tact to expand notions of childhood agency by turning to Hopkinson's (2000) work, which narratively and discursively represents the child of slavery in the arrivant and its agencies.

Science Fiction, the Future, and Afrofuturism

The genre of science fiction is a specifically Euro-American cultural formation in which adult desires for the future are represented through the figure of the white European child, who often stands in for the future. Kay Sambell (2004) critiques representations of childhood agency in *the* classic science fiction subgenre, the dystopia, and George Orwell's *1984* in particular. While the dystopian novel offers a critical commentary of the present through dismal extrapolations of the future, it also, by virtue of its conceptual constraints as a totalizing *dys* (bad) -*topia* (place), renders the redemptive arc of the hero as an impossibility (i.e., Orwell's Winston whose disillusionment with a totalitarian state and subsequent dissent is broken and transformed by coercive re-education into patriotism). Within the grammar of this literary space, there is a paradoxical relationship that creates dilemmas for adult authors by positioning them between grim hopeless futures and nostalgia for romantic, white, innocent, and increasingly agentic figures of the child who represent hopefulness. These dilemmas often manifest in the uncritical reproduction of romantic and utopic versions of childhood that are exclusionary of Black life and inattentive to the racial and colonial politics of childhood.

In *So Long Been Dreaming,* edited with Uppinder Mehan, Hopkinson (2004) reminds us that while the recurring meme of science fiction involves futuristic exploration, typically by male characters, into foreign spaces to colonize the natives and their lands, "for many of us, that's not a thrilling adventure story [or future]; its non-fiction, and we are on the wrong side of the strange-looking ship that appears out of nowhere" (ii). This trope continues in contemporary science fiction cinema through the figure of the agentic child in which the futuristic narrative follows the "boy pal" (Neustader 1989, 231). For example, the television series *Lost in Space* (2018–present) features the white male child and his Black alloy alien robot while on an intergalactic mission to colonize a new world in the wake of humankind's destruction of the earth. This contemporary cinematographic text is a remake of its 1965 predecessor of the same name, which was inspired by Johann David Wyss's

(1812/1991) novel *The Swiss Family Robinson*— a colonial castaway narrative in which sea (versus space) faring European's arrive and independently survive on the *terra nullius* frontier (Weaver-Hightower 2007). Drawing on an Afro-Caribbean cultural archive, Hopkinson disrupts the genre of science fiction by imagining Afrofuturistic childhoods that destabilize these colonial futures.

Afrofuturism refuses and reinvents anti-Black visions of tomorrow. The first usage of the term "Afrofuturism" was introduced in Mark Dery's (1994) "Black to the Future" interview essay with Black U.S. science fiction authors Samuel Delaney, Greg Tate, and Tricia Rose. They define Afrofuturism as "Speculative fiction that treats African-American themes and addresses African-American concerns in the context of twentieth-century techno-culture— and, more generally, African-American signification that appropriates images of technology and a prosthetically enhanced future. . . " (Dery 1994, 180). Afrofuturistic aesthetics emerged in North American Black artistic movements such as the jazz of the 1930s to 1960s in the work of George Schuyler, Sun Ra, and Miles Davis and would extend into the late twentieth century to artists including musicians George Clinton and Parliament Funkadelic, Erykah Badu, and Missy Elliot, and the work of eminent science fiction writer, Octavia Butler. In the twenty-first century, Black cultural production continues to push Afrofuturist boundaries through the music of Janelle Monae, the recent Black Panther films, and writers, such as Nnedi Okorafor, Karen Lord, N.K. Jemisin, as well as the work of Nalo Hopkinson that is at the center of this analysis.

For some, this North American genealogy dislocates Afrofuturist ontoepistemologies from African intellectualism to the extent that it has "nothing to do with Africa" (Bristow 2012, 25). However, this stance dismisses what Cedric Robinson (1983/2020) calls the Black radical tradition, which recognizes "an African tradition that grounded collective resistance [often interpreted as human agency] by Blacks to slavery and colonial imperialism" (169). Paul Gilroy (1993), less convinced of a singular "tradition" across the African diaspora, views Black transcultural, diasporic, and international cultural formations as part of a "rhizomorphic, fractal structure" (4) that he calls the Black Atlantic. Importantly, the hybridization and creolization characteristic of displaced Africans is not only limited to the Caribbean and New World but also has a recursive effect on Europe, Africa, and Asia. Thus, Afrofuturism can be understood as a "Diasporic techno-cultural 'Pan-African'" (Samatar 2015, quoted in Anderson and Jones 2016) hybridized form of expression Black people have been engaged in since the dawn of modernity.

The political project of Afrofuturism is deeply connected to the past as "an extension of historical recovery projects that Black Atlantic intellectuals have engaged in for well over 200 years" (Yaszek 2006, 47). This recovery project is akin to what Saidiya Hartman (2008) calls critical fabulation or the use of imaginative and speculative writing to extrapolate the archival traces of the enslaved whose stories and lives have been lost to the Middle Passage. As an ensemble of counter-memories that contest colonial archives, Afrofuturism identifies the foundational trauma of slavery as the origin of modernity (Eshun 2003). As such, it remembers that for African arrivants, the apocalypse of slavery has already come. For Black people, the postapocalypse is not some distant future but can also define the present (Maynard 2018). The postapocalyptic present can be thought of as a continuation of what Hartman (2008) refers to as the afterlife of slavery or the "racial calculus and political arithmetic that were entrenched centuries ago . . . [that produces in the present] . . . skewed life chances, limited access to health and education, premature death, incarceration, [and] impoverishment" (6).

It is from within this present postapocalypse that Christina Sharpe (2016) theorizes Black non/being in the *longue durée* of the wake of slavery or the breach and disturbance of the surface of the water left behind the slave ship. The wake is a metaphor for the aftermath of slavery and its effects which continues into the present through neo-imperial circuits of cultural and capital production. These circuits continue to force migrating and fleeing Black bodies into "liquid graves" (Philip 2008, 201). Take for example the sixty-two migrants, including twelve children, who drowned in their passage from Turkey to Italy with passengers from Afghanistan, Somalia, and Pakistan (Marsi 2023). Sharpe (2016) returns to the hold of the slave ship in which Black people exist as chattel and is therefore devoid of humanity and its agency. She reminds us that within the hold, the Black "*child* is not 'child'" (Sharpe 2016, 77), but rather a fungible commodity who inherits the nonhuman being status of its mother. However, "As loathsome as life inside this zone of enslavement might be, it is a zone of hope and natality" (Roberts 2015, 118). It is from this wake where Black humanism and being is structured, imagined, performed, and claimed through multiple forms of agency required in the pursuit of freedom.

It is from this present of non/being in the wake that Afrofuturism conjures a future that also holds the continuances of the past. The work of Ghanian-British author Kodwo Eshun (2003) is particularly helpful in understanding Afrofuturism's political stakes in the future. For Eshun (2003), the future is a commodity that is produced and circulated through the "futures industry" (291) ranging from the natural sciences that predict the future (weather) to artistic forms such as science fiction literature. In this global industry, "African social reality is overdetermined by intimidating global scenarios, doomsday economic projections, weather predictions, medical reports on AIDS, and life-expectancy forecasts, all of which predict decades of immiseration" (291-292). As such, Afrofuturism is a form of what Eshun (2003) calls chronopolitics or acts that emerge from the wake to resist and dismantle these overdeterminations of the future. Engagement in the production and study of Afrofuturist texts is a chronopolitical act that is "concerned with the possibilities for intervention within the dimension of the predictive, the projected, the proleptic, the envisioned, the virtual, the anticipatory and the future conditional" (Eshun 2003, 293) in the past and future, through the present. It is a place where, as Lisa Yaszek (2006) says, Afrofuturists are engaged in reclaiming a "history of the future" (44) that insists on not imagining away the colonial past and present.

Decolonization, Futurity, and Afrofuturity

The future conditional of Afrofuturism that I am interested in is its decolonial possibilities. For Danielle Becker (2016), the decolonial potentials of Afrofuturism can be understood through their similar temporal practices. As they explain, "Afrofuturism makes use of the past to disrupt the present and to create a future imaginary so does the decolonial, in something of a reversal, seek to change the present and future by acknowledging and disrupting the power of the past" (Becker 2019, 17). Afrofuturism also resembles decolonial conversations in and across North American settler occupied polities that are also attentive to temporality. For example, in Tuck and Gaztambide-Fernández's (2012) critique of interventions that resist settler futures, they note that North American settler contexts operate through "a triad of relationships, between the (white [but not always]) settlers, the Indigenous inhabitants and chattel slaves who are removed from their homelands to work stolen land" (74). For Tuck and Gaztambide-Fernández (2012), drawing on the work of Andrew Baldwin (2012), futurity signals the ways in which, "the future is rendered knowable through specific practices (i.e., calculation, imagination, and performance) and, in turn, intervenes upon the present" (173). Futurity recognizes *the* future not only as the yet-to-be but also as an object of the present that is oriented toward the yet-to-be. In this way, the future, which the child often stands in for, can be imagined in ways that resist settler futures. Thus, Afrofuturity reaches from the present, through diasporas, through the multiplicities of the Black Atlantic, across the middle passage, to Black collective memories of enslavement and ancestral African epistemologies as continual renewals for freedom, presence, and futures.

THEORY AND READING STRATEGY

In the opening of this study, I centered two scenes from the novel in which the child, Tan-Tan, is dislocated and subsequently arrives, the first is after she is kidnapped by her father Antonio as he flees to New Half-Way Tree where they immediately encounter an Indigenous figure Chichibud; the second is when Tan-Tan arrives to Chichibud's homeland after killing Antonio as he raped her. Of particular importance is the address of the narrator, eshu, named after the West African Yoruba deity, to Tan-Tan's unborn child, Taubman. The novel opens as Tan-Tan goes into labour with Taubman and closes with Taubman's arrival. Such incidents of arrival are recurrent throughout the novel as the child first experiences a dislocation, which is followed by an arrival. I read this recurrence as constitutive of an ongoing state of arrivance. Therefore, I expand on the concept of arrivance here to read the multiple instances of the child's geographic dislocations and arrivals to theorize the web of relational agencies the arrivant is situated within. In what follows, I trace the notion of arrivance to Caribbean and Indigenous African reinventions of home in the wake of the afterlife of slavery.

Arrivance, Futurity, and Childhood Agency

One notion of arrivant holds currency through Jodi Byrd's (2011) often cited understanding to "signify those people *forced* [emphasis added] into the Americas through the violence of European and Anglo-American colonialism and imperialism around the globe" (xix). Byrd (2011) uses this term to distinguish between settler colonialism and arrivant colonialism. For Manu Vimalassery, Juliana Hu Pegues, and Alyosha Goldstein (2016), the term arrivant dismantles the term settler, which is "both inadequate and somehow monstrously wrong" (8) as a descriptor for the social position of chattel slaves and indentured laborers (and their descendants) forced to the New World to assume presence and futures on usurped Indigenous homeland. Despite wide ranging interventions made through this understanding of arrivants, reading them as exclusively *forced* is at risk of further stripping arrivants of agency when in fact imperial force is continuously met with resistance through multiple relations and thus forms of agency. This misrepresentation of the enslaved as without agency perpetuates false narratives that reinforces ongoing systems of colonization (Roberts 2015).

For the Barbadian poet Kamau Brathwaite, who inspired Byrd's (2011) theorization, arrivant is an agentic social position "of active continuance, of active Indigenous conjuring, or active arrival at a ground of temporal beginning and therefore possibility in the impossibility of return" (Byrd 2019, 211) to a lost home. Roberts' (2015) notion of marronage *as* freedom is a helpful heuristic which links arrivance to enslavement in terms of the often-disavowed agency of the enslaved. Roberts' (2015) argues that any conception of freedom is in a dialectic relationship with enslavement and to understand freedom, scholars must look to the agency of the enslaved and practices of marronage or agentic "flight from slavery" (3). Additionally, Vimalassery et al. (2016) remind us that "arrival would be no arrival, except in relation to the indigenous" (9) which helps to resist narratives of Indigenous absence that emanate from doctrines such as *terra nullius*. These relationships constitute the agencies between arrivants and the Indigenous. The terms of active arrival in the wake of slavery are critical to reading the arrivant child's shifting and multiplying agencies. Therefore, I first read *Midnight Robber* paying close attention to how the trauma of slavery and the presence of Indigeneity inform the narrative and the arrivant child's agency.

Enslavement and dislocation required arrivants to reinvent the meanings and practices of home through relationships with Indigenous peoples. Taíno historian, Erica Neeganagwedgin (2015), notes that many Taíno people fled European enslavement by going into the hills of Jamaica to form alliances with Indigenous African arrivants. These alliances would form maroon societies or the liminal and interstitial spaces between enslavement and freedom (Roberts 2015). In fact, the word *maroon* is etymologically derived from the vocabulary of the Arawaks and Taíno of the Caribbean. Its Spanish form, *cimarrón*, linked Indigenous flight from European enslavement to the hills of Hispaniola. The maroon functioned as a site of cultural exchange, hybridity, and alliance formation. These functions are evident in Brathwaite's (1978) opening to *The Arrivants: A New World Trilogy* in the epigraph which quotes The Kumina Queen, Imogene Kennedy, an arrivant, spiritual leader, and practitioner of Kumina, an African Indigenous and Jamaican religious form when she says:

> Well, muh ol' arrivance . . . is from Africa . . . . That's muh ol' arrivants family. Muh gran'muddah an' muh gran'fadda. Well, they came out here as slavely . . . you unnerstan'? Well, when them came now, I doan belongs to Africa, I belongs to Jamaica. I born here.
> Well, muh gran 'parents, she teach me some of the African languages an' the rest I get it at the cotton -tree root . . . I take twenty-one days to get all the balance. . . . (Brathwaite 1978, epigraph)

De Line and O'Shaughnessy (2018) unpack Kennedy's use of the word arrivance. They suggest that Kennedy's "ol' arrivants family" could be read as "whole" arrivants family or Kennedy's search for "balance" and wholeness in the fragmented plantocratic Caribbean. They note that her connection to her African Indigeneity through the cotton tree also establishes her connection to the Taíno for whom the cotton-tree, or *ceiba*, is also an important life-giving spiritual relative. Attention to Indigenous–arrivant relationships destabilizes the representational logics of colonial discourses (Vimalassery et al. 2016) such as the absent presence of Indigeneity (Vizenor 1994) and their perpetual elimination (Wolfe 1999) that operate to secure settler futurity (Tuck and Gaztambide-Fernández 2012).

Additionally, Indigenous, arrivant, and settler relationships to land are important in the conceptualization and making of home. For P'urhépecha scholar Michael Lerma (2012), settlers often relate to land as "a resource employed for utility" while Indigenous peoples view their traditional "homelands" as part of an "interdependent" and "living relationship" (76–77). For arrivants brought to the "chained and welcoming port[s]" of the New World (Brathwaite 1967, 11), land is an ambivalent figure that is neither commodity nor home, but representative of freedom and thus the possibility of a "profoundly anti-colonial practice of making home" (De Line and O'Shaughnessy 2018, 142). In turn, I use the term "homeland" when referring to Indigenous relationships to home and land, while for settlers and arrivants, I use "home" and "land" separately since they are not always interdependent. Thus, with the understanding that arrivance implies an agentic position of making home between arrivants and Indigenous people, I am attentive to Hopkinson's (2000) narration of home and the relationships that resist and produce home beyond colonial conventions. The relationships Hopkinson (2000) narrates in this formulation of home helps to support the idea that agency is contingent and relational. In turn, this helps to illustrate my argument that the arrivant child and the im/possibilities of home are constructed through the doublebind of losing one's home and having to make home on stolen Indigenous homeland.

Building on the two reading strategies outlined above, I read through the relationships between the novel characters depicted in fig 8.1. I first consider how Hopkinson narrates the child's agency through the trauma of slavery

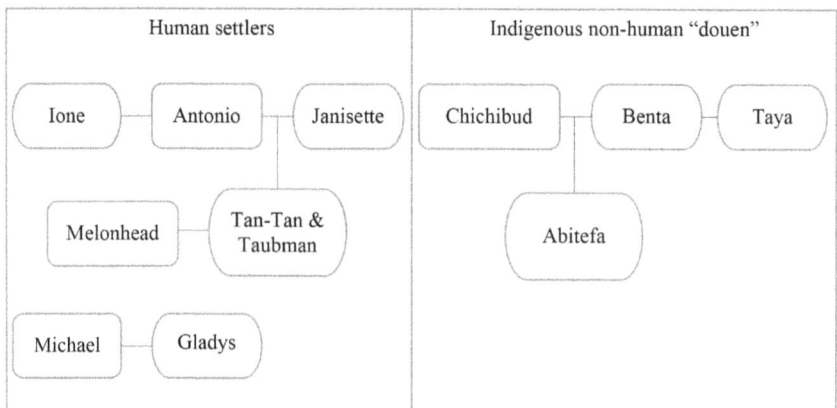

Figure 8.1   Familial and community relations in *Midnight Robber.* **Original chart created by author.**

and the precarities of arrivance. I argue that these frames create the futuristic conditions that psychically split the child, giving birth to multiple agencies of the self rooted in resistance to colonial violence. Second, I turn to consider the im/possibilities of making home on Indigenous home/land. Here, I argue that the cultivation of the child's resistive agencies as she tries to make a new home is contingent on the relationship of care provided by the Indigenous. Paradoxically, this care invites settler aggression which ultimately destabilizes conventional notions of home and invites new formations through the space of the maroon.

ARRIVANCE, THE TRAUMA OF SLAVERY, AND CHILDHOOD AGENCY AS RESISTANCE AND REFUSAL

Hopkinson (2000) introduces her young protagonist through the universal figure of the innocent and dependent child with little to no agency, but by the end of the novel, she is an agentic figure that resists colonial violence and logic. The shift from helpless child to resistive agent draws on both an individualized capacity concept of agency and contingent and relational forms of agency. In this first section of the analysis, I focus on how Hopkinson (2000) draws on individualized but multiple forms of agency necessary for survival in the wake of the afterlife of slavery and its waves of arrivance. First, I argue that Hopkinson (2000) draws on the trope of rape and more specifically the child of rape, to represent the collective violence and lingering trauma of colonization. Second, I argue that Hopkinson (2000), like Frantz Fanon, turns to the psychology of the arrivant to explore what agency means on colonized and contested land. More specifically, she draws on traumatic colonial processes of subject formation and the psychic splitting of the self, what Fanon (1967) refers to as double consciousness, to speak to the generative effects of colonization in the agentic, resistive, and destabilizing figure of the Midnight Robber.

Hopkinson (2000) connects childhood innocence and dependence to a history of trans-Atlantic slavery. For example, the story begins on the "civilized" home planet named "Toussaint" after the Haitian slave revolt leader Toussaint Louverture. The narrative space devoted to life on Toussaint constitutes the first-third of the novel in which the arrivant child is generally seen not heard. Tan-Tan is conceived in between the antagonisms of her parents and is a pawn in her mother, Ione's, strategy to garner the attention of her womanizing husband, Antonio. For Antonio, the child is a figure of desire immediately ensconced in a male chauvinistic paternalist hierarchy as "Someone who would listen to him, look up to him. Like Ione when she'd been a green young woman" (Hopkinson 2000, 6). Throughout her time in Toussaint,

Tan-Tan is referred to as "doux-doux" a Trinidadian term of endearment meaning sweetness inherited from French colonizers, and she is a figure of "pureness." Her home life is a conventional heteronormative arrangement she shares with her mother and father. Home is a place of "play" with her caregivers, Nursie and eshu, on whom she is dependent. They are all technologically connected to Granny Nanny, the web-based benevolent and surveilling artificial intelligence named after the Jamaican maroon leader. Together, they protect Tan-Tan from adult affairs, conflict, and suffering. In short, the Afrofuturistic arrivant child in "civilized" space is a figure of innocence but with little agency similar to that of her enslaved ancestors.

After these innocent and passive origins, Hopkinson (2000) examines the trauma of slavery through arrivance and the trope of childhood rape. After accidentally killing his wife's lover, Antonio manages to flee Toussaint and kidnaps Tan-Tan in the process. They travel to the "rough" prison planet New Half-Way tree by way of an interdimensional shifting pod in which they are confined like "long time ago Africans" (Hopkinson 2000, 74). This marks the arrivant child's first dislocation from her home and arrival to the New World. The pair is immediately greeted in the bush by the Indigenous figure, Chichibud, who guides them to the safety of a human settlement, Junjuh. In these first moments in relationship with the Indigenous, the child shifts from being a passive object to an active agent at the center of the narrative. After the ordeal of dislocation and arrival, the narrative leaps forward two years to Tan-Tan's ninth birthday celebrations after which the father rapes the child for the first time. In her struggle to make meaning during the violence, Tan-Tan first presumes that she must be "very bad for Daddy to do her so" (Hopkinson 2000, 140). However, her ambivalence toward the father takes hold as "Daddy's hands were hurting, even though his mouth smiled at her like the old Daddy . . . Daddy was two daddies" (Hopkinson 2000, 140). Under the weight of these psychic contradictions, Tan-Tan "felt her own self split in two to try to understand, to accommodate them both. Antonio, good Antonio smiled at her with his face. Good Tan-Tan smiled back. She closed her mind to what bad Antonio was doing to her bad body" (Hopkinson 2000, 40). Tan-Tan then proceeds to mentally escape the violence by directing her gaze to a toy figure of the resistive Robber Queen whom she internalizes. No longer is she good and innocent Tan-Tan but in the midst of violence a new part of the self is birthed, "Tan-Tan the Robber Queen . . . the one who born on a faraway planet, who travel to this place to rob the rich in their idleness and help the poor in their humility" (Hopkinson 2000, 140), who is now impervious to cruelty and instead evokes fear in the hearts of men. Here, the arrivant child's consciousness is split much in the same way that Fanon (1967) describes the crumbling of his "corporeal schema" (84) within the enclosing circle of white imperial violence.

For Sielke (2002), representations of rape function as a rhetorical device that stands in for other social, political, and economic conflicts. Rape here functions as a symbol of colonial violence in its fragmenting effects and lingering traumas that continue to haunt the arrivant child through to the very end of the novel. For example, in her dreams, Tan-Tan is "chased by a thing she couldn't see" (264). This chase extends beyond the child protagonists' psyche into the broader plot as she is chased by settlers seeking revenge and retributive justice for the killing of Antonio, the colonial patriarch. The connection between rape and colonization is made explicit later in the novel as Tan-Tan says, "He rape me . . . He put this baby in me, like the one before. He was forever trying to *plant* me, like I was his soil to harvest" (260). Across these moments, Hopkinson (2000) is drawing on a colonial literary tradition in which the figure of the racialized woman is the passive victim of male colonizers. For example, Jenny Sharpe (1993) argues that the literary figure of the racialized and colonized woman is representative of colonized territory and contributed to an Orientalizing discourse that perpetuated colonization beyond the pages of the European novel. Similarly, Gayatri Spivak refers to the colonized and more broadly the postcolonial condition as "The child of rape" (29) or a product of racialized and gendered colonial violence.

However, in the same foundational rape scene, Hopkinson (2000) speaks to the generative effects of violence by resisting the trope of the passive female victim in spite of the persistence and lingering effects of colonial trauma. Colonial violence splits the arrivant child giving birth to the Robber Queen, a female version of the traditionally male Midnight Robber. The Midnight Robber is a bombastic figure from the Caribbean carnival archive with Indigenous African (Akan) roots in the griot (storyteller). He is an agentic trickster that embodies "resistance to officialdom" (Zobel Marshall 2016, 210) such as the civilizing discourses and practices of colonial imperialism, its technologies of enslavement, and its idealizations of childhood. Spivak's (2009) metonymic link between the postcolonial condition and "The child of rape" (29) is helpful in unpacking these generative effects in this scene of foundational trauma that Sigmund Freud (1917) famously said offers a glimpse into "the constitution of the human ego" (247). Spivak (2009) condemns the violence of rape, but she also does not ostracize the child. Instead, she sees this child as an "enabling violation" (Spivak 2009, 29) and something to hold a deconstructive position toward. Such a position can, for example, work to undo taken-for-granted child–adult binaries, its hierarchies of generational power, and individualized distributions of agency. It can recognize the closely linked, malleable, and interchangeable categories of childhood and adulthood, its mobilization in colonial imperial discourse (Nandy 1984), and trans-Atlantic slavery (King 2011; Webster 2021) and redeploy it as a figure that is menacing and destabilizing to colonial logics. Hopkinson (2000) achieves this in Tan-Tan, the arrivant child of rape and the birth of another agency of the self in the Robber Queen.

After this foundational rape scene, there is the longest chronological break from Tan-Tan's ninth birthday to her sixteenth. This period of narratological forgetting continues to play with literary models of psychic trauma (Balaev 2018) and extends to the next major break in the plot where she is dislocated from the human settlement leading to another arrival to the douen homeland, the Daddy Tree. In her bid for adulthood and its freedoms, Tan-Tan actively plans with her friend, Melonhead, to move from Junjuh to the town of Sweet Pone as a couple. A drunken Antonio overhears this and erupts into a rage. Melonhead tries to protect Tan-Tan, but she asks him to leave after which Antonio proceeds to rape her, for the last time. With a knife on her waist, given to her as a birthday present from her stepmother, Janisette, the resistive part of the self acts to kill the father, "Her hand found it. The scabbard. With the knife inside . . . . It must have been the Robber Queen . . . who . . . got the knife braced at her breastbone just as Antonio slammed his heavy body right onto the blade" (Hopkinson 2000, 168). In the midst of repeated violence, Tan-Tan the Robber Queen, resistor of officialdom, returns to kill the colonial patriarch. In this scene, Hopkinson (2000) displaces the intention of action to the repressed part of the self that returns to protect the self from harm with the revolutionary kind of violence directed toward the institutions of colonialism in the form of the patriarch. In this way, the arrivant child and its historicity destabilize the unity of the agent through a Freudian splitting of the self to create an unconscious agent within that reads and acts in the world to administer justice, even from under the penetrative force of colonial violence.

Extending the logics of psychoanalytic trauma, if the subject cannot accept the losses that precipitate from ruptural violence (i.e., the loss of nation in war or subjecthood in rape) into a cohesive and life affirming self-narrative, she exists in a state of sorrow and dejection. Freud (1917) calls this state *melancholia*, and it is a site of "critical agency" (Freud 1917, 240) often in the form of self-criticism such as the feeling of inferiority held by the colonized subject. This is evident throughout the narrative as Tan-Tan berates herself as a "stupid," "idiotic," "bitch," and "killer." One reading understands Tan-Tan as being in a melancholic state, subject to the unpredictable return of losses that she cannot reconcile as part of the self, such as the loss of selfhood through rape or the ambivalent patriarch that haunts her dreams. However, postcolonial scholar Ranjana Khanna (2003) inverts this depressive state by directing the "melancholic's manic critical agency into the unworking of conformity, and into the critique of the status quo" (23). From this perspective, the revolutionary political violence necessary to destabilize and decolonize the status quo, such as the arrivant child's killing of the father, can be understood as an agentic refusal by a part of the self. This part of the self will not accept the loss of ideals such as "the right of subjecthood and the right not to be exploited" (Khanna 2003, 23) through the rape of trans-Atlantic slavery and imperial colonialism. Thus, the arrivant child's agency is not a universal unitary capacity that she possesses, instead, it is a multiple, diverse, and discordant mode of resistance and refusal rooted in colonial history.

IM/POSSIBILITIES OF HOME, CONTINGENT CHILDHOOD AGENCIES, AND THE DESTABILIZING FIGURE OF THE ARRIVANT CHILD

After killing Antonio, Chichibud finds Tan-Tan in an immobile state of shock. Fully aware of both Tan-Tan's ongoing abuse and settler societies retributive justice, Chichibud and his wife, Benta, relocate Tan-Tan to the Indigenous homeland in the Daddy Tree where they can care for her as she heals. However, the arrivant child's movements across the contradictions and paradoxes on usurped Indigenous homeland destabilize communities, relationships, and thus agency. In this final section of the analysis, I open by considering the historical relationships arrivants, settlers, and indigenous have to home/land and each other. Next, I trace how the arrivant child destabilizes these relationships. More specifically, I argue that Hopkinson (2000) challenges individualized forms of agency by attending to the contingent agencies the arrivant child is part of, as she seeks, that elusive and prized object of desire—home.

Here, we might recall that for scholars of relational agency, agency is distributed between human, nonhuman, and more-than-human interactants. Agency only appears among beings in and through relationships such that the multiple social relationships at the centers of production "*constitute the very structure and form of agency itself*" (Burkitt 2016, 336). In the relational context of the New World and Hopkinson's (2000) universe, both settlers and arrivants must reckon with the loss of home on the ancestral homelands of Indigenous peoples. The etiologies of these losses are distinct, thereby forming drastically different relations between settlers, arrivants, the Indigenous, and home/lands. Settler presence in the New World stems from social decay at home and the search for a new home and comes with an endowed sense of superiority that relates to others as inferior. This happens through various ideological discourses and practices such as colonial paternalism and the mission to progress and civilize the childlike savage, convictions of manifest destiny, and arrogant declarations of sovereignty on an others homeland (Veracini 2010). For settlers, land is not an active agent but rather a passive commodity (Lerma 2012) that is often cleared (Seed 1995) of all living, nonliving, and more-than-human beings, or a logic of elimination (Wolfe 1999) at the center of colonial formations of home. In contrast, Indigenous relationships to homeland are material, real, concrete, metaphysical, intellectual, and spiritual (Lerma 2012). Take for example the Oglala Lakota leader Crazy Horse that fought against United States settlers who said "The Great Spirit gave us this country as a home" (Lerma 2012, 75) or for Indigenous Hawaiians the statement "Land is our mother" is not a metaphor (Meyer 2008, 219). In these relationships, land is an active and caring parental figure with whom home, identity, life, and thus agency are contingent.

Hopkinson (2000) represents these different relationships starkly through the trope of home and representations of space. She first does this with attention to the organization of space depicted in Tan-Tan's arrivals to both the human settlement, Junjuh, and the Indigenous homeland, the Daddy Tree. For example, when Tan-Tan and Antonio were on their way to Junjuh after their first arrival at New Half-Way Tree, ". . . one minute they were beating their way through bush, then the bush got less dense, fewer trees, more shrubs. Next minute they turned the corner to see *cleared earth* [emphasis added]" (Hopkinson 2000, 119). In contrast to the human settlement, Tan-Tan's arrival to the Indigenous homeland is less clear to her. As Benta swoops into the forest canopy after Tan-Tan's rescue, they eventually land on what seemed like the ground. Eventually, she realizes that it is not the ground but rather "Big branches everywhere, so big they disappeared into the shadows like trails . . . . This place was a massive tree, so big she couldn't see all of it" (Hopkinson 2002, 178). Again, the notable difference here is that settler relationships to land and arrangements of home involve clearing the land of life and history while Indigenous relationships to homeland are dependent on, and in union with, its living interactants.

Meanwhile, arrivants to the New World must navigate settler and Indigenous ideological and spatial arrangements of home/land in attempts to make home. According to Silva (2009), for those living in diaspora home is both "a place of belonging" and an "elusive, seductive and prized" (Silva 2009, 694) object of relation. The arrivant is abducted from their homeland, transformed into chattel, and forced to occupy stolen Indigenous land (Byrd 2002). Before any notion of home can be realized, flight from bondage would have to be prioritized by the enslaved. Roberts (2015) calls the flight from bondage marronage which he understands *as* freedom. Marronage as freedom is the action of flight from enslavement that destabilizes the economic productivity of the colonies, both the Caribbean plantation and settlements on the "frontier" (Maynard 2017). It is from this social position of inevitable flight, movement, and action that the arrivant establishes relationships to the lands of the New World which represent the possibility of home. Importantly, home is contingent on the allied relationship between African arrivants and Indigenous people such as the Taíno (Neeganagwedgin 2015) for whom the land *is* home and who is also subject to the violent encroachment and enslavement of settlers. Thus, for arrivants, the conditions of arrival and desires for home and freedom necessitate fundamentally different relationships to Indigenous people, their homelands, and the structure of agency itself.

Hopkinson's (2000) arrivant children (Tan-Tan and Taubman) destabilizes the relationships narratively set up between settler and Indigenous cultures, their relationships to land, and conceptions of home, which is the focus of the remainder of this section. Again, for Vimalassery et al. (2016), the arrivant is an inherently destabilizing presence that challenges the Indigenous–settler binary and the very idea of home. After arriving to the hidden Indigenous homeland, Tan-Tan must learn to survive and Chichibud and Benta agree that their daughter, Abitefa, a large bird-like figure also learning to do the same would accompany Tan-Tan in the forest from day to day. Abitefa shows her another douen secret, the foundry. The douen are teaching themselves metallurgy to resist the violent aggression of human settlers and also plan to trade with them, which requires travel to a settlement. Tan-Tan is eager for belonging and wants to be among her own kind and asks to join Chichibud and Benta. However, they deny her request saying there is "Too much danger" (Hopkinson 2000, 231). Tan-Tan is upset and insists that she is not going to be a bother and that because she is human, they would not endanger her. Chichibud explains, "The danger is you, not them. We can't take the risk that you tell them about we. Tan-Tan felt cold. They would never let her go" (Hopkinson 2000, 232). Here, the arrivant child, while having been rescued from the confinements and the retributive justice of settlers, remains in captivity on Indigenous homeland. Thus, the arrivant child is caught in a double bind situation where in order to heal and survive in the New World through Indigenous care and homeland, they must surrender to a certain degree of captivity reminiscent of enslavement or take flight from such confinements.

However, another wave of impending arrivance in the unborn child of rape, Taubman, compels Tan-Tan to resist captivity and venture into settler society. One day while out in the forest with Abitefa, Tan-Tan tells her that she is pregnant with her father's child, the child of rape saying, "Oh, God; I making baby for my own father . . . What I go do? Tell me what? . . . And what I go call it, eh? Son or brother? . . . I can't give birth to this thing, Abitefa. Is a monster. I rip one of the brutes out of me once, I could do it twice" (Hopkinson 2000, 233). Abitefa doesn't quite understand Tan-Tan's desire to get rid of the child since she sees it as a gift from the Daddy Tree, a living more-than-human interactant rooted in the homeland. Nonetheless, she agrees to help Tan-Tan go to a human settlement to get an abortion against the warnings from the adults Benta and Chichibud. Here, the unborn child of rape is depicted as a monstrous figure representative of colonial violence that the mother, also a child of rape, wants to violently rip out. Reading with Christina Sharpe (2016), the womb of the Black arrivant mother functions "much like the ships hold . . . turning the birth canal into another domestic Middle Passage" (74) that brings forth a nonhuman being and monstrous child. Hopkinson (2000) is attentive to this metaphor in the unborn and monstrous child of rape and its "premature death" (Hartman 2008) through the social institution of slavery. However, Hopkinson (2000) also imagines life-affirming possibilities for the child that refuses this position devoid of agency. Instead, the unborn child of rape actively moves the protagonist from within the hold of her womb to leave the safety and care of the Indigenous homeland and return to settler space to, as I will demonstrate shortly, pursue freedom and decolonial conventions of home.

Tan-Tan and Abitefa arrive to the human settlement, Chigger Bite, for Tan-Tan to get an abortion. They agree that it is too dangerous for Abitefa to go into town with her, so she waits on the edge of the forest, "a shadow place between two peoples" (Hopkinson 2000, 298) or what can be read as the maroon, and to which I will return momentarily. In this first arrival to Chigger Bite, the repressed Robber Queen is awakened by the abuse of an adult child by his mother. The abrupt return of the repressed intervenes to mete out justice which only stops as Tan-Tan remembers her own abuse. She leaves the village without an abortion and returns to Abitefa. On her walk back, Tan-Tan is filled with pride as she remembers the voice of the Robber Queen and eagerly tells her tale of triumph to Abitefa. No longer concerned with getting an abortion, Tan-Tan the Robber Queen, or the critical agent within, grows bolder and she repeatedly returns to the settlement to bring justice to the downtrodden. However, an overly confident and agentic Tan-Tan the Robber Queen is ambushed in one venture leading to Abitefa, a large bird-like figure, having to rescue her. After recovery, Tan-Tan again returns to the settlement and learns that people imagine the Robber Queen as a nonhuman being with fiery eyes and large wings, which she revels in. In this series of events, the arrivant child's sense of agency is growing and continues to be emboldened. However, this agency is contingent on Indigenous intervention that settlers misrecognize and appropriate into their mythology which pleases the arrivant. Thus, the arrivants individualized sense of agency comes by way of her complicity in the erasure of Indigeneity.

Hopkinson (2000) dismantles this growing sense of individualized agency through the arrivants' movements between and across geographies. These movements invite the aggression of settlers that destabilize Indigenous territory and homeland. After continued forays into human settlements and the growing myth of Tan-Tan the Robber Queen, Tan-Tan is tracked down by her widowed stepmother, Janisette, who intends to bring her back to the settlement to be punished. This encounter is brief but deadly as Benta's sister, Taya, is killed. After fending off Janisette, the douen decide to destroy their Daddy Tree and take flight to other Daddy Tree's but Tan-Tan and Abitefa are exiled and soon "living in misery" (Hopkinson 2000, 283). Just before departure, Tan-Tan expresses her sorrow to a grieving Benta who says, "is not you make the gun, is not you fire the gun. But it's your *actions* [emphasis added] brings you to this path, so it's good you sorry" (Hopkinson 2000, 275). Benta's words illustrate how "action," the measure of possessive agency, is not limited to the individual but is distributed across multiple social relationships. It is the differentials of power embedded in these relations that structure the agency of the subject. For example, Janisette's intention to return the child to settler society is a kind of "enforced belonging" (Harris 2019, 219) similar to enslaved African arrivants into the United States. Arrivants constructed as nonhuman beings are excluded from discourses of citizenship while they are forcibly included in the nation as laborers. In this double-bind situation, Hopkinson (2000) unravels the arrivant child's growing capacity to act through the recursive effects of its actions. This ultimately results in the weakening of the arrivant's relationship with the Indigenous, and in turn the agency of the arrivant.

After the destruction of the Daddy Tree, Tan-Tan and Abitefa are surviving in maroon shadows of human settlements, but soon Tan-Tan is faced with the option to be part of a conventional notion of home. They eventually make their way to Sweet Pone settlement, where Tan-Tan reunites with her childhood friend Melonhead and where she must face a revengeful Janisette. After speaking back to Janisette and exposing her as complicit in Antonio's violence, Melonhead asks Tan-Tan to come home with him. Just as they reach his door, the pangs of labor begin to knock. Instead of going into Melonhead's home, she tells him that she must return home. Having visited her camp in the "shadow place" (Hopkinson 2000, 298), he is shocked and confused and asks, "What home? Where?" (Hopkinson 2000, 327) illustrating the settler's failure to recognize anti-colonial conceptions of home (De Line and O'Shaughnessy 2018). Tan-Tan replies, "I have to go back in the bush to Abitefa . . . [then] she turned on her heel and started walking, with or without him" (Hopkinson 2000, 327). The arrivant child's active and intentional refusal of settler conventions of home are a practice of freedom *as* marronage or the flight from enslavement and the "perpetual domesticity" (Roberts 2015, 70) of settler society, particularly for women. For Roberts (2015), the relations of slavery are more than, as Orlando Patterson (1982) suggests, a dehumanizing set of property relations that yields social death. For Roberts (2015), slavery is a social institution in dialectic relation to freedom. This freedom is not someplace, but rather "flight from the zone of nonbeing . . . [that]creates the possibility for actualizing revolutions against slavery through the natality embedded in its processes of movement" (20). Here, Roberts (2015) is drawing on Hannah Arendt's

(1958) concept of natality which refers to "the new beginning inherent in birth [that] can make itself felt in the world only because the newcomer possesses the capacity of beginning something anew, that is, of acting" (9). Natality then requires a universal kind of agency that is inherent to newness, either by birth or by new cultural or social beginnings, such as those made in the maroon. The arrivant child's rejection of settler conceptions of home and return to the maroon is a disavowal of the presumed lacking agency of the enslaved. This disavowal is replaced with the arrivant's irreducible and indeterminate capacity for newness, creativity, rebirth, and freedom that is part of the condition of being birthed into the social order. It is through this indeterminate capacity that the arrivant child insists on returning to the agencies constituted in the relationship between the arrivant and the Indigenous, thereby effectively destabilizing settler orders symbolized through notions of home.

Hopkinson's (2000) attention to the agencies of natality in the processes of working toward freedom is made quite explicit in the arrival of the unborn child of rape, Taubman. As Tan-Tan hikes back to camp, the narrator, eshu, interrupts in the final scene of arrival to address Taubman. Eshu explains to Taubman how through nanomite technology transferred to him by his mother that they could be tracked by the artificial intelligence Granny Nanny. This has created a connection to the web and the voices of its ancestors unlike that of others on Toussaint. While others could hear the song of the ancestors through a bio-integrated earpiece, Taubman could *feel* the songs of the ancestors through the "the body . . . as one living connection . . . a bodystring [that] will sing to Nanny tune" (Hopkinson 2000, 328). In this way, the child is a more-than-human "weave" in Granny Nanny's web. The narrative returns to the labor scene where Tan-Tan looks at the "little bit of person in her arms . . . He had Antonio's face, but they were her features too, *hers*. Her son was not a monster" (Hopkinson 2000, 329). The child is greeted by Melonhead and Abitefa when his mother names him "Taubman: The human bridge from slavery to freedom" (Hopkinson 2000, 329). The natality embedded in the processes of marronage, or the arrivant child's flight from the confinements of colonial conventions of home, gives birth to a new Afrofuturistic subject. This subject resists an exclusively individualized notion of agency in its characterization as a bridge or the relationship itself between the trauma of slavery and a present and future of liberation. The Afrofuturist arrivant child's agencies are the relationships between arrivants (Tan-Tan and Taubman), settlers (Melonhead), and the Indigenous (Abitefa), who occupy a future home not predicated on the elimination of the Indigenous. Hopkinson's (2000) children are a testament to the idea that any notion of an individualized capacity to act is contingent on the terms of the relationships in which the subject is located.

CONCLUSIONS: ARRIVANT CHILDHOODS AND AFROFUTURITY

Hopkinson's (2000) writing of *Midnight Robber* and the representations of childhood it offers is a form of Afrofuturity or an act in the present that destabilizes colonial archives of the past toward Black arrivant counter-futures. These counter-futures are an important intervention to the current management of colonial geographies manifest in the nation-state and its borders, which actual arrivant children continue to encounter through displacement. In this final section, I first connect representational practices, in general terms, and Afrofuturism, in particular, to the experiences and futures of actual arrivant children. Next, I outline three contributions Afrofuturity makes to discourses of childhood. Finally, I call for the practice of Afrofuturity to extend to childhood studies.

Adult idealizations of childhood as a universal state of innocence, ignorance, and dependence does little to protect children or remedy colonial histories of childhood abuse and trauma that have created the conditions necessary to try and "save the child." In fact, the continued production of childhood in these ways operates to perpetuate the very violence it tries to distance itself from. Carly McLaughlin (2018) examines the material effects of representational practices surrounding children seeking asylum in the United Kingdom in the wake of the dead two-year-old Syrian boy, Alan Kurdi, whose image lying face down on the shore stirred global emotions. McLaughlin (2018) looks at the media campaign surrounding the 2016 "Dubs Amendment" which sought to reform the United Kingdom immigration act in response to the dismal living conditions of predominantly Middle Eastern and African children in the French refugee camp the "Calais Jungle." According to McLaughlin (2018), the campaign, and humanitarian organizations more generally, adopted a "child first, migrant second" (1758) rhetoric in their efforts to persuade the British public and lawmakers to create pathways to citizenship for child migrants in a growing anti-immigration climate. Importantly, the shift in public sentiment was made possible through images and representations that appealed to the universalist figure of the ahistorical and apolitical innocent child. McLaughlin (2018) argues that the idealized image of the innocent child in the public imaginary precluded the media imagery of actual racialized children from the camp. The image of the racialized child, caught in a longstanding colonial racial hierarchy, would quickly be reconfigured in the media to "unchildlike" and undocumented criminal noncitizens that threatened British sovereignty and ultimately stymied efforts to help migrants. Therefore, if "representational practices around asylum-seeking children rely on codes that preclude demonstrations of resilience, maturity and agency in these children, and suppress bodily markers of gender and race that would detract from their perceived childness" (McLaughlin 2018, 1758), then Afrofuturity offers an important intervention through the production of new decolonial codes of childhood.

Hopkinson's (2000) practice of Afrofuturity attends to the arrivant child as a category that is neither the universally innocent recipient of adult protection nor a wellspring of personal agency necessary to redeem adults from dismal futures of their own creation. Rather, the Afrofuturistic arrivant child is a complex historical, political, and relational subject situated in the contradictions and paradoxes of colonial space. This figure of the child offers three interventions to dominant constructions of childhood. First, Afrofuturity and its refusal to imagine away colonialism and slavery as part of the history of childhood recognizes that any discussion of agency must attend to that of the enslaved. This logic follows Roberts's (2015) insistence that any notion of freedom can only be understood in dialectic relationship to the enslaved. In a fragmented and porous archive like that of the Middle Passage in which the subject and her voice are rarely centered, the critical fabulations of Afrofuturism can speculate on what childhood agency means in a dialectical relationship to the ongoing enslavement, detainment, capture, incarceration, and dislocation of arrivants. The second contribution that Hopkinson's (2000) text offers is very particular and situational attention to the paradoxes and double binds of settler contexts that are formed between Indigenous, settler, and arrivant desires, cultures, and relationships to land. Sukaina Hirji (2021) defines the double bind as a "dammed if you do, dammed if you don't" (649) choice situation conditioned by intersecting systems of oppression. These intersecting systems undermine agency to the extent that it is "impossible for an agent not to be complicit in their own oppression" (668). The British-Somali poet, Warsan Shire's (2011) poem "Home" illustrates these binds when she says, "no one leaves home unless home is the mouth of a shark . . . you have to understand, that no one puts their children in a boat unless the water is safer than the land." These double binds mean that for some children, their actions, regardless of their capacity, make them complicit in their own oppression. Hopkinson (2008) illustrates this through Tan-Tan's actions that invite settler aggression and the destruction of the Indigenous homeland which ultimately leads to her own diminished agency. Understanding these double binds helps to understand that childhood agency is not exclusively measured by what the agent directly and intentionally *does*, but also by what they indirectly and unintentionally *undo*. For Hopkinson (2008), the dammed if you do, damned if you don't structure of some children's agency is destabilizing to that elusive prize for the diasporic subject—home. Finally, Afrofuturity offers a vision of the future, in the present that is not immiserating to Black, brown, and Indigenous children. Hopkinson's (2008) very act of imagining from the wake of the afterlife of slavery and her return to the natality and hybridity of the maroon opens the possibility of inventing decolonial orders of home, belonging, and inclusion for the transitory and stateless casualties of colonial imperialism and its ongoing circuits of immiseration.

I opened this chapter with the proposition that the destabilizing and decolonial effects of Afrofuturism on the Euro-American genre of science fiction is a form of Afrofuturity that could be incorporated into the interdisciplinary field of childhood studies to bring about a similar and urgent destabilization. At its core, Afrofuturism is a manifestation of Black desires for a future in which Blackness is a source of joy and life, not misery and death. Olga Nieuwenhuys (2012), in an editorial for *Childhood*, called for a similar kind of attention to the positive life-affirming aspects of children's lives from the Global South through attention to postcolonial childhoods. Nieuwenhuys (2012) makes the claim that the normative dominance of Northern over Southern childhoods studies in the field is linked to "an overproduction of knowledge based in disciplinary strongholds that resist critique of their Eurocentrism" (4) and, given the requirement of racial difference to colonization, I add their white supremacy. This glaring absence of racial difference in both scholars and scholarship in the field is understandable and curious. Perhaps, childhood like "The human is a pointless and treacherous category" (Eshun 1998, 005) to scholars of color and leads to important but adjacent fields such as the recent emergence of Black girlhood studies and Black boyhood studies. However, while Black, brown, and Indigenous people have historically been located outside of the category of "the human"— a human always imagined to be a white European adult—we have also been relegated to the status of perpetual child races to be civilized into adults by an imperial paternalism. Childhood then, in its dominant form, continues to be an inescapable organizing principle and as an interdisciplinary field of study, an important site of knowledge production. Thus, it is my assertion that childhood studies should and can be Blackened, browned, and decolonized through sustained attention to the future(s), childhood and otherwise, longed for from the margins. Childhood studies can become a field invested in Afrofuturity and the futurity of other marginalized subjects by turning to archives and creating futures in which the cipher of humanity is no longer the universal white, innocent, and agentic child that holds the promise of continued racist and colonial global orders.

REFERENCES

Alanen, Leena. 2009. "Generational Order." In *The Palgrave Handbook of Childhood Studies*, edited by Jens Qvortrup, William A. Corsaro, Michael-Sebastian Honig, and Gill Valentine, 159–74. Basingstoke: Palgrave Macmillan.

Balaev, Michelle. 2018. "Trauma Studies." In *A Companion to Literary Theory*, edited by David H. Richter, 260–371. Chichester, West Sussex: Wiley Blackwell.

Balagopalan, Sarada. 2021. "Precarity and the Question of Children's Relationalities." *Childhood* 28 (3): 327–32. https://doi.org/10.1177/09075682211021748.

Baldwin, Andrew. 2012. "Whiteness and Futurity: Towards a Research Agenda." *Progress in Human Geography* 36 (2): 172–87. https://doi.org/10.1177/0309132511414603.

Becker, Danielle. 2019."Afrofuturism and Decolonisation: Using Black Panther as Methodology." *Image & Text* 33: 1-21.

Bernstein, Robin. 2011. *Racial Innocence: Performing American Childhood from Slavery to Civil Rights*. New York: New York University Press.

Blomley, N. 2003. "Law, Property, and the Geography of Violence: The Frontier, the Survey, and the Grid." *Annals of the Association of American Geographers* 93 (1): 121–41.

Bollig, Sabine and Helga Kelle. 2016. "Children as Participants in Practices: The Challenges of Practice Theories to An Actor-Centred Sociology of Childhood." In *Reconceptualising Agency and Childhood*, edited by Florian Esser, Meike S. Baader, Tanja Betz, and Beatrice Hungerland, 34–47. Taylor & Francis.

Brathwaite, Kamau. 1973. *The Arrivants: A New World Trilogy*. Oxford: Oxford University Press.

Bristow, Tegan. 2012. "We Want the Funk: What Is Afrofuturism to the Situation of Digital Arts in Africa?" *Technoetic Arts* 1: 25–32.

Burman, Erica. 2017. *Deconstructing Developmental Psychology*, 3rd edn. London: Routledge, Taylor & Francis Group.

Byrd, Jodi Ann. 2002. "Colonialism's Cacophony: Natives and Arrivants at the Limits of Postcolonial Theory". ProQuest Dissertations Publishing.

Byrd, Jodi A. 2011. *The Transit of Empire: Indigenous Critiques of Colonialism*. Minneapolis: University of Minnesota Press.

Burkitt, Ian. 2016. "Relational Agency: Relational Sociology, Agency and Interaction." *European Journal of Social Theory* 19 (3): 322–39. https://doi.org/10.1177/1368431015591426.

Cannella, Gaile Sloan and Radhika Viruru. 2004. *Childhood and Postcolonization: Power, Education, and Contemporary Practice*. New York: RoutledgeFalmer.

Castro, Ingrid E., Jessica Clark, and Gary Westfahl. 2019. *Child and Youth Agency in Science Fiction: Travel, Technology, Time*. Lanham: Lexington Books.

De Line, Sebastian and Frances H. O'Shaughnessy. 2018. "Waves of Arrivance." *Junctures: The Journal for Thematic Dialogue* 19: 138–145.

Dery, Mark. 1994. "Black to the Future: Interviews with Samuel R. Delany, Greg Tate, and Tricia Rose." In *Flame Wars*, edited by Mark Dery, 179-222. Duke University Press.

Dyer, Hannah. 2017. "Queer Futurity and Childhood Innocence: Beyond the Injury of Development." *Global Studies of Childhood* 7 (3): 290–302. https://doi.org/10.1177/2043610616671056.

Eshun, Kodwo. 1998. *More Brilliant Than the Sun: Adventures in Sonic Fiction*. London: Quartet Books.

Eshun, Kodwo. 2017. "Further Considerations on Afrofuturism." In *Science Fiction Criticism: An Anthology of Essential Writings*, edited by Rob Latham, 458–69. London: Bloomsbury Academic. Bloomsbury Collections. http://dx.doi.org/10.5040/9781474248655.0044.

Esser, Florian, Meike S. Baader, Tanja Betz, and Beatrice Hungerland. 2016. *Reconceptualising Agency and Childhood: New Perspectives in Childhood Studies*. New York: Taylor & Francis. https://doi.org/10.4324/9781315722245.

Esser, Florian. 2016. "Neither 'Thick' nor 'Thin': Reconceptualising Agency and Childhood Relationally." In *Reconceptualising Agency and Childhood*, edited by Florian Esser, Meike S. Baader, Tanja Betz, and Beatrice Hungerland, 48–60. Taylor & Francis.

Fanon, Frantz. 1967/2008. *Black Skin, White Masks*. Grove Press.

Freud, Sigmund. 1917. "Mourning and Melancholia." In *The Standard Edition of the Complete Psychological Works of Sigmund Freud*, edited by James Strachey, vol. 14, 237–58. London: Hogarth Press.

Frie, Roger. 2002. "Modernism or Postmodernism?: Binswanger, Sullivan, and the Problem of Agency in Contemporary Psychoanalysis." *Contemporary Psychoanalysis* 38 (4): 635–73. https://doi.org/10.1080/00107530.2002.10747190.

Garlen, Julie C., Debbie Sonu, Lisa Farley, and Sandra Chang-Kredl. 2022. "Agency as Assemblage: Using Childhood Artefacts and Memories to Examine Children's Relations with Schooling." *Journal of Childhood, Education & Society* 3 (2): 122–38.

Gill-Peterson, Julian. 2015. "The Value of the Future: The Child as Human Capital and the Neoliberal Labor of Race." *Women's Studies Quarterly* 43 (1/2): 181–96. https://doi.org/10.1353/wsq.2015.0023.

Gilroy, Paul. 1993. *The Black Atlantic: Modernity and Double Consciousness*. Cambridge: Harvard University Press.

Harris, Cheryl I. 2019. "Of Blackness and Indigeneity: Comments on Jodi A. Byrd's 'Weather with You: Settler Colonialism, Antiblackness, and the Grounded Relationalities of Resistance.'" *Critical Ethnic Studies* 5 (1–2): 215–28. https://doi.org/10.5749/jcritethnstud.5.1-2.0215.

Hartman, Saidiya V. 2008. *Lose Your Mother: A Journey Along the Atlantic Slave Route*. First paperback edition. New York: Farrar, Straus & Giroux.

Hirji, Sukaina. 2021. "Oppressive Double Binds." *Ethics* 131 (4): 643–69. https://doi.org/10.1086/713943.

Hopkinson, N. 1998. *Brown Girl in the Ring*. New York: Warner Books.

Hopkinson, N. 2000. *Midnight Robber*. New York: Warner Books.

Hopkinson, Nalo. 2003. *The Salt Roads*. New York: Warner Books.

Mehan, Uppinder and Nalo Hopkinson. 2004. *So Long Been Dreaming: Postcolonial Science Fiction & Fantasy*. Vancouver: Arsenal Pulp Press.

James, Allison, Chris Jenks, and Alan Prout. 1998. *Theorizing childhood*. Cambridge: Polity Press.

Jones, Charles E. and Reynaldo Anderson. 2016. *Afrofuturism 2.0: the Rise of Astro-Blackness*. Edited by Charles E. Jones and Reynaldo Anderson. Lanham: Lexington Books.

Khanna, Ranjana. 2003. *Dark Continents: Psychoanalysis and Colonialism*. Durham: Duke University Press.

King, W. 2011. *Stolen Childhood: Slave Youth in Nineteenth-Century America*. Indiana University Press.

Land, Nicole. 2022. "Thinking Metabolically with Shivering, Sweating and Feminist Science Studies in Early Childhood Education." *Curriculum Inquiry*. ahead-of-print (ahead-of-print): 1–19. https://doi.org/10.1080/03626784.2022.2149026.

Lerma, Michael. 2012. "Indigeneity and Homeland: Land, History, Ceremony, and Language." *American Indian Culture and Research Journal* 36 (3): 75–97. https://doi.org/10.17953/aicr.36.3.m5gm12061202kx80.

Marsi, Federica. 2023. "Mediterranean Shipwreck: Stories of Tragedy Emerge After 62 Drown." Accessed March 6, 2023. https://www.aljazeera.com/news/2023/2/27/tragic-scene-refugees-in-shock-after-shipwreck-off-italy.

Mawhinney, Janet Lee. 1998. "'Giving up the Ghost': Disrupting the (Re)production of White Privilege in Anti-Racist Pedagogy and Organizational Change". ProQuest Dissertations Publishing.

Maynard, Robyn. 2017. *Policing Black Lives: State Violence in Canada from Slavery to the Present*. Black Point: Fernwood Publishing.

Maynard, Robyn. 2018. "Reading Black Resistance through Afrofuturism: Notes on Post-Apocalyptic Blackness and Black Rebel Cyborgs in Canada." *Topia (Montreal)* 39: 29–47. https://doi.org/10.3138/topia.39.04.

Meyer, M. A. 2008. "Indigenous and Authentic: Hawaiian Epistemology and the Triangulation of Meaning." 2014. In *The Global Intercultural Communication Reader*, 148–64. Routledge. https://doi.org/10.4324/9780203508534-18.

Nandy, Ashis. 1984. "Reconstructing Childhood: A Critique of the Ideology of Adulthood." *Alternatives: Global, Local, Political* 10 (3): 359–75. https://doi.org/10.1177/030437548401000303.

Neeganagwedgin, Erica. 2015. "Rooted in the Land: Taíno Identity, Oral History and Stories of Reclamation in Contemporary Contexts." *AlterNative: an International Journal of Indigenous Peoples* 11 (4): 376–88.

Neustadter, Roger. 1989. "Phone Home: From Childhood Amnesia to the Catcher in Sci-Fi—The Transformation of Childhood in Contemporary Science Fiction Films." *Youth & Society* 20 (3): 227–40. https://doi.org/10.1177/0044118X89020003001.

Nxumalo, Fikile, Veronica Pacini-Ketchabaw, and Mary Rowan. 2011. "Lunch Time at the Child Care Centre: Neoliberal Assemblages in Early Childhood Education." *Journal of Pedagogy* 2 (2): 195–223.

Oswell, David. 2013. *The Agency of Children: From Family to Global Human Rights*. Cambridge: Cambridge University Press.

Passoth, Jan-Hendrik, Birgit Peuker, and Michael Schillmeier. 2012. "Introduction." In *Agency Without Actors?: New Approaches to Collective Action,* edited by Jan-Hendrik Passoth, Michael W. J. Schillmeier, and Birgit Maria Peuker, 1-11. London: Routledge.

Patterson, Orlando. 1982. *Slavery and Social Death: A Comparative Study*. Cambridge: Harvard University Press.

Philip, Marlene Nourbese, and Setaey Adamu. Boateng. 2008. *Zong!* Middletown: Wesleyan University Press.
Raithelhuber, Eberhard. 2016. "Extending Agency: The Merit of Relational Approaches for Childhood Studies." In *Reconceptualising Agency and Childhood*, edited by Florian Esser, Meike S. Baader, Tanja Betz, and Beatrice Hungerland, 89–101. Taylor & Francis.
Roberts, Neil. 2015. *Freedom as Marronage*. Chicago: The University of Chicago Press.
Robinson, Cedric J. 2020. *Black Marxism*. Revised and Updated Third Edition. Chapel Hill: The University of North Carolina Press.
Rollo, Toby. 2018. "Feral Children: Settler Colonialism, Progress, and the Figure of the Child." *Settler Colonial Studies* 8 (1): 60–79.
Samatar, Sofia. 2017. "Toward a Planetary History of Afrofuturism." *Research in African Literatures* 48 (4): 175–91. https://doi.org/10.2979/reseafrilite.48.4.12.
Sambell, Kay. 2004. "Carnivalizing the Future: A New Approach to Theorizing Childhood and Adulthood in Science Fiction for Young Readers." *The Lion and the Unicorn (Brooklyn)* 28 (2): 247–67. https://doi.org/10.1353/uni.2004.0026.
Saranillio, Dean Itsuji. 2018. "Haunani-Kay Trask and Settler Colonial and Relational Critique: Alternatives to Binary Analyses of Power." *Verge: Studies in Global Asias* 4 (2): 36–44.
Seed, Patricia. 1995. *Ceremonies of Possession in Europe's Conquest of the New World, 1492–1640*. Cambridge: Cambridge University Press.
Sen, Satadru. 2004. "A Juvenile Periphery: The Geographies of Literary Childhood In Colonial Bengal." *Journal of Colonialism and Colonial History* 5 (1). https://doi.org/10.1353/cch.2004.0039.
Sharpe, Christina Elizabeth. 2016. *In the Wake: On Blackness and Being*. Durham: Duke University Press. https://doi.org/10.1515/9780822373452.
Sharpe, Jenny. 1993. *Allegories of Empire: The Figure of Woman in the Colonial Text*. University of Minnesota Press.
Shire, Warsan. 2020. "Home." Accessed March 6, 2023. https://www.facinghistory.org/resource-library/home-warsan-shire.
Sielke, Sabine. 2002. *Reading Rape: The Rhetoric of Sexual Violence in American Literature and Culture, 1790–1990*. Princeton: Princeton University Press.
Silva, Kumarini. 2009. "Oh, Give Me a Home: Diasporic Longings of Home and Belonging." *Social Identities* 15 (5): 693–706. https://doi.org/10.1080/13504630903205332.
Spivak, Gayatri Chakravorty, Donna Landry, and Gerald M. MacLean. 1996. *The Spivak Reader: Selected Works of Gayatri Chakravorty Spivak*. New York: Routledge.
Taylor, Affrica, Veronica Pacini-Ketchabaw, Sandrina de Finney, and Mindy Blaise. 2016. "Inheriting the Ecological Legacies of Settler Colonialism." *Environmental Humanities* 7 (1): 129–32.
Tisdall, E. Kay M. and Samantha Punch. 2012. "Not So 'New'? Looking Critically at Childhood Studies." *Children's Geographies* 10 (3): 249–64.
Tuck, Eve and Rubén A. Gaztambide-Fernández. 2013. "Curriculum, Replacement, and Settler Futurity." *Journal of Curriculum Theorizing* 29 (1): 72–89.

Tuck, Eve, Marcia McKenzie, and Kate McCoy. 2014. "Land Education: Indigenous, Post-Colonial, and Decolonizing Perspectives on Place and Environmental Education Research." *Environmental Education Research* 20 (1): 1–23. https://doi.org/10.1080/13504622.2013.877708.

Veracini, Lorenzo. 2010. *Settler Colonialism: A Theoretical Overview*. Basingstoke, Hampshire: Palgrave Macmillan.

Vimalassery, Manu, Juliana Hu Pegues, and Alyosha Goldstein. 2016. "Introduction On Colonial Unknowing." *Theory & Event* 19 (4).

Vizenor, Gerald Robert. 1994. *Manifest Manners: Postindian Warriors of Survivance*. Hanover: Wesleyan University Press.

Weaver-Hightower, Rebecca. 2007. *Empire Islands: Castaways, Cannibals, and Fantasies of Conquest*. Minneapolis: University of Minnesota Press.

Webster, Crystal Lynn. 2021. *Beyond the Boundaries of Childhood African American Children in the Antebellum North*. Chapel Hill: The University of North Carolina Press.

Wolfe, Patrick. 1999. *Settler Colonialism and the Transformation of Anthropology the Politics and Poetics of an Ethnographic Event*. London: Continuum International Publishing.

Wyss, Johann D. 1812/1991. *The Swiss Family Robinson*. Oxford Paperbacks.

Yaszek, Lisa. 2006. "Afrofuturism, Science Fiction, and the History of the Future." *Socialism and Democracy* 20 (3): 41–60. https://doi.org/10.1080/08854300600950236.

Zobel Marshall, Emily. 2016. "Resistance Through 'Robber-Talk': Storytelling Strategies and the Carnival Trickster." *Caribbean Quarterly* 62 (2): 210–26. https://doi.org/10.1080/00086495.2016.1203178.

Chapter 9

Troubling Innocence

Staging Scenes of Black Youth Pleasures and Possibilities

Dominique C. Hill and Durell M. Callier

dark phrases of womanhood
of never havin been a girl
half-notes scattered
without rhythm/no tune
distraught laughter fallin
over a black girl's shoulder [...]

        somebody/anybody
        sing a black girl's song

                bring her out
                to know herself
                to know you
                but sing her rhythms
                carin/struggle/hard times
                sing her song of life [...]

        sing the song of her possibilities [...]
        let her be born
        let her be born
        & handled warmly.

In Ruth Nicole Brown's (2009) *Black Girlhood Celebration,* she defines Black girlhood as "the representations, memories, and lived experiences of being and becoming in a body marked as youthful, Black, and female.

Black girlhood then is not dependent, then, on age, physical maturity, or any essential category of identity" (1). We begin here with her definition and the epigraph from Ntozake Shange because it sets the stage for understanding the stakes of limiting narratives of childhood, alongside the imperative to expansively recognize "Black girl[hood]'s song" (Shange 1975, 4). Both Shange (1975) and Brown (2009, 2013), in their grappling with the lived realities of Black girls, women, femmes, and those who center celebrating the full spectrum of Black girlhood, offer important insights into understanding the ways that racialized gender and sexuality (i.e., Black genders and sexualities) in and under white supremacy and colonization negate and obliterate the very idea of the subject position and the categories of child, childhood, girlhood, and human. In tow of such configurations is the denial of innocence in the traditional sense of the word where Blackness blots out naivety, non-knowing, and exemption from responsibility. Our argument here is not to negate how this also maps onto the Black body in general (Spillers 1987), inclusive of Black men/boys, Black boyhood (see Bost, Bruce, and Manning 2019; Boutte and Bryan 2021; Poulson-Bryant 2005) those who may identify as or be identified as girls, women, femmes (Ellison 2019), or gender expansive, nonbinary, and trans identified Black folx (Ellison 2019) but to dedicate focused attention to girlhood.

Under the rubric of Black girlhood studies, pivots are made away from the normative assumptions that girlhood is a bounded phase in time, that innocence is a quality attributed to childhood, and that girlhood and childhood are equivalents. These movements decenter innocence and trouble historical frameworks, which configure childhood (and later girlhood) as linear and inevitably distinct progressions toward adulthood. While we focus here on terms often configured through a sex/gender binary, our point here is to mark more so the ways theories of childhood tend to mark it and more recently girlhood as stops on the road to adulthood and its "matured counterparts," wo/man/hood. Our usage of the word adulthood does not foreclose the reality of how it is a troublesome social category, imbued with false binaries such as sex/gender and that all of these terms have cultural particularity not often centered in popular debates. That is to say, not all individuals marked and/or raised as girls need to/desire/can or will become women and not all individuals raised/marked as boys will/need to/can or desire to become men. We want to underscore fluidity and agency that is simultaneously held in the messiness of identity, alongside the foreclosure of self-actualizing any of these terms because of how Black subjectivity is denied access to such terms, personhood, and the accordant rights, privileges, and dignity.

In *10 Years of Black Girlhood Celebration,* Kwakye, Hill, and Callier (2017) named two key offerings of the field: "a better understanding of how they [Black girls] survive and thwart systemic violence and persistent inequalities, and a celebration of their ingenious approaches to real and imagined social change" (1). To celebrate Black girls is to "sing a black girl's song" with the spirit in which it was told. To celebrate amidst the machinations, conceptualizations, and grammars that render Black girls as only "half notes scattered" (Shange 1975, 19) requires transgression and a different orientation to girlhood. Such a re-orientation demands that Black girls' pleasures—joy, aspirations, erotic knowing (Lorde 1984), and sexuality—take front and center. Moreover, "holding celebration as a central tenet to scholarship involving Black girlhood is an academic side-eye to theories, tropes, and representations promoted and sustained by the simultaneous pathologization and hyper(in)visibility of Black girls" (Hill 2021, 550). This chapter expands the narrative of childhood beyond a bounded state of innocence only afforded certain bodies. "Troubling Innocence: Staging Scenes of Black Youth Pleasures and Possibilities" demonstrates how performance reorients contemporary understandings of childhood beyond innocence by (i) illuminating the complex lives of Black youth, (ii) exemplifying how race, class, gender, and sexuality trouble contemporary notions of childhood, and (iii) highlighting real and imagined scenes of pleasure for youth as a necessary juxtaposition to commonly held believes of Black youth and specifically Black queer girls' access to pleasure, agency, and knowledge.

Drawing upon Black performance theory (DeFrantz and Gonzalez 2014), Black feminist theory and creative practice (Bambara 1996; Shange 1975), and queer of color theories (Brockenbrough 2013; Cohen 2019; Ferguson 2004), this chapter extends the tradition of storytelling and employs critical fabulation to stage scenes of Black girlhood. Our intentional centering of pleasure through the Black girlhood studies ethos of celebration advances a queer articulation of childhood—one that does not insist on naivety nor safety. This troubling of innocence is taken up in this paper as the scenes devised traverse the mundane and spectacular violence that Black girls experience. Furthermore, we trouble innocence by locating alongside material and discursive violence reimagined possibilities for otherwise by centering (Black girls') pleasure. Extending our work on gaze and theorizing pleasure (Callier and Hill 2019) through the performance "Bodies on display," we advance pleasure as a heuristic and an embodiment of Black living amidst figurative and literal forms of death as well as many forms of violence; it makes plain the vastness of Blackness in the face of abjection and focuses on what becomes possible when childhood is embraced as a failed project.

Shange's (1975) *for colored girls who have considered suicide/when the rainbow is enuf* provides a useful primer to our thinking beyond innocence, as she confronts the reality in the above passage of "never havin been a girl." Yet she asks, and demands of us, "somebody/anybody sing a black girl's song" (Shange 1975, 4). A treatise on the lived reality of Black girl/

womanhood, *for colored girls* illuminates the both/and neither/nor liminality of Black girlhood and womanhood while documenting complex negotiations of their hyperinvisibility and visibility. Bringing together poetry and movement, a choreopoem is a set of poems arranged as a whole, inclusive of movement and music. Instead of being a succession of individual poems, the poems taken together tell a coherent embodied story, borrowing from the theatricality, aesthetics, dance and gestures of Black expressive culture (i.e., theatre). Shange's *for colored girls* is the first iteration of the chorepoem and has been taken up by other artists and researchers like Marc Bamuthi Joseph's (2006) *Word Becomes Flesh*. In this tradition, what follows is our own reckoning of singing Black girls' songs as a means to center Black girls' experiences, knowledge, and ways of being—necessary ingredients for expanding our contemporary understandings of childhood and girlhood in particular.

Guided by excerpts from the choreopoem's opening poem, "dark phrases," each section of this chapter takes up a portion of that poem as a means to broaden narratives of Black childhood, queerness, and pleasure. Accordingly, the chapter is organized around four sections. Section one, "dark phrases of womanhood" examines the often-overlooked realities and discordant narratives that foreclose innocence to Black youth. In section two, "somebody/anybody sing a black girl's song" we provide an overview of performance in education and reflect on our own staged performance *Bodies on Display* to demonstrate how performance provides a juncture to reorient and uncover what else is imaginatively and creatively possible for Black youth and those who love them. Section three "bring her out/to know herself" utilizes pleasure as an analytical frame in examining a contemporary case of Dynasia Clark, a Black girl denied the affordances of innocence, and what those realities can teach us about the contours of and contradictions of Black girlhood, innocence, and childhood. The final section "sing the song of her possibilities" offers speculative accounts of what else could happen if we centered Black girls' pleasures' and needs. We conclude with a coda that takes up the call to "let her be born," an invitation to stakeholders in the lives of Black girls, to make room for their self-determination, including the practice of pleasure.

In this way, performances of Blackqueer pleasure and a Blackqueer body performing pleasure, such as the scenes featured in this chapter, are transgressive acts that have the potential "to note and redress harm in complicated ways" (Callier and Hill 2019, 52). To see Black girls through a Blackqueer gaze is to make space for Dynasia specifically and Black girls generally to be read through a celebratory lens (Brown 2009). That pleasure serves as a method of enacting and recognizing Black possibilities, Black girls come to know themselves with an interiority. Through this conceptualization, Black girls are invited to be seen, see, and therefore know themselves anew.

SOMEBODY/ANYBODY SING A BLACK GIRL'S SONG: COMING TO PERFORMANCE IN EDUCATION

To "sing a black girl's song" (Shange 1975) properly requires a recognition that Black girls are more than the pain the world insists on inflicting upon them and more than their "prematurely knowing" (Jacobs 1861, 42). As described above, racialized gender and its interplay with childhood render Black girlhood a place of contention and denied autonomy. As scholar-artists committed to Black girls and actors in the project of Black girlhood, we work from the paradigm of celebration and analytical frame of Black girlhood studies. An inter/undisciplined field, it "makes visible creative, intellectual, and cultural production of Black girls and Black girlhood while simultaneously illumining the dearth of attention afforded Black girls and Black girlhood" (Hill 2018, 385). Attendant to visual and material culture, intellectual, practice, and political contributions, this field knows Black girls to be knowledge and culture producers, trendsetters, and pedagogues. As we labor in this field, we bring forth methodologies and frames that maintain the interiority of young people's lives, our responsibilities to them, and the telling of their stories. Our praxis of telling Black girl stories is informed by our time in the arts-based healing collective, Black girlhood celebration space of Saving Our Lives, Hear Our Truths (Brown 2009). Organized by an expansive notion of girlhood that transcends age and biology, Saving Our Lives, Hear Our Truths (SOLHOT), rethinks the categories of youth, childhood, girl, and innocence. We extend this work to consider how they map onto and against Black, queer, youth. As the terrain of violence endured by youth of color and queer youth of color continues to broaden, this reorientation is increasingly important. Such violence includes but is not limited to the loss of life at the hands of police and vigilantes, increased assaults on the dignity of transgender and nonbinary youth within state legislatures and school policies, and an enduring expansion of systems of capture. In using the term "capture," we are describing the totalizing effects of practices and policies that swiftly and intentionally move students away from schools into prisons, and/or hold them, their families, and communities structurally in place, making exiting poverty, actualizing autonomy, or moving toward greater senses of freedom— freedom to breathe, to stylize as one desires, to vote, etc. —near impossibilities.

Our studies and co-conspiring with Black youth in particular directed us to interrogate the power of gaze and how it gives shape to their educational experiences and to investigate the ingredients of gazes that constrain Black expression and flourishing. In previous scholarship, we grapple with these complex realities (Callier and Hill 2019; Hill 2021) to consider how Black youth are denied the protections of childhood because they are marked as criminal, problematic, and unable to inhabit the location of innocence. The way that Blackness is so often mapped onto hegemonic scripts of assumed wrongness highlights the ways that anti-Blackness is a ubiquitous bulwark in the lives of Black youth. To combat the discursive and material impacts of these foreclosures, we turn to performance as a liberatory space to provide narratives that foreground what Black youth teach and create amidst violence, hyper(in)visibility, and harm. Moreover, as theory, method, and event, performance within educational practice and discourse becomes a tool for attuning to and shifting gazes that do not serve the enactment of Black life. Whether engaging in what performance can teach us within and beyond the classroom (performance pedagogy), or analyzing the spectacular and mundane daily dramas of our lives and living (performance theory), or exploring worldmaking as praxis (performing), the space of performance opens up other registers for analyses, embraces diverse ways of knowing, and imagines differently our relationships to power. We take its potential seriously, as illustrated by our creation of the performance *Bodies on Display* as praxis work in staging Black life and centering pleasure as something that need not be earned but as rightfully part of our survival.

In March 2016, *Bodies on Display* was performed at the University of Alabama's "Discerning Diverse Voices Symposium." Imagined as a live-art installation vis-à-vis a living mobile museum, the performance used our bodies—through self-authored poetry, movement, and a series of visual images created by Callier—to make more visible the lived realities of Blackqueerness and stage a dynamic conversation about the interwoven relationships of race, gender, and sexuality. As an analytic, Blackqueer attunes to the ways that racialized sexuality and gender queers Black people regardless of their sexual practice and romantic affiliations (Callier 2020). Drawing upon women of color feminisms, queer of color critique, and Black queer theory, Blackqueer highlights how state apparati, specifically education, are undergirded by and reifies anti-Blackness. It also demonstrates how Black youth and their communities are constructed as aberrant precisely because of how their performances of gender and sexuality are seen as nonnormative. The conjoining of the words Black and queer on the page denotes an intentional language shift to explore processes of racialization and how Black people are queered by the state.

Drawing from an amassed archive of media coverage, our life histories, personal journal entries and reflections, we created poetry to synthesize and make sense of the archive informing our show and the questions we were seeking to explore through performance. Structured around three concepts—pain, pleasure, and possibility—the performance offered a critique of larger discourses of anti-Black and anti-queer sentiments and their mappings onto our everyday lived experiences. Through original poetry, *Bodies on Display* considered the pain, pleasure, and possibilities endured by Black and queer bodies. The performance itself revealed the cultural curriculum that circulates to define Black and queer bodies and illustrate how that the Blackqueer body imagines itself beyond such scripts. Creating an avenue for us to talk, *Bodies on Display* allowed us to productively revisit and disassemble Blackness, queerness, and Blackqueerness.

To turn away from the oft overwrought and viralized abused, dispossessed, and disposable Black body is an intentional choice to decenter Blackqueer's proximity to harm, violence, and even death and foreground Blackqueer alterity (Callier and Hill 2019, 33). Upon initial reflection on the "pleasure" section of *Bodies on Display*, we introduce three important shifts for how we think about Blackness that ultimately aid in seeing the fullness and humanity of Blackqueer people. First, it brings visibility to pleasure, an often invisible or presumed unavailable resource to be accessed by Blackness, especially in the current milieu plagued by Black death, police violence, and Black youth disappearing. Second, it forces viewers to reckon with Black bodies doing things and being themselves in ways that denote sovereignty, self-definition, and joy (Dillard 2016). Third, it intentionally narrows the frame of gaze to examine Black, queer bodies' relationship(s) to pleasure and what constitutes pleasure for these bodies and individuals. Agreeing with Diamond (1996) that "it is impossible to write the pleasurable embodiments we call performance without tangling with the cultural stories, traditions, and political contestations that comprise our sense of history" (1), we focused on pleasure and possibility while pain remained backgrounded. The act of staging Black pleasure revealed for us and the audience the ways Black folk, through their play and insistence on joy, survive heteronormative, white supremacist, and pathology-centered gazes. It also allowed us to imagine how pleasure as an analytic facilitates Black youth to flourish without the tag of innocent. Although violence in its various forms is quotidian in the lives of Black youth, they are not strangers to playing, experiencing joy, and crafting worlds of survival built upon their creativity and genius. To forecast Blackqueer pleasure in the future while expanding who can enact and experience it, we utilize pleasure as a framework and method for seeing more wholly the life of Dynasia Clark and specifically her graduation day.

DARK PHRASES OF WOMANHOOD/OF NEVER HAVIN BEEN A GIRL: BLACK YOUTH STEREOTYPES AND THE DIFFICULTY WITH INNOCENCE

How does the reality of "never havin been a girl" (Shange 1975) shape Black girlhood and womanhood? What are those "dark phrases of womanhood" that haunt the contours of Black girls' imaginaries and possibilities? How do they inform Black women's lived realities? And what is the relationship between the impossibility of girlness and the specter of womanhood as it relates to Black girls/women's pleasure? These questions trouble the very notions of Black girlhood and childhood. Not only foreclosed possibilities for Black people because of how systems of domination force "adultification" and "adult-like duties" onto us, but these categories are also conceived outside of Blackness. What is a Black child within a white colonial gaze, other than an object to be owned, accumulated, and denied humanity and the attributed rights, privileges, and faculties of the category of the human? And within a post-emancipation United States context, in particular, is a Black child ever a child if they are consistently seen as a threat to whiteness, especially white femininity and masculinity? This section takes up the various types of stereotypes and tropes that characterize Black childhoods and how these racist, sexist, and gender-specific ideologies shape the life experiences and possibilities of Black youth. What immediately follows is a brief overview of the ways Black childhood has been framed within a U.S. context, moving to more specific and nuanced discourses that surround Black girls/girlhood.

The social category "child" and its imagined corresponding experience, childhood, is fraught with tensions relating to language, racialization, and context. In *Stolen Childhoods*, Wilma King (2011) traces how for Black children, childhood was snatched and replaced with "enter[ing] the workplace early" and being "subjected to arbitrary authority, punishment, and separation, just as enslaved adults" (xxi-xxii). Within this same white imaginary, Black people are thereby reduced to bodies, tools for laboring, which afforded the production of "the Black body" (Young 2010). Conceptualized as, "an idea of the black body [that] has been and continues to be projected across actual physical bodies," this body becomes a figure which people latch onto never having to acknowledge or come to know the girl, the woman, the human behind the image (Young 2010, 4). As a mode of domination and practice of denying Black folk personhood, McKittrick (2006) describes Black femininity as a critical geography and one charged with loss, insurgence, and abjection: "The 'not-quite' spaces of black femininity are unacknowledged spaces of sexual violence, violence, stereotype, and sociospatial marginalization; erased, erasable, hidden, resistant geographies and women that are, due to persistent and public forms of objectification, not readily decipherable" (61).

Racialized gender and its corresponding racial sexual oppression, as outlined in the Combahee River Collective Statement (1979), calculate living breathing bodies adorned by women and girls as read, evaluated, and deciphered through historical tropes that posit Black bodies as labor, which are productive to the extent that they labor in service of ideologies (white supremacy), paradigms (dualism), and political economies (capitalism) foundational to the society. The tropes contrived and circulated must conspire with how a society is organized; they must serve a function that is larger than (sometimes oppositional to) their personal survival and vision for their lives. In a discussion of this abstract body in the context of urban America, Tolman (1996) works to debunk myths surrounding sexuality of the "Urban" or non-white and almost always Black girl. Tolman (1996) states, "It is not hard to flesh out a single face, a single body, for The Urban Girl. This stereotype is not a real person but a unidimensional stick figure who lives in the public imagination rather than on the streets of urban America" (Tolman 1996, 255). Through language interrogation as related to urban girls, Tolman illustrates the pertinent role language and labeling has in the reification of dichotomous framings of girls along racial and class lines. Interviewing suburban and urban girls, she found that in the case of those living in urban settings, more times than not they would forgo acting on their desires to concede to safety.

As a "a set of political commitments that are independent from data about actual occurrences of lawbreaking," carcerality and its divergent modes corroborate with the racialized histories and participate in the denial of Black girl and woman personhood (Richie and Martensen 2020, 2). Carceral logics suture perceived (and assigned deviance) criminal designation and foreclosures of childhood innocence. For instance, in the Black Girls Matter (2015) publication, a national report examining educational policies and their impacts on girls' of color in-school experiences, they reported Black girls are six times more likely to be suspended. Drawing data from surveys collected from a sample of predominantly white (more than 70%) and female (more than 60%) adults about Black girls across four age groups, Epstein et al. (2017) found that Black girls are assumed more adult in all age ranges beginning at age five. While adultification, the idea of designating more responsibility and culpability on youth because of their race, is not bound by gender, the particularities of Black girl adultification is specific to the ways racial-sexual histories conjoin to allot delinquent branding and harsher treatment in disciplinary measures.

The loud Black girl archetype follows in step with the Black woman archetype Sapphire. This stereotype describes a supposed overbearing, loud, and even malicious Black woman caricature circulated post antebellum and popularized in mid-1900s popular culture, as described by P.B. Scott (1976). Examining gender's impact on academic achievement, Signithia Fordham's (1993) study reveals that Black girls who fared best in school—good grades, high test scores, and support from teachers—did not disrupt the assumed social order between Black boys and girls. On the other hand, their "loud Black girl" counterparts, who also had good grades, scored lower on standardized tests and received less teacher support. These findings highlight that traditional gender roles and conceptions of femininity inform the gaze of in-school authority figures and contribute to teachers' perceptions of Black girls. Similarly, Lei's (2003) ethnographic study in a different high school examines the role of stereotypes in framing Asian boys and Black girls, finding that girls' behavior and "loudness" proved in opposition to gender expectations held by most teachers. Importantly, all teachers assumed that Black girls' volume was unacceptable and would stifle their academic success. In a similar way, Black girls are rewarded for more servitude-like qualities. Linda Grant's (1994) examination of six first-grade classrooms and the roles Black girls are expected to adopt found that girls are introduced to and encouraged to adopt the specific roles of "helper, enforcer, or go-between" (43). In this study, girls were rewarded by Black and white teachers for their behavior and less for academics. Resembling the Mammy, these roles cater in different ways to the needs of others and indicate that Black girls' comportment is fundamental to how they are seen and supported. Furthermore, these roles center on the services Black girls can provide, and therefore the extent to which their bodies can be of use. Characterized as loudies (Morris 2007), thugs (Brown-Manning 2013), divas (Cox 2009), bad (Bryan 2020), good or ghetto (Jones 2010), the ways that Black youth and, more specifically, Black girls are read in larger society directly impacts the protections and opportunities afforded.

"Dark phrases" as Shange's poem highlights are those names used to codify the grammars described by Spillers (1987), which derive from being simultaneously distinct and yet unknown, a disposable necessity wherein, "My country needs me, and if I were not here, I would have to be invented" (65). Dark phrases are both things stated and the result of others' reading and corresponding treatment of Black girls in and out of schools. Such phrases build a lexicon that, unless intentionally in search of, erase the idea of a Black girl figure all together. Knowing otherwise, Harriet Jacobs, in her autobiography, names "prematurely knowing" as a manifestation of "dark phrases" (1861, 28). Both the 1975 poem and our analysis point to the cumulative impacts of systems of domination and their role in ordering the lives of Black girls. Careful to mark a process wherein young, enslaved girls are stripped of naivety; Jacobs importantly indicts the system of slavery and the man responsible for depriving her of a life unburdened by sexual violation. Jacobs is intentional to make clear processes and choices made on the behalf of others to construct and preclude access to certain locations. As Callier and Hill (2019) urge, "when power and gaze converge in the absence of critical reflexivity, they reproduce the status quo" (13). Different from but in conversation with adultification, Jacobs, awareness of an otherwise, does not deny the girl because of one's social location but rather archives the complexity of Black girlhood in such a context. Ensnared by the arrangements of slavery, Jacobs knows to craft a song of life, of process, one that mobilizes a consciousness where her sighs and breaths are lyrics.

BRING HER OUT/TO KNOW HERSELF: THEORIZING PLEASURE AT THE NEXUS OF BLACKNESS, QUEERNESS, AND GIRLHOOD

On June 2, 2020, Lamar High school in Darlington, South Carolina, denied graduating senior Dynasia Clark the right and pleasure of walking. The prioritization of policy over celebration made Dynasia an unnecessary target of body policing, racial-sexual oppression, and anti-celebratory gaze. If there was such a policy as "Love Black girls," what would this day, this moment entail? What processes may have unfolded in the name of transformative education for a teacher's decision to foreclose on a Black girl's celebration? Providing a pathway to think about these possibilities, Garner et al. discuss the central role of pleasure and its utility to Black girl praxis:

> Black girlhood pleasure as a method of anti-respectability, then, must move us away from dominant desires to only know Black girls through deficit frames or to name Black girls' vulnerabilities due to their social locations within a society that has never cared for or about Black girls. To do so, we argue, requires a rootedness in Black girls' aesthetics of love, reliability, funk, and performance Arriving at this mode of anti-respectability methodology required individual and collective unlearning that allowed us to hear Black girls differently. (Garner et al. 2019, 191)

To sing a Black girl's song necessitates a keen ear and a will to be disrespectful to policies that negate their humanity, dignity, and sense of self.

Escorted off the graduation field while adorned in an outfit that was compliant with the school's formal dress code policy in both attire and clothing aesthetic—wrinkle-free, tucked-in and buttoned dress shirt, shiny oxfords, belted slacks, bow tie, dress socks, and suspenders—school authority misheard or could not hear Dynasia. On a day that signaled achievement and a rite of passage event (graduation) to which family, community members, and all other stakeholders in the lives of youth are invited to join in on, Dynasia's family and anyone else there to celebrate her were relegated to commemorating her elsewhere. The standard dress code emphasized wearing "decent, clean, and properly worn" clothing. The deliberate attention Dynasia gave to her outfit choice, including its alignment with the daily school year dress policy, was overlooked and instead they chose to underscore her decision not to "dress like a girl." Ruminating on the tight containers Black girls are asked to navigate, especially as related to sexuality, Jessica Robinson (2012) asks, "Can we be for Black girls and against their sexuality?" (223) This question begs a conversation about the ways the category girl, when tied to innocence, also presumably distances those occupying the subject from sexuality. Again, Black girlhood studies, and specifically the ethos of celebration, instead require that school authorities hear differently. The question is again, one of policy: What if Lamar High School believed who Black girls said they were, in this case openly gay, a lover of pants and ties, looking clean, and being actualized?

Part of an intimate school community, Lamar high school has a student population of less than 300 students and 18 teachers. Such a learning community size ensures that staff and administrators are familiar with Dynasia as a student and likely her shifting understanding of the world and her desires. Yet, during an interview, Dynasia is baffled and annoyed at the school's decision:

> Well dey already know how I am . . . so dey already know that I'm not going to wear a dress . . . so I didn't think dey would be like, "oh well you can't walk" because dey already know me, I been goin to school here for four years [. . .]

As she pretended not to know her, the school principal's gaze was both faulty and harmful. Although it is well-known that Black girls are overrepresented in suspension and expulsion rates and experience both symbolic and physical violence in school, less interrogated are the harms enacted when they are policed for and denied their rights to embodiment and self-definition. While this formative event did not result in physical death, it animates the ways the multiplicity of race and gender policing coalesce and incite figurative death upon Black girls or what Patricia Williams (1987) describes as "spirit murdering." While a variety of names can be offered to describe such accounts, spirit murdering maps relationships between carceral logics, Blackness, and quality of life. Defined as a "crime, an offense so deeply painful and assaultive," Williams seeks to document racism as a pervasive agent of foreclosure and denial of humane living (129). To catalog racism's legal presence as well as its incessant effects on culture, representation, and self-concept or as Williams describes, how "the legacy of killing finds its way into cultural expectations, archetypes, and 'isms'" (156). This conceptualization recognizes this form of death as significant, pervasive, and sewn into systems and even syntax and grammar, as Spillers (1987) warns.

Dynasia's sartorial choices signaled a power she was able to and comfortable with accessing—the erotic. Articulated by Lorde (1984), as a resource for identifying, conjuring, and enriching internally derived pleasure, "the erotic" serves as both a reminder and urge ". . . that my deep and irreplaceable knowledge of my capacity for joy comes to demand from all of my life that it be lived within the knowledge that such satisfaction is possible and does not have to be called marriage, nor god, nor an *afterlife*" (57). Dynasia knew, because she fashioned it so, that a dress was unnecessary and actually antithetical to her showing up in celebration of her achievement. Instead, she showed up trusting that the school knew her and more so what knowing her meant. Dynasia was a queer subject, a designation that exceeded her sexual orientation. When transcending queer solely as a descriptor of sexual orientation and using it to describe both a proximity and a politic, Carbado, McBride, and Weise (2002) reference it as a signification of nonconformity—ideologically and identity wise. They describe contributors to the collection of *Black Like Us* as:

> queer in terms of how they defined and embodied their racial identity, queer in terms of their conception and performance of their gender, queer in how they articulated and practiced politics, as well as queer in their intimate relationships and sense of sexual identity. (xiv-xv)

The gender binary enforced through graduation attire regulation coalesced with anti-queer violence to deny Black girl celebration. As a form of anti-queer violence and anti-Black antagonism, gender regulation bars celebrating girls. Already marred by the popularization of Blackness as perverted and its related agendering of Black girls and women, the lack of reverence afforded is rationalized and possibility is obscured. Under such a gaze, Dynasia's unconventional gender expression, Blackness, self-identification as a lesbian, and will to be known was misheard as wrong, defiant, and in opposition to policy. And yet, the Lamar High School belief statement states, "Cultural sensitivity is essential to success and well being in our global society" (Lamar High School Beliefs Statement), which is inconsistent with their treatment of Dynasia. Whether it is homophobic bullying as perpetrated by peers, anti-Black racism as experienced through school curricula and staff, or the policing of expressive (racialized) genders vis-à-vis school policies, it is precisely this experience of spirit murdering that Black queer youth must consistently endure. Marred by these realities, Black childhood and girlhood highlight the enduring and ubiquitous often ignored truth about oppression in the lives of Black girls and Black girls in particular. To craft scenes of Black girl pleasure is to, as Shange (1975) demands, "sing the song of her possibilities." Furthermore, to emphasize (or sing) her possibilities is to consciously name Black girlhood a site of pleasure while rewriting how Black girls utilize the erotic even as their bodies archive violence.

SING THE SONG OF HER POSSIBILITIES: STAGING SCENES OF BLACK GIRLHOOD

Through an ethos of celebration, Black girlhood studies' takes very seriously the interiority of Black girls lives and lived experiences—to believe them, the real and imagined stories they tell and what they know. Leaning into storytelling as well as the impulse of Black queer studies to create research that engages, "anti-oppressive knowledge production" (Brokenbrough and Boatwright 2013), we take up critical fabulation vis-à-vis performance theorizing to enliven the nuanced textures of violence Black (gender) queer girls experience while imagining otherwise possibilities for justice and their embodied sense of knowing.

In order to do this, we employ storytelling in the tradition of Black arts educator, cultural worker, and Black girl storyteller Toni Cade Bambara. Known for her essays and stories about Black life, Bambara's work reveals the praxis and possibility of culturally relevant pedagogy and culturally situated knowledge to illuminate Black genius, history, and liberatory practices. Notably within her 1996 collection of short essays and stories, *Deep Sightings and Rescue Missions: Fictions, Essays, and Conversations,* edited by Toni Morrison, Bambara's attunement to the power of storytelling actualizes liberatory education by and in service to Black people. Molded by an "outdoor university" of Black cultural spaces (e.g., beauty salons, trade unions, race uplift organizations, religious, political and artist collectives, etc.) that documented and affirmed Black life, Bambara notes how stories told within and across these spaces shaped her identity and sense of what it meant to be a member of a community. Taking up this liberatory education praxis, she uses storytelling as a cultural worker to provide counternarratives to ahistorical and deficit understandings of Black life, upending and filling in gaps within official archives.

Following Bambara and Shange's tradition, to use the creative arts to "sing the song of her possibilities," in the context of Dynasia's story would mean to provide counterstories that redress the silences of the official archive of the events that happened to her on graduation day. In this vein, we create new songs, new stories, to undo, intervene into, and altogether stop the forces—racism, sexism, homophobia, transphobia, white supremacy, etc.—that rob Black girls of their girlhood. The "spirit murdering," which Dynasia endured as evidenced in her affect on her interviews, does not have to be the only way the story goes. What follows are performative responses and imagined possibilities for Dynasia. We ask and answer: What happens when Black girls' pleasure is centered? How does *knowing* a Black girl change how we would interact and show up for her? How can Black girls and Black girlhood in all of their complexity be celebrated? These questions and the stories that unfold below point to other ways educators, administrators, and those who care about Black youth and Black (gender) queer girls in particular can operate differently to provide alternative, just, joy-filled possibilities for them.

> In true fashion, like the actualized self that she was—was becoming, Dynasia was ready to deliver her actualitorian speech. See, unlike other stellar magnet schools, Lamar didn't have a traditional valedictorian and salutatorian speech. No, they thought a real *valedictum* speech, to honor the Latin form relating to

leave taking, should come from one most prepared to take flight. As outlined in the Lamar Community and School Collaboratory handbook, to take leave— "was of the utmost importance and would be recognized publicly at commencement and other celebratory events to aid others in their own becoming." Hence, the actualitorian was zoe who had actualized themselves. And having been the one to dare to be herself—from the way she dressed, to how she walked, to who she loved, and let love her, to how she knew *who* she was—Lamar couldn't help but choose Dynasia Clark—self-actualization personified.

Mounting the podium with the saunter and style of a confident lion, Dynasia was prepared to address all who had gathered. She began by thanking everyone and saying, "It kinda was hard at first, being myself." Unfurling more of the speech she had penned on the folded up piece of paper. "I was told I should reflect on how I became myself and how you can too. Simple, I just remember a game I use to play growing up. The words go . . ."

down down baby down by the roller coaster
sweet sweet baby
i'll never let you go

"Because I'll never let me go" she said to herself out loud, breaking the singsong. Some of the audience caught slightly off guard as they were just remembering this handgame they played under a South Carolina sun.

shimmy shimmy cocoa pop
shimmy shimmy pow
grandma grandma sick in bed
she called the doctor and the doctor said

Some now were standing up, getting ready for their favorite part of this familiar game.

A kinetic memory coming back to them, of their days when imaginations ran free, and were used to get the rhythm of the head, hands, feet, and hoooooot dog. Dynasia, seeing that the crowd was with her, says out loud, "and this was always my favorite part."

let's get the rhythm of the head
  ding dong
let's get the rhythm of the hands
  clap clap
let's get the rhythm of the feet
  stomp stomp
let's get the rhythm of the hottttt dogggg

"And sometimes I would change the words, to get my confidence goin right and remind myself in my body."

let's get the rhythm of the self
  i'm fine

let's get the rhythm of my style
  be you
let's get the rhythm of my joy
  ha ha
let's get the rhythm of my freeeeeeedommmm

At least that's one way the story goes, and another version of it goes,

Eenie meanie miney moe, won't catch this Black girl she's on the go! Runnin late as fly girls do, today started off as nothing short of magical. Dynasia could feel it in the air when she woke. This uncontrollable sense of joy washed over her, beaming from ear to ear she had only felt *this good* a handful of times. See on count of the fact that Black don't crack and do shine, specifically at a high achieving school like Lamar, the Bureau of Black Joy (BBJ) was in full effect. Rallying to the aid of all Black souls in this anti-Black world, the BBJ's motto is, "Joynow, joy tomorrow, joy forever." If you aren't familiar with the BBJ or Black folx, and Black folx joy, you might ask a silly question, like what's so special about joy, why joy, why devote a whole fancy-sophisticated-organization to it? Well the BBJ has an answer for that too. Because Blackness is joy, contrary to popular belief, because joy is our birthright, and because if Blackness is joy and our birthright the joy is and must be Blackness, ya dig.

And so on count on all these things, the BBJ had already determined that on this day here, they was fittin to set it all the way off for Dynasia. Not like the tragic impossibility of life and a future for Black masculine of center lesbians like Cleo but, you know a real, live, amazing sort of set it off. Starting the morning with the soundtrack of Bill Wither's, *Lovely Day* heard floating in the distance, nothing and I mean nothing could change the fact that Dynasia was fittin to walk right cross that stage.

With the BBJ on the job, there were no rain clouds in the sky. Imagine that! Even on count that all the experts had said it would. The scuff mark that would have appeared on Dynasia's fresh shoes, ruining a perfectly laid out fit, couldn't seem to take, try as it did. Just no obstacle or weapon as the old folks would say could prosper. Not even the likes of principals turned Atlas, because the weight of the world really was on their shoulders, could mess with her day.

Flyin past the principal to line up, Dynasia got an unexpected glance. The first thought, wondering why there were pants where a dress "should be," or stockings, or bare legs. The next thought, wondering why penny loafers were where respectable heels "should be." So unimaginative, limiting, and not even what the day was about. The Bureau on its job, in a blink, wisped those thoughts right on out her head. I mean after all, isn't a principal, your pal, and not the (gender) police? She chuckled to herself, unable to remember what it was she was thinking. Remembering just how much she *knew* Dynasia, that because she *knew* her, she loved her, because she *knew-loved* her, she *saw* her as she was. Of course she'd let her walk, just as she was. The Bureau of Black Joy was working overtime that day, but then again when is it not? Black joy, got some?

Or another version that also circulates,

stopped more than once by a teacher who thought this dress code just ain't right or so the story goes. Every time they thought to say a curse at Dynasia something just wouldn't click right in they mind. Almost like they had been fixed not to ruin lil Black girls' special days. Almost like they remembered their own lil black girl selves or recalled some conversation with her, how she made them feel warm and alive inside how she was this precious thing they just couldn't bare to see have her dreams squashed that day. Any other day they knew they might succumb to the snap judgment of by the book policies, a book which might make hypocrites of them one day because they loved kids but this book did not reflect that same love. And today on count of it being so much joy, the families all beaming with pride, saying thank you Mr. Johnson, Ms. Smith, Dr. Clark y'all did our babies good. Thank you, thank you, thank you. Each of them feeling this, feeling good for the first time in a while, feeling at all, they couldn't scratch this out they head, couldn't fix they lips to yell outta line, nah you can't walk today, sorry thems the rules, couldn't catch themselves killin nobodies dreams that day. And so, it was each one of them just smiled at Dynasia, gesturing her on to her rightful place in the line, and smiled as she walked on cross the stage and smiled even wider as they heard her name and remembered that this was the choice that they madee today. A good choice.

And so it goes.

Or so we are told . . .

She walked. She walked right on. Head high, knowing that dignity was her birthright. A girl who knew what she deserved. She was her own. Enough. She deserved to be celebrated. She was. She knew. She. Knew.

Coda: Sensing Pleasure, Sensing *her*

let her be born
let her be born
& handled warmly. (Shange 1975, 5)

We end our chapter here with reiterating the need for centering pleasure in our understanding of Black youth lived experiences. Performance as a pedagogical practice, strategy, and laboratory for imagining the world we deserve is one way to locate pleasure and its possibilities for more expansive ways to know Black youth and to challenge the deleterious impacts of systems of domination. What might it mean to use the space of the creative, as illustrated above, for educators to problem solve with young people? What alternative language would be introduced to create policies as well as systems of shared accountability and mutual respect? It is our belief that the creative provides a playground for us to imagine and enact a more just world. We see performance also as a site of potential within academic texts and for researchers to similarly imagine creative solutions. Performance centers bodies, incites emotion, and creates connection. The challenge resides in our ability to move from that place where we suspend reality for a moment, to then actualize a different world once the "story, play, performance" ends.

Building off of our assertion that "performance is an intimate space to speak Blackness into its own existence, a space to imagine and practice freedom, a space for unbridled pleasures" (Callier and Hill 2019, 52), the speculative scenes above present a set of possibilities for Dynasia forged through different policy. As a "set of ideas or plans that is used as a basis for making decisions, especially in politics, economics, or business," policy is de jure and de facto (Meaning of Policy in Longman Dictionary of Contemporary English). Each of the crafted scenes, grounded in a celebration ethos, introduce multiple potential opportunities for pleasure, while creatively providing redress to the disembodying experiences endured by and robbing Dynasia of enjoying a special moment. Importantly, celebration is oriented around a different set of assumptions about Black girls that, if applied, would generate new policy in schools and responses to Black girls being themselves. One of the impacts of racism, colonization, white supremacy, homophobia, and gender policing is theft—the stealing of time, resources, opportunity, life, joy, pleasure, innocence, childhood—that Black youth, and in particular Black masculine, presenting girls like Dynasia experience. Combatting this theft, even if only imaginatively, demonstrates ways that Black, queer youth can and do craft scenes of pleasure. Furthermore, the imaginative text above offers a critique of normative views of childhood that help to move understandings of childhood beyond innocence.

Take for instance the remixing of a rhyme "Eenie, meenie, Minie, Mo" in the counterstory we provide of Dynasia. Originally rooted in racist history and a narration of the capture and subsequent brutalization of Black people and their bodies, the rhyme in our retelling becomes an opportunity of escape. Moving Dynasia beyond the carceral encampments (e.g., plantation, school, prisons, etc.), she is a freed Black subject, a Blackqueer subject on the go. The rhyme in its original intent and in our remixing underscores the way childhood as a failed project is often denied to Black youth, and the ways they creatively take flight from this space of confinement.

As Shange's opening poem, "dark phases" comes to an end, the words, in the above epigram provide a directive and possibility that if one allows, calls for a living and breathing Black girlhood. A type of living and breathing Black girlhood in which she is "handled warmly," as Shange states that we extend here to educators, policy makers, and those invested in the well-being of Black girls. The counterstories we fashion here and elsewhere are to combat deficit appraisals of their being and make room for sum total of all Black girls be. It is in this spirit that we hope you might also join us to "let her be born & handled warmly" (Shange 1975, 5). That we might praise where we tear down. See genius, autonomy, creativity at play and encourage it where we often see something in need of correction. Or said differently, let *her* be celebrated. To let the Dynasias of the world walk across the stage, to class, in their neighborhood without harm and harassment, is to know Black girls have a song to sing and know her enough that to sing it alongside her.

REFERENCES

Bambara, Toni Cade. 1996. *Deep Sightings and Rescue Missions: Fiction, Essays, and Conversations.* New York: Vintage.
Bost, Darius, La Marr Jurelle Bruce, and Brandon J. Manning. 2019. "Introduction: Black Masculinities and the Matter of Vulnerability." *The Black Scholar* 49 (2): 1–10. https://doi.org/10.1080/00064246.2019.1581970
Boutte, Gloria and Nathaniel Bryan. 2021. "When Will Black Children Be Well? Interrupting Anti-Black Violence in Early Childhood Classrooms and Schools." *Contemporary Issues in Early Childhood* 22 (3): 232–243. https://doi.org/10.1177/1463949119890598
Brockenbrough, Ed. 2013. "Introduction to the Special Issue: Queers of Color and Anti- oppressive Knowledge Production." *Curriculum Inquiry* 43 (4): 426–440. https://doi.org/10.1111/curi.12023
Brockenbrough, Ed and Tomás Boatwright. 2013. "In the MAC: Creating Safe Spaces for Transgender Youth of Color." In *Cultural Transformations: Youth and Pedagogies of Possibility*, edited by Korina Jocson, 165–182. Cambridge, MA: Harvard Education Press.
Brown, Ruth Nicole. 2013. *Hear Our Truths: The Creative Potential of Black Girlhood.* Urbana, IL: University of Illinois Press.
Brown, Ruth Nicole. 2009. *Black Girlhood Celebration: Toward a Hip-Hop Feminist Pedagogy.* Peter Lang.
Brown-Manning, Robyn. 2013. *We Don't Give Birth to Thugs; We Give Birth to Children: The Emotional Journeys of African-American Mothers Raising Sons under American Racism.* PhD diss. City University of New York.
Bryan, Nathaniel. 2020. "Shaking the 'Bad Boys': Troubling the Criminalization of Black Boys' Childhood Play, Hegemonic White Masculinity and Femininity, and the School Playground-to-Prison Pipeline." *Race Ethnicity and Education* 23 (5): 673–692.
Callier, Durell M. and Dominique C. Hill. 2019. *Who Look at Me?!: Shifting the Gaze of Education Through Blackness, Queerness, and the Body.* Brill | Sense.
Carbado, Devon, Dwight A. McBride, and Donald Weise, eds. 2011. *Black Like Us: A Century of Lesbian, Gay, and Bisexual African American Fiction.* Cleis Press Start.
Cohen, Cathy. 2019. "The Radical Potential of Queer? Twenty Years Later." *GLQ: A Journal of Lesbian and Gay Studies* 25 (1): 140–144.
"Combahee River Collective: A Black Feminist Statement." *Off Our Backs* 9, no. 6 (1979): 6–8.

Cox, Aimee. 2009. "Thugs, Black Divas, and Gendered Aspirations." *Souls* 11 (2): 113–141.

Crenshaw, Kimberlé, Priscilla Ocen, and Jyoti Nanda, "Black Girls Matter: Pushed Out, Overpoliced and Underprotected," *Columbia Law School Faculty Scholarship Archive*, January 1, 2015, https://scholarship.law.columbia.edu/faculty_scholarship/3227.

DeFrantz, Thomas, and Anita Gonzalez, eds. 2014. *Black Performance Theory*. Duke University Press.

Dillard, Cynthia B. 2016. "We Are Still Here: Declarations of Love and Sovereignty in Black Life Under Siege." *Educational Studies* 52 (3): 201–215.

Ferguson, Roderick A. 2004. *Aberrations in Black: Toward a Queer of Color Critique*. University of Minnesota Press.

Fordham, Signithia. 1993. "'Those Loud Blackgirls:' (Black) Women Silence, and Gender "Passing" in the Academy." *Anthropology and Education Quarterly* 24 (1): 3–32.

Grant, Linda. 1994. "Helpers, Enforcers, and Go-Betweens: Black Girls in Elementary Schools." In *Women of Color in U.S. Society*, edited by Bonnie Thorton Dill and Maxine Baca Zinn, 2nd edn, 43–63. Temple University Press.

Hill, Dominique C. 2021. "And Who Will Revere the Black Girl." *Gender & Society* 35 (4): 546–556.

Hill, Dominique C. 2018. "Black Girl Pedagogies: Layered Lessons on Reliability." *Curriculum Inquiry* 48 (3): 383–405.

Jacobs, Harriet. 1861. *Incidents in the Life of a Slave Girl*. Thayer and Eldrige.

Jones, Nikki. 2010. *Between Good and Ghetto: African American Girls and Inner-City Violence*. Rutgers University Press.

King, Wilma. 2011. *Stolen Childhood: Slave Youth in Nineteenth-Century America*. Indiana University Press.

Kwakye, Chamara Jewel, Dominique C. Hill, and Durell M. Callier. 2017. "10 Years of Black Girlhood Celebration: A Pedagogy of Doing." *Departures in Critical Qualitative Research* 6 (3): 1–10.

Lamar High School. "Beliefs Statement." Accessed February 5, 2021. http://lhs.dcsdschools.org/about_us/beliefs_statement

Lei, Joy L. 2003. (Un)necessary Toughness?: Those "Loud Black Girls" and Those "Quiet Asian Boys." *Anthropology and Education Quarterly* 34 (2): 158–181.

Lorde, Audre. 1984. *Sister Outsider*. Berkeley, CA: Crossing Press.

McKittrick, Katherine. 2006. *Demonic Grounds: Black Women and the Cartographies of Struggle*. University of Minnesota Press.

Morris, Edward W. 2007. "'Ladies' or 'Loudies'? Perceptions and Experiences of Black Girls in Classrooms." *Youth & Society* 38 (4): 490–515.

"Policy | Meaning of Policy in Longman Dictionary of Contemporary English | LDOCE." Accessed March 26, 2022. https://www.ldoceonline.com/dictionary/policy

Poulson-Bryant, Scott. 2011. *Hung: A Meditation on the Measure of Black Men in America*. Crown.

Richie, Beth E., and Kayla M. Martensen. 2020. "Resisting Carcerality, Embracing Abolition: Implications for Feminist Social Work Practice." *Affilia* 35 (1): 12–16. https://doi.org/10.1177/0886109919897576.

Scott, Patricia Bell. 1976. "Debunking Sapphire: Toward a Non-Racist and Non-Sexist Social Science." *Journal of Sociology and Social Welfare* 4 (6): 864.

Shange, Ntozake. 1975. *For Colored Girls Who Have Considered Suicide / When the Rainbow is Enuf.* Macmillian Publishing Company.

Spillers, Hortense J. 1987. "Mama's Baby, Papa's Maybe: An American Grammar Book." In *The Transgender Studies Reader Remix*, edited by Susan Stryker and Dylan Mcarthy Blackston, 93–104. Routledge.

Tolman, Deborah. 1996. "Adolescent Girls' Sexuality: Debunking the Myth of the Urban Girl." In *Urban Girls: Resisting Stereotypes, Creating Identities*, edited by Bonnie J. Ross Leadbeater and Niobe Way, 255–271. New York University Press.

Toliver, Stephanie Renee. 2018. "Alterity and Innocence: The Hunger Games, Rue, and Black Girl Adultification." *Journal of Children's Literature* 44 (2): 4–15.

Williams, Patricia. 1987. "Spirit-Murdering the Messenger: The Discourse of Finger-pointing as the Law's Response to Racism." *University of Miami Law Review* 42 (1): 127–158.

Young, Harvey. 2010. *Embodying Black Experience: Stillness, Critical Memory, and the Black Body.* University of Michigan Press.

Index

abandonment, 133, 157, 175
abduction, 181, 184
ability, 13, 33, 35–36, 52, 67–68, 80, 84, 88, 157, 159, 183, 185, 236
abjection, 221, 226
abortion, 207–8
absence, 19, 37, 52, 105, 156–58, 164–65, 174–75, 183, 199, 228
academic achievement, 42–47, 51, 227
academy, 17, 104–5, 115, 117, 123
action, 45, 80, 104, 109, 116, 123, 137, 144, 147–48, 204, 206, 209
activism, 60, 74, 84, 117
actualization, 233
administrators, 38, 40–41, 54, 159, 230, 232
adolescence, 7, 70–72, 162–63, 167
adolescents, 61, 68–69, 71–72, 160, 162–63, 167
adulthood, 16–17, 35, 60–61, 66–69, 71–72, 82–84, 89, 160, 167, 203–4, 220
adultification, 16, 33–34, 38–39, 45, 50, 52–53, 59–61, 63, 66, 68, 72–74, 79, 226–28
adultism, 17, 60, 64, 67, 72–74, 86, 132–36, 141, 143, 145–48
adultness, 60, 73–74
adults, 1–2, 5, 7, 10, 16–18, 30–31, 35, 38, 53, 60–74, 79, 81, 85, 109, 118, 129, 133–35, 140–42, 145–46, 155, 160, 163, 167, 178, 180–81, 185, 207, 212–13, 226–27
advantages, 60, 66, 71–72, 180
advocacy, 17
aesthetics, 19, 195, 222, 229
affective, 80, 164
Afghanistan, 196
Africa, 2, 48, 90, 129–33, 137, 148, 195, 199
Afrofuturism, 191–97, 211–18
Afrofuturity, 189, 192, 197, 211–13
afterlife, 196, 198, 201, 212, 230
ageism, 134, 146
agency, 8, 13–15, 17–20, 34–35, 72, 93, 123, 146, 171, 180, 189–96, 198–212, 220–21
agentic, 10, 18, 68, 176, 180, 190, 194, 198–201, 203–4, 208
agreements, 116–17, 121, 173
ahistorical, 168, 211, 232
alterity, 225
ambiguity, 16, 68, 72
ambivalence, 60, 72, 202
Americans, 66, 70–71
ancestors, 7, 202, 210
ancestral, 172, 197, 205
antiblackness, 74
antidiscrimination, 74
antiqueer, 231

241

antiracism, 36, 60–61, 65–66, 72–74
anxieties, 4, 71, 91, 190
appropriation, 106, 108, 180
archives, 192, 196, 211, 228, 232
arrival, 19, 107, 191, 198–99, 202, 204, 206–8, 210
arrivance, 19, 191, 198–202, 207
arrivants, 19, 190–91, 193, 196, 198–200, 205–10, 212
artistic, 30, 118, 195–96
artists, 4, 195, 222–23
assemblages, 193
assessment, 157–59, 164–67
assimilation, 53, 89
attitudes, 47, 141, 143
autobiographical, 20, 175
autoethnography, 32, 39
autonomy, 16–17, 67, 72, 82, 104, 109–10, 113–14, 116–17, 143, 223
awareness, 8, 94, 103, 123, 177, 179, 181, 183, 228

babies, 184, 235
Balagopalan, Sarada, 162–63, 190
becomings, 7, 134, 143
beginnings, 81, 106, 210
behavioral, 80, 83, 86–88
beings, 5, 7, 34–35, 70, 82, 85, 93, 134, 140, 143, 147, 193, 205, 209
beliefs, 106, 135, 141, 143, 145
Bernstein, Robin, 3–4, 14, 60–61, 63, 69, 164–65, 176, 193
Bertrand, Jane, 83
Bhalla, Alok, 173
Bharucha, Col., 176, 184
Bhasin, Kamala, 172–74
binaries, 16, 92, 168, 203, 220
biological, 5, 31, 35, 84, 90, 162
biomedical, 84–85
Blackness, 16–17, 34, 42, 52, 80, 86–87, 92, 94, 220–21, 224–26, 230–31, 234, 236–37
Blackqueerness, 224–25
Blackwell, 74, 132

bodies, 15, 17–18, 29, 39, 52, 70, 89–91, 143, 159, 164–65, 167, 196, 221, 224–26, 228, 231, 235–36
bolder, 208
bondage, 30, 47, 206
boundaries, 14, 68, 84, 90, 94, 156, 158, 161, 163–65, 181, 195
bourgeois, 7, 104–5
Boutte, Gloria, 36, 220
boyhood, 172, 220
Brathwaite, Kamau, 191, 198–200
brutality, 173, 182, 185
Burman, Erica, 7, 9, 31, 88, 192

Cairns, James, 71
Calvinist, 164–65
Canada, 1, 21, 30–38, 40–41, 46, 48, 51–53, 79, 103, 190, 192
capacities, 9–10, 50, 83, 144–46, 190
capitalism, 103–4, 106, 115, 117, 123, 226
carcerality, 74, 227
Caribbean, 19, 29, 32, 40, 190–92, 195, 198–99, 203, 206
carnival, 189, 203
Caruth, Cathy, 173–74, 176
Castañeda, Claudia, 71
caste, 18, 156, 159, 161–64, 167–68, 172, 177, 184–85
Castillo, Hernández, 111
categories, 61, 73, 105, 141, 162, 172, 185, 203, 220, 223, 226
celebration, 119, 177, 221, 223, 229–31, 236
centrality, 104, 113, 171, 176, 192
Chang-Kredl, Sandra, 193
chattel, 194, 196–98, 206
chauvinistic, 18, 201
childhood, 2–21, 30–32, 34–37, 39–41, 44–45, 47, 50–53, 59–64, 66–69, 71–74, 79–95, 104–5, 108–12, 114, 123, 130–32, 134–35, 156–57, 159–69, 171–72, 175–80, 182–83, 185, 190–95, 201–3, 209, 211–13, 220–23, 226–27, 231, 236

Index

childishness, 60, 72–74
childism, 17, 132, 134–36, 140, 143, 146–47
children, 1–21, 30–40, 42–54, 59–74, 79–91, 93–95, 104–5, 107–12, 114–15, 117–24, 129–48, 155–68, 171–73, 175–78, 180–85, 190–93, 196, 207, 210–13, 226
China, 95
choices, 135, 228, 230
circuits, 190, 196
citizen, 18, 73, 140, 162
citizenship, 13, 67, 71, 84, 209, 211
civilization, 7, 159–60, 162
classroom, 37, 41, 43–45, 51, 224
collaboration, 110–11, 117, 122–23
collective, 40, 93, 104–5, 108, 112–19, 122–23, 173, 184, 195, 197, 201, 223, 229
colonial, 6–7, 10, 14, 16–19, 31, 51, 63, 80–81, 84, 86, 95, 103–6, 109–11, 113, 155–56, 159–69, 178, 189–92, 194–97, 199–201, 203–5, 207, 209–13, 226
colonialism, 2, 13, 73, 82, 89, 91, 103–4, 106, 132, 190–91, 198, 204–5, 212
colonization, 2–3, 19–20, 105, 109, 190, 198, 201, 203, 220, 236
communities, 17, 48, 62, 84, 87, 104–5, 107–11, 113–16, 119, 137, 145, 147, 162–63, 174, 186, 205, 223–24
compassion, 38, 47, 51, 69, 164, 181
complexities, 13, 33, 37, 74
complicity, 14, 208
común, 104, 111, 124
concepts, 19, 31, 35, 37, 52, 132, 135, 145, 168, 224
conceptualization, 18, 80, 171, 200, 222, 230
connections, 34, 85–86, 90–91, 95, 173, 177
connotations, 92, 157–58
consciousness, 89–90, 175, 201–2, 228
consequences, 16, 52, 130, 132–33, 141, 144–45, 157–59, 161, 163–65, 167

constructions, 10, 13, 30, 36, 51, 61, 80–85, 89–91, 94, 177, 180, 212
contexts, 3, 8–9, 12–13, 15, 17–18, 20, 35, 104–5, 107–12, 117, 123–24, 130, 173, 180, 192–93, 197, 212
continuity, 104, 107, 119, 121, 160
contradictions, 60–61, 202, 205, 212, 222
corporal, 131, 138–39, 144–45
counternarratives, 21, 232
counterstories, 232, 236
COVID, 1, 3, 21, 121, 130–31, 136
creativity, 210, 225
criminalization, 65, 72, 94
critiques, 9, 14, 59, 74, 81–82, 89, 94, 164, 191–92, 194
culpability, 67, 227
curriculum, 11, 43, 46–50, 225

DAP, 11
Darling-Hammond, Linda, 31, 38, 46, 52
Darwinism, 5, 70
decolonization, 105, 111, 118, 123
deficits, 84, 88, 92, 229, 232, 236
defilement, 137–39, 144
denial, 89, 145, 220, 227, 230
dependence, 9, 201, 211
depravity, 164–65
destabilizing, 191, 201, 203, 207, 210, 212–13
developmentalism, 7, 11, 16–17, 80, 87–89, 134–35, 143, 146, 192
deviance, 86, 162, 227
dialectic, 198, 209, 212
diaspora, 107, 195, 206
differences, 106–7, 172, 192
dignity, 60, 110, 117, 122, 143, 220, 223, 229, 235
disability, 32, 134, 138–39
discourse, 3–4, 7–9, 11, 14, 17–19, 21, 39, 90, 132–33, 136, 146, 164, 174, 180, 203, 224, 239
discrimination, 19–20, 36, 38, 42, 51–53, 86, 107, 109, 134–35, 142, 145

244 Index

dislocation, 11, 189, 190, 192, 198–99, 202, 212
dismantling, 31, 43, 51, 82, 93–95, 134–35
displacement, 111, 172, 211
dispossession, 3, 6, 111, 191
disruption, 36, 80, 88, 191
diversity, 11, 17, 19, 29, 41–42, 45, 104, 108–11, 117, 124
doctrine, 4, 164–65, 199
dominance, 12, 14, 61, 69, 84, 94
Douglass, Frederick, 69
Duschinsky, Robbie, 3, 7, 176, 178, 180

education, 3–5, 9, 11–12, 15–17, 21, 30–34, 36–40, 43–46, 49–54, 74, 82–83, 94, 103, 105, 108, 110, 136–39, 142–43, 163, 166, 186, 194, 196, 222–24, 229, 232, 237
educators, 33, 38, 50, 53–54, 79, 232, 235–36
elimination, 137–39, 141, 200, 205, 210
emancipation, 69, 192, 226
embodiment, 11, 32, 36, 51–52, 82, 85, 161, 163, 221, 222, 225, 230–32
emotions, 30, 91, 211
Enlightenment, 17, 80, 82, 84–85, 87, 89–92, 164–65
enslavement, 2, 6, 64, 194, 196–99, 203, 206–7, 209, 212
environments, 37, 40, 42–43, 50, 53–54, 108
epidemic, 1–2, 17
epistemology, 7, 12, 15, 32–34, 82, 89, 91, 146, 168–69, 197
Epstein, 32–33, 38, 71, 227
erasure, 7, 15, 18, 86, 156, 164–65, 168, 191, 208
erotic, 180, 221, 230–31
Esser, Florian, 13, 192–93
establishment, 12, 69–70, 83, 185
ethnography, 33, 118, 228
ethos, 178, 221, 229, 231, 236
eugenics, 6, 70, 83, 86
Eurocentrism, 7, 14, 16, 29, 46–47, 49–51, 89, 112

Evans-Winters, Venus, 37
exclusion, 13, 16–17, 40–42, 45, 49, 52–54, 59, 63, 66, 71, 164
exclusionary, 74, 80, 82, 89, 91–92, 95, 130, 168–69, 176, 186, 194

failure, 15, 36, 42, 45–46, 50, 53, 94, 161, 209
families, 17, 62, 64–65, 73, 110, 114, 116, 118, 121, 123, 132, 174–75, 223, 235
Fanon, Frantz, 201–2
Farley, Lisa, 3, 14, 31, 81, 91–93, 193
Feldman, Shoshana, 174
femininity, 74, 92, 183, 226–27
feminism, 15, 21, 30, 32–34, 39–40, 74, 82, 148, 155, 174–76, 221, 224
Ferguson, Ann, 65
Ferguson, Roderick, 221
fiction, 10, 18–19, 173, 175, 190–92, 194–96
Fordham, Signithia, 227
Foucault, Michel, 9, 178
freedom, 6, 9, 14, 16, 18, 94, 114, 131, 143, 157, 193–94, 196–200, 206–10, 212, 223, 236
Freud, Sigmund, 11, 173, 175, 203–4
futurity, 95, 197–98, 200

García-Moren, Claudia, 130, 133, 146
Garlen, Julie, 1–6, 8, 10, 12, 14, 16, 18, 20, 31, 35, 59–61, 63, 74, 80–81, 89, 91, 94–95, 130, 157–58, 164–65, 176, 193
Gaztambide-Fernández, Rubén, 197, 200
gender, 18–19, 21, 33, 37, 40–42, 49, 51–52, 74, 82, 92, 134, 138–39, 141, 143, 149–51, 159, 172, 174–75, 177, 185–87, 211, 220–21, 223–24, 226–28, 230–32, 234, 236
genealogy, 115, 178, 192, 195
geographies, 74, 168–69, 189, 191–92, 208, 211, 226
geography, 12–13, 226
girlhood, 13, 18, 172, 181, 219–23, 225–26, 228–29, 231–32, 236

girls, 15–16, 19, 29–34, 36–46, 48–54, 74, 85, 117, 121, 129–31, 133, 136–37, 142–43, 145, 178, 181, 184, 220–23, 226–32, 234–36
Gorman, 84–85, 94
government, 4, 6, 37, 103, 112, 114–16, 131, 135–39, 141–42, 146
Griffin, Rachel, 32, 39
guilt, 67, 157–58, 183

Hardt, Michael, 111, 113
Hartman, Saidiya, 196, 208
Hawkes, Gail, 178, 180
hegemony, 3, 7–9, 16, 19, 21, 83, 88–89, 104–7, 109, 114, 146, 224
Henriques, Julian, 9
heteromasculinity, 92–93
heteronormativity, 80, 82, 202, 225
heteropatriarchy, 81, 91, 95
heterosexuality, 90, 92
hierarchy, 7, 14, 73, 85–86, 89, 91–94, 106–7, 156, 167–68, 201, 203, 211
Higonnet, Anne, 62, 67, 71
Hindus, 172–73, 181
histories, 9–10, 18–19, 33–34, 37, 47–51, 84, 88, 91, 106, 155, 168, 173–74, 178, 211, 224, 227
HIV, 137–39
homeland, 189, 191, 197–98, 200, 204–8, 212
Hopkinson, Nalo, 18–19, 189, 191–92, 194–95, 200–212
Howe, Brian, 31, 35
Howe, Samuel G., 54
humanism, 82, 89, 92–95, 177, 196
humanness, 67, 90, 93–94, 160
hybridity, 68–70, 72, 199, 212

ideals, 16, 31, 52, 80, 91, 205
ideas, 9, 79–81, 83–84, 86–88, 90–91, 95, 105–7, 110, 115–16, 156, 163, 168, 192, 236
identities, 13, 16, 21, 30, 33–34, 36–37, 40–41, 45–46, 48–52, 68, 80, 113
ideology, 16–17, 21, 61–62, 68, 72–73, 80, 89, 92, 107, 117, 155, 168–69, 226

ignorance, 3–4, 18, 59, 82, 157–58, 164–66, 176, 211
imagination, 4, 62, 84, 123, 134, 197, 227, 233
immigration, 2, 6, 29, 34, 70, 211
implementation, 116, 133, 145–46
implications, 17, 32, 34, 81, 90, 132, 156, 159, 164, 166
impossibility, 10, 19, 32, 91, 164, 194, 198, 223, 226, 234
inadequacies, 132, 136, 140, 142, 146–47
incarceration, 46, 62, 94, 196, 212
inclusion, 20, 108, 146, 168
Indigeneity, 109–10, 199, 208
Indigenous, 2–3, 6–7, 14, 17, 19–20, 48–49, 54, 81, 84, 88–91, 93, 103–17, 119, 122–23, 173, 189–92, 197–203, 205–10, 212–14
inequality, 16, 34, 38, 45, 52, 103, 109, 133, 146–47, 162, 164, 168, 221
inequity, 15, 30–32, 34–36, 44, 52–53, 94, 132
infantilization, 16, 60, 63, 65–69, 71–74, 84, 86–87
injustice, 20, 87, 146–47, 191
innocence, 1, 3–7, 10, 14–16, 18–21, 29–35, 37, 39, 41–43, 45, 47, 49–51, 53, 61–63, 69, 72–74, 79–89, 91, 93, 95, 155, 157, 159, 161, 163–65, 167–69, 171, 173, 175–81, 183, 185–87, 191, 201–2, 211, 219–23, 225, 227, 229, 231, 233, 235
insanity, 83, 86, 178
institutionalization, 63–64, 66, 90, 167
institutions, 4, 12, 36, 60, 63, 65–67, 112, 116, 144, 147, 158–60, 162, 164, 180, 204
interiority, 11, 222–23, 231
intersectionality, 13, 33, 49, 51–52, 74
intervention, 3, 5, 14, 19, 61–63, 65–66, 72–73, 83–88, 95, 142, 191, 197–98, 208, 211–12
invisibility, 10, 14, 175, 185
irrationality, 85, 88, 90

Jamaica, 192, 199
Jenks, Chris, 10, 71, 171, 192
Jensen, Frances E., 70
Jocson, Korina, 237
justice, 14, 18, 56, 74, 103–4, 133, 136, 145–46, 155–60, 164–69, 190, 203–5, 207–8, 232
juvenile, 18, 70, 74, 155–60, 162–69, 178, 185

Kenneally, Noah, 82, 86
Kennedy, Imogene, 199
Kessler, Shirley, 11
Kinsella, Anne, 16, 82, 86–87
Konstantoni, Kristina, 13, 59
Kumar, Shailesh, 159
Kyegombe, Nambusi, 132–33

Lang, James, 21, 133, 186, 237
languages, 110–11, 173, 199
Leblanc, Stephanie, 16, 86
LeFrançois, Brenda, 16, 60, 80, 84–87, 91, 94–95
legislation, 132, 140, 155–57
Lerma, Michael, 200, 205–6
lessons, 48
liberation, 103, 118, 123, 189, 210
Lima-Kerckhoff, Ashley, 46
liminal, 85, 123, 164–65, 199, 222
linear, 8, 10, 20, 31, 84, 177, 192, 220
literature, 10, 12, 14, 18, 34, 38, 71–72, 85, 118, 133, 136, 146, 156, 164, 171–74, 183, 186–87, 192, 196
Locke, John, 11, 63, 67–68, 82, 84, 89–90, 164–65
logics, 3, 7–8, 16, 18–19, 72–73, 81, 84, 89–92, 94–95, 159, 162–63, 191, 199, 203–4, 227, 230
Lorde, Audrey, 221, 230
Louverture, Toussaint, 201–2, 210

maddening, 16, 79, 81, 91, 93–94
madness, 16–17, 74, 80, 84–91, 93–94
malleability, 16, 18, 155–57, 159–61, 163–64, 166–69, 203

manifestation, 32–33, 44, 45, 50, 52, 60, 72, 228
marginalization, 12, 17, 18, 20, 30, 33, 37, 40, 48, 50, 52, 86, 103, 105, 109, 134–35, 140, 164–65, 168, 176, 226
marriage, 6, 130, 137, 141, 148, 181, 184, 230
marronage, 193–94, 198–99, 206, 209–10
masculinity, 84, 92–93, 226
masturbation, 85
maturation, 172, 182–85
maturity, 18, 20, 71, 211, 220
McClelland, Sara I., 129
McInerney, Brandon, 92–93
McKinney, Kim, 1
McKittrick, Katherine, 30, 226
McLaughlin, Carly, 211–12
McNamee, Sally, 8, 10
media, 12, 29, 40–41, 43, 45, 61, 71, 80, 155, 173, 211, 224
medicalization, 80, 85–87, 89, 92–94
Meiners, Erica R., 3, 7, 14, 59, 67
melancholia, 204
memories, 177, 196–97, 219
metaphor, 20, 191, 196, 206, 208
methodology, 12, 32, 105, 113, 117–20, 132, 146, 223, 229
methods, 9, 32, 39, 50, 106, 108, 111, 113, 123, 133, 136, 143, 222, 224–25, 229
Mexico, 17, 103, 105–7, 109, 115, 123–24
migrants, 196, 211
Milner, Richard H., 37
miscegenation, 69–70
miseducation, 16, 33, 40, 43, 45, 47–50, 53
misrepresentation, 40, 43, 45, 49, 54, 198
mobilization, 156, 164, 203
modernism, 80, 82, 89, 177, 193
modernity, 90, 106–7, 111, 159–60, 167–69, 178, 186, 194–96
Mohanram, Radhika, 89–90

monstrous, 69–72, 198, 207–8
morality, 4, 178
Morss, John R., 9
mortality, 1–2, 179
movement, 5–9, 11, 17, 21, 87–88, 103–5, 110–15, 117, 123, 131, 135, 176, 195, 205–9, 220, 222, 224
multidimensional, 1, 116
multiplicity, 168–69, 230
Muslims, 172–73, 181
mutilation, 137–40
myth, 3, 10, 18, 35, 37, 74, 95, 179–80, 182, 185, 208
myths, 72, 227

NAEYC, 11
NAFTA, 103, 112
naivety, 35, 220–21, 228
Nandy, Ashis, 3, 61, 66, 72, 160, 168–69, 203
narratives, 19, 32, 39–40, 43–45, 54, 105, 109, 172–75, 185, 198–99, 220, 222, 224
natality, 196, 209–10, 212
nationalism, 18, 171, 174–75, 177–78, 184–87
neocolonial, 123
neoliberal, 112, 114–15
neoliberalism, 117
Neuman, R. P., 85
Neustadter, Roger, 4, 194
Nigeria, 2
nonbinary, 220, 223
nonhuman, 189, 196, 205, 208–9
normalcy, 86, 94
normalization, 11, 15, 20, 30–31, 33, 35–37, 44, 51, 70, 84, 92, 111, 178
normativity, 8, 10, 15–18, 37, 60, 70, 80–82, 84–86, 91–93, 134–35, 163, 171, 176–78, 180, 184–85, 220, 236
nostalgia, 171, 194
Nutt, Amy E., 70, 74
Nxumalo, Fikile, 14, 82, 190

offenders, 70, 74, 133, 138–39, 145, 158, 160, 163

ontoepistemologies, 89, 195
oppression, 12, 16, 33–34, 36–37, 40, 51–53, 60, 63, 65–66, 74, 103, 113, 122, 134, 191, 212, 226, 229, 231
Orwell, George, 194
O'Shaughnessy, Frances H., 199–200, 209
Oswell, David, 193
othered, 5, 90, 175, 181
otherness, 90, 93
overrepresentation, 12, 90, 230

Pacini-Ketchabaw, Veronica, 190
Pakistan, 172, 177, 181, 196
Palestine, 2
pandemic, 1–3, 21, 121, 136, 148
Pandey, Gyanendra, 171, 173, 178, 185
paradigmatic, 62, 175
paradigms, 8, 112, 192–93, 223, 226
paradox, 16, 51, 59–61, 63, 65, 66, 68–74, 194, 201, 205, 212
Parkes, Jenny, 133, 136
participation, 13, 17, 90, 103, 105, 107–8, 110, 116–18, 121–24, 138–42, 146, 164, 166, 168, 183, 193
paternalism, 81, 143, 184, 189, 201, 205
pathologies, 69
pathologization, 16, 69, 70, 84–89, 91, 221, 225
patriarchy, 47, 67, 184
pedagogical, 6, 45, 48, 49, 51, 54, 235
pedagogy, 5, 11, 16, 40, 74, 224, 232
peers, 30, 38, 41, 43, 53, 131, 144–46, 231
perceptions, 33, 105, 176, 228
performativity, 232
periphery, 159–61, 164, 166, 168–69
personhood, 8, 67, 82, 85, 220, 226–27
perspectives, 8, 11–17, 20, 32, 40, 47–49, 53, 74, 85–86, 107–8, 159, 175, 177
Philippe, Ariès, 21
philosophy, 4, 46, 63, 67, 70, 83, 87, 147
Piaget, Jean, 8, 83
plasticity, 156, 162

policies, 2, 15, 17, 31, 33, 36–37, 40, 51, 53–54, 62, 65, 74, 112, 132, 134–47, 223, 227, 229, 231, 235
Poole, Jennifer M., 80, 86–87
Popkewitz, Thomas S., 21
populations, 12, 82, 84, 87, 93–94, 105, 109, 156, 161
pornography, 131
positivism, 4, 94
possibilities, 2, 7, 17, 19, 74, 103, 105, 111, 116, 122–24, 156, 164, 191–92, 197, 200–201, 205, 208, 219, 221–22, 224, 226, 229, 231–32, 235–36
possibility, 111, 191, 198, 200, 206, 209, 224–25, 231–32, 235–37
postcolonialism, 156–57, 159, 175, 177, 186, 190, 203–4, 213
Postman, Neil, 71
postmodernism, 8, 9, 21, 191, 193
poststructuralism, 9, 193
poverty, 1, 3, 10, 38, 103, 109, 163, 223
Pratt, Richard, 2
praxis, 13, 105, 113, 117, 147, 223–24, 229, 232
prejudice, 20, 38, 47, 107, 135
prevention, 130–33, 135, 137–42, 144, 146–47
principle, 5, 7, 11, 62–63, 65, 73, 108, 117, 140, 142, 147, 157
priorities, 13, 15, 36, 53, 115
privilege, 66, 67, 71–72, 93, 116, 122, 180, 185, 220, 226
problematize, 19, 31, 107, 113, 156, 171
prohibition, 137–40
prostitution, 131, 175, 181
protagonism, 105, 107, 123
protagonist, 18, 30, 172, 175, 190, 201, 203, 208
Prout, Alan, 7, 10, 31, 34–35, 192
psychiatrization, 16, 85, 91, 94
psychoanalysis, 10–11, 173, 174, 186, 193
psychology, 5, 7–9, 20, 21, 35, 80, 83–84, 87, 91, 94, 140, 192, 201
psychosocial, 183
Punjab, 172, 185

purity, 34–35, 61, 69, 80, 85, 157, 165, 177

queerness, 19, 222, 224, 225, 229
Qvortrup, Jens, 10, 12, 134

Raby, Rebecca, 91
racial, 4, 6–7, 13–14, 16, 21, 29, 32–33, 35–36, 38, 42, 47–54, 59, 63, 69, 74, 86, 89, 92, 94, 106–7, 168–69, 186, 194, 196, 211, 226–27, 229, 231
racialization, 3, 13, 19, 31, 33, 36, 49, 63, 80–82, 84, 86–91, 93–94, 109, 191, 203, 211, 220, 223–24, 226, 227, 231
racism, 3, 7, 9, 12, 14, 16, 19–20, 31, 34, 36–37, 42, 43, 47–48, 50–53, 59–61, 63–65, 67–74, 85, 87–89, 91, 94, 103, 107, 110, 123, 134, 226, 230–32, 236–37
Rasmussen, Kim, 172, 180
rationalism, 69, 90, 94
rationality, 17, 20, 72, 80–91, 93–94, 109, 113, 180
recapitulation, 5–7, 83, 86
reconceptualization, 11, 34, 191, 192
redemption, 4–5, 8, 18, 194
redress, 19, 222, 232, 236
reflexivity, 193, 228
reform, 5, 8, 15, 37, 146, 148, 159–61, 163, 178, 211
reformatories, 64, 66, 160, 163
reformatory, 156, 159–63, 167–69
reforms, 132, 147
refugees, 3, 164, 172, 211
refusal, 19, 30, 95, 191, 201, 204–5, 209, 212
reimagining, 17, 19, 94, 95, 155, 221
relationships, 5, 13, 19, 20, 62, 74, 84, 90, 94, 106–10, 112–14, 116–19, 122–23, 133, 138–39, 144, 148, 180, 189–91, 193–94, 197, 198, 200–202, 205–7, 209–10, 212, 224–26, 230–31
representation, 6, 7, 18, 29, 40, 43, 48, 50, 81, 123, 136, 171–72, 175, 176,

185–87, 194, 203, 206, 211, 219, 221, 230
reproduction, 65, 72, 83, 107, 111, 168, 193–94
resistance, 12, 16–18, 86, 93–94, 103, 111, 113–15, 117, 145, 201, 203, 205
responsibilities, 9, 15, 34, 36, 40, 49, 51, 66, 68, 82, 109, 144, 157–59, 164–65, 178, 220, 223, 227
rhetoric, 7, 59, 89, 155, 164–65, 203, 211
Rhodes, Jesse H., 69
Richie, Beth E., 227
Robinson, Cedric, 195
Rollo, Toby, 60–61, 69, 72–73, 79, 81–82, 190
Romanticism, 4, 82, 194, 224
Rousseau, Jean-Jacques, 4, 11, 61–62, 82–83, 164–65
Runswick-Cole, Katherine, 13, 88
Russo, Jasna, 84, 95

safety, 17, 21, 80, 158, 167, 202, 208, 221, 227
sanism, 16, 79–81, 83, 85–87, 89, 91–94
Satadru, Sen, 168–69
savage, 5–6, 61, 68, 70, 72, 82, 205
savagery, 6–7, 83, 174
savior, 68–70, 74, 183
schooling, 2, 5, 11, 13, 16, 32, 39–40, 45, 52, 93, 190
schools, 2, 5, 15–16, 21, 29, 30, 32, 34, 37, 39–41, 43, 45–47, 49–54, 64–66, 73, 109, 112, 118, 123, 129–30, 137, 141–43, 146, 159–60, 162, 163, 167–69, 223, 228, 232, 236
selfhood, 11, 189, 204
separation, 109, 161, 171–72, 178, 226
settlement, 34, 189, 202, 204, 206–9
settlers, 2, 19, 31, 48, 81, 89, 189–91, 197–98, 200–201, 203, 205–10, 212
sexism, 34, 37, 52–53, 85, 88, 134, 226, 232
sexuality, 18–19, 35, 74, 85, 92–93, 134, 158, 164–65, 177–78, 180, 183, 220–21, 224, 227, 229

sexualization, 39
Shalaby, Carla, 79, 83
Shange, Ntozake, 220–23, 225, 228, 231–32, 235–36
Sharpe, Christina, 196, 207
Sharpe, Jenny, 203
Sheldon, H. White, 59
Sheley, Joseph F., 67, 74
Sidhva, Dina, 136
Sidhwa, Bapsi, 18, 171, 175–77, 179–80, 183–84
Sikhs, 172–73, 181–82
silence, 52–54, 91–92, 116, 141, 144, 145, 148, 172–73, 175, 184–86, 193
Silva, Kumarini, 206
Singh, Deepak, 159, 168–69
Singh, Preeti, 175
slavery, 19, 21, 64, 87, 90–91, 186, 190–91, 193–96, 198–203, 205, 208–10, 212, 228
socialization, 8, 10, 35, 104, 107–8, 110–11, 119, 123, 160
sociology, 8–10, 12, 21, 35
sociopolitical, 132–33, 145–46
sociospatial, 226
solidarity, 110, 113, 185
Sonu, Debbie, 32, 193
sovereignty, 7, 111, 113, 205, 211, 225
Spandler, Helen, 84
spatiality, 31, 104, 177, 180, 181, 206
Specht, Jacqueline, 87
speculative fiction, 19, 189, 195, 196, 222, 236
Spillers, Hortense, 220, 228, 230
Spivak, Gayatri Chakravorty, 175, 203
Spyrou, Spyros, 31, 86
Sserwanja, Quraish, 136
Stahler-Sholk, Richard, 112
stakeholders, 138–39, 141, 145, 146, 222, 229
Steedman, Carolyn, 11
Stenberg, Shari J., 69
stereotypes, 30, 41, 42, 44, 46, 47, 225–28
stories, 17, 21, 30, 173, 185, 196, 223, 225, 231–32

storytelling, 221, 231–32
strategies, 33, 53, 115, 117, 121, 132–33, 137, 144–46, 200
students, 2, 15, 29–30, 36, 41, 43–49, 65, 93, 109, 223, 230
subcontinent, 18, 171–72, 185
subjecthood, 177, 204–5
subjectification, 18, 155, 164–65
subjectivity, 8, 32, 84, 87, 90, 93, 109–10, 114–15, 167, 220
subversion, 18, 171–72, 177–78, 180, 181, 185
success, 43, 46, 51, 161, 228, 231
suicide, 2, 21, 221
surveillance, 74, 104, 129, 143, 178, 182, 202
survival, 53, 70, 106, 138–39, 201, 224–25, 227
Swadener, Beth Blue, 11
systemic, 16, 31, 36, 37, 85–86, 134–35, 220
systems, 15–16, 30–33, 36, 45–46, 51–53, 63, 66, 85–87, 90–91, 94, 134, 162, 164, 167, 198, 212, 223, 226, 228, 230, 235
Szulc, Andrea, 109

Taíno, 199, 206
Tarc, Aparna, 2
Tatum, Beverly D., 59, 61
Taubman, 198, 207, 210
TDSB, 43, 46, 51
teachers, 7, 21, 29–30, 38, 40–54, 74, 80, 94, 109, 119, 131, 137, 227–30, 235
technology, 4, 164–65, 190, 195, 203, 210
teenage, 74, 130, 137, 141
teens, 19, 21, 74
Temmerman, Marleen, 133–34
temporality, 31, 71–72, 80, 82, 83, 93–94, 176–77, 191, 197–98
tensions, 17, 31, 132, 140, 142–43, 146–47, 190, 193, 226
textbooks, 62, 83

theories, 3, 5–6, 9, 11, 16, 19, 21, 50, 71, 80, 82–84, 89–91, 177, 193–94, 220–21
theorists, 104, 106, 173, 193
theorizing, 39–40, 51, 88, 94–95, 190, 221, 229, 232
theory, 5–8, 10–12, 65, 70–71, 73, 74, 83, 106, 113, 174, 197, 221, 224
Tisdall, E. Kay M., 13, 34, 192
Todorov, Tzvetan, 112
tolerance, 65, 74, 138–39, 164
Tolman, Deborah, 227
Toronto, 30, 32, 39–40, 45–46, 52, 54, 74, 186, 192
trans, 94, 164, 201, 203, 205, 220
transformation, 47, 49, 107, 108, 110, 113–14, 117, 122–23, 134, 178, 194, 206
transgender, 2, 92–93, 223
transgression, 69, 172, 182, 221
transgressive, 181, 222
transness, 92
transphobia, 88, 232
trauma, 15, 19, 47, 51, 53, 171–76, 177, 179, 182–87, 189–91, 196, 199–204, 210–21
truth, 6, 9, 62, 94, 179, 183, 223, 231
Tuck, Eve, 197, 200
Twum-Danso Imoh, Afua, 14
Tylor, Affrica, 106

Uganda, 17, 129–33, 135–53
UNCRC, 8, 131, 142–43, 146
UNICEF, 1–2, 131, 135
universalism, 4, 17, 31, 35, 65, 211
unpacking, 49, 59, 61, 63, 65, 67–69, 71, 73, 156, 203

Varga, Donna, 81–84, 86–88, 91
victims, 17, 133, 145, 164, 174, 183–84, 203
violence, 3, 7, 14–15, 17–18, 30, 44, 47, 54, 59, 66, 69, 73–74, 80, 86, 89, 91, 111, 113, 129–33, 135, 137–41, 144–53, 155, 158, 164–65, 171–78,

180–82, 184–87, 189–91, 198, 201–4, 207, 209, 211, 220–21, 223–26, 230–32
virginity, 129–30, 143
Viruru, Radhika, 109, 190
Vizenor, Gerald, 199
Voronka, Jijian, 91, 94

Walkerdine, Valerie, 8–9, 31
Watson, Drew, 83, 95
weaponization, 16, 60, 61, 63–64, 66, 68
Weaver-Hightower, Rebecca, 195
Weinfeld, Morton, 36
Weise, Donald, 231
welfare, 16, 21, 64, 112, 131, 148
whiteness, 6–7, 42, 44, 52, 82, 91–92, 226
white supremacy, 6–7, 19, 44, 47, 49, 66, 68–72, 81, 83–86, 91, 134, 144, 220, 225, 226, 232, 236

Wickersham, Joan, 1
womanhood, 184, 219, 222, 225–26
Wynter, Sylvia, 6, 16, 86, 88, 90, 93–94
Wyss, Johann D., 194

Yoruba, 198
Yousif, Nadine, 1
youth, 2, 16, 19, 21, 32, 37, 60, 64–65, 67, 70–71, 73, 74, 86, 89, 93, 114–15, 134–35, 138–39, 141, 155, 160, 183–84, 190, 221–29, 231–32, 235–36

Zapatismo, 105, 114–15
Zapatista, 17, 103–5, 107, 109–19, 121–23
Zelizer, Viviana, 10, 61–62
Zimmerman, Cathy, 133, 146
Zobel Marshall, Emily, 203

About the Contributors

Sebastian Barajas is a PhD candidate in the Department of Childhood Studies at Rutgers University–Camden. Their dissertation investigates how alternative education settings navigate power and inequality. With an undergraduate degree in Western classics from St. John's College, Annapolis, Sebastian's work spans from youth rights activism to childist critiques of the concept of privilege. Sebastian's vision for the field of childhood studies is to see it deepen its intersectional critique of ageist/adultist norms and institutions and to explore alternatives to them.

Durell M. Callier is an artist-scholar, who employs Black feminist and queer methodologies to explore the interconnectivity of race, gender, sexuality, and culture. His research documents, analyzes, and interrogates the lived experience of Black youth and their communities and illuminates the role art can play in responding to anti-Black and anti-queer violence. Callier is co-founder of Hill L. Waters (HLW), an arts-based research collaborative that enacts Black queer world making as embodied pedagogy. He is co-author of two books, *Who look at me?!: Shifting the Gaze of Education Through Blackness, Queerness, and the Body* (Brill, 2019), and *Performative Intergenerational Dialogues of a Black Quartet: Qualitative Inquiries on Race, Gender, Sexualities, and Culture* (Routledge, 2022).

Mayurika Chakravorty teaches in the Department of English and the Institute of Interdisciplinary Studies (Childhood and Youth Studies program), Carleton University, Canada. Her research focuses on fantasy and science fiction; children's literature; and the representation of children in literature and media.

Adam Davies (they/them) is an Ontario Certified Teacher, Registered Early Childhood Educator, and Assistant Professor in Family Relations and Human Development at the University of Guelph. Adam holds a PhD in curriculum studies and teacher development from the Ontario Institute for Studies in Education, University of Guelph, and is a neurodivergent, queer, and mentally disabled white settler activist, scholar, and educator. Adam's work centres around disability justice, equity, anti-oppressive practices, and emancipatory approaches to early childhood education and K-12 schooling. Adam works and lives on the unceded lands of the Mississaugas of the Credit First Nation and gives thanks for the land that they continue to work in relation with.

Julie C. Garlen is a critical cultural theorist with interests in childhood, education, and curriculum studies. She is currently the director of the Institute of Interdisciplinary Studies and a professor of childhood and youth studies at Carleton University in Ottawa, Canada. Previously, she worked in as an elementary school teacher and an early childhood teacher educator in the U.S. South, where her work on cultural studies of education and children's popular culture led to the publication of two volumes co-edited with Jennifer Sandlin: *Teaching with Disney* (Peter Lang, 2016) and *Disney, Culture and Curriculum* (Routledge, 2016). More recently, she has focused on understanding how the Western myth of childhood innocence informs work with and understandings of children in North American contexts.

Dominique C. Hill, |scholar-artist, vulnerability guide, facilitator, through written and performed scholarship, examines Black embodiment, youth culture, and creative healing practices. Raised by three generations of women who know the power of prayer and libations, Hill's living, art, and research is grounded in collectivity and imagination. Hill continues this intergenerational and spiritual work as a homegirl of Saving Our Lives, Hear Our Truths (SOLHOT), a core member of Street Dance Activism and divine guide of the 28 Day Global Dance Meditation, and co-visionary of Hill L. Waters (HLW), Blackqueer worldmaking collective, Hill is co-author of the recently published *Performative Intergenerational Dialogues of a Black Quartet* (Routledge, 2022) and W*ho look at me?!: Shifting the Gaze of Education Through Blackness, Queerness, and the Body* (Brill|Sense, 2019). Hill extends the field of Black Girlhood Studies as an assistant professor of Women's Studies at Colgate University.

Anusha Iyer is a doctoral student in the Department of Childhood Studies at Rutgers University. In the past, she has worked in the development sector in India researching on adolescence, children, gender, and education in rural and urban parts of India. Her current research lies at the intersection of nationalist agendas and childhoods in the Indian context specifically focusing on the themes of dissent as deviance and young people in politics.

Doris Kakuru is associate professor in child and youth care at the University of Victoria. Her research interests include violence against children and youth, adolescent motherhood, gendered children's rights, and children and youth in urban poverty.

Kisha McPherson is an educator and scholar with over 15 years of research and teaching experience in critical race, cultural studies, social justice, and media education. Her research and scholarship are focused on the impact of media, education policies, and contemporary representations of Blackness, on the identity and development of Black youth. Dr. McPherson is interested in utilizing Black feminist approaches to research, community engagement, and education, to develop and contribute to anti-oppressive pedagogies and practices, which aim to support Black youth in both formal academic and community spaces. Dr. McPherson is an assistant professor in the Department of Professional Communications at Toronto Metropolitan University (TMU).

Kathia Núñez Patiño holds a PhD in educational research from the Educational Research Institute at the University of Veracruz and a master's in social anthropology from CIESAS (Centro de Investigaciones y Estudios Superiores en Antropología Social) Southeast. She is a member of the National System of Level 1 Researchers and was a coordinator of the Network of Community Defenders for Human Rights (2001–2003). She is also a member of the academic body "Childhood and Youth in Contexts of Diversity." Her research interests include anthropology of education, childhood studies, Indigenous education, and autonomous education. Dr. Núñez Patiño is a founding member of the Latin American Network for Research and Reflection with Girls, Boys, and Youth (REIR).

Chanelle Perrier-Telemaque is a development practitioner with over 12 years of local and international experience with a focus on youth mentorship in underserved communities. To date, she has held many roles within nongovernmental organizational settings, as well as the public sector; some of these positions have included project coordinator and senior manager of international programming. Chanelle began her academic career by earning a Bachelor of Arts in International Development from York University in Toronto. Upon completing her postgraduate certificate in international development from Humber College, she relocated to Barbados where she underwent a master of Science in Gender and Development Studies at The University of West Indies Cave Hill. Her major research project investigated the support-mothering experiences of second-generation African-Caribbean women, born and raised in Toronto, Canada. Currently, Chanelle is a third-year doctoral student in the Critical Disability Studies program at York University. Her dissertation explores Blackness, disability, and embodiment in an effort to examine the complex implications of sistering disabled siblings, as performed by second-generation African-Caribbean women.

Neil T. Ramjewan is a PhD candidate at the University of Toronto's, Ontario Institute for Studies in Education (OISE) in the department of Curriculum and Pedagogy. Neil's scholarship turns to histories and literatures of resistance and survivance to reinvent and reconfigure universalist conceptions of childhood that operate to marginalize racialized children and childify racialized adults as part of ongoing colonial projects. Neil is an instructor for the Childhood and Youth Studies program at Carleton University and has experience working with children and youth as an Ontario Certified Teacher (OCT).

Milton Keynes UK
Ingram Content Group UK Ltd.
UKHW020632160224
437918UK00002B/4